Alexander Roberts, James Sir Donaldson

The works of Lactantius

Ante-Nicene Christian Library Volume 22

Alexander Roberts, James Sir Donaldson

The works of Lactantius
Ante-Nicene Christian Library Volume 22

ISBN/EAN: 9783742854605

Manufactured in Europe, USA, Canada, Australia, Japa

Cover: Foto ©Lupo / pixelio.de

Manufactured and distributed by brebook publishing software (www.brebook.com)

Alexander Roberts, James Sir Donaldson

The works of Lactantius

NOTICE TO SUBSCRIBERS.

———◆———

EDINBURGH, *November* 1871.

MESSRS. CLARK have pleasure in issuing to the Subscribers to the ANTE-NICENE LIBRARY the first issue of Sixth Year (Volumes XXI. and XXII.), viz. The WRITINGS of LACTANTIUS, in Two Volumes, with the addition of Various FRAGMENTS.

The next and final issue will comprise the Completion of ORIGEN, and a Volume of LITURGIES. The whole Series will thus be finished in Twenty-four Volumes.

Messrs. CLARK beg respectfully to request an early remittance of Subscriptions for Sixth Year.

They also invite attention to the Series of Translations of the Works of
ST. AUGUSTINE,
on the same plan as the ANTE-NICENE LIBRARY.

The first issue,

THE CITY OF GOD,

in Two Volumes, is now ready, and Prospectuses will be forwarded on application. They especially hope for the support of their Friends the Subscribers to the ANTE-NICENE LIBRARY.

ANTE-NICENE

CHRISTIAN LIBRARY:

TRANSLATIONS OF
THE WRITINGS OF THE FATHERS

DOWN TO A.D. 325.

EDITED BY THE
REV. ALEXANDER ROBERTS, D.D.,
AND
JAMES DONALDSON, LL.D.

VOL. XXII.

THE WORKS OF LACTANTIUS, VOL. II.

TOGETHER WITH

THE TESTAMENTS OF THE TWELVE PATRIARCHS AND FRAGMENTS
OF THE SECOND AND THIRD CENTURIES.

EDINBURGH:
T. & T. CLARK, 38, GEORGE STREET.
MDCCCLXXI.

PRINTED BY MURRAY AND GIBB,

FOR

T. & T. CLARK, EDINBURGH.

LONDON, ... HAMILTON, ADAMS, AND CO.
DUBLIN, ... JOHN ROBERTSON AND CO.
NEW YORK, . . . C. SCRIBNER AND CO.

THE WORKS

OF

LACTANTIUS.

Translated by

WILLIAM FLETCHER, D.D.,
HEAD-MASTER OF QUEEN ELIZABETH'S SCHOOL, WIMBORNE, DORSET.

IN TWO VOLUMES.

VOL. II.

EDINBURGH:
T. & T. CLARK, 38, GEORGE STREET.
MDCCCLXXI.

CONTENTS.

	PAGE
A Treatise on the Anger of God,	1
On the Workmanship of God, or the Formation of Man,	49
The Epitome of the Divine Institutes,	92
Of the Manner in which the Persecutors died,	164
Fragments of Lactantius Firmianus,	212
The Phœnix,	214
A Poem on the Passion of the Lord,	220
Poem on Easter,	223
Index,	229

A TREATISE ON THE ANGER OF GOD,

ADDRESSED TO DONATUS.

Chap. I.—*Of divine and human wisdom.*

I HAVE often observed, Donatus, that many persons hold this opinion, which some philosophers also have maintained, that God is not subject to anger; since the divine nature is either altogether beneficent, and that it is inconsistent with His surpassing and excellent power to do injury to any one; or, at any rate, He takes no notice of us at all, so that no advantage comes to us from His goodness, and no evil from His ill-will. But the error of these men, because it is very great, and tends to overthrow the condition of human life, must be refuted by us, lest you yourself also should be deceived, being incited by the authority of men who deem themselves wise. Nor, however, are we so arrogant as to boast that the truth is comprehended by our intellect; but we follow the teaching of God, who alone is able to know and to reveal secret things. But the philosophers, being destitute of this teaching, have imagined that the nature of things can be ascertained by conjecture. But this is impossible; because the mind of man, enclosed in the dark abode of the body, is far removed from the perception of truth: and in this the divine nature differs from the human, that ignorance is the property of the human, knowledge of the divine nature.

On which account we have need of some light to dispel the darkness by which the reflection of man is overspread, since, while we live in mortal flesh, we are unable to divine by our senses. But the light of the human mind is God, and he who has known and admitted Him into his breast will acknowledge the mystery of the truth with an enlightened heart; but when God and heavenly instruction are removed, all things are full of errors. And Socrates, though he was the most learned of all the philosophers, yet, that he might prove the ignorance of the others, who thought that they possessed something, rightly said that he knew nothing, except one thing—that he knew nothing. For he understood that that learning had nothing certain, nothing true in itself; nor, as some imagine, did he pretend[1] to learning that he might refute others, but he saw the truth in some measure. And he testified even on his trial (as is related by Plato) that there was no human wisdom. He so despised, derided, and cast aside the learning in which the philosophers then boasted, that he professed that very thing as the greatest learning, that he had learnt that he knew nothing. If, therefore, there is no human wisdom, as Socrates taught, as Plato handed down, it is evident that the knowledge of the truth is divine, and belongs to no other than to God. Therefore God must be known, in whom alone is the truth. He is the Parent of the world, and the Framer of all things; who is not seen with the eyes, and is scarcely distinguished by the mind; whose religion is accustomed to be attacked in many ways by those who have neither been able to attain true wisdom, nor to comprehend the system of the great and heavenly secret.

CHAP. II.—*Of the truth and its steps, and of God.*

For since there are many steps by which the ascent is made to the abode of truth, it is not easy for any one to reach the summit. For when the eyes are darkened by the brightness of the truth, they who are unable to maintain a firm step fall back to the level ground.[2] Now the first step is to understand false religions, and to throw aside the impious worship of gods which are made by the hand of man. But the second step is to perceive with the mind that there is but one supreme God, whose power and providence made the world from the beginning, and afterwards continues to govern it. The third step is to know His Servant and Messenger,[3] whom He sent as His ambassador to the earth, by whose teaching being freed from the error in which we were held entangled, and formed to the

---

[1] "Simulavit;" others read "dissimulavit," concealed his knowledge.
[2] "Revolvuntur in planum."
[3] Thus our Lord Himself speaks, John xvii. 3 : " This is life eternal, that they may know Thee, the only true God, and Jesus Christ, whom Thou hast sent."

worship of the true God, we might learn righteousness. From all of these steps, as I have said, there is a rapid and easy gliding to a downfall,[1] unless the feet are firmly planted with unshaken stedfastness.

We see those shaken off from the first step, who, though they understand things which are false, do not, however, discover that which is true; and though they despised earthly and frail images, do not betake themselves to the worship of God, of whom they are ignorant. But viewing with admiration the elements of the universe, they worship the heaven, the earth, the sea, the sun, the moon, and the other heavenly bodies.

But we have already reproved their ignorance in the second book of the *Divine Institutes*.[2] But we say that those fall from the second step, who, though they understand that there is but one supreme God, nevertheless, ensnared by the philosophers, and captivated by false arguments, entertain opinions concerning that excellent majesty far removed from the truth; who either deny that God has any figure, or think that He is moved by no affection, because every affection is a sign of weakness, which has no existence in God. But they are precipitated from the third step, who, though they know the Ambassador of God, who is also the Builder of the divine and immortal temple,[3] either do not receive Him, or receive Him otherwise than faith demands; whom we have partly refuted in the fourth book of the above-named work.[4] And we will hereafter refute more carefully, when we shall begin to reply to all the sects, which, while they dispute,[5] have destroyed the truth.

But now we will argue against those who, falling from the second step, entertain wrong sentiments respecting the supreme God. For some say that He neither does a kindness to any one, nor becomes angry, but in security and quietness enjoys the advantages of His own immortality. Others, indeed, take away anger, but leave to God kindness; for they think that a nature excelling in the greatest virtue, while it ought not to be malevolent, ought also to be benevolent. Thus all the philosophers are agreed on the subject of anger, but are at variance respecting kindness. But, that my speech may descend in order to

---

[1] "Ad ruinam."   [2] Ch. v. and vi.
[3] The temple built of living stones, 1 Pet. ii. 5.   [4] Ch. x. etc.
[5] "Dum disputant;" other editions read, "dum dissipant."

the proposed subject, a division of this kind must be made and followed by me, since anger and kindness are different, and opposed to one another. Either anger must be attributed to God, and kindness taken from Him; or both alike must be taken from Him; or anger must be taken away, and kindness attributed to Him; or neither must be taken away. The nature of the case admits of nothing else besides these; so that the truth, which is sought for, must necessarily be found in some one of these. Let us consider them separately, that reason and arrangement may conduct us to the hiding-place of truth.

CHAP. III.—*Of the good and evil things in human affairs, and of their author.*

First, no one ever said this respecting God, that He is only subject to anger, and is not influenced by kindness. For it is unsuitable to God, that He should be endowed with a power of this kind, by which He may injure and do harm, but be unable to profit and to do good. What means, therefore, what hope of safety, is proposed to men, if God is the author of evils only? For if this is so, that venerable majesty will now be drawn out, not to the power of the judge, to whom it is permitted to preserve and set at liberty, but to the office of the torturer and executioner. But whereas we see that there are not only evils in human affairs, but also goods, it is plain that if God is the author of evils, there must be another who does things contrary to God, and gives to us good things. If there is such an one, by what name must he be called? Why is he who injures us more known to us than He who benefits us? But if this can be nothing besides God, it is absurd and vain to suppose that the divine power, than which nothing is greater or better, is able to injure, but unable to benefit; and accordingly no one has ever existed who ventured to assert this, because it is neither reasonable nor in any way credible. And because this is agreed upon, let us pass on and seek after the truth elsewhere.

CHAP. IV.—*Of God and His affections, and the censure of Epicurus.*

That which follows is concerning the school of Epicurus; that as there is no anger in God, so indeed there is no kindness. For when Epicurus thought that it was inconsistent with God to injure and to inflict harm, which for the most part arises from the affection of anger, he took away from Him beneficence also, since he saw that it followed that if God has anger, He must also have kindness. Therefore, lest he should concede to Him a vice, he deprived Him also of virtue. From this, he says, He is happy and uncorrupted, because He cares about nothing, and neither takes trouble Himself nor occasions it to another. Therefore He is not God, if He is neither moved, which is peculiar to a living being, nor does anything impossible for man, which is peculiar to God, if He has no will at all, no action, in short, no administration, which is worthy of God. And what greater, what more worthy administration can be attributed to God, than the government of the world, and especially of the human race, to which all earthly things are subject?

What happiness, then, can there be in God, if He is always inactive, being at rest and unmoveable? if He is deaf to those who pray to Him, and blind to His worshippers? What is so worthy of God, and so befitting to Him, as providence? But if He cares for nothing, and foresees nothing, He has lost all His divinity. What else does he say, who takes from God all power and all substance, except that there is no God at all? In short, Marcus Tullius relates that it was said by Posidonius, that Epicurus understood that there were no gods, but that he said those things which he spoke respecting the gods for the sake of driving away odium; and so that he leaves the gods in words, but takes them away in reality, since he gives them no motion, no office. But if this is so, what can be more deceitful than him? And this ought to be foreign to the character of a wise and weighty man. But if he understood one thing and spoke another, what else is he to be called than a deceiver, double-tongued, wicked, and moreover foolish? But Epicurus was not so crafty as to say those things with the desire of deceiving, when he consigned these things also by his writings to everlasting remembrance; but he erred through ignorance of the truth. For, being led from the beginning by the probability[1] of a single opinion, he necessarily fell into those things which followed. For the first opinion was, that anger was not consistent with the character of God. And when this

---

[1] "Verisimilitudine," *i.e.* likeness of truth.

appeared to him to be true and unassailable,[1] he was unable to refuse the consequences; because one affection being removed, necessity itself compelled him to remove from God the other affections also. Thus, he who is not subject to anger is plainly uninfluenced by kindness, which is the opposite feeling to anger. Now, if there is neither anger nor kindness in Him, it is manifest that there is neither fear, nor joy, nor grief, nor pity. For all the affections have one system, one motion,[2] which cannot be the case with God. But if there is no affection in God, because whatever is subject to affections is weak, it follows that there is in Him neither the care of anything, nor providence.

The disputation of the wise man[3] extends thus far: he was silent as to the other things which follow; namely, that because there is in Him neither care nor providence, therefore there is no reflection nor any perception in Him, by which it is effected that He has no existence at all. Thus, when he had gradually descended, he remained on the last step, because he now saw the precipice. But what does it avail to have remained silent, and concealed the danger? Necessity compelled him even against his will to fall. For he said that which he did not mean, because he so arranged his argument that he necessarily came to that point which he wished to avoid. You see, therefore, to what point he comes, when anger is removed and taken away from God. In short, either no one believes that, or a very few, and they the guilty and the wicked, who hope for impunity for their sins. But if this also is found to be false, that there is neither anger nor kindness in God, let us come to that which is put in the third place.

CHAP. V.—*The opinion of the Stoics concerning God; of His anger and kindness.*

The Stoics and some others are supposed to have entertained much better sentiments respecting the divine nature, who say that there is kindness in God, but not anger. A very pleasing and popular speech, that God is not subject to such littleness of mind as to imagine that He is injured by any one, since it is impossible for Him to be injured; so that that serene and holy majesty is excited, disturbed, and maddened, which is the part

---
[1] "Inexpugnabile," impregnable. [2] "Commotio."
[3] Epicurus: it seems to be spoken with some irony.

of human frailty. For they say that anger is a commotion and perturbation of the mind, which is inconsistent with God. But if anger is unbecoming to a man, provided he be of wisdom and authority (since, when it falls upon the mind of any one, as a violent tempest it excites such waves that it changes the condition of the mind, the eyes gleam, the countenance trembles, the tongue stammers, the teeth chatter, the countenance is alternately stained now with redness spread over it, now with white paleness), how much more is so foul a change unbecoming to God! And if man, when he has authority and power, inflicts widespread injury through anger, sheds blood, overthrows cities, destroys communities, reduces provinces to desolation, how much more is it to be believed that God, since He has power over the whole human race, and over the universe itself, would have been about to destroy all things if He were angry!

Therefore they think that so great and so pernicious an evil ought to be absent from Him. And if anger and excitement are absent from Him, because it is disfiguring and injurious, and He inflicts injury on no one, they think that nothing else remains, except that He is mild, calm, propitious, beneficent, the preserver. For thus at length He may be called the common Father of all, and the best and greatest, which His divine and heavenly nature demands. For if among men it appears praiseworthy to do good rather than to injure, to restore to life[1] rather than to kill, to save rather than to destroy, and innocence is not undeservedly numbered among the virtues,— and he who does these things is loved, esteemed, honoured, and celebrated with all blessings and vows,—in short, on account of his deserts and benefits is judged to be most like to God; how much more right is it that God Himself, who excels in divine and perfect virtues, and who is removed from all earthly taint, should conciliate[2] the whole race of man by divine and heavenly benefits! Those things are spoken speciously and in a popular manner, and they allure many to believe them; but they who entertain these sentiments approach nearer indeed to the truth, but they partly fail, not sufficiently considering the nature of the case. For if God is not angry with the impious and the unrighteous, it is clear that He does not love the pious and the

[1] "Vivificare."   [2] "Promereri."

righteous. Therefore the error of those is more consistent who take away at once both anger and kindness. For in opposite matters it is necessary to be moved to both sides or to neither. Thus, he who loves the good also hates the wicked, and he who does not hate the wicked does not love the good; because the loving of the good arises from the hatred of the wicked, and the hating of the wicked has its rise from the love of the good. There is no one who loves life without a hatred of death, nor who is desirous of light, but he who avoids darkness. These things are so connected by nature, that the one cannot exist without the other.

If any master has in his household a good and a bad servant, it is evident that he does not hate them both, or confer upon both benefits and honours; for if he does this, he is both unjust and foolish. But he addresses the one who is good with friendly words, and honours him, and sets him over his house and household, and all his affairs; but punishes the bad one with reproaches, with stripes, with nakedness, with hunger, with thirst, with fetters: so that the latter may be an example to others to keep them from sinning, and the former to conciliate them; so that fear may restrain some, and honour may excite others. He, therefore, who loves also hates, and he who hates also loves; for there are those who ought to be loved, and there are those who ought to be hated. And as he who loves confers good things on those whom he loves, so he who hates inflicts evils upon those whom he hates; which argument, because it is true, can in no way be refuted. Therefore the opinion of those is vain and false, who, when they attribute the one to God, take away the other, not less than the opinion of those who take away both. But the latter,[1] as we have shown, in part do not err, but retain that which is the better of the two; whereas the former,[2] led on by the accurate method of their reasoning, fall into the greatest error, because they have assumed premises which are altogether false. For they ought not to have reasoned thus: Because God is not liable to anger, therefore He is not moved by kindness; but in this manner: Because God is moved by kindness, therefore He is also liable to anger. For if it had been certain and undoubted that God is not liable to anger, then the other point would necessarily be arrived at.

[1] The Stoics.   [2] The Epicureans.

But since the question as to whether God is angry is more open to doubt, while it is almost perfectly plain that He is kind, it is absurd to wish to subvert that which is certain by means of an uncertainty, since it is easier to confirm uncertain things by means of those which are certain.

CHAP. VI.—*That God is angry.*

These are the opinions entertained by the philosophers respecting God. But if we have discovered that these things which have been spoken are false, there remains that one last resource, in which alone the truth can be found, which has never been embraced by philosophers, nor at any time defended: that it follows that God is angry, since He is moved by kindness. This opinion is to be maintained and asserted by us; for[1] this is the sum and turning-point on which the whole of piety and religion depend: and no honour can be due to God, if He affords nothing to His worshippers; and no fear, if He is not angry with him who does not worship Him.

CHAP. VII.—*Of man, and the brute animals, and religion.*

Though philosophers have often turned aside from reason through their ignorance of the truth, and have fallen into inextricable errors (for that is wont to happen to these which happens to a traveller ignorant of the way, and not confessing that he is ignorant,—namely, that he wanders about, while he is ashamed to inquire from those whom he meets), no philosopher, however, has ever made the assertion that there is no difference between man and the brutes. Nor has any one at all, provided that he wished to appear wise, reduced a rational animal to the level of the mute and irrational; which some ignorant persons do, resembling the brutes themselves, who, wishing to give themselves up to the indulgence of their appetite and pleasure, say that they are born on the same principle as all living animals, which it is impious for man to say. For who is so unlearned as not to know, who is so void of understanding as not to perceive, that there is something divine in man? I do not as yet come to the excellences of the soul and of the intellect, by which there is a manifest affinity between man and God. Does not the position of the body itself, and the fashion

[1] "In eo enim summa omnis et cardo religionis pietatisque versatur."

of the countenance, declare that we are not on a level with the dumb creation? Their nature is prostrated to the ground and to their pasture, and has nothing in common with the heaven, which they do not look upon. But man, with his erect position, with his elevated countenance raised to the contemplation of the universe, compares his features with God, and reason recognises reason.[1]

And on this account there is no animal, as Cicero says,[2] except man, which has any knowledge of God. For he alone is furnished with wisdom, so that he alone understands religion; and this is the chief or only difference between man and the dumb animals. For the other things which appear to be peculiar to man, even if there are not such in the dumb animals, nevertheless may appear to be similar. Speech is peculiar to man; yet even in these there is a certain resemblance to speech. For they both distinguish one another by their voices; and when they are angry, they send forth a sound resembling altercation; and when they see one another after an interval of time, they show the office of congratulation by their voice. To us, indeed, their voices appear uncouth,[3] as ours perhaps do to them; but to themselves, who understand one another, they are words. In short, in every affection they utter distinct expressions of voice by which they may show their state of mind. Laughter also is peculiar to man; and yet we see certain indications of joy in other animals, when they use passionate gestures[4] with a view to sports, hang down[5] their ears, contract their mouth, smooth their forehead, relax their eyes to sportiveness. What is so peculiar to man as reason and the foreseeing of the future? But there are animals which open several outlets in different directions from their lairs, that if any danger comes upon them, an escape may be open for them shut in; but they would not do this unless they possessed intelligence and reflection. Others are provident for the future, as "ants, when they plunder a great heap of corn, mindful of the winter, and lay it up in their dwelling;"[6] as bees, which "alone know a country and fixed abodes; and mindful of the

---

[1] The reason of man, man's rational nature, recognises the divine reason, *i.e.* God.
[2] *De Legibus*, i. 8.   [3] "Incondita," unformed, or rude.
[4] "Ad lusum gestiunt."   [5] "Demulcent."   [6] Virg. *Æn.* iv. 402.

winter which is to come, they practise labour in the summer, and lay up their gains as a common stock."[1]

It would be a long task if I should wish to trace out the things most resembling the skill of man, which are accustomed to be done by the separate tribes of animals. But if, in the case of all these things which are wont to be ascribed to man, there is found to be some resemblance even in the dumb animals, it is evident that religion is the only thing of which no trace can be found in the dumb animals, nor any indication. For justice is peculiar to religion, and to this no other animal attains. For man alone bears rule; the other animals are subjected[2] to him. But the worship of God is ascribed to justice; and he who does not embrace this, being far removed from the nature of man, will live the life of the brutes under the form of man. But since we differ from the other animals almost in this respect alone, that we alone of all perceive the divine might and power, while in the others there is no understanding of God, it is surely impossible that in this respect either the dumb animals should have more wisdom, or human nature should be unwise, since all living creatures, and the whole system of nature, are subject to man on account of his wisdom. Wherefore if reason, if the force of man in this respect, excels and surpasses the rest of living creatures, inasmuch as he alone is capable of the knowledge of God, it is evident that religion can in no way be overthrown.

CHAP. VIII.—*Of religion.*

But religion is overthrown if we believe Epicurus speaking thus: "For the nature of gods must ever in itself of necessity enjoy immortality together with supreme repose, far removed and withdrawn from our concerns; since, exempt from every pain, exempt from all dangers, strong in its own resources, not wanting aught of us, it is neither gained by favours nor moved by anger."[3] Now, when he says these things, does he think that any worship is to be paid to God, or does he entirely overthrow religion? For if God confers nothing good on any one, if He repays the obedience of His worshipper with no favour, what is so senseless, what so foolish, as to build temples, to offer sacrifices, to present gifts, to diminish our property,

[1] Virg. *Georg.* iv. 155.   [2] "Conciliata sunt."   [3] Lucret. ii. 646.

that we may obtain nothing?[1] But (it will be said) it is right that an excellent nature should be honoured. What honour can be due to a being who pays no regard to us, and is ungrateful? Can we be bound in any manner to him who has nothing in common with us? "Farewell to God," says Cicero,[2] "if He is such as to be influenced by no favour, and by no affection of men. For why should I say 'may He be propitious?' for He can be propitious to no one." What can be spoken more contemptible with respect to God? Farewell to Him, he says, that is, let Him depart and retire, since He is able to profit no one. But if God takes no trouble, nor occasions trouble to another, why then should we not commit crimes as often as it shall be in our power to escape the notice of men,[3] and to cheat the public laws? Wherever we shall obtain a favourable opportunity of escaping notice, let us take advantage of the occasion: let us take away the property of others, either without bloodshed or even with blood, if there is nothing else besides the laws to be reverenced.

While Epicurus entertains these sentiments, he altogether destroys religion; and when this is taken away, confusion and perturbation of life will follow. But if religion cannot be taken away without destroying our hold of wisdom, by which we are separated from the brutes, and of justice, by which the public life may be more secure, how can religion itself be maintained or guarded without fear? For that which is not feared is despised, and that which is despised is plainly not reverenced. Thus it comes to pass that religion, and majesty, and honour exist together with fear; but there is no fear where no one is angry. Whether, therefore, you take away from God kindness, or anger, or both, religion must be taken away, without which the life of men is full of folly, of wickedness, and enormity. For conscience greatly curbs men, if we believe that we are living in the sight of God; if we imagine not only that the actions which we perform are seen from above, but also that our thoughts and our words are heard by God. But it is profitable to believe this, as some imagine, not for the sake of the truth, but of utility, since laws cannot punish conscience unless some terror from above hangs over to restrain offences.

---

[1] *i.e.* without any result.
[2] *De Nat. Deor.* i. 44.
[3] "Hominum conscientiam fallere."

Therefore religion is altogether false, and there is no divinity; but all things are made up by skilful men, in order that they may live more uprightly and innocently. This is a great question, and foreign to the subject which we have proposed; but because it necessarily occurs, it ought to be handled, however briefly.

CHAP. IX.—*Of the providence of God, and of opinions opposed to it.*

When the philosophers of former times had agreed in their opinions respecting providence, and there was no doubt but that the world was set in order by God and reason, and was governed by reason, Protagoras, in the times of Socrates, was the first of all who said that it was not clear to him whether there was any divinity or not. And this disputation of his was judged so impious, and so contrary to the truth and to religion, that the Athenians both banished him from their territories, and burnt in a public assembly those books of his in which these statements were contained. But there is no need to speak respecting his opinions, because he pronounced nothing certain. After these things Socrates and his disciple Plato, and those who flowed forth from the school of Plato like rivulets into different directions, namely, the Stoics and Peripatetics, were of the same opinion as those who went before them.

Afterwards Epicurus said that there was indeed a God, because it was necessary that there should be in the world some being of surpassing excellence, distinction, and blessedness; yet that there was no providence, and thus that the world itself was ordered by no plan, nor art, nor workmanship, but that the universe was made up of certain minute and indivisible seeds. But I do not see what can be said more repugnant to the truth. For if there is a God, as God He is manifestly provident; nor can divinity be attributed to Him in any other way than if He retains the past, and knows the present, and foresees the future. Therefore, in taking away providence, he also denied the existence of God. But when he openly acknowledged the existence of God, at the same time he also admitted His providence; for the one cannot exist at all, or be understood without the other. But in those later times in which philosophy had now lost its vigour,[1] there lived a certain Diagoras

[1] "Defloruerat."

of Melos, who altogether denied the existence of God, and on account of this sentiment was called atheist;[1] also Theodorus of Cyrene: both of whom, because they were unable to discover anything new, all things having already been said and found out, preferred even, in opposition to the truth, to deny that in which all preceding philosophers had agreed without any ambiguity. These are they who attacked providence, which had been asserted and defended through so many ages by so many intellects. What then? Shall we refute those trifling and inactive philosophers by reason, or by the authority of distinguished men, or rather by both? But we must hasten onwards, lest our speech should wander too far from our subject.

CHAP. X.—*Of the origin of the world, and the nature of affairs, and the providence of God.*

They who do not admit that the world was made by divine providence, either say that it is composed of first principles coming together at random, or that it suddenly came into existence by nature, but hold, as Straton does, that nature has in itself the power of production and of diminution, but that it has neither sensibility nor figure, so that we may understand that all things were produced spontaneously, without any artificer or author. Each opinion is vain and impossible. But this happens to those who are ignorant of the truth, that they devise anything, rather than perceive that which the nature of the subject[2] requires. First of all, with respect to those minute seeds, by the meeting together of which they say that the whole world came into existence,[3] I ask where or whence they are. Who has seen them at any time? who has perceived them? who has heard them? Had none but Leucippus eyes? had he alone a mind, who assuredly alone of all men was blind and senseless, since he spoke those things which no sick man could have uttered in his ravings,[4] or one asleep in his dreams?

The ancient philosophers argued that all things were made up of four elements. He would not admit this, lest he should appear to tread in the footsteps of others; but he held that there were other first principles of the elements themselves, which can neither be seen, nor touched, nor be perceived by any part of the body. They are so minute, he says, that there

[1] ἄθεος. [2] "Ratio." [3] "Coiisse." [4] "Delirare posset."

is no edge of a sword so fine that they can be cut and divided by it. From which circumstance he gave them the name of atoms. But it occurred to him, that if they all had one and the same nature, they could not make up different objects of so great a variety as we see to be present in the world. He said, therefore, that there were smooth and rough ones, and round, and angular, and hooked. How much better had it been to be silent, than to have a tongue for such miserable and empty uses! And, indeed, I fear lest he who thinks these things worthy of refutation, should appear no less to rave. Let us, however, reply as to one who says something.[1] If they are soft[2] and round, it is plain that they cannot lay hold of one another, so as to make some body; as, though any one should wish to bind together millet into one combination,[3] the very softness of the grains would not permit them to come together into a mass. If they are rough, and angular, and hooked, so that they may be able to cohere, then they are divisible, and capable of being cut; for hooks and angles must project,[4] so that they may possibly be cut off.

Therefore that which is able to be cut off and torn away, will be able both to be seen and held. "These," he says, "flutter about with restless motions through empty space, and are carried hither and thither, just as we see little particles of dust in the sun when it has introduced its rays and light through a window. From these there arise trees and herbs, and all fruits of the earth; from these, animals, and water, and fire, and all things are produced, and are again resolved into the same elements." This can be borne as long as the inquiry is respecting small matters. Even the world itself was made up of these. He has reached to the full extent of perfect madness: it seems impossible that anything further should be said, and yet he found something to add. "Since everything," he says, "is infinite, and nothing can be empty, it follows of necessity that there are innumerable worlds." What force of atoms had been so great, that masses so incalculable should be collected from such minute elements? And first of all I ask, What is the nature or origin of those seeds? For if all things are from them, whence shall we say that they them-

---

[1] *i.e.* something to the purpose. [2] "Lenia;" others read "lævia," smooth.
[3] "Coagmentationem." [4] "Eminere," to stand out prominently.

selves are? what nature supplied such an abundance of matter for the making of innumerable worlds? But let us grant that he raved with impunity concerning worlds; let us speak respecting this in which we are, and which we see. He says that all things are made from minute bodies which are incapable of division. If this were so, no object would ever need the seed of its own kind. Birds would be born without eggs, or eggs without bringing forth; likewise the rest of the living creatures without coition: trees and the productions of the earth would not have their own seeds, which we daily handle and sow. Why does a corn-field arise from grain, and again grain from a corn-field? In short, if the meeting together and collecting of atoms would effect all things, all things would grow together in the air, since atoms flutter about through empty space. Why cannot the herb, why cannot the tree or grain, arise or be increased without earth, without roots, without moisture, without seed? From which it is evident that nothing is made up from atoms, since everything has its own peculiar and fixed nature, its own seed, its own law given from the beginning. Finally, Lucretius, as though forgetful of atoms, which he was maintaining, in order that he might refute those who say that all things are produced from nothing, employed these arguments, which might have weighed against himself. For he thus spoke: "If things came from nothing, any kind might be born of anything; nothing would require seed."[1] Likewise afterwards: "We must admit, therefore, that nothing can come from nothing, since things require seed before they can severally be born, and be brought out into the buxom fields of air."[2] Who would imagine that he had brain when he said these things, and did not see that they were contrary to one another? For that nothing is made by means of atoms, is apparent from this, that everything has a definite[3] seed, unless by chance we shall believe that the nature both of fire and water is derived from atoms. Why should I say, that if materials of the greatest hardness are struck together with a violent blow, fire is struck out? Are atoms concealed in the steel, or in the flint? Who shut them in? or why do they not leap forth spontaneously? or how could the seeds of fire remain in a material of the greatest coldness?

[1] Lucret. i. 160.   [2] Lucret. i. 206.   [3] "Certum."

I leave the subject of the flint and steel. If you hold in the sun an orb of crystal filled with water, fire is kindled from the light which is reflected from the water, even in the most severe cold. Must we then believe that fire is contained in the water? And yet fire cannot be kindled from the sun even in summer. If you shall breathe upon wax, or if a light vapour shall touch anything—either the hard surface[1] of marble or a plate of metal—water is gradually condensed by means of the most minute drops. Also from the exhalation of the earth or sea mist is formed, which either, being dispersed, moistens whatever it has covered, or being collected, is carried aloft by the wind to high mountains, and compressed into cloud, and sends down great rains. Where, then, do we say that fluids are produced? Is it in the vapour? or in the exhalation? or in the wind? But nothing can be formed in that which is neither touched nor seen. Why should I speak of animals, in whose bodies we see nothing formed without plan, without arrangement, without utility, without beauty, so that the most skilful and careful marking out[2] of all the parts and members repels the idea of accident and chance? But let us suppose it possible that the limbs, and bones, and nerves, and blood should be made up of atoms. What of the senses, the reflection, the memory, the mind, the natural capacity: from what seeds can they be compacted?[3] He says, From the most minute. There are therefore others of greater size. How, then, are they indivisible?

In the next place, if the things which are not seen are formed from invisible seeds, it follows that those which are seen are from visible seeds. Why, then, does no one see them? But whether any one regards the invisible parts which are in man, or the parts which can be touched, and which are visible, who does not see that both parts exist in accordance with design?[4] How, then, can bodies which meet together without design effect anything reasonable?[5] For we see that there is nothing in the whole world which has not in itself very great and wonderful design. And since this is above the sense and capacity of man, to what can it be more rightly attributed than to the divine providence? If a statue, the resemblance of man, is

---

[1] "Crustam marmoris." [2] "Descriptio." [3] "Coagmentari."
[4] "Ratio." [5] "Rationale."

made by the exercise of design and art, shall we suppose that man himself is made up of fragments which come together at random? And what resemblance to the truth is there in the thing produced,[1] when the greatest and most surpassing skill[2] can imitate nothing more than the mere outline and extreme lineaments[3] of the body? Was the skill of man able to give to his production any motion or sensibility? I say nothing of the exercise of the sight, of hearing, and of smelling, and the wonderful uses of the other members, either those which are in sight or those which are hidden from view. What artificer could have fabricated either the heart of man, or the voice, or his very wisdom? Does any man of sound mind, therefore, think that that which man cannot do by reason and judgment, may be accomplished by a meeting together of atoms everywhere adhering to each other? You see into what foolish ravings they have fallen, while they are unwilling to assign to God the making and the care of all things.

Let us, however, concede to them that the things which are earthly are made from atoms: are the things also which are heavenly? They say that the gods are without contamination, eternal, and blessed; and they grant to them alone an exemption, so that they do not appear to be made up of a meeting together of atoms. For if the gods also had been made up of these, they would be liable to be dispersed, the seeds at length being resolved, and returning to their own nature. Therefore, if there is something which the atoms could not produce, why may we not judge in the same way of the others? But I ask why the gods did not build for themselves a dwelling-place before those first elements produced the world? It is manifest that, unless the atoms had come together and made the heaven, the gods would still be suspended through the midst of empty space. By what counsel, then, by what plan, did the atoms from a confused mass collect themselves, so that from some the earth below was formed into a globe, and the heaven stretched out above, adorned with so great a variety of constellations that nothing can be conceived more embellished? Can he, therefore, who sees such and so great objects, imagine that they were made without any design, without any providence, without any divine intelligence, but that such great and

---

[1] "Ficto."   [2] "Artificium."   [3] "Umbram et extrema lineamenta."

wonderful things arose out of fine and minute atoms? Does it not resemble a prodigy, that there should be any human being who might say these things, or that there should be those who might believe them?—as Democritus, who was his hearer, or Epicurus, to whom all folly flowed forth from the fountain of Leucippus. But, as others say, the world was made by Nature, which is without perception and figure. But this is much more absurd. If Nature made the world, it must have made it by judgment and intelligence; for it is he that makes something who has either the inclination to make it, or knowledge. If nature is without perception and figure, how can that be made by it which has both perception and figure, unless by chance any one thinks that the fabric of animals, which is so delicate, could have been formed and animated by that which is without perception, or that that figure of heaven, which is prepared with such foresight for the uses of living beings, suddenly came into existence by some accident or other, without a builder, without an artificer?

"If there is anything," says Chrysippus, "which effects those things which man, though he is endowed with reason, cannot do, that assuredly is greater, and stronger, and wiser than man." But man cannot make heavenly things; therefore that which shall produce or has produced these things surpasses man in art, in design, in skill, and in power. Who, therefore, can it be but God? But Nature, which they suppose to be, as it were, the mother of all things, if it has not a mind, will effect nothing, will contrive nothing; for where there is no reflection there is neither motion nor efficacy. But if it uses counsel for the commencement of anything, reason for its arrangement, art for its accomplishment, energy for its consummation, and power to govern and control, why should it be called Nature rather than God? Or if a concourse of atoms, or Nature without mind, made those things which we see, I ask why it was able to make the heaven, but unable to make a city or a house? why it made mountains of marble, but did not make columns and statues? But ought not atoms to have come together to effect these things, since they leave no position untried? For concerning Nature, which has no mind, it is no wonder that it forgot to do these things. What, then, is the case? It is plain that God, when He commenced this work of the world,—than which nothing can be better arranged with respect to order, nor more befitting as to utility, nor more adorned as to beauty, nor greater as to bulk,—Himself made the things which could not be made by man; and among these also man himself, to whom He gave a portion of His own wisdom, and furnished him with reason, as much as earthly frailty was capable of receiving, that he might make for himself the things which were necessary for his own uses.

But if in the commonwealth of this world, so to speak, there is no providence which rules, no God who administers, no sense at all prevails in this nature of things. From what source therefore will it be believed that the human mind, with its skill and its intelligence, had its origin? For if the body of man was made from the ground, from which circumstance man received his name;[1] it follows that the soul, which has intelligence, and is the ruler of the body, which the limbs obey as a king and commander, which can neither be looked upon nor comprehended, could not have come to man except from a wise nature. But as mind and soul govern everybody, so also does God govern the world. For it is not probable that lesser and humble things bear rule, but that greater and highest things do not bear rule. In short, Marcus Cicero, in his *Tusculan Disputations*, and in his *Consolation*, says: "No origin of souls can be found on earth. For there is nothing, he says, mixed and compound[2] in souls, or which may appear to be produced and made up from the earth; nothing moist or airy,[3] or of the nature of fire. For in these natures there is nothing which has the force of memory, of mind and reflection, which both retains the past and foresees the future, and is able to comprise the present; which things alone are divine For no source will ever be found from which they are able to come to man, unless it be from God." Since, therefore, with the exception of two or three vain calumniators, it is agreed upon that the world is governed by providence, as also it was made, and there is no one who ventures to prefer the opinion of Diagoras and Theodorus, or the empty fiction of Leucippus, or the levity of Democritus and Epicurus, either to the authority of those seven ancient men who were called wise, or to that of Pythagoras or of Socrates or Plato, and the other philosophers who judged that there is a providence; therefore that opinion also is false, by which they think

[1] " Homo " ab " humo." [2] " Concretum." [3] " Flabile."

that religion was instituted by wise men for the sake of terror and fear, in order that ignorant men might abstain from sins.

But if this is true, it follows that we are derided by the wise men of old. But if they invented religion for the sake of deceiving us, and moreover of deceiving the whole human race, therefore they were not wise, because falsehood is not consistent with the character of the wise man. But grant that they were wise; what great success in falsehood was it, that they were able to deceive not only the unlearned, but Plato also, and Socrates, and so easily to delude Pythagoras, Zeno, and Aristotle, the chiefs of the greatest sects? There is therefore a divine providence, as those men whom I have named perceived, by the energy and power of which all things which we see were both made and are governed. For so vast a system of things,[1] such arrangement and such regularity in preserving the settled orders and times, could neither at first have arisen without a provident artificer, or have existed so many ages without a powerful inhabitant, or have been perpetually governed without a skilful and intelligent[2] ruler; and reason itself declares this. For whatever exists which has reason, must have arisen from reason. Now reason is the part of an intelligent and wise nature; but a wise and intelligent nature can be nothing else than God. Now the world, since it has reason, by which it is both governed and kept together, was therefore made by God. But if God is the maker and ruler of the world, then religion is rightly and truly established; for honour and worship are due to the author and common parent of all things.

CHAP. XI.—*Of God, and that the one God, and by whose providence the world is governed and exists.*

Since it is agreed upon concerning providence, it follows that we show whether it is to be believed that it belongs to many, or rather to one only. We have sufficiently taught, as I think, in our *Institutions*, that there cannot be many gods; because, if the divine energy and power be distributed among several, it must necessarily be diminished. But that which is lessened is plainly mortal; but if He is not mortal, He can neither be lessened nor divided. Therefore there is but one God, in whom complete energy and power can neither be lessened

---

[1] "Tanta rerum magnitudo."   [2] "Sentiente;" others read "sciente."

nor increased. But if there are many, while they separately have something of power and authority, the sum itself decreases; nor will they separately be able to have the whole, which they have in common with others: so much will be wanting to each as the others shall possess. There cannot therefore be many rulers in this world, nor many masters in one house, nor many pilots in one ship, nor many leaders in one herd or flock, nor many queens in one swarm. But there could not have been many suns in heaven, as there are not several souls in one body; so entirely does the whole of nature agree in unity. But if the world

"Is nourished by a soul,
A spirit whose celestial flame
Glows in each member of the frame,
And stirs the mighty whole," [1]

it is evident from the testimony of the poet, that there is one God who inhabits the world, since the whole body cannot be inhabited and governed except by one mind. Therefore all divine power must be in one person, by whose will and command all things are ruled; and therefore He is so great, that He cannot be described in words by man, or estimated by the senses. From what source, therefore, did the opinion or persuasion [2] respecting many gods come to men? Without doubt, all those who are worshipped as gods were men, and were also the earliest and greatest kings; but who is ignorant that they were invested with divine honours after death, either on account of the virtue by which they had profited the race of men, or that they obtained immortal memory on account of the benefits and inventions by which they had adorned human life? And not only men, but women also. And this, both the most ancient writers of Greece, whom they call *theologi*,[3] and also Roman writers following and imitating the Greeks, teach; of whom especially Euhemerus and our Ennius, who point out the birth-days, marriages, offspring, governments, exploits, deaths, and tombs [4] of all of them. And Tullius, following them, in his third book, *On the Nature of the Gods*, destroyed the public

---

[1] Virg. Æn. vi. 726.
[2] "Persuasiove;" most editions read "persuasione," but the meaning is not so good.
[3] θεολόγοι.   [4] "Sepulcra;" others read "simulacra."

religions; but neither he himself nor any other person was able to introduce the true one, of which he was ignorant. And thus he himself testified that that which was false was evident; that the truth, however, lay concealed. "Would to heaven," he says, "that I could as easily discover true things as refute those that are false!"[1] And this he proclaimed not with dissimulation as an academic, but truly and in accordance with the feeling of his mind, because the truth cannot be uprooted from human perceptions: that which the foresight of man was able to attain to, he attained to, that he might expose false things. For whatever is fictitious and false, because it is supported by no reason, is easily destroyed. There is therefore one God, the source and origin of all things, as Plato both felt and taught in the *Timæus*, whose majesty he declares to be so great, that it can neither be comprehended by the mind nor be expressed by the tongue.

Hermes bears the same testimony, whom Cicero asserts[2] to be reckoned by the Egyptians among the number of the gods. I speak of him who, on account of his excellence and knowledge of many arts, was called Trismegistus; and he was far more ancient not only than Plato, but than Pythagoras, and those seven wise men. In Xenophon,[3] Socrates, as he discourses, says that "the form of God ought not to be inquired about;" and Plato, in his *Book of Laws*,[4] says: "What God is, ought not to be the subject of inquiry, because it can neither be found out nor related." Pythagoras also admits that there is but one God, saying that there is an incorporeal mind, which, being diffused and stretched through all nature, gives vital perception to all living creatures; but Antisthenes, in his *Physics*, said that there was but one natural God, although the nations and cities have gods of their own people. Aristotle, with his followers the Peripatetics, and Zeno with his followers the Stoics, say nearly the same things. Truly it would be a long task to follow up the opinions of all separately, who, although they used different names, nevertheless agreed in one power which governed the world. But, however, though philosophers and poets, and those, in short, who worship the gods, often acknowledge the supreme God, yet no one ever inquired into,

[1] *De Nat. Deor.* i. 32.
[2] *Memor.* iv. 3.
[3] *De Nat. Deor.* iii. 22.
[4] *Lib.* vii.

no one discussed, the subject of His worship and honours; with that persuasion, in truth, with which, always believing Him to be bounteous and incorruptible, they think[1] that He is neither angry with any one, nor stands in need of any worship. Thus there can be no religion where there is no fear.

Chap. XII.—*Of religion and the fear of God.*

Now, since we have replied to the impious and detestable wisdom,[2] or rather senselessness of some, let us return to our proposed subject. We have said that, if religion is taken away, neither wisdom nor justice can be retained: wisdom, because the understanding of the divine nature, in which we differ from the brutes, is found in man alone; justice, because unless God, who cannot be deceived, shall restrain our desires, we shall live wickedly and impiously. Therefore, that our actions should be viewed by God, pertains not only to the usefulness of common life, but even to the truth; because, if religion and justice are taken away, having lost our reason, we either descend to the senselessness[3] of the herds; or to the savageness of the beasts, yea, even more so, since the beasts spare animals of their own kind. What will be more savage, what more unmerciful, than man, if, the fear of a superior being taken away, he shall be able either to escape the notice of or to despise the might of the laws? It is therefore the fear of God alone which guards the mutual society of men, by which life itself is sustained, protected, and governed. But that fear is taken away if man is persuaded that God is without anger; for that He is moved and indignant when unjust actions are done, not only the common advantage, but even reason itself, and truth, persuade us. We must again return to the former subjects, that, as we have taught that the world was made by God, we may teach why it was made.

Chap. XIII.—*Of the advantage and use of the world and of the seasons.*

If any one considers the whole government of the world, he

---

[1] "Arbitrantur;" some editions have "arbitrabantur," which appears preferable.
[2] "Prudentiæ;" another reading is "imprudentiæ."
[3] "Stultitiam."

will certainly understand how true is the opinion of the Stoics, who say that the world was made on our account. For all the things of which the world is composed, and which it produces from itself, are adapted to the use of man. Man, accordingly, uses fire for the purpose of warmth and light, and of softening his food, and for the working of iron; he uses springs for drinking, and for baths; he uses rivers for irrigating the fields, and assigning boundaries to countries; he uses the earth for receiving a variety of fruits, the hills for planting vineyards, the mountains for the use of trees and firewood,[1] the plains for crops of grain; he uses the sea not only for commerce, and for receiving supplies from distant countries, but also for abundance of every kind of fish. But if he makes use of these elements to which he is nearest, there is no doubt that he uses the heaven also, since the offices even of heavenly things are regulated for the fertility of the earth from which we live. The sun, with its ceaseless courses and unequal intervals,[2] completes its annual circles, and either at his rising draws forth the day for labour, or at his setting brings on the night for repose; and at one time by his departure farther towards the south, at another time by his approach nearer towards the north, he causes the vicissitudes of winter and summer, so that both by the moistures and frosts of winter the earth becomes enriched for fruitfulness, and by the heats of summer either the produce of grass[3] is hardened by maturity, or that which is in moist places, being seethed and heated, becomes ripened. The moon also, which governs the time of night, regulates her monthly courses by the alternate loss and recovery of light,[4] and by the brightness of her shining illumines the nights obscure with gloomy darkness, so that journeys in the summer heat, and expeditions, and works, may be performed without labour and inconvenience; since

"By night the light stubble, by night
The dry meadows are better mown."[5]

The other heavenly bodies also, either at their rising or setting,

[1] "Lignorum."
[2] "Spatiis." The word properly refers to a racecourse.
[3] "Herbidæ fruges."   [4] "Amissi ac recepti luminis vicibus."
[5] Virg. *Georg.* i. 289.

supply favourable times[1] by their fixed positions.[2] Moreover, they also afford guidance to ships, that they may not wander through the boundless deep with uncertain course, since the pilot duly observing them arrives at the harbour of the shore at which he aims.[3] Clouds are attracted by the breath of the winds, that the fields of sown grain may be watered with showers, that the vines may abound with produce, and the trees with fruits. And these things are exhibited by a succession of changes throughout the year, that nothing may at any time be wanting by which the life of men is sustained. But[4] (it is said) the same earth nourishes the other living creatures, and by the produce of the same even the dumb animals are fed. Has not God laboured also for the sake of the dumb animals? By no means; because they are void of reason. On the contrary, we understand that even these themselves in the same manner were made by God for the use of man, partly for food, partly for clothing, partly to assist him in his work; so that it is manifest that the divine providence wished to furnish and adorn the life of men with an abundance of objects and resources, and on this account He both filled the air with birds, and the sea with fishes, and the earth with quadrupeds. But the Academics, arguing against the Stoics, are accustomed to ask why, if God made all things for the sake of men, many things are found even opposed, and hostile, and injurious to us, as well in the sea as on the land. And the Stoics, without any regard to the truth, most foolishly repelled this. For they say that there are many things among natural productions,[5] and reckoned among animals, the utility of which hitherto[6] escapes notice, but that this is discovered in process of the times, as necessity and use have already discovered many things which were unknown in former ages. What utility, then, can be discovered in mice, in beetles, in serpents, which are troublesome and pernicious to man? Is it that some medicine lies concealed in them? If there is any, it will at some time be found out, namely, as a

---

[1] "Opportunitates temporum."
[2] "Certis stationibus." Others read "sationibus," for certain kinds of sowing; but "statio" is applied to the stars by Seneca and Pliny.
[3] "Designati."
[4] An objection is here met and answered.
[5] "Gignentium."   [6] "Adhuc," omitted in many manuscripts.

remedy against evils, whereas they complain that it is altogether evil. They say that the viper, when burnt and reduced to ashes, is a remedy for the bite of the same beast. How much better had it been that it should not exist at all, than that a remedy should be required against it drawn from itself?

They might then have answered with more conciseness and truth after this manner. When God had formed man as it were His own image, that which was the completion of His workmanship, He breathed wisdom into him alone, so that he might bring all things into subjection to his own authority and government, and make use of all the advantages of the world. And yet He set before him both good and evil things, inasmuch as He gave to him wisdom, the whole nature of which is employed in discerning things evil and good: for no one can choose better things, and know what is good, unless he at the same time knows to reject and avoid the things which are evil. They are both mutually connected with each other, so that, the one being taken away, the other must also be taken away. Therefore, good and evil things being set before it, then at length wisdom discharges its office, and desires the good for usefulness, but rejects the evil for safety. Therefore, as innumerable good things have been given which it might enjoy, so also have evils, against which it might guard. For if there is no evil, no danger—nothing, in short, which can injure man—all the material of wisdom is taken away, and will be unnecessary for man. For if only good things are placed in sight, what need is there of reflection, of understanding, of knowledge, of reason? since, wherever he shall extend his hand, that is befitting and adapted to nature: so that if any one should wish to place a most exquisite dinner before infants, who as yet have no taste, it is plain that each will desire that to which either impulse, or hunger, or even accident, shall attract them; and whatever they shall take, it will be useful and salutary to them. What injury will it therefore be for them always to remain as they are, and always to be infants and unacquainted with affairs? But if you add a mixture either of bitter things, or things useless, or even poisonous, they are plainly deceived through their ignorance of good and evil, unless wisdom is added to them, by which they may have the rejection of evil things and the choice of good things.

You see, therefore, that we have greater need of wisdom on account of evils; and unless these things had been proposed to us, we should not be a rational animal. But if this account is true, which the Stoics were in no manner able to see, that argument also of Epicurus is done away. God, he says, either wishes to take away evils, and is unable; or He is able, and is unwilling; or He is neither willing nor able, or He is both willing and able. If He is willing and is unable, He is feeble, which is not in accordance with the character of God; if He is able and unwilling, He is envious, which is equally at variance with God; if He is neither willing nor able, He is both envious and feeble, and therefore not God; if He is both willing and able, which alone is suitable to God, from what source then are evils? or why does He not remove them? I know that many of the philosophers, who defend providence, are accustomed to be disturbed by this argument, and are almost driven against their will to admit that God takes no interest in anything, which Epicurus especially aims at; but having examined the matter, we easily do away with this formidable argument. For God is able to do whatever He wishes, and there is no weakness or envy in God. He is able, therefore, to take away evils; but He does not wish to do so, and yet He is not on that account envious. For on this account He does not take them away, because He at the same time gives wisdom, as I have shown; and there is more of goodness and pleasure in wisdom than of annoyance in evils. For wisdom causes us even to know God, and by that knowledge to attain to immortality, which is the chief good. Therefore, unless we first know evil, we shall be unable to know good. But Epicurus did not see this, nor did any other, that if evils are taken away, wisdom is in like manner taken away; and that no traces of virtue remain in man, the nature of which consists in enduring and overcoming the bitterness of evils. And thus, for the sake of a slight gain[1] in the taking away of evils, we should be deprived of a good, which is very great, and true, and peculiar to us. It is plain, therefore, that all things are proposed for the sake of man, as well evils as also goods.

[1] "Propter exiguum compendium sublatorum malorum."

Chap. XIV.—*Why God made man.*

It follows that I show for what purpose God made man himself. As He contrived the world for the sake of man, so He formed man himself on His own account, as it were a priest of a divine temple, a spectator of His works and of heavenly objects. For he is the only being who, since he is intelligent and capable of reason, is able to understand God, to admire His works, and perceive His energy and power; for on this account he is furnished with judgment, intelligence, and prudence. On this account he alone, beyond the other living creatures, has been made with an upright body and attitude, so that he seems to have been raised up for the contemplation of his Parent. On this account he alone has received language, and a tongue the interpreter of his thought, that he may be able to declare the majesty of his Lord. Lastly, for this cause all things were placed under his control, that he himself might be under the control of God, their Maker and Creator. If God, therefore, designed man to be a worshipper of Himself, and on this account gave him so much honour, that he might rule over all things; it is plainly most just that he should worship Him[1] who bestowed upon him such great gifts, and love man, who is united with us in the participation of the divine justice. For it is not right that a worshipper of God should be injured by a worshipper of God. From which it is understood that man was made for the sake of religion and justice. And of this matter Marcus Tullius is a witness in his books respecting the Laws, since he thus speaks:[2] "But of all things concerning which learned men dispute, nothing is of greater consequence than that it should be altogether understood that we are born to justice." And if this is most true, it follows that God will have all men to be just, that is, to have God and man as objects of their affection; to honour God in truth as a Father, and to love man as a brother: for in these two things the whole of justice is comprised. But he who either fails to acknowledge God or acts injuriously to man, lives unjustly and contrary to his nature, and in this manner disturbs the divine institution and law.

---

[1] "Et Deum colere," etc. Some editions read, "et eum, qui tanta præstiterit," omitting the word "colere."
[2] i. 10.

CHAP. XV.—*Whence sins extended to man.*

Here perhaps some one may ask, Whence sins extended to man, or what perversion distorted the rule of the divine institution to worse things, so that, though he was born to justice, he nevertheless performs unjust works. I have already in a former place explained, that God at the same time set before him good and evil, and that He loves the good, and hates the evil which is contrary to this; but that He permitted the evil on this account, that the good also might shine forth, since, as I have often taught, we understand that the one cannot exist without the other; in short, that the world itself is made up of two elements opposing and connected with one another, of fire and moisture, and that light could not have been made unless there had also been darkness, since there cannot be a higher place without a lower, nor a rising without a setting, nor warmth without cold, nor softness without hardness. Thus also we are composed of two substances equally opposed to one another—soul and body: the one of which is assigned to the heaven, because it is slight and not to be handled; the other to the earth, because it is capable of being laid hold of: the one is firm[1] and eternal, the other frail and mortal. Therefore good clings to the one, and evil to the other: light, life, and justice to the one; darkness, death, and injustice to the other. Hence there arose among men the corruption of their nature, so that it was necessary that a law should be established, by which vices might be prohibited, and the duties of virtue be enjoined. Since, therefore, there are good and evil things in the affairs of men, the nature of which I have set forth, it must be that God is moved to both sides, both to favour when He sees that just things are done, and to anger when He perceives unjust things.

But Epicurus opposes us, and says: "If there is in God the affection of joy leading Him to favour, and of hatred influencing Him to anger, He must of necessity have both fear, and inclination, and desire, and the other affections which belong to human weakness." It does not follow that he who is angry must fear, or that he who feels joy must grieve; in short, they who are liable to anger are less timid, and they who are of a

---
[1] "Solidum."

joyful temperament are less affected with grief. What need is there to speak of the affections of humanity, to which our nature yields? Let us weigh the divine necessity; for I am unwilling to speak of nature, since it is believed that our God was never born. The affection of fear has a subject-matter in man, but it has none in God. Man, inasmuch as he is liable to many accidents and dangers, fears lest any greater violence should arise which may strike, despoil, lacerate, dash down, and destroy him. But God, who is liable neither to want, nor injury, nor pain, nor death, can by no means fear, because there is nothing which can offer violence to Him. Also the reason and cause of desire is manifest in man. For, inasmuch as he was made frail and mortal, it was necessary that another and different sex should be made, by union with which offspring might be produced to continue the perpetuity of his race. But this desire has no place in God, because frailty and death are far removed from Him; nor is there with Him any female in whose union He is able to rejoice; nor does He stand in need of succession, since He will live for ever. The same things may be said respecting envy and passion, to which, from sure and manifest causes, man is liable, but to which God is by no means liable. But, in truth, favour and anger and pity have their substance[1] in God, and that greatest and matchless power employs them for the preservation of the world.

CHAP. XVI.—*Of God, and His anger and affections.*

Some one will ask what this substance is. First of all, when evils befall them, men in their dejected state for the most part have recourse to God: they appease and entreat Him, believing that He is able to repel injuries from them. He has therefore an occasion of exercising pity; for He is not so unmerciful and a despiser of men as to refuse aid to those who are in distress. Very many, also, who are persuaded that justice is pleasing to God, both worship Him who is Lord and Parent of all, and with continual prayers and repeated vows offer gifts and sacrifices, follow up His name with praises, striving to gain His favour by just and good works. There is therefore a reason, on account of which God may and ought to favour them. For if there is nothing so befitting God as beneficence, and nothing

[1] "Materia" = subjective existence.

so unsuited to His character as to be ungrateful, it is necessary that He should make some return for the services of those who are excellent, and who lead a holy life, that He may not be liable to the charge of ingratitude, which is worthy of blame[1] even in the case of a man. But, on the contrary, others are daring[2] and wicked, who pollute all things with their lusts, harass with slaughters, practise fraud, plunder, commit perjury, neither spare relatives nor parents, neglect the laws, and even God Himself.

Anger, therefore, has a befitting occasion[3] in God. For it is not right that, when He sees such things, He should not be moved, and arise to take vengeance upon the wicked, and destroy the pestilent and guilty, so as to promote the interests of all good men. Thus even in anger itself there is also contained a showing of kindness.[4] Therefore the arguments are found to be empty and false, either of those who, when they will not admit that God is angry, will have it that He shows kindness, because this, indeed, cannot take place without anger; or of those who think that there is no emotion of the mind in God. And because there are some affections to which God is not liable, as desire, fear, avarice, grief, and envy, they have said that He is entirely free from all affection. For He is not liable to these, because they are vicious affections; but as to those which belong to virtue,—that is, anger towards the wicked, regard towards the good, pity towards the afflicted,—inasmuch as they are worthy of the divine power, He has affections of His own,[5] both just and true. And if He is not possessed of them, the life of man will be thrown into confusion, and the condition of things will come to such disturbance that the laws will be despised and overpowered, and audacity alone reign, so that no one can at length be in safety unless he who excels[6] in strength. Thus all the earth will be laid waste, as it were, by a common robbery. But now, since the wicked expect punishment, and the good hope for favour, and the afflicted look for aid, there is place for virtues, and crimes are more rare. But[7] it is said, ofttimes the wicked are more prosperous, and the good more wretched, and the just are

---

[1] "Criminosa."   [2] "Facinorosi."   [3] "Materia."
[4] "Gratificatio."   [5] "Proprios."   [6] "Prævaleat."
[7] An objection is here met and answered.

harassed with impunity by the unjust. We will hereafter consider why these things happen. In the meantime let us explain respecting anger, whether there be any in God; whether He takes no notice at all, and is unmoved at those things which are done with impiety.

CHAP. XVII.—*Of God, His care and anger.*

God, says Epicurus, regards nothing; therefore He has no power. For he who has power must of necessity regard affairs. For if He has power, and does not use it, what so great cause is there that, I will not say our race, but even the universe itself, should be contemptible in His sight? On this account he says He is pure [1] and happy, because He is always at rest.[2] To whom, then, has the administration of so great affairs been entrusted,[3] if these things which we see to be governed by the highest judgment are neglected by God? or how can he who lives and perceives be at rest? For rest belongs either to sleep or to death. But sleep has not rest. For when we are asleep, the body indeed is at rest, but the soul is restless and agitated: it forms for itself images which it may behold, so that it exercises its natural power of motion by a variety of visions, and calls itself away from false things, until the limbs are satiated, and receive vigour from rest. Therefore eternal rest belongs to death alone. Now if death does not affect God, it follows that God is never at rest. But in what can the action of God consist, but in the administration of the world? But if God carries on the care of the world, it follows that He cares for the life of men, and takes notice of the acts of individuals, and He earnestly desires that they should be wise and good. This is the will of God, this the divine law; and he who follows and observes this is beloved by God. It is necessary that He should be moved with anger against the man who has broken or despised this eternal and divine law. If, he says, God does harm to any one, therefore He is not good. They are deceived by no slight error who defame all censure, whether human or divine, with the name of bitterness and malice, thinking that He ought to be called injurious [4] who visits the injurious with punishment. But if this is so, it follows that we have injurious laws, which enact punishment for offenders, and injurious judges

[1] "Incorruptus."   [2] "Quietus."   [3] "Cessit."   [4] "Nocentes."

who inflict capital punishments on those convicted of crime. But if the law is just which awards to the transgressor his due, and if the judge is called upright and good when he punishes crimes (for he guards the safety of good men who punishes the evil), it follows that God, when He opposes the evil, is not injurious; but he himself is injurious who either injures an innocent man, or spares an injurious person that he may injure many.

I would gladly ask from those who represent God as immoveable,[1] if any one had property, a house, a household[2] of slaves, and his slaves, despising the forbearance of their master, should attack all things, and themselves take the enjoyment of his goods, if his household should honour them, while the master was despised by all, insulted, and deserted: could he be a wise man who should not avenge the insults, but permit those over whom he had power to have the enjoyment of his property? Can such forbearance be found in any one?—if, indeed, it is to be called forbearance, and not rather a kind of insensible stupor. But it is easy to endure contempt. What if those things were done which are spoken of by Cicero?[3] "For I ask, if any head of a family,[4] when his children had been put to death by a slave, his wife slain and his house set on fire, should not exact most severe punishment from that slave, whether he would appear to be kind and merciful, or inhuman and most cruel?" But if to pardon deeds of this kind is the part of cruelty rather than of kindness,[5] it is not therefore the part of goodness in God not to be moved at those things which are done unjustly. For the world is, as it were, the house of God, and men, as it were, His slaves; and if His name is a mockery to them, what kind or amount of forbearance is it to give[6] up His own honours, to see wicked and unjust things done, and not to be indignant, which is peculiar and natural to Him who is displeased with sins! To be angry, therefore, is the part of reason: for thus faults are removed, and licentiousness is curbed; and this is plainly in accordance with justice and wisdom.

But the Stoics did not see that there is a distinction between

---

[1] "Immobilem" = not subject to emotions.   [2] "Familiam."
[3] In *Catal.* iv. 6.   [4] "Paterfamilias," the master of a house.
[5] "Pietatis."   [6] "Ut cedat."

right and wrong, that there is a just and also an unjust anger; and because they did not find a remedy for the matter, they wished altogether to remove it. But the Peripatetics said that it was not to be cut out, but moderated; to whom we have made a sufficient reply in the sixth book of the *Institutions*. Now, that the philosophers were ignorant of the nature of anger, is plain from their definitions, which Seneca enumerated in the books which he composed on the subject of anger. "Anger is," he says, "the desire of avenging an injury." Others, as Posidonius says, describe it as the desire of punishing him by whom you think that you have been unfairly injured. Some have thus defined it: "Anger is an incitement of the mind to injure him who either has committed an injury, or who has wished to do so." The definition of Aristotle does not differ greatly from ours; for he says that "anger is the desire of requiting pain." This is the unjust anger, concerning which we spoke before, which is contained even in the dumb animals; but it is to be restrained in man, lest he should rush to some very great evil through rage. This cannot exist in God, because He cannot be injured;[1] but it is found in man, inasmuch as he is frail. For the inflicting[2] of injury inflames[3] anguish, and anguish produces a desire of revenge. Where, then, is that just anger against offenders? For this is evidently not the desire of revenge, inasmuch as no injury precedes. I do not speak of those who sin against the laws; for although a judge may be angry with these without incurring blame, let us, however, suppose that he ought to be of a sedate mind when he sentences the guilty to punishment, because he is the executor[4] of the laws, not of his own spirit or power; for so they wish it who endeavour to extirpate anger. But I speak of those in particular who are in our own power, as slaves, children, wives, and pupils; for when we see these offend, we are incited to restrain them.

For it cannot fail to be, that he who is just and good is displeased with things which are bad, and that he who is displeased with evil is moved when he sees it practised. Therefore we arise to take vengeance, not because we have been injured, but

[1] "Illaesibilis est." Others read "stabilis est," he is firm. The reading of the text is confirmed by "laesio" in the next clause.
[2] "Laesio."   [3] "Inurit," burns in.   [4] "Minister."

that discipline may be preserved, morals may be corrected, and licentiousness be suppressed. This is just anger; and as it is necessary in man for the correction of wickedness, so manifestly is it necessary in God, from whom an example comes to man. For as we ought to restrain those who are subject to our power, so also ought God to restrain the offences of all. And in order that He may do this, He must be angry; because it is natural for one who is good to be moved and incited at the fault of another. Therefore they ought to have given this definition: Anger is an emotion of the mind arousing itself for the restraining of faults. For the definition given by Cicero, " Anger is the desire of taking vengeance," does not differ much from those already mentioned. But that anger which we may call either fury or rage ought not to exist even in man, because it is altogether vicious; but the anger which relates to the correction of vices ought not to be taken away from man; nor can it be taken away from God, because it is both serviceable for the affairs of men, and necessary.

CHAP. XVIII.—*Of the punishment of faults, that it cannot take place without anger.*

What need is there, they say, of anger, since faults can be corrected without this affection? But there is no one who can calmly see any one committing an offence. This may perhaps be possible in him who presides over the laws, because the deed is not committed before his eyes, but it is brought before him as a doubtful matter from another quarter. Nor can any wickedness be so manifest, that there is no place for a defence; and therefore it is possible that a judge may not be moved against him who may possibly be found to be innocent; and when the detected crime shall have come to light, he now no longer uses his own opinion, but that of the laws. It may be granted that he does that which he does without anger; for he has that which he may follow. We, undoubtedly, when an offence is committed by our household at home, whether we see or perceive it, must be indignant; for the very sight of a sin is unbecoming. For he who is altogether unmoved either approves of faults, which is more disgraceful and unjust, or avoids the trouble of reproving them, which a tranquil spirit and a quiet mind despises and refuses, unless anger shall have aroused and incited it. But when any one is moved, and yet through unseasonable leniency grants pardon more frequently than is necessary, or at all times, he evidently both destroys the life of those whose audacity he is fostering for greater crimes, and furnishes himself with a perpetual source of annoyances. Therefore the restraining of one's anger in the case of sins is faulty.

Archytas of Tarentum is praised, who, when he had found everything ruined[1] on his estate, rebuking the fault of his bailiff, said, "Wretch, I would have beaten you to death if I had not been angry." They consider this to be a singular example of forbearance; but influenced by authority, they do not see how foolishly he spoke and acted. For if (as Plato says) no prudent man punishes because there is an offence, but to prevent the occurrence of an offence, it is evident how evil an example this wise man put forth. For if slaves shall perceive that their master uses violence when he is not angry, and abstains from violence[2] when he is angry, it is evident that they will not commit slight offences, lest they should be beaten; but will commit the greatest offences, that they may arouse the anger of the perverse man, and escape with impunity. But I should praise him if, when he was enraged, he had given space to his anger, that the excitement of his mind might calm down through the interval of time, and his chastisement might be confined within moderate limits. Therefore, on account of the magnitude of the anger, punishment ought not to have been inflicted, but to have been delayed, lest it should inflict[3] upon the offender pain greater than is just, or occasion an outburst of fury in the punisher. But now, how is it equitable or wise, that any one should be punished on account of a slight offence, and should be unpunished on account of a very great one? But if he had learned the nature and causes of things, he never would have professed so unsuitable a forbearance, that a wicked slave should rejoice that his master has been angry with him. For as God has furnished the human body with many and various senses which are necessary for the use of life, so also He has assigned to the soul various affections by which the course of life might be regulated; and as He has given desire for the

---

[1] "Corrupta esse omnia."   [2] "Parcere."
[3] "Inureret," *i.e.* should burn in, or brand.

sake of producing offspring, so has He given anger for the sake of restraining faults.

But they who are ignorant of the ends of good and evil things, as they employ sensual desire for the purposes of corruption and pleasure, in the same manner make use of anger and passion for the inflicting of injury, while they are angry with those whom they regard with hatred. Therefore they are angry even with those who commit no offence, even with their equals, or even with their superiors. Hence they daily rush to monstrous[1] deeds; hence tragedies often arise. Therefore Archytas would be deserving of praise, if, when he had been enraged against any citizen or equal who injured him, he had curbed himself, and by forbearance mitigated the impetuosity of his fury. This self-restraint is glorious, by which any great evil which impends is restrained; but it is a fault not to check the faults of slaves and children; for through their escaping without punishment they will proceed to greater evil. In this case anger is not to be restrained; but even if it is in a state of inactivity,[2] it must be aroused. But that which we say respecting man, we also say respecting God, who made man like to Himself. I omit making mention of the figure of God, because the Stoics say that God has no form, and another great subject will arise if we should wish to refute them. I only speak respecting the soul. If it belongs[3] to God to reflect, to be wise, to understand, to foresee, to excel, and of all animals man alone has these qualities, it follows that he was made after the likeness of God; but on this account he goes on to vice, because, being mingled with frailty derived from earth, he is unable to preserve pure and uncontaminated that which he has received from God, unless he is imbued with the precepts of justice by the same God.

CHAP. XIX.—*Of the soul and body, and of providence.*

But since he is made up, as we have said, of two parts, soul and body, the virtues are contained in the one, and vices in the other, and they mutually oppose each other. For the good properties of the soul, which consist in restraining lusts, are contrary to the body; and the good properties of the body, which

---

[1] "Immania," *i.e.* of an inhuman character.
[2] "Jacet."
[3] "Deo subjacet."

consist in every kind of pleasure, are hostile to the soul. But if the virtue of the soul shall have resisted the desires, and suppressed them, he will be truly like to God. From which it is evident that the soul of man, which is capable of divine virtue, is not mortal. But there is this distinction, that since virtue is attended with bitterness, and the attraction of pleasure is sweet, great numbers are overcome and are drawn aside to the pleasantness; but they who have given themselves up to the body and earthly things are pressed to the earth, and are unable to attain to the favour of the divine bounty, because they have polluted themselves with the defilements of vices. But they who, following God, and in obedience to Him, have despised the desires of the body, and, preferring virtue to pleasures, have preserved innocence and righteousness, these God recognises as like to Himself.

Since, therefore, He has laid down a most holy law, and wishes all men to be innocent and beneficent, is it possible that He should not be angry when He sees that His law is despised, that virtue is rejected, and pleasure made the object of pursuit? But if He is the governor of the world, as He ought to be, He surely does not despise that which is even of the greatest importance in the whole world. If He has foresight, as it is befitting that God should have, it is plain that He consults the interests of the human race, in order that our life may be more abundantly supplied, and better, and safer. If He is the Father and God of all, He is undoubtedly delighted with the virtues of men, and provoked by their vices. Therefore He loves the just, and hates the wicked. There is no need (one says) of hatred; for He once for all has fixed a reward for the good, and punishment for the wicked. But if any one lives justly and innocently, and at the same time neither worships God nor has any regard for Him, as Aristides, and Timon,[1] and others of the philosophers, will he escape[2] with impunity, because, though he has obeyed the law of God, he has nevertheless despised God Himself? There is therefore something on

---

[1] Others read "Cimon." If the reading Timon be retained, the reference is not to Timon who is called "the Misanthrope," but to Timon the philosopher of Phlius, who lived in the time of Ptolemy Philadelphus, and belonged to the sect of the Sceptics.

[2] "Cedetne huic impune."

account of which God may be angry with one rebelling against Him, as it were, in reliance upon His integrity. If He can be angry with this man on account of his pride, why not more so with the sinner, who has despised the law together with the Lawgiver? The judge cannot pardon offences, because he is subject to the will of another. But God can pardon, because He is Himself the arbitrator[1] and judge of His own law; and when He laid down this, He did not surely deprive Himself of all power, but He has the liberty of bestowing pardon.

CHAP. XX.—*Of offences, and the mercy of God.*

If He is able to pardon, He is therefore able also to be angry. Why, then, some one will say, does it often occur, that they who sin are prosperous, and they who live piously are wretched? Because fugitives and disinherited[2] persons live without restraint, and they who are under the discipline of a father or master live in a more strict and frugal manner. For virtue is proved and fixed[3] by means of ills; vices by means of pleasure. Nor, however, ought he who sins to hope for lasting impunity, because there is no lasting happiness.

"But, in truth, the last day is always to be looked for by man; and no one ought to be called happy before his death and last funeral rites,"[4] as the not inelegant poet says. It is the end which proves happiness, and no one is able to escape the judgment of God, either when alive or after death. For He has the power both to cast down the living from on high, and to punish the dead with eternal torments. Nay, he says, if God is angry, He ought to have inflicted vengeance at once, and to have punished every one according to his desert. But (it is replied) if He had done this, no one would survive. For there is no one who offends in no respect, and there are many things which excite to the commission of sin—age, intemperance, want, opportunity, reward. To such an extent is the frailty of the flesh with which we are clothed liable to sin, that unless God were indulgent to this necessity, perhaps too few would live. On this account He is most patient, and restrains His anger. For because there is in Him perfect virtue, it follows of necessity that His patience also is perfect, which is itself also a

[1] "Disceptator." [2] "Abdicati."
[3] "Constat." [4] Ovid, *Metam.* iii. 153.

virtue. How many men, from having been sinners, have afterwards become righteous; from being injurious, have become good; from being wicked, have become temperate! How many who were in early life base, and condemned by the judgment of all, afterwards have turned out praiseworthy! But it is plain that this could not happen if punishment followed every offence.

The public laws condemn those who are manifestly guilty; but there are great numbers whose offences are concealed, great numbers who restrain the accuser either by entreaties or by reward, great numbers who elude justice by favour or influence. But if the divine censure should condemn all those who escape the punishment of men, there would be few or even no men on the earth. In short, even that one reason for destroying the human race might have been a just one, that men, despising the living God, pay divine honour to earthly and frail images, as though they were of heaven, adoring works made by human hands. And though God their Creator made them of elevated countenance and upright figure, and raised them to the contemplation of the heaven and the knowledge of God, they have preferred, like cattle, to bend themselves to the earth. For he is low, and curved, and bent downward, who, turning away from the sight of heaven and God his Father, worships things of the earth, which he ought to have trodden upon, that is, things made and fashioned from earth. Therefore, amidst such great impiety and such great sins of men, the forbearance of God attains this object, that men, condemning the errors of their past life, correct themselves. In short, there are many who are just and good; and these having laid aside the worship of earthly things, acknowledge the majesty of the one and only God. But though the forbearance of God is very great and most useful; yet, although late, He punishes the guilty, and does not suffer them to proceed further, when He sees that they are incorrigible.

CHAP. XXI.—*Of the anger of God and man.*

There remains one question, and that the last. For some one will perhaps say, that God is so far from being angry, that in His precepts He even forbids man to be angry. I might say that the anger of man ought to be curbed, because he is often angry unjustly; and he has immediate emotion, because he is only for a time.[1] Therefore, lest those things should be done which the low, and those of moderate station, and great kings do in their anger, his rage ought to have been moderated and suppressed, lest, being out of his mind,[2] he should commit some inexpiable crime. But God is not angry for a short time,[3] because He is eternal and of perfect virtue, and He is never angry unless deservedly. But, however, the matter is not so; for if He should altogether prohibit anger, He Himself would have been in some measure the censurer of His own workmanship, since He from the beginning had inserted anger in the liver[4] of man, since it is believed that the cause of this emotion is contained in the moisture of the gall. Therefore He does not altogether prohibit anger, because that affection is necessarily given, but He forbids us to persevere in anger. For the anger of mortals ought to be mortal; for if it is lasting, enmity is strengthened to lasting destruction. Then, again, when He enjoined us to be angry, and yet not to sin, it is plain that He did not tear up anger by the roots, but restrained it, that in every correction we might preserve moderation and justice. Therefore He who commands us to be angry is manifestly Himself angry; He who enjoins us to be quickly appeased is manifestly Himself easy to be appeased: for He has enjoined those things which are just and useful for the interests of society.[5]

But because I had said that the anger of God is not for a time[6] only, as is the case with man, who becomes inflamed with an immediate[7] excitement, and on account of his frailty is unable easily to govern himself, we ought to understand that because God is eternal, His anger also remains to eternity; but, on the other hand, that because He is endued with the greatest excellence, He controls His anger, and is not ruled by it, but that He regulates it according to His will. And it is plain that this is not opposed to that which has just been said. For

---

[1] "Temporalis."
[2] "Mentis impos," *i.e.* not having possession of his mind, opposed to "mentis compos." Some editions add, " in bile."
[3] "Ad præsens."   [4] As supposed to be the seat of the passions.
[5] "Rebus communibus."   [6] "Temporalem."
[7] "Præsentanea." The word is applied to a remedy which operates instantaneously.

if His anger had been altogether immortal, there would be no place after a fault for satisfaction or kind feeling, though He Himself commands men to be reconciled before the setting of the sun.[1] But the divine anger remains for ever against those who ever sin. Therefore God is appeased not by incense or a victim, not by costly offerings, which things are all corruptible, but by a reformation of the morals: and he who ceases to sin renders the anger of God mortal. For this reason He does not immediately[2] punish every one who is guilty, that man may have the opportunity of coming to a right mind,[3] and correcting himself.

CHAP. XXII.—*Of sins, and the verses of the Sibyls respecting them recited.*

This is what I had to say, most beloved Donatus, respecting the anger of God, that you might know how to refute those who represent God as being without emotions.[4] It only remains that, after the practice of Cicero, I should use an epilogue by way of peroration. As he did in the *Tusculan Disputations*, when discoursing on the subject of death, so we in this work ought to bring forward divine testimonies, which may be believed, to refute the persuasion of those who, believing that God is without anger, destroy all religion, without which, as we have shown, we are either equal to the brutes in savageness, or to the cattle in foolishness; for it is in religion only—that is, in the knowledge of the supreme God—that wisdom consists. All the prophets, being filled with the Divine Spirit, speak nothing else than of the favour of God towards the righteous, and His anger against the ungodly. And their testimony is indeed sufficient for us; but because it is not believed by those who make a display of wisdom by their hair and dress,[5] it was necessary to refute them by reason and arguments. For they act so preposterously,[6] that human things give authority to divine things, whereas divine things ought rather to give authority to human. But let us now leave these things, lest we should produce no effect upon them, and the subject should be in-

---

[1] See Eph. iv. 26.   [2] "Ad præsens."
[3] "Resipiscendi."   [4] "Immobilem."
[5] The philosophers wore long hair and cloaks. See *Instit.* iii. 25.
[6] "Præpostere," *i.e.* in a reversed order, putting the last first.

definitely drawn out. Let us therefore seek those testimonies which they can either believe, or at any rate not oppose.

Authors of great number and weight have made mention of the Sibyls; of the Greeks, Aristo the Chian, and Apollodorus the Erythræan; of our writers, Varro and Fenestella. All these relate that the Erythræan Sibyl was distinguished and noble beyond the rest. Apollodorus, indeed, boasts of her as his own citizen and countrywoman. But Fenestella also relates that ambassadors were sent by the senate to Erythræ, that the verses of this Sibyl might be conveyed to Rome, and that the consuls Curio and Octavius might take care that they should be placed in the Capitol, which had then been restored under the care of Quintus Catulus. In her writings, verses of this kind are found respecting the supreme God and Maker of the world: " The incorruptible and eternal Maker who dwells in the heaven, holding forth good to the good, a much greater reward, but stirring up anger and rage against the evil and unjust." Again, in another place, enumerating the deeds by which God is especially moved to anger, she introduced these things: " Avoid unlawful services, and serve the living God. Abstain from adultery and impurity; bring up a pure generation of children; do not kill: for the Immortal will be angry with every one who may sin." Therefore He is angry with sinners.

CHAP. XXIII.—*Of the anger of God and the punishment of sins, and a recital of the verses of the Sibyls respecting it; and, moreover, a reproof and exhortation.*

But because it is related by most learned men that there have been many Sibyls, the testimony of one may not be sufficient to confirm the truth, as we purpose to do. The volumes, indeed, of the Cumæan Sibyl, in which are written the fates of the Romans, are kept secret; but the writings of all the others are, for the most part, not prohibited from being in common use. And of these another, denouncing the anger of God against all nations on account of the impiety of men, thus began: " Since great anger is coming upon a disobedient world, I disclose the commands of God to the last age, prophesying to all men from city to city."

Another (Sibyl) also said, that the deluge was caused by the indignation of God against the unrighteous in a former age, that the wickedness of the human race might be extinguished: "From the time when, the God of heaven being enraged against the cities themselves and all men, a deluge having burst forth, the sea covered the earth." In like manner she foretold a conflagration about to take place hereafter, in which the impiety of men should again be destroyed: "And at some time, God no longer soothing His anger, but increasing it, and destroying the race of men, and laying waste the whole of it by fire." From which mention is thus made concerning Jupiter by Ovid:[1] "He remembers also that it is fated that the time shall come in which the sea, the earth, and the palace of heaven, being caught by fire, shall be burnt, and the curiously wrought framework of the world[2] be in danger." And this must come to pass at the time when the honour and worship of the Supreme shall have perished among men. The same (Sibyl), however, testifying that He was appeased by reformation[3] of conduct and self-improvement, added these things: "But, ye mortals, in pity[4] turn yourselves now, and do not lead the great God to every kind of anger." And also a little later: "He will not destroy, but will again restrain His anger, if you all practise valuable piety in your minds." Then another Sibyl declares that the Father of heavenly and earthly things ought to be loved, lest His indignation should arise, to the destruction of men: "Lest by chance the immortal God should be angry, and destroy the whole race of men, their life and shameless race, it is befitting that we love the wise, ever-living God the Father."

From these things it is evident that the arguments of the philosophers are vain, who imagine that God is without anger, and among His other praises reckon that which is most useless, detracting from Him that which is most salutary for human affairs, by which majesty itself exists. For this earthly kingdom and government, unless guarded by fear, is broken down. Take away anger from a king, and he will not only cease to be obeyed, but he will even be cast down headlong from his height. Yea, rather, take away this affection from any person of low

---

[1] *Metam.* i. 256.   [2] "Moles operosa laboret."
[3] "Pœnitentiâ factorum."
[4] ἰλίω. Others read, ὦ μέλεοι, O wretched.

degree, and who will not plunder him? who will not deride him? who will not treat him with injury? Thus he will be able to have neither clothing, nor an abode, nor food, since others will deprive him of whatever he has; much less can we suppose that the majesty of the heavenly government can exist without anger and fear. The Milesian Apollo being consulted concerning the religion of the Jews, inserted these things in his answer: " God, the King and Father of all, before whom the earth trembles, and the heaven and sea, and whom the recesses of Tartarus and the demons dread."

If He is so mild, as the philosophers will have it, how is it that not only the demons and ministers of such great power, but even the heaven and earth, and the whole system of the universe, tremble at His presence? For if no one submits to the service of another except by compulsion, it follows that all government exists by fear, and fear by anger. For if any one is not aroused against one who is unwilling to obey, it will not be possible for him to be compelled to obedience. Let any one consult his own feelings; he will at once understand that no one can be subdued to the command of another without anger and chastisement. Therefore, where there shall be no anger, there will be no authority. But God has authority; therefore also He must have anger, in which authority consists. Therefore let no one, induced by the empty prating[1] of the philosophers, train himself to the contempt of God, which is the greatest impiety. We all are bound both to love Him, because He is our Father; and to reverence Him, because He is our Lord: both to pay Him honour, because He is bounteous; and to fear Him, because He is severe: each character in Him is worthy of reverence.[2] Who can preserve his piety, and yet fail to love the parent of his life? or who can with impunity despise Him who, as ruler of all things, has true and everlasting power over all? If you consider Him in the character of Father, He supplies to us our entrance to the light which we enjoy: through Him we live, through Him we have entered into the abode[3] of this world. If you contemplate Him as God, it is He who nourishes us with innumerable resources: it is He who sustains us, we dwell in His house, we are His

---

[1] " Vaniloquentia."   [2] " Venerabilis."
[3] " Hospitium," *i.e.* a place of hospitality.

household;[1] and if we are less obedient than was befitting, and less attentive to our duty[2] than the endless merits of our Master and Parent demanded: nevertheless it is of great avail to our obtaining pardon, if we retain the worship and knowledge of Him; if, laying aside low and earthly affairs and goods, we meditate upon heavenly and divine things which are everlasting. And that we may be able to do this, God must be followed by us, God must be adored and loved; since there is in Him the substance[3] of things, the principle[4] of the virtues, and the source of all that is good.

For what is greater in power than God, or more perfect in reason, or brighter in clearness? And since He begat us to wisdom, and produced us to righteousness, it is not allowable for man to forsake God, who is the giver of intelligence and life, and to serve earthly and frail things, or, intent upon seeking temporal goods, to turn aside from innocence and piety. Vicious and deadly pleasures do not render a man happy; nor does opulence, which is the inciter of lusts; nor empty ambition; nor frail honours, by which the human soul, being ensnared and enslaved to the body, is condemned[5] to eternal death: but innocence and righteousness alone, the lawful and due reward of which is immortality, which God from the beginning appointed for holy and uncorrupted minds, which keep themselves pure and uncontaminated from vices, and from every earthly impurity. Of this heavenly and eternal reward they cannot be partakers, who have polluted their conscience by deeds of violence, frauds, rapine, and deceits; and who, by injuries inflicted upon men, by impious actions, have branded themselves[6] with indelible stains. Accordingly it is befitting that all who wish deservedly to be called wise, who wish to be called men, should despise frail things, should trample upon earthly things, and should look down upon base[7] things, that they may be able to be united in a most blissful relationship with God.

Let impiety and discords be removed; let turbulent and deadly dissensions be allayed,[8] by which human societies and

---

[1] "Familia," a household of slaves.
[2] "Officiosa," *i.e.* familia.
[3] "Materia rerum."
[4] "Ratio virtutum."
[5] "Æterna morte damnatur."
[6] "Ineluibiles sibi maculas inusserunt."
[7] "Humilia."
[8] "Sopiantur," *i.e.* be lulled to sleep.

the divine union of the public league are broken in upon, divided, and dispersed; as far as we can, let us aim at being good and bounteous: if we have a supply of wealth and resources, let it not be devoted to the pleasure of a single person, but bestowed on the welfare of many. For pleasure is as shortlived as the body to which it does service. But justice and kindness are as immortal as the mind and soul, which by good works attain to the likeness of God. Let God be consecrated by us, not in temples, but in our heart. All things which are made by the hand are destructible.[1] Let us cleanse this temple, which is defiled not by smoke or dust, but by evil thoughts; which is lighted not by blazing tapers, but by the brightness and light of wisdom. And if we believe that God is always present in this temple, to whose divinity the secrets of the heart are open, we shall so live as always to have Him propitious, and never to fear His anger.

[1] "Destructilia." The word is used by Prudentius.

ON THE WORKMANSHIP OF GOD,

OR THE FORMATION OF MAN.

A TREATISE ADDRESSED TO HIS PUPIL DEMETRIANUS.

CHAP. I.—*The introduction, and exhortation to Demetrianus.*

HOW disturbed I am, and in the greatest necessities, you will be able to judge from this little book which I have written to you, Demetrianus, almost in unadorned words, as the mediocrity of my talent permitted, that you might know my daily pursuit, and that I might not be wanting to you, even now an instructor, but of a more honourable subject and of a better system. For if you afforded yourself a ready hearer in literature, which did nothing else than form the style, how much more teachable ought you to be in these true studies, which have reference even to the life! And I now profess to you, that I am hindered by no necessity of circumstance or time from composing something by which the philosophers of our sect[1] which we uphold may become better instructed and more learned for the future, although they now have a bad reputation, and are commonly reproved, as living otherwise than is befitting for wise men, and as concealing their vices under the covering of a name; whereas they ought either to have remedied them, or to have altogether avoided them, that they might render the name of wisdom happy and uncorrupted, their life itself agreeing with their precepts. I, however, shrink from no labour that I may at once instruct ourselves and others. For I am not able to forget myself, and especially at that time when it is most necessary for me to remember; as also you do not forget yourself, as I hope and wish. For although the necessity of the state may turn you aside from true and

[1] *i.e.* Christians.

just works, yet it is impossible that a mind conscious of rectitude should not from time to time look to the heaven.

I indeed rejoice that all things which are esteemed blessings turn out prosperously to you, but only on condition of their changing nothing of your state of mind. For I fear lest custom and the pleasantness of these subjects should, as usually happens, creep by degrees into your mind. Therefore I advise you,

"And repeating it, will again and again advise you,"[1]

not to believe that you have these enjoyments of the earth as great or true blessings, since they are not only deceitful because they are doubtful, but also treacherous because they are pleasant. For you know how crafty that wrestler and adversary of ours is, and also often violent, as we now see that he is. He employs all these things which are able to entice as snares, and with such subtilty that they escape the notice of the eyes of the mind, so that they cannot be avoided by the foresight of man. Therefore it is the highest prudence to advance step by step, since he occupies the passes on both sides, and secretly places stumbling-blocks for our feet. Accordingly I advise you, either to disregard, if you are able according to your virtue, your prosperity in which you live, or not to admire it greatly. Remember your true parent, and in what[2] city you have given your name, and of what rank you have been. You understand assuredly what I say. For I do not charge you with pride, of which there is not even a suspicion in your case; but the things which I say are to be referred to the mind, not to the body, the whole system of which has been arranged on this account, that it may be in subjection to the soul as to a master, and may be ruled by its will. For it is in a certain manner an earthen vessel in which the soul, that is, the true man himself, is contained, and that vessel indeed not made by Prometheus, as the poets say, but by that supreme Creator and Artificer of the world, God, whose divine providence and most perfect excellence it is neither possible to comprehend by the perception, nor to express in word.

I will attempt, however, since mention has been made of the body and soul, to explain the nature of each, as far as the weakness of my understanding sees through; and I think that this duty is especially to be undertaken on this account, because Marcus

[1] Virg. Æn. iii. 436.   [2] *i.e.* have been initiated by baptism.

Tullius, a man of remarkable talent, in his fourth book on the Republic, when he had attempted to do this, concluded a subject of wide extent within narrow limits, lightly selecting the chief points. And that there might be no excuse, because he had not followed up this subject, he testified that neither inclination nor attention had been wanting to him. For in his first book concerning the Laws, when he was concisely summing up the same subject, he thus spoke: "Scipio, as it appears to me, has sufficiently expressed this subject in those books which you have read." Afterwards, however, in his second book concerning the Nature of the Gods, he endeavoured to follow up the same subject more extensively. But since he did not express it sufficiently even there, I will approach this office, and will take upon myself boldly to explain that which a man of the greatest eloquence has almost left untouched. Perhaps you may blame me for attempting to discuss something in matters of obscurity, when you see that there have been men of such rashness who are commonly called philosophers, that they scrutinized those things which God willed to be abstruse and hidden, and investigated the nature of things in heaven and on earth, which are far removed from us, and cannot be examined[1] by the eyes, nor touched by the hand, nor perceived by the senses; and yet they so dispute concerning the nature of these things, as to wish that the things which they bring forward may appear to be proved and known. What reason is there, I pray, why any one should think it an invidious thing in us, if we wish to look into and contemplate the system of our body, which is not altogether obscure, because from the very offices of the limbs, and the uses of the several parts, it is permitted us to understand with what great power of providence each part has been made?

CHAP. II.—*Of the production of the beasts and of man.*

For our Creator and Parent, God, has given to man perception and reason, that it might be evident from this that we are descended from Him, because He Himself is intelligence, He Himself is perception and reason. Since He did not give that power of reason to the other animals, He provided beforehand in what manner their life might be more safe. For He clothed

[1] "Contrectari."

them all with their own natural hair,[1] in order that they might more easily be able to endure the severity of frosts and colds. Moreover, He has appointed to every kind its own peculiar defence for the repelling of attacks from without; so that they may either oppose the stronger animals with natural weapons, or the feebler ones may withdraw themselves from danger by the swiftness of their flight, or those which require at once both strength and swiftness may protect themselves by craft, or guard themselves in hiding-places. And so others of them either poise themselves aloft with light plumage, or are supported by hoofs, or are furnished with horns; some have arms in their mouth— namely, their teeth—or hooked talons on their feet; and none of them is destitute of a defence for its own protection.

But if any fall as a prey to the greater animals, that their race might not utterly perish, they have either been banished to that region where the greater ones cannot exist, or they have received a more abundant fruitfulness in production, that food might be supplied from them to the beasts which are nourished by blood, and yet their very multitude might survive the slaughter inflicted upon them, so as to preserve the race. But He made man—reason being granted to him, and the power of perceiving and speaking being given to him—destitute of those things which are given to the other animals, because wisdom was able to supply those things which the condition of nature had denied to him. He made him naked and defenceless, because he could be armed by his talent, and clothed by his reason. But it cannot be expressed how wonderfully the absence of those things which are given to the brutes contributes to the beauty of man. For if He had given to man the teeth of wild beasts, or horns, or claws, or hoofs, or a tail, or hairs of various colour, who cannot perceive how misshapen an animal he would be, as the dumb animals, if they were made naked and defenceless? For if you take from these the natural clothing of their body, or those things by which they are armed of themselves, they can be neither beautiful nor safe, so that they appear wonderfully furnished if you think of utility, and wonderfully adorned if you think of appearance: in such a wonderful manner is utility combined with beauty.

But with reference to man, whom He formed an eternal and

[1] "Omnes enim suis ex se pilis." Others read, "pellibus texit."

immortal being, He did not arm him, as the others, without, but within; nor did He place his protection in the body, but in the soul: since it would have been superfluous, when He had given him that which was of the greatest value, to cover him with bodily defences, especially when they hindered the beauty of the human body. On which account I am accustomed to wonder at the senselessness of the philosophers who follow Epicurus, who blame the works of nature, that they may show that the world is prepared and governed by no providence; but they ascribe the origin of all things to indivisible and solid bodies, from the fortuitous meetings of which they say that all things are and were produced. I pass by the things relating to the world itself with which they find fault, in which matter they are ridiculously mad; I assume that which belongs to the subject of which we are now treating.

CHAP. III.—*Of the condition of the beasts and man.*

They complain that man is born in a more feeble and frail condition than that in which the other animals are born: for that these, as soon as they are produced from the womb, immediately raise themselves on their feet, and express their joy by running to and fro, and are at once fit for enduring the air, inasmuch as they have come forth to the light protected by natural coverings; but man, on the contrary, being naked and defenceless, is cast forth, and driven, as it were, from a shipwreck, to the miseries of this life; who is neither able to move himself from the place where he has been born,[1] nor to seek the nourishment of milk, nor to endure the injury of time. Therefore they say that Nature is not the mother of the human race, but a stepmother, who has dealt so liberally with the dumb creation, but has so produced man, that, without resources, and without strength, and destitute of all aid, he can do nothing else than give tokens[2] of the state of his frailty by wailing and lamentations; " as well he may, whose destiny it is to go through in life so many ills."[3]

And when they say these things they are believed to be very wise, because every one without consideration is displeased with his own condition; but I contend that they are never more foolish than when they say these things. For when I consider

[1] " Effusus est."   [2] " Ominari."   [3] Lucret. v. 228.

the condition of things, I understand that nothing ought to have been otherwise than it is—not to say could have been otherwise, for God is able to do all things: but it must be, that that most provident majesty made that which was better and more right.

I should like, therefore, to ask those censurers of the divine works, what they think to be wanting in man, on account of his being born in a more feeble condition. Do they think that men are, on this account, brought up worse? or that they advance the less to the greatest strength of age? or that weakness is a hindrance to their growth or safety, since reason bestows[1] the things which are wanting? But, they say, the bringing up of man costs the greatest labours: in truth, the condition of the brute creation is better, because all these, when they have brought forth their young, have no care except for their own food; from which it is effected that, their teats being spontaneously distended, the nourishment of milk is supplied to their offspring, and that they seek this nourishment by the compulsion of nature, without any trouble on the part of the mothers. How is it with birds, which have a different nature? do they not undergo the greatest labours in bringing up their young, so that they sometimes appear to have something of human intelligence? For they either build their nests of mud, or construct them with twigs and leaves, and they sit upon the eggs without taking food; and since it has not been given to them to nourish their young from their own bodies, they convey to them food, and spend whole days in going to and fro in this manner; but by night they defend, cherish, and protect them. What more can men do? unless it be this only, that they do not drive away their young when grown up, but retain them bound by perpetual relationship and the bond of affection. Why should I say that the offspring of birds is much more fragile than that of man? inasmuch as they do not bring forth the animal itself from the body of the mother, but that which, being warmed by the nourishment and heat of the body of the mother, produces the animal; and this, even when animated by breath, being unfledged and tender, is not only without the power of flying, but even of walking. Would he not, therefore, be most senseless, if any one should think that nature has

[1] "Dependit."

dealt badly with birds, first, because they are twice born, and then because they are so weak, that they have to be nourished by food sought with labour by their parents? But they select the stronger, and pass by the more feeble animals.

I ask, therefore, from those who prefer the condition of the beasts to their own, what they would choose if God should give them the choice: would they prefer the wisdom of man together with his weakness, or the strength of the beasts together with their nature? In truth, they are not so much like the beasts as not to prefer even a much more fragile condition, provided that it be human, to that strength of theirs unattended with reason. But, in truth, prudent men neither desire the reason of man together with frailty, nor the strength of the dumb animals without reason. Therefore it is nothing so repugnant or contradictory,[1] that either reason or the condition of nature should of necessity prepare each animal. If it is furnished with natural protection, reason is superfluous. For what will it contrive?[2] what will it do? or what will it plan? or in what will it display that light of the intellect, when Nature of its own accord grants those things which are able to be the result of reason? But if it be endued with reason, what need will there be of defences for the body, when reason once granted is able to supply the office of nature? And this has such power for the adorning and protection of man, that nothing greater or better can be given by God. Finally, since man is possessed of a body which is not great, and of slight strength, and of infirm health, nevertheless, since he has received that which is of greater value, he is better equipped than the other animals, and more adorned. For though he is born frail and feeble, yet he is safe from all the dumb animals, and all those which are born with greater strength, though they are able to bear patiently the inclemency of the sky, yet are unable to be safe from man. Thus it comes to pass that reason bestows more on man than nature does on the dumb animals; since, in their case, neither greatness of strength nor firmness of body can prevent them from being oppressed by us, or from being made subject to our power.

Can any one, then, when he sees that even elephants,[3] with

---

[1] "Contrarium."   [2] "Excogitabit."
[3] "Boves Lucas." Elephants are said to have been so called, because they were first seen by the Romans in Lucania.

their vast bodies and strength, are subservient to man, complain respecting God, the Maker of all things, because he has received moderate strength, and a small body; and not estimate according to their deserts the divine benefits towards himself, which is the part of an ungrateful man, or (to speak more truly) of a madman? Plato, I believe, that he might refute these ungrateful men, gave thanks to nature that he was born a man.[1] How much better and more soundly did he act, who perceived that the condition of man was better, than they did who would have preferred that they had been born beasts! For if God should happen to change them into those animals whose condition they prefer to their own, they would now immediately desire to return to their previous state, and would with great outcries eagerly demand their former condition, because strength and firmness of body are not of such consequence. that you should be without the office of the tongue; or the free course of birds through the air, that you should be without the hands. For the hands are of greater service than the lightness and use of the wings; the tongue is of greater service than the strength of the whole body. What madness is it, therefore, to prefer those things which, if they were given, you would refuse to receive!

CHAP. IV.—*Of the weakness of man.*

They also complain that man is liable to diseases, and to untimely death. They are indignant, it appears, that they are not born gods. By no means, they say; but we show from this, that man was made with no foresight, which ought to have been otherwise. What if I shall show, that this very thing was foreseen with great reason, that he might be able to be harassed by diseases, and that his life might often be cut short in the midst of its course? For, since God had known that the animal which He had made, of its own accord passed to death, that it might be capable of receiving death itself, which is the dissolution of nature, He gave to it frailty, which might find an approach for death in order to the dissolution of the animal. For if it had been of such strength that disease and sickness could not approach it, not even could death, since death is the

[1] Some editions here add: "But what is the nature of this, it does not belong to the present subject to consider."

consequence of diseases. But how could a premature death be absent from him, for whom a mature death had been appointed? Assuredly they wish that no man should die, unless when he has completed his hundredth year. How can they maintain their consistency in so great an opposition of circumstances? For, in order that no one may be capable of dying before a hundred years, something of the strength which is immortal must be given to him; and when this is granted, the condition of death must necessarily be excluded. But of what kind can that be, which can render a man firm and impregnable against diseases and attacks from without? For, inasmuch as he is composed of bones, and nerves, and flesh, and blood, which of these can be so firm as to repel frailty and death? That man, therefore, may not be liable to dissolution before that time which they think ought to have been appointed for him, of what material will they assign to him a body? All things which can be seen and touched are frail. It remains that they seek something from heaven, since there is nothing on earth which is not weak.

Since, therefore, man had to be so formed by God, that he should at some time be mortal, the matter itself required that he should be made with a frail and earthly body. It is necessary, therefore, that he should at some time receive death, since he is possessed of a body; for every body is liable to dissolution and to death. Therefore they are most foolish who complain of premature death, since the condition of nature makes a place for it. Thus it will follow that he is subject also to diseases; for nature does not admit that infirmity can be absent from that body which is at some time to undergo dissolution. But let us suppose it to be possible, as they wish, that man is not born under those conditions by which he is subject to disease or death, unless, having completed the course of his life, he shall have arrived at the extremity of old age. They do not, therefore, see what would be the consequence if it were so arranged, that it would be plainly impossible to die at another time; but if any one can be deprived of nourishment by another, it will be possible for him to die. Therefore the case requires that man, who cannot die before an appointed day, should have no need of the nourishment of food, because it may be taken from him; but if he shall have no need of food, he will now not be a man, but will become a god. Therefore, as I have already said, they who complain of the frailty of man, make this complaint especially, that they were not born immortal and everlasting. No one ought to die unless he is old. On this account, in truth, he ought to die, because he is not God. But mortality cannot be united with immortality: for if a man is mortal in old age, he cannot be immortal in youth; neither is the condition of death foreign to him who is at some time about to die; nor is there any immortality to which a limit is appointed. Thus it comes to pass, that the exclusion of immortality for ever, and the reception of mortality for a time, place man in such a condition that he is at some time mortal.

Therefore the necessity is in all points suitable,[1] that he ought not to have been otherwise than he is, and that it was impossible. But they do not see the order of consequences, because they have once committed an error in the main point itself. For the divine providence having been excluded from the affairs of men, it necessarily followed that all things were produced of their own accord. Hence they invented the notion of those blows and fortuitous meetings together of minute seeds, because they did not see the origin of things. And when they had thrown themselves into this difficulty, necessity now compelled them to think that souls were born together with bodies, and in like manner were extinguished together with bodies; for they had made the assumption, that nothing was made by the divine mind. And they were unable to prove this in any other way, than by showing that there were some things in which the system of providence appeared to be at fault.[2] Therefore they blamed those things in which providence wonderfully expressed its divinity, as those things which I have related concerning diseases and premature death; whereas they ought to have considered, these things being assumed, what would be the necessary consequences (but those things which I have spoken are the consequences) if he were not liable to diseases, and did not require a dwelling, nor clothing. For why should he fear the winds, or rains, or colds, the power of which consists in this, that they bring diseases? For on this account he has received wisdom, that he may guard his frailty against things that would injure him. The necessary consequence is, that

[1] "Quadrat."   [2] "Claudicare."

since he is liable to diseases for the sake of retaining his wisdom, he must also be liable to death; because he to whom death does not come, must of necessity be firm. But infirmity has in itself the condition of death; but where there shall be firmness, neither can old age have any place, nor death, which follows old age.

Moreover, if death were appointed for a fixed age, man would become most arrogant, and would be destitute of all humanity. For almost all the rights of humanity, by which we are united with one another, arise from fear and the consciousness of frailty. In short, all the more feeble and timid animals herd together, that, since they are unable to protect themselves by strength, they may protect themselves by their multitude; but the stronger animals seek solitudes, since they trust in their force and strength. If man also, in the same manner, had sufficient strength for the repelling of dangers, and did not stand in need of the assistance of any other, what society would there be? or what system? what humanity? or what would be more harsh than man? what more brutal? what more savage? But since he is feeble, and not able to live by himself apart from man, he desires society, that his life, passed in intercourse with others, may become both more adorned and more safe. You see, therefore, that the whole reason of man centres most of all in this, that he is born naked and fragile, that he is attacked by diseases, that he is punished by premature death. And if these things should be taken away from man, reason also, and wisdom, must necessarily be taken away. But I am discussing too long respecting things which are manifest, since it is clear that nothing ever was made, or could have been made, without providence. And if I should now wish to discuss respecting all its works in order, the subject would be infinite. But I have purposed to speak so much concerning the body of man only, that I may show in it the power of divine providence, how great it has been in those things only which are easy of comprehension and open; for those things which relate to the soul can neither be subjected to the eyes, nor comprehended. Now we speak concerning the vessel itself of man, which we see.

CHAP. V.—*Of the figures and limbs of animals.*

In the beginning, when God was forming the animals, He did

not wish to conglobate[1] and collect them into a round shape, that they might be able easily to put themselves in motion for walking, and to turn themselves in any direction; but from the highest part of the body He lengthened out the head. He also carried out to a greater length some of the limbs, which are called feet, that, being fixed on the ground with alternate motions, they might lead forward the animal wherever his inclination had borne him, or the necessity of seeking food had called him. Moreover, He made four limbs standing out from the very vessel of the body: two behind, which are in all animals—the feet; also two close to the head and neck, which supply various uses to animals. For in cattle and wild beasts they are feet like the hinder ones; but in man they are hands, which are produced not for walking, but for acting and controlling.[2] There is also a third class, in which those former limbs are neither feet nor hands; but wings, which, having feathers arranged in order, supply the use of flying. Thus one formation has different forms and uses; and that He might firmly hold together the density itself of the body, by binding together greater and small bones, He compacted a kind of keel, which we call the spine; and He did not think fit to form it of one continued bone, lest the animal should not have the power of walking and bending itself. From its middle part, as it were, He has extended in a different direction transverse and flat bones, by which, being slightly curved, and almost drawn together to themselves as into a circle, the inward organs[3] may be covered, that those parts which needed to be soft and less strong might be protected by the encircling of a solid framework.[4] But at the end of that joining together which we have said to resemble the keel of a ship, He placed the head, in which might be the government of the whole living creature; and this name was given to it, as indeed Varro writes to Cicero, because from this the senses and the nerves take their beginning.

But those parts, which we have said to be lengthened out from the body, either for the sake of walking, or of acting, or of

---

[1] "Conglobare," to gather into a ball.
[2] "Temperandum." Others read "tenendum."
[3] "Viscera." This word includes the heart, lungs, liver, stomach, and intestines.
[4] "Cratis," properly "wicker-work."

flying, He would have to consist of bones, neither too long, for the sake of rapidity of motion, nor too short, for the sake of firmness, but of a few, and those large. For either they are two as in man, or four as in a quadruped. And these He did not make solid, lest in walking sluggishness and weight should retard; but He made them hollow, and full of marrow within, to preserve the vigour of the body. And again, He did not make them equally extended to the end; but He conglobated their extremities with coarse knots, that they might be able more easily to be bound with sinews, and to be turned more easily, from which they are called joints.[1] These knots He made firmly solid, and covered with a soft kind of covering, which is called cartilage; for this purpose, that they might be bent without galling or any sense of pain. He did not, however, form these after one fashion. For He made some simple and round into an orb, in those joints at least in which it was befitting that the limbs should move in all directions, as in the shoulders, since it is necessary that the hands should move and be twisted about in any direction; but others He made broad, and equal, and round towards one part, and that plainly in those places where only it was necessary for the limbs to be bent, as in the knees, and in the elbows, and in the hands themselves. For as it was at the same time pleasant to the sight, and useful, that the hands should move in every direction from that position from which they spring; so assuredly, if this same thing should happen to the elbows, a motion of that kind would be at once superfluous and unbecoming. For then the hand, having lost the dignity which it now has, through its excessive flexibility,[2] would appear like the trunk of an elephant; and man would be altogether snake-handed,[3]—an instance of which has been wonderfully effected in that monstrous beast. For God, who wished to display His providence and power by a wonderful variety of many things, inasmuch as He had not extended the head of that animal to such a length that he might be able to touch the earth with his mouth, which would have been horrible and hideous, and because He had so armed the mouth itself with extended tusks, that even if he touched the earth the tusks would still deprive him of the power of feeding, He lengthened out be-

[1] "Vertibula."   [2] "Mobilitas."
[3] "Anguimanus,"—a word applied by Lucretius to the elephant.

tween these from the top of the forehead a soft and flexible limb, by which he might be able to grasp and lay hold of anything, lest the prominent magnitude of the tusks, or the shortness of the neck, should interfere with the arrangement for taking food.

CHAP. VI.—*Of the error of Epicurus, and of the limbs and their use.*

I cannot here be prevented from again showing the folly of Epicurus. For all the ravings of Lucretius belong to him, who, in order that he might show that animals are not produced by any contrivance of the divine mind, but, as he is wont to say, by chance, said that in the beginning of the world innumerable other animals of wonderful form and magnitude were produced; but that they were unable to be permanent, because either the power of taking food, or the method of uniting and generating, had failed them. It is evident that, in order to make a place for his atoms flying about through the boundless and empty space, he wished to exclude the divine providence. But when he saw that a wonderful system of providence is contained in all things which breathe, what vanity was it (O mischievous one!) to say that there had been animals of immense size, in which the system of production ceased!

Since, therefore, all things which we see are produced with reference to a plan—for nothing but a plan[1] can effect this very condition of being born—it is manifest that nothing could have been born without a plan. For it was previously foreseen in the formation of everything, how it should use the service of the limbs for the necessaries of life; and how the offspring, being produced from the union of bodies, might preserve all living creatures by their several species. For if a skilful architect, when he designs to construct some great building, first of all considers what will be the effect[2] of the complete building, and previously ascertains by measurement what situation is suitable for a light weight, in what place a massive part of the structure will stand, what will be the intervals between the columns, what or where will be the descents and outlets of the falling waters and the reservoirs,—he first, I say, foresees these things, that he

[1] "Ratio." Nearly equivalent in this place to "providentia."
[2] "Summa."

may begin together with the very foundations whatever things are necessary for the work when now completed,—why should any one suppose that, in the contrivance of animals, God did not foresee what things were necessary for living, before giving life itself? For it is manifest that life could not exist, unless those things by which it exists were previously arranged.

Therefore Epicurus saw in the bodies of animals the skill of a divine plan; but that he might carry into effect that which he had before imprudently assumed, he added another absurdity agreeing with the former. For he said that the eyes were not produced for seeing, nor the ears for hearing, nor the feet for walking, since these members were produced before there was the exercise of seeing, hearing, and walking; but that all the offices of these members arose from them after their production. I fear lest the refutation of such extravagant and ridiculous stories should appear to be no less foolish; but it pleases me to be foolish, since we are dealing with a foolish man, lest he should think himself too clever. What do you say, Epicurus? Were not the eyes produced for seeing? Why, then, do they see? Their use, he says, afterwards showed itself. Therefore they were produced for the sake of seeing, since they can do nothing else but see. Likewise, in the case of the other limbs, use itself shows for what purpose they were produced. For it is plain that this use could have no existence, unless all the limbs had been made with such arrangement and foresight, that they might be able to have their use.

For what if you should say, that birds were not made to fly, nor wild beasts to rage, nor fishes to swim, nor men to be wise, when it is evident that living creatures are subject to that natural disposition and office to which each was created? But it is evident that he who has lost the main point itself of the truth must always be in error. For if all things are produced not by providence, but by a fortuitous meeting together of atoms, why does it never happen by chance, that those first principles meet together in such a way as to make an animal of such a kind, that it might rather hear with its nostrils, smell with its eyes, and see[1] with its ears? For if the first principles leave no kind of position untried, monstrous productions of this kind ought daily to have been brought forth, in

---

[1] "Cernerst," to see so as to distinguish; a stronger word than "video."

which the arrangement of the limbs might be distorted,[1] and the use far different from that which prevails. But since all the races of animals, and all the limbs, observe their own laws and arrangements, and the uses assigned to them, it is plain that nothing is made by chance, since a perpetual arrangement of the divine plan is preserved. But we will refute Epicurus at another time. Now let us discuss the subject of providence, as we have begun.

CHAP. VII.—*Of all the parts of the body.*

God therefore connected and bound together the parts which strengthen[2] the body, which we call bones, being knotted and joined to one another by sinews, which the mind might make use of, as bands,[3] if it should wish to hasten forward or to lag behind; and, indeed, without any labour or effort, but with a very slight inclination, it might moderate and guide the mass of the whole body. But He covered these with the inward organs,[4] as was befitting to each place, that the parts which were solid might be enclosed and concealed. Also He mixed with the inward organs, veins as streams divided through the whole body, through which the moisture and the blood, running in different directions, might bedew all the limbs with the vital juices; and He fashioned these inward organs after that manner which was befitting to each kind and situation, and covered them with skin drawn over them, which He either adorned with beauty only, or covered with thick hair, or fenced with scales, or adorned with brilliant feathers. But that is a wonderful contrivance of God, that one arrangement and one state exhibits innumerable varieties of animals. For in almost all things which breathe there is the same connection and arrangement of the limbs. For first of all is the head, and annexed to this the neck; also the breast adjoined to the neck, and the shoulders projecting from it, the belly adhering to the breast; also the organs of generation subjoined to the belly; in the last place, the thighs and feet. Nor do the limbs only keep their own course and position in all, but also the parts of the limbs. For in the head itself alone the ears occupy a fixed position, the eyes a fixed position, likewise the nostrils, the

---

[1] "Præposterus;" having the last first, and the first last.
[2] "Solidamenta corporis." [3] "Retinaculis." [4] "Visceribus."

mouth also, and in it the teeth and tongue. And though all these things are the same in all animals, yet there is an infinite and manifold diversity of the things formed; because those things of which I have spoken, being either more drawn out or more contracted, are comprehended by lineaments differing in various ways. What! is not that divine, that in so great a multitude of living creatures each animal is most excellent in its own class and species?—so that if any part should be taken from one to another, the necessary result would be, that nothing would be more embarrassed for use, nothing more unshapely to look upon; as if you should give a prolonged neck to an elephant, or a short neck to a camel; or if you should attach feet or hair to serpents, in which the length of the body equally stretched out required nothing else, except that being marked as to their backs with spots, and supporting themselves by their smooth scales, with winding courses they should glide into slippery tracts. But in quadrupeds the same designer lengthened out the arrangement of the spine, which is drawn out from the top of the head to a greater length on the outside of the body, and pointed it into a tail, that the parts of the body which are offensive might either be covered on account of their unsightliness, or be protected on account of their tenderness, so that by its motion certain minute and injurious animals might be driven away from the body; and if you should take away this member, the animal would be imperfect and weak. But where there is reason and the hand, that is not so necessary as a covering of hair. To such an extent are all things most befittingly arranged, each in its own class, that nothing can be conceived more unbecoming than a quadruped which is naked, or a man that is covered.

But, however, though nakedness itself on the part of man tends in a wonderful manner to beauty, yet it was not adapted to his head; for what great deformity there would be in this, is evident from baldness. Therefore He clothed the head with hair; and because it was about to be on the top, He added it as an ornament, as it were, to the highest summit of the building. And this ornament is not collected into a circle, or rounded into the figure of a cap, lest it should be unsightly by leaving some parts bare; but it is freely poured forth in some places, and withdrawn in others, according to the comeliness of each place. Therefore, the forehead entrenched by a circumference, and the hair put forth from the temples before the ears, and the uppermost parts of these being surrounded after the manner of a crown, and all the back part of the head covered, display an appearance of wonderful comeliness. Then the nature of the beard contributes in an incredible degree to distinguish the maturity of bodies, or to the distinction of sex, or to the beauty of manliness and strength; so that it appears that the system of the whole work would not have been in agreement, if anything had been made otherwise than it is.

CHAP. VIII.—*Of the parts of man: the eyes and ears.*

Now I will show the plan of the whole man, and will explain the uses and habits of the several members which are exposed to view in the body, or concealed. When, therefore, God had determined of all the animals to make man alone heavenly, and all the rest earthly, He raised him erect[1] to the contemplation of the heaven, and made him a biped, doubtless that he might look to the same quarter from which he derives his origin; but He depressed the others to the earth, that, inasmuch as they have no expectation of immortality, being cast down with their whole body to the ground, they might be subservient to their appetite and food. And thus the right reason and elevated position of man alone, and his countenance, shared with and closely resembling God his Father, bespeak his origin and Maker. His mind, nearly divine, because it has obtained the rule not only over the animals which are on the earth, but even over his own body, being situated in the highest part, the head, as in a lofty citadel, looks out upon and observes all things. He formed this its palace, not drawn out and extended, as in the case of the dumb animals, but like an orb and a globe, because all[2] roundness belongs to a perfect plan and figure. Therefore the mind and that divine fire is covered with it,[3] as with a vault;[4] and when He had covered its highest top with a natural garment, He alike furnished and adorned the front part, which is called the face, with the necessary services of the members.

[1] "Rigidum."
[2] "Omnis." Others read "orbis."
[3] *i.e.* the head.
[4] "Cœlo." Some believed that the soul was of fire.

And first, He closed the orbs of the eyes with concave apertures, from which boring[1] Varro thought that the forehead[2] derived its name; and He would have these to be neither less nor more than two, because no number is more perfect as to appearance than that of two: as also He made the ears two, the doubleness[3] of which bears with it an incredible degree of beauty, both because each part is adorned with a resemblance, and that voices coming from both sides[4] may more easily be collected. For the form itself is fashioned after a wonderful manner: because He would not have their apertures to be naked and uncovered, which would have been less becoming and less useful; since the voice might fly beyond the narrow space of simple caverns, and be scattered, did not the apertures themselves confine it, received through hollow windings and kept back from reverberation, like those small vessels, by the application of which narrow-mouthed vessels are accustomed to be filled.

These ears, then, which have their name from the drinking[5] in of voices, from which Virgil says,[6]

"And with these ears I drank in his voice;"

or because the Greeks call the voice itself αὐδήν, from hearing, —the ears (*aures*) were named as though *audes* by the change of a letter,—God would not form of soft skins, which, hanging down and flaccid, might take away beauty; nor of hard and solid bones, lest, being stiff and immoveable, they should be inconvenient for use. But He designed that which might be between these, that a softer cartilage might bind them, and that they might have at once a befitting and flexible firmness. In these the office of hearing only is placed, as that of seeing is in the eyes, the acuteness of which is especially inexplicable and wonderful; for He covered their orbs, presenting the similitude of gems in that part with which they had to see, with transparent membranes, that the images of objects placed opposite them, being refracted[7] as in a mirror, might penetrate to the innermost perception. Through these membranes, therefore, that faculty which is called the mind sees those things which are

---

[1] "Foratu," the process of boring; "foramen," the aperture thus made.
[2] "Frontem."   [3] "Duplicitas."   [4] "Altrinsecus."
[5] "Hauriendis," from which "aures" is said to be formed.
[6] *Æneid,* iv. 359.   [7] "Refulgentes."

without; lest you should happen to think that we see either by the striking[1] of the images, as the philosophers discuss, since the office of seeing ought to be in that which sees, not in that which is seen; or in the tension of the air together with the eyesight; or in the outpouring of the rays: since, if it were so, we should see the ray towards which we turn with our eyes, until the air, being extended together with the eyesight, or the rays being poured out, should arrive at the object which was to be seen.

But since we see at the same moment of time, and for the most part, while engaged on other business, we nevertheless behold all things which are placed opposite to us, it is more true and evident that it is the mind which, through the eyes, sees those things which are placed opposite to it, as though through windows covered with pellucid crystal or transparent stone;[2] and therefore the mind and inclination are often known from the eyes. For the refutation of which Lucretius[3] employed a very senseless argument. For if the mind, he says, sees through the eyes, it would see better if the eyes were torn out and dug up, inasmuch as doors being torn up together with the doorposts let in more light than if they were covered. Truly his eyes, or rather those of Epicurus who taught him, ought to have been dug out, that they might not see, that the torn-out orbs, and the burst fibres of the eyes, and the blood flowing through the veins, and the flesh increasing from wounds, and the scars drawn over at last can admit no light; unless by chance he would have it that eyes are produced resembling ears, so that we should see not so much with eyes as with apertures, than which there can be nothing more unsightly or more useless. For how little should we be able to see, if from the innermost recesses of the head the mind should pay attention through slight fissures of caverns; as, if any one should wish to look through a stalk of hemlock, he would see no more than the capability of the stalk itself admitted! For sight, therefore, it was rather needful that the members should be collected together into an orb, that the sight might be spread in breadth and the parts which adjoined them in the front of the face, that they might freely behold all things. Therefore the un-

[1] "Imaginum incursione." [2] According to some, "talc."
[3] iii. 368.

speakable power of the divine providence made two orbs most resembling each other, and so bound them together that they might be able not only to be altogether turned, but to be moved and directed with moderation.[1] And He willed that the orbs themselves should be full of a pure and clear moisture, in the middle part of which sparks of lights might be kept shut up, which we call the pupils, in which, being pure and delicate, are contained the faculty and method of seeing. The mind therefore directs itself through these orbs that it may see, and the sight of both the eyes is mingled and joined together in a wonderful manner.

CHAP. IX.—*Of the senses and their power.*

It pleases me in this place to censure the folly of those who, while they wish to show that the senses are false, collect many instances in which the eyes are deceived; and among them this also, that all things appear double to the mad and intoxicated, as though the cause of that error were obscure. For it happens on this account, because there are two eyes. But hear how it happens. The sight of the eyes consists in the exertion of the soul. Therefore, since the mind, as has been above said, uses the eyes as windows, this happens not only to those who are intoxicated or mad, but even to those who are of sound mind, and sober. For if you place any object too near, it will appear double, for there is a certain interval and space in which the sight of the eyes meets together. Likewise, if you call the soul back as if to reflection, and relax the exertion of the mind, then the sight of each eye is drawn asunder, and they each begin to see separately.

If you, again, exert the mind and direct the eyesight, whatever appeared double unites into one. What wonder, therefore, if the mind, impaired by poison and the powerful influence of wine, cannot direct itself to seeing, as the feet cannot to walking when they are weak through the numbness of the sinews, or if the force of madness raging against the brain disunites the agreement of the eyes?—which is so true, that in the case of one-eyed[2] men, if they become either mad or intoxicated, it can by no means happen that they see any object double. Wherefore, if the reason is evident why the eyes are deceived, it is clear that the senses are not false: for they either are not de-

[1] "Cum modo," in a measured degree.   [2] "Luscis."

ceived if they are pure and sound; or if they are deceived, yet the mind is not deceived which recognises their error.

CHAP. X.—*Of the outer limbs of man, and their use.*

But let us return to the works of God. That the eyes, therefore, might be better protected from injury, He concealed them with the coverings of the eyelashes,[1] from which Varro thinks that the eyes[2] derived their name. For even the eyelids themselves, in which there is the power of rapid motion, and to which throbbing[3] gives their name, being protected by hairs standing in order, afford a most becoming fence to the eyes; the continual motion of which, meeting with incomprehensible rapidity, does not impede the course of the sight, and relieves the eyes.[4] For the pupil—that is, the transparent membrane—which ought not to be drained and to become dry, unless it is cleansed by continual moisture so that it shines clearly, loses its power.[5] Why should I speak of the summits of the eyebrows themselves, furnished with short hair? Do they not, as it were by mounds, both afford protection to the eyes, so that nothing may fall into them from above, and at the same time ornament? And the nose, arising from the confines of these, and stretched out, as it were, with an equal ridge, at once serves to separate and to protect the two eyes. Below also, a not unbecoming swelling of the cheeks, gently rising after the similitude of hills, makes the eyes safer on every side; and it has been provided by the great Artificer, that if there shall happen to be a more violent blow, it may be repelled by the projecting parts. But the upper part of the nose as far as the middle has been made solid; but the lower part has been made with a softened cartilage annexed to it, that it may be pliant[6] to the use of the fingers. Moreover, in this, though a single member, three offices are placed: one, that of drawing the breath; the second, that of smelling; the third, that the secretions of the brain may escape through its caverns. And in how wonderful, how divine a manner did God contrive these also, so

---

[1] "Ciliorum." The word properly denotes the edge of the eyelid, in which the eyelash is fixed; said to be derived from "cilleo," to move.
[2] "Oculi," as though derived from "occulere," to conceal.
[3] "Palpitatio." Hence "palpebræ," the eyelids.
[4] "Reficit obtutum."   [5] "Obsolescit."   [6] "Tractabilis."

that the very cavity of the nose should not deform the beauty of the face!—which would certainly have been the case if one single aperture only were open. But He enclosed and divided that, as though by a wall drawn through the middle, and made it most beautiful by the very circumstance of its being double.[1] From which we understand of how much weight the twofold number, made firm by one simple connection, is to the perfection of things.

For though the body is one, yet the whole could not be made up of single members, unless it were that there should be parts on the right hand or on the left. Therefore, as the two feet and also hands not only avail to some utility and practice either of walking or of doing something, but also bestow an admirable character and comeliness; so in the head, which is, as it were, the crown of the divine work, the hearing has been divided by the great Artificer into two ears, and the sight into two eyes, and the smelling into two nostrils, because the brain, in which is contained the system of the sensation, although it is one, yet is divided into two parts by the intervening membrane. But the heart also, which appears to be the abode of wisdom, although it is one, yet has two recesses within, in which are contained the living fountains of blood, divided by an intervening barrier: that as in the world itself the chief control, being twofold from simple matter, or simple from a twofold matter, governs and keeps together the whole; so in the body, all the parts, being constructed of two, might present an inseparable unity. Also how useful and how becoming is the appearance and the opening of the mouth transversely cannot be expressed; the use of which consists in two offices, that of taking food and speaking.

The tongue enclosed within, which by its motions divides the voice into words, and is the interpreter of the mind, cannot, however, by itself alone fulfil the office of speaking, unless it strikes its edge against the palate, unless aided by striking against the teeth or by the compression of the lips. The teeth, however, contribute more to speaking: for infants do not begin to speak before they have teeth; and old men, when they have lost their teeth, so lisp that they appear to have returned afresh to infancy. But these things relate to man alone, or to birds, in which the tongue, being pointed and vibrating with fixed

[1] "Ipsa duplicitate."

motions, expresses innumerable inflexions of songs and various kinds of sounds. It has, moreover, another office also, which it exercises in all, and this alone in the dumb animals, that it collects the food when bruised and ground by the teeth, and by its force presses it down when collected into balls, and transmits it to the belly. Accordingly, Varro thinks that the name of tongue was given to it from binding[1] the food. It also assists the beasts in drinking: for with the tongue stretched out and hollowed they draw water; and when they have taken it in the hollow[2] of the tongue, lest by slowness and delay it should flow away, they dash[3] it against the palate with swift rapidity. This, therefore, is covered by the concave part of the palate as by a shell,[4] and God has surrounded it with the enclosure of the teeth as with a wall.

But He has adorned the teeth themselves, which are arranged in order in a wonderful manner, lest, being bare and exposed,[5] they should be a terror rather than an ornament, with soft gums, which are so named from producing teeth, and then with the coverings of the lips; and the hardness of the teeth, as in a millstone, is greater and rougher than in the other bones, that they might be sufficient for bruising the food and pasture. But how befittingly has He divided[6] the lips themselves, which as it were before were united! the upper of which, under the very middle of the nostrils, He has marked with a kind of slight cavity, as with a valley: He has gracefully spread out[7] the lower for the sake of beauty. For, as far as relates to the receiving of flavour, he is deceived, whoever he is, who thinks that this sense resides in the palate; for it is the tongue by which flavours are perceived, and not the whole of it: for the parts of it which are more tender on either side, draw in the flavour with the most delicate perceptions. And though nothing is diminished from that which is eaten or drunk, yet the flavour in an indescribable manner penetrates to the sense, in the same way in which the taking of the smell detracts nothing from any material.

And how beautiful the other parts are can scarcely be expressed. The chin, gently drawn down from the cheeks, and

---

[1] "Lingua," as though from "ligando." [2] "Linguæ sinu."
[3] "Complodunt."   [4] "Testudine."   [5] "Restricti."
[6] "Intercidit."   [7] "Foras molliter explicavit."

the lower part of it so closed that the lightly imprinted division appears to mark its extreme point: the neck stiff and well rounded: the shoulders let down as though by gentle ridges from the neck: the fore-arms[1] powerful, and braced[2] by sinews for firmness: the great strength of the upper-arms[3] standing out with remarkable muscles: the useful and becoming bending of the elbows. What shall I say of the hands, the ministers of reason and wisdom? which the most skilful Creator made with a flat and moderately concave bend, that if anything was to be held, it might conveniently rest upon them, and terminated them in the fingers; in which it is difficult to explain whether the appearance or the usefulness is greater. For the perfection and completeness of their number, and the comeliness of their order and gradation, and the flexible bending of the equal joints, and the round form of the nails, comprising and strengthening the tips of the fingers with concave coverings, lest the softness of the flesh should yield in holding any object, afford great adornment. But this is convenient for use in wonderful ways, that one separated from the rest rises together with the hand itself, and is enlarged[4] in a different direction, which, offering itself as though to meet the others, possesses all the power of holding and doing either alone, or in a special manner, as the guide and director of them all; from which also it received the name of thumb,[5] because it prevails among the others by force and power. It has two joints standing out, not as the others, three; but one is annexed by flesh to the hand for the sake of beauty: for if it had been with three joints, and itself separate, the foul and unbecoming appearance would have deprived the hand of all grace.

Again, the breadth of the breast, being elevated, and exposed to the eyes, displays a wonderful dignity of its condition; of which this is the cause, that God appears to have made man only, as it were, reclining with his face upward: for scarcely any other animal is able to lie upon its back. But He appears to have formed the dumb animals as though lying on one side,

---

[1] "Brachia." The fore-arms, from the hand to the elbow.
[2] "Substricta."
[3] "Lacerti." The arm from the elbow to the shoulder.
[4] "Maturius funditur."
[5] *i.e.* "pollex," as though from "polleo," to prevail.

and to have pressed them to the earth. For this reason He gave them a narrow breast, and removed from sight, and prostrate[1] towards the earth. But He made that of man open and erect, because, being full of reason given from heaven, it was not befitting that it should be humble or unbecoming. The nipples also gently rising, and crowned with darker and small orbs, add something of beauty; being given to females for the nourishment of their young, to males for grace only, that the breast might not appear misshapen, and, as it were, mutilated. Below this is placed the flat surface of the belly, about the middle of which the navel distinguishes by a not unbecoming mark, being made for this purpose, that through it the young, while it is in the womb, may be nourished.

CHAP. XI.—*Of the intestines in man, and their use.*

It necessarily follows that I should begin to speak of the inward parts also, to which has been assigned not beauty, because they are concealed from view, but incredible utility, since it was necessary that this earthly body should be nourished with some moisture from food and drink, as the earth itself is by showers and frosts. The most provident Artificer placed in the middle of it a receptacle for articles of food, by means of which, when digested and liquefied, it might distribute the vital juices to all the members. But since man is composed of body and soul, that receptacle of which I have spoken above affords nourishment only to the body; to the soul, in truth, He has given another abode. For He has made a kind of intestines soft and thin,[2] which we call the lungs, into which the breath might pass by an alternate interchange;[3] and He did not form this after the fashion of the uterus, lest the breath should all at once be poured forth, or at once inflate it. And on this account He did not make it a full intestine,[4] but capable of being inflated, and admitting the air, so that it might gradually receive the breath ; while the vital air is spread through that thinness, and might again gradually give it back, while it spreads itself

---

[1] "Abjectum."
[2] "Rarum," *i.e.* loose in texture.
[3] "Reciprocâ vicissitudine."
[4] "Ne plenum quidem." Some editions omit "ne," but it seems to be required by the sense; the lungs not being compact and solid, as the liver, but of a slighter substance.

forth from it: for the very alternation of blowing and breathing,[1] and the process of respiration, support life in the body.

Since, therefore, there are in man two receptacles,—one of the air which nourishes the soul,[2] the other of the food which nourishes the body,—there must be two tubes[3] through the neck for food, and for breath, the upper of which leads from the mouth to the belly, the lower from the nostrils to the lungs. And the plan and nature of these are different: for the passage which is from the mouth has been made soft, and which when closed always adheres[4] to itself, as the mouth itself; since drink and food, being corporeal, make for themselves a space for passage, by moving aside and opening the gullet. The breath, on the other hand, which is incorporeal and thin, because it was unable to make for itself a space, has received an open way, which is called the windpipe. This is composed of flexible and soft bones, as though of rings fitted together after the manner of a hemlock stalk,[5] and adhering together; and this passage is always open. For the breath can have no cessation in passing; because it, which is always passing to and fro, is checked as by a kind of obstacle through means of a portion of a member usefully sent down from the brain, and which is called the uvula, lest, drawn by pestilential air, it should come with impetuosity and spoil the slightness[6] of its abode, or bring the whole violence of the injury upon the inner receptacles. And on this account also the nostrils are slightly open, which are therefore so named, because either smell or breath does not cease to flow[7] through these, which are, as it were, the doors of this tube. Yet this breathing-tube lies open[8] not only to the nostrils, but also to the mouth in the extreme regions of the palate, where the risings of[9] the jaws, looking towards the uvula, begin to raise themselves into a swelling. And the reason of this arrangement is not obscure: for we should not have the power of speaking if the windpipe were open to the nostrils

---

[1] "Flandi et spirandi." The former word denotes the process of sending forth, the latter of inhaling, the air.
[2] "Animam," the vital principle, as differing from the rational.
[3] "Fistulas." [4] "Cohæreat sibi."
[5] "In cicutæ modum." [6] "Teneritudinem domicilii."
[7] "Nare;" hence "nares," the nostrils. [8] "Interpatet."
[9] "Colles faucium." Others read "toles," *i.e.* the tonsils.

only, as the path of the gullet is to the mouth only; nor could the breath proceeding from it cause the voice, without the service of the tongue.

Therefore the divine skill opened a way for the voice from that breathing-tube, so that the tongue might be able to discharge its office, and by its strokes divide into words the even[1] course of the voice itself. And this passage, if by any means it is intercepted, must necessarily cause dumbness. For he is assuredly mistaken, whoever thinks that there is any other cause why men are dumb. For they are not tongue-tied, as is commonly believed; but they pour forth that vocal breath through the nostrils, as though bellowing,[2] because there is either no passage at all for the voice to the mouth, or it is not so open as to be able to send forth the full voice. And this generally comes to pass by nature; sometimes also it happens by accident that this entrance is blocked up and does not transmit the voice to the tongue, and thus makes those who can speak dumb. And when this happens, the hearing also must necessarily be blocked up; so that because it cannot emit the voice, it is also incapable of admitting it. Therefore this passage has been opened for the purpose of speaking. It also affords this advantage, that in frequenting the bath,[3] because the nostrils are not able to endure the heat, the hot air is taken in by the mouth; also, if phlegm contracted by cold shall have happened to stop up the breathing pores of the nostrils, we may be able to draw the air through the mouth, lest, if the passage[4] should be obstructed, the breath should be stifled. But the food being received into the stomach, and mixed with the moisture of the drink, when it has now been digested by the heat, its juice, being in an indescribable manner diffused through the limbs, bedews and invigorates the whole body.

The manifold coils also of the intestines, and their length rolled together on themselves, and yet fastened with one band, are a wonderful work of God. For when the stomach has sent forth from itself the food softened, it is gradually thrust forth through those windings of the intestines, so that whatever of

---

[1] "Inoffensum tenorem," *i.e.* without obstruction, not striking against any object—smooth.

[2] "Quasi mugiens."

[3] "In lavacris celebrandis."

[4] "Obstructâ meandi facultate."

the moisture by which the body is nourished is in them, is divided to all the members. And yet, lest in any place it should happen to adhere and remain fixed, which might have taken place on account of the turnings of the coils,[1] which often turn back to themselves, and which could not have happened without injury, He has spread over[2] these from within a thicker juice, that the secretions of the belly might more easily work their way through the slippery substance to their outlets. It is also a most skilful arrangement, that the bladder, which birds do not use, though it is separated from the intestines, and has no tube by which it may draw the urine from them, is nevertheless filled and distended with moisture. And it is not difficult to see how this comes to pass. For the parts of the intestines which receive the food and drink from the belly are more open than the other coils, and much more delicate. These entwine themselves around and encompass the bladder; and when the meat and the drink have arrived at these parts in a mixed state, the excrement becomes more solid, and passes through, but all the moisture is strained through those tender parts,[3] and the bladder, the membrane of which is equally fine and delicate, absorbs and collects it, so as to send it forth where nature has opened an outlet.

CHAP. XII.—*De utero, et conceptione atque sexibus.*[4]

De utero quoque et conceptione, quoniam de internis loquimur, dici necesse est, ne quid præterisse videamur; quæ quamquam in operto latent, sensum tamen atque intelligentiam latere non possunt. Vena in maribus, quæ seminium continet, duplex est, paulo interior, quam illud humoris obscœni receptaculum. Sicut enim renes duo sunt, itemque testes, ita et venæ seminales duæ, in una tamen compage cohærentes; quod videmus in corporibus animalium, cùm interfecta[5] patefiunt. Sed illa dexterior masculinum continet semen, sinisterior fœmininum; et omnino in toto corpore pars dextra masculina est, sinistra vero fœminina. Ipsum semen quidam putant ex medullis tantum, quidam ex

---

[1] "Voluminum flexiones." [2] "Oblevit ea intrinsecus crassiore succo."
[3] "Per illam teneritudinem."
[4] It has been judged advisable not to translate this and the first part of the next chapter.
[5] Alii legunt "intersecta."

omni corpore ad venam genitalem confluere, ibique concrescere. Sed hoc, humana mens, quomodo fiat, non potest comprehendere. Item in fœminis uterus in duas se dividit partes, quæ in diversum diffusæ ac reflexæ, circumplicantur, sicut arietis cornua. Quæ pars in dextram retorquetur, masculina est; quæ in sinistram, fœminina.

Conceptum igitur Varro et Aristoteles sic fieri arbitrantur. Aiunt non tantum maribus inesse semen, verum etiam fœminis, et inde plerumque matribus similes procreari; sed earum semen sanguinem esse purgatum, quod si recte cum virili mixtum sit, utraque concreta et simul coagulata informari: et primum quidem cor hominis effingi, quod in eo sit et vita omnis et sapientia; denique totum opus quadragesimo die consummari. Ex abortionibus hæc fortasse collecta sunt. In avium tamen fœtibus primum oculos fingi dubium non est, quod in ovis sæpe deprehendimus. Unde fieri non posse arbitror, quin fictio a capite sumat exordium.

Similitudines autem in corporibus filiorum sic fieri putant. Cum semina inter se permixta coalescunt, si virile superaverit, patri similem provenire, seu marem, seu fœminam; si muliebre prævaluerit, progeniem cujusque sexus ad imaginem respondere maternam. Id autem prævalet e duobus, quod fuerit uberius; alterum enim quodammodo amplectitur et includit: hinc plerumque fieri, ut unius tantum lineamenta prætendat. Si vero æqua fuerit ex pari semente permixtio, figuras quoque misceri, ut soboles illa communis aut neutrum referre videatur, quia totum ex altero non habet; aut utrumque, quia partem de singulis mutuata est. Nam in corporibus animalium videmus aut confundi parentum colores, ac fieri tertium neutri generantium simile; aut utriusque sic exprimi, ut discoloribus membris per omne corpus concors mixtura varietur. Dispares quoque naturæ hoc modo fieri putantur. Cum forte in lævam uteri partem masculinæ stirpis semen inciderit, marem quidem gigni opinatio est; sed quia sit in fœminina parte conceptus, aliquid in se habere fœmineum, supra quam decus virile patiatur; vel formam insignem, vel nimium candorem, vel corporis levitatem, vel artus delicatos, vel staturam brevem, vel vocem gracilem, vel animum imbecillum, vel ex his plura. Item, si partem in dextram semen fœminini sexus influxerit, fœminam quidem procreari; sed quoniam in masculina parte concepta sit, habere in se aliquid virilitatis, ultra quam sexus ratio permittat; aut valida membra, aut immoderatam longitudinem, aut fuscum colorem, aut hispidam faciem, aut vultum indecorum, aut vocem robustam, aut animum audacem, aut ex his plura.

Si verò masculinum in dexteram, fœmininum in sinistram pervenerit, utrosque fœtus recte provenire; ut et fœminis per omnia naturæ suæ decus constet, et maribus tam mente, quam corpore robur virile servetur. Istud vero ipsum quam mirabile institutum Dei, quod ad conservationem generum singulorum, duos sexus maris ac fœminæ machinatus est; quibus inter se per voluptatis illecebras copulatis, successiva soboles pareretur, ne omne genus viventium conditio mortalitatis extingueret. Sed plus roboris maribus attributum est, quo facilius ad patientiam jugi maritalis fœminæ cogerentur. Vir itaque nominatus est, quod major in eo vis est, quàm in fœmina; et hinc virtus nomen accepit. Item mulier (ut Varro interpretatur) a mollitie, immutata et detracta littera, velut mollier; cui suscepto fœtu, cùm partus appropinquare jam cœpit, turgescentes mammæ dulcibus succis distenduntur, et ad nutrimenta nascentis fontibus lacteis fœcundum pectus exuberat. Nec enim decebat aliud quàm ut sapiens animal a corde alimoniam duceret. Idque ipsum solertissimè comparatum est, ut candens ac pinguis humor teneritudinem novi corporis irrigaret, donec ad capiendos fortiores cibos, et dentibus instruatur, et viribus roboretur. Sed redeamus ad propositum, ut cætera, quæ supersunt, breviter explicemus.

CHAP. XIII.—*Of the lower members.*

Poteram nunc ego ipsorum quoque genitalium membrorum mirificam rationem tibi exponere, nisi me pudor ab hujusmodi sermone revocaret: itaque a nobis indumento verecundiæ, quæ sunt pudenda velentur. Quod ad hanc rem attinet, queri satis est, homines impios ac profanos summum nefas admittere, qui divinum et admirabile Dei opus, ad propagandam successionem inexcogitabili ratione provisum et effectum, vel ad turpissimos quæstus, vel ad obscœnæ libidinis pudenda opera convertunt, ut jam nihil aliud ex re sanctissima petant, quam inanem et sterilem voluptatem.

How is it with respect to the other parts of the body? Are they without order and beauty? The flesh rounded off into the buttocks, how adapted to the office of sitting! and this also more firm than in the other limbs, lest by the pressure of the bulk of the body it should give way to the bones. Also the length of the thighs drawn out, and strengthened by broader muscles, in order that it might more easily sustain the weight of the body; and as this is gradually contracted, it is bounded[1] by the knees, the comely joints[2] of which supply a bend which is most adapted for walking and sitting. Also the legs not drawn out in an equal manner, lest an unbecoming figure should deform the feet; but they are at once strengthened and adorned by well-turned[3] calves gently standing out and gradually diminishing.

But in the soles of the feet there is the same plan as in the hands, but yet very different: for since these are, as it were, the foundations of the whole body,[4] the admirable Artificer has not made them of a round appearance, lest man should be unable to stand, or should need other feet for standing, as is the case with quadrupeds; but He has formed them of a longer and more extended shape, that they might make the body firm by their flatness,[5] from which circumstance their name was given to them. The toes are of the same number with the fingers, for the sake of appearance rather than utility; and on this account they are both joined together, and short, and put together by gradations; and that which is the greatest of these, since it was not befitting that it should be separated from the others, as in the hand, has been so arranged in order, that it appears to differ from the others in magnitude and the small space which intervenes. This beautiful union[6] of them strengthens the pressure of the feet with no slight aid; for we cannot be excited to running, unless, our toes being pressed against the ground, and resting upon the soil, we take an impetus and a spring. I appear to have explained all things of which the plan is capable of being understood. I now come to those things which are either doubtful or obscure.

CHAP. XIV.—*Of the unknown purpose of some of the intestines.*

It is evident that there are many things in the body, the

---

[1] " Genua determinant." [2] " Nodi." [3] " Teretes."
[4] " Corporis." Other editions have " operis," *i.e.* of the whole work.
[5] " Planitie," hence " planta."
[6] " Germanitas," a brotherhood, or close connection.

force and purpose of which no one can perceive but He who made them. Can any one suppose that he is able to relate what is the advantage, and what the effect, of that slight transparent membrane by which the stomach is netted over and covered? What the twofold resemblance of the kidneys? which Varro says are so named because streams of foul moisture arise from these; which is far from being the case, because, rising on either side of the spine, they are united, and are separated from the intestines. What is the use of the spleen? what of the liver? which organs appear as it were to be made up [1] of disordered blood. What of the very bitter moisture of the gall? what of the heart? unless we shall happen to think that they ought to be believed, who think that the affection of anger is placed in the gall, that of fear in the heart, of joy in the spleen. But they will have it that the office of the liver is, by its embrace and heat, to digest the food in the stomach; some think that the desires of the amorous passions are contained in the liver.

First of all, the acuteness of the human sense is unable to perceive these things, because their offices lie concealed; nor, when laid open, do they show their uses. For, if it were so, perhaps the more gentle animals would either have no gall at all, or less than the wild beasts; the more timid ones would have more heart, the more lustful would have more liver, the more playful more spleen. As, therefore, we perceive that we hear with our ears, that we see with our eyes, that we smell with our nostrils; so assuredly we should perceive that we are angry with the gall, that we desire with the liver, that we rejoice with the spleen. Since, therefore, we do not at all perceive from what part those affections come, it is possible that they may come from another source, and that those organs may have a different effect to that which we suppose; but we cannot, however, prove that they who discuss these things speak falsely. But I think that all things which relate to the motions of the mind and soul, are of so obscure and profound a nature, that it is beyond the power of man to see through them clearly. This, however, ought to be sure and undoubted, that so many objects and so many organs have one and the same office—to retain the soul in the body. But what office is particularly assigned to each, who

[1] Concreta esse.

can know, except the Designer, to whom alone His own work is known?

Chap. xv.—*Of the voice.*

But what account can we give of the voice? Grammarians, indeed, and philosophers, define the voice to be air struck by the breath; from which words[1] derive their name: which is plainly false. For the voice is not produced outside of the mouth, but within, and therefore that opinion is more probable, that the breath, being compressed, when it has struck against the obstacle presented by the throat, forces out the sound of the voice: as when we send down the breath into an open hemlock stalk, having applied it to the lips, and the breath, reverberating from the hollow of the stalk, and rolled back from the bottom, while it returns[2] to that descending through meeting with itself, striving for an outlet, produces a sound; and the wind, rebounding by itself, is animated into vocal breath. Now, whether this is true, God, who is the designer, may see. For the voice appears to arise not from the mouth, but from the innermost breast. In fine, even when the mouth is closed, a sound such as is possible is emitted from the nostrils. Moreover, also, the voice is not affected by that greatest breath with which we gasp, but with a light and not compressed breath, as often as we wish. It has not therefore been comprehended in what manner it takes place, or what it is altogether. And do not imagine that I am now falling into the opinion of the Academy, for all things are not incomprehensible. For as it must be confessed that many things are unknown, since God has willed that they should exceed the understanding of man; so, however, it must be acknowledged that there are many which may both be perceived by the senses and comprehended by the reason. But we shall devote an entire treatise to the refutation of the philosophers. Let us therefore finish the course over which we are now running.

Chap. xvi.—*Of the mind and its seat.*

That the nature of the mind is also incomprehensible, who

---

[1] "Verba," as though derived from "verbero," to strike.

[2] Dum ad descendentem occursu suo redit. Others read, "Dum descendentem reddit."

can be ignorant, but he who is altogether destitute of mind, since it is not known in what place the mind is situated, or of what nature it is? Therefore various things have been discussed by philosophers concerning its nature and place. But I will not conceal what my own sentiments are: not that I should affirm that it is so (for it is the part of a foolish person to do this in a doubtful matter); but that when I have set forth the difficulty of the matter, you may understand how great is the magnitude of the divine works. Some would have it, that the seat of the mind is in the breast. But if this is so, how wonderful is it, that a faculty which is situated in an obscure and dark habitation should be employed in so great a light of reason and intelligence; then that the senses from every part of the body come together to it, so that it appears to be present in any quarter of the limbs! Others have said that its seat is in the brain: and, indeed, they have used probable arguments, saying that it was doubtless befitting that that which had the government of the whole body should especially have its abode in the highest place, as though in the citadel of the body; and that nothing should be in a more elevated position than that which governs the whole by reason, just as the Lord Himself, and Ruler of the universe, is in the highest place. Then they say that the organs which are the ministers of each sense, that is, of hearing, and seeing, and smelling, are situated in the head, and that the channels of all these lead not to the breast, but to the brain: otherwise we must be more slow in the exercise of our senses, until the power of sensation by a long course should descend through the neck even to the breast. These, in truth, do not greatly err, or perchance not at all.

For the mind, which exercises control over the body, appears to be placed in the highest part, the head, as God is in heaven; but when it is engaged in any reflection, it appears to pass to the breast, and, as it were, to withdraw to some secret recess, that it may elicit and draw forth counsel, as it were, from a hidden treasury. And therefore, when we are intent upon reflection, and when the mind, being occupied, has withdrawn itself to the inner depth,[1] we are accustomed neither to hear the things which sound about us, nor to see the things which stand in our way. But whether this is the case, it is assuredly

---

[1] In altum se abdiderit.

a matter of admiration how this takes place, since there is no passage from the brain to the breast. But if it is not so, nevertheless it is no less a matter of admiration that, by some divine plan or other, it is caused that it appears to be so. Can any fail to admire that that living and heavenly faculty which is called the mind or the soul, is of such volubility[1] that it does not rest even then when it is asleep; of such rapidity, that it surveys the whole heaven at one moment of time; and, if it wills, flies over seas, traverses lands and cities,—in short, places in its own sight all things which it pleases, however far and widely they are removed?

And does any one wonder if the divine mind of God, being extended[2] through all parts of the universe, runs to and fro, and rules all things, governs all things, being everywhere present, everywhere diffused; when the strength and power of the human mind, though enclosed within a mortal body, is so great, that it can in no way be restrained even by the barriers of this heavy and slothful body, to which it is bound, from bestowing upon itself, in its impatience of rest, the power of wandering without restraint? Whether, therefore, the mind has its dwelling in the head or in the breast, can any one comprehend what power of reason effects, that that incomprehensible faculty either remains fixed in the marrow of the brain, or in that blood divided into two parts[3] which is enclosed in the heart; and not infer from this very circumstance how great is the power of God, because the soul does not see itself, or of what nature or where it is; and if it did see, yet it would not be able to perceive in what manner an incorporeal substance is united with one which is corporeal? Or if the mind has no fixed locality, but runs here and there scattered through the whole body,— which is possible, and was asserted by Xenocrates, the disciple of Plato,—then, inasmuch as intelligence is present in every part of the body, it cannot be understood what that mind is, or what its qualities are, since its nature is so subtle and refined, that, though infused into solid organs by a living and, as it were, ardent perception, it is mingled with all the members.

But take care that you never think it probable, as Aristoxenus said, that the mind has no existence, but that the power of perception exists from the constitution of the body and the

---

[1] Mobilitatis. [2] Intenta discurrit. [3] Bipartito.

construction of the organs, as harmony does in the case of the lyre. For musicians call the stretching and sounding of the strings to entire strains, without any striking of notes in agreement with them, harmony. They will have it, therefore, that the soul in man exists in a manner like that by which harmonious modulation exists on the lyre; namely, that the firm uniting of the separate parts of the body and the vigour of all the limbs agreeing together, makes that perceptible motion, and adjusts[1] the mind, as well-stretched things produce harmonious sound. And as, in the lyre, when anything has been interrupted or relaxed, the whole method of the strain is disturbed and destroyed; so in the body, when any part of the limbs receives an injury, the whole are weakened, and all being corrupted and thrown into confusion, the power of perception is destroyed: and this is called death. But he, if he had possessed any mind, would never have transferred harmony from the lyre to man. For the lyre cannot of its own accord send forth a sound, so that there can be in this any comparison and resemblance to a living person; but the soul both reflects and is moved of its own accord. But if there were in us anything resembling harmony, it would be moved by a blow from without, as the strings of the lyre are by the hands; whereas without the handling of the artificer, and the stroke of the fingers, they lie mute and motionless. But doubtless he[2] ought to have beaten by the hand, that he might at length observe; for his mind, badly compacted from his members, was in a state of torpor.

CHAP. XVII.—*Of the soul, and the opinion of philosophers concerning it.*

It remains to speak of the soul, although its system and nature cannot be perceived. Nor, therefore, do we fail to understand that the soul is immortal, since whatever is vigorous and is in motion by itself at all times, and cannot be seen or touched, must be eternal. But what the soul is, is not yet agreed upon by philosophers, and perhaps will never be agreed upon. For some have said that it is blood, others that it is fire, others wind, from which it has received its name of "anima," or "animus," because in Greek the wind is called "ane-

---

[1] Concinnet.
[2] Aristoxenus, whose opinion has been mentioned above.

mos,"[1] and yet none of these appears to have spoken anything. For if the soul appears to be extinguished when the blood is poured forth through a wound, or is exhausted by the heat of fevers, it does not therefore follow that the system of the soul is to be placed in the material of the blood; as though a question should arise as to the nature of the light which we make use of, and the answer should be given that it is oil, for when that is consumed the light is extinguished: since they are plainly different, but the one is the nourishment of the other. Therefore the soul appears to be like light, since it is not itself blood, but is nourished by the moisture of the blood, as light is by oil.

But they who have supposed it to be fire made use of this argument, that when the soul is present the body is warm, but on its departure the body grows cold. But fire is both without perception and is seen, and burns when touched. But the soul is both endowed with perception and cannot be seen, and does not burn. From which it is evident that the soul is something like God. But they who suppose that it is wind are deceived by this, because we appear to live by drawing breath from the air. Varro gives this definition: "The soul is air conceived in the mouth, warmed in the lungs, heated in the heart, diffused into the body." These things are most plainly false. For I say that the nature of things of this kind is not so obscure, that we do not even understand what cannot be true. If any one should say to me that the heaven is of brass, or crystal, or, as Empedocles says, that it is frozen air, must I at once assent because I do not know of what material the heaven is? For as I know not this, I know that. Therefore the soul is not air conceived in the mouth, because the soul is produced much before air can be conceived in the mouth. For it is not introduced into the body after birth, as it appears to some philosophers, but immediately after conception, when the divine necessity has formed the offspring in the womb; for it so lives within the bowels of its mother, that it is increased in growth, and delights to bound with repeated beatings. In short, there must be a miscarriage if the living young within shall die. The other parts of the definition have reference to this, that during those nine months in which we were in the womb we

[1] ἄνεμος.

appear to have been dead. None, therefore, of these three opinions is true. We cannot, however, say that they who held these sentiments were false to such an extent that they said nothing at all; for we live at once by the blood, and heat, and breath. But since the soul exists in the body by the union of all these, they did not express what it was in its own proper sense;[1] for as it cannot be seen, so it cannot be expressed.

CHAP. XVIII.—*Of the soul and the mind, and their affections.*

There follows another, and in itself an inexplicable inquiry: Whether the soul and the mind are the same, or there be one faculty by which we live, and another by which we perceive and have discernment. There are not wanting arguments on either side. For they who say that they are one faculty make use of this argument, that we cannot live without perception, nor perceive without life, and therefore that that which is incapable of separation cannot be different; but that whatever it is, it has the office of living and the method of perception. On which account two[2] Epicurean poets speak of the mind and the soul indifferently. But they who say that they are different argue in this way: That the mind is one thing, and the soul another, may be understood from this, that the mind may be extinguished while the soul is uninjured, which is accustomed to happen in the case of the insane; also, that the soul is put to rest[3] by death, the mind by sleep, and indeed in such a manner that it is not only ignorant of what is taking place,[4] or where it is, but it is even deceived by the contemplation of false objects. And how this takes place cannot accurately be perceived; why it takes place can be perceived. For we can by no means rest unless the mind is kept occupied by the similitudes[5] of visions. But the mind lies hid, oppressed with sleep, as fire buried[6] by ashes drawn over it; but if you stir it a little it again blazes, and, as it were, wakes up.[7] Therefore it is called away by images,[8] until the limbs, bedewed with sleep, are

---

[1] Proprie.

[2] Lucretius is undoubtedly one of the poets here referred to; some think that Virgil, others that Horace, is the second.

[3] Sopiatur.

[4] Quid fiat. Others read "quid faciat."

[5] Imaginibus.

[6] Sopitus.

[7] Evigilat.

[8] Simulacris.

invigorated; for the body while the perception is awake, although it lies motionless, yet is not at rest, because the perception burns in it, and vibrates as a flame, and keeps all the limbs bound to itself.

But when the mind is transferred from its application to the contemplation of images, then at length the whole body is resolved into rest. But the mind is transferred from dark thought, when, under the influence of darkness, it has begun to be alone with itself. While it is intent upon those things concerning which it is reflecting, sleep suddenly creeps on, and the thought itself imperceptibly turns aside to the nearest appearances:[1] thus it begins also to see those things which it had placed before its eyes. Then it proceeds further, and finds diversions[2] for itself, that it may not interrupt the most healthy repose of the body. For as the mind is diverted in the day by true sights, so that it does not sleep; so is it diverted in the night by false sights, so that it is not aroused. For if it perceives no images, it will follow of necessity either that it is awake, or that it is asleep in perpetual death. Therefore the system of dreaming has been given by God for the sake of sleeping; and, indeed, it has been given to all animals in common; but this especially to man, that when God gave this system on account of rest, He left to Himself the power of teaching man future events by means of the dream.[3] For narratives often testify that there have been dreams which have had an immediate and a remarkable accomplishment,[4] and the answers of our prophets have been after the character of a dream.[5] On which account they are not always true, nor always false, as Virgil testified,[6] who supposed that there were two gates for the passage of dreams. But those which are false are seen for the sake of sleeping; those which are true are sent by God, that by this revelation we may learn impending goods or evils.

[1] Species.   [2] Avocamenta.
[3] Thus Joseph and Daniel were interpreters of dreams; and the prophet Joel (ii. 28) foretells this as a mark of the last days, "Your old men shall dream dreams, your young men shall see visions."
[4] Quorum præsens et admirabilis fuerit eventus.
[5] Ex parte somnii constiterunt. Some editions read, "ex parte somniis constituerunt."
[6] Æneid, vi. 804.

Chap. XIX.—*Of the soul, and it given by God.*

A question also may arise respecting this, whether the soul is produced from the father, or rather from the mother, or indeed from both. But I think that this judgment is to be formed as though in a doubtful matter.[1] For nothing is true of these three opinions, because souls are produced neither from both nor from either. For a body may be produced from a body, since something is contributed from both; but a soul cannot be produced from souls, because nothing can depart from a slight and incomprehensible subject. Therefore the manner of the production of souls belongs entirely to God alone.

"In fine, we are all sprung from a heavenly seed, all have that same Father," as Lucretius[2] says. For nothing but what is mortal can be generated from mortals. Nor ought he to be deemed a father who in no way perceives that he has transmitted or breathed a soul from his own; nor, if he perceives it, comprehends in his mind when or in what manner that effect is produced.

From this it is evident that souls are not given by parents, but by one and the same God and Father of all, who alone has the law and method of their birth, since He alone produces them. For the part of the earthly parent is nothing more than with a sense of pleasure to emit the moisture of the body, in which is the material of birth, or to receive it; and to this work man's power is limited,[3] nor has he any further power. Therefore men wish for the birth of sons, because they do not themselves bring it about. Everything beyond this is the work of God,—namely, the conception itself, and the moulding of the body, and the breathing in of life, and the bringing forth in safety, and whatever afterwards contributes to the preservation of man: it is His gift that we breathe, that we live, and are vigorous. For, besides that we owe it to His bounty that we are safe in body, and that He supplies us with nourishment from various sources, He also gives to man wisdom, which no earthly father can by any means give; and therefore it often happens that foolish sons are born from wise parents, and wise

---

[1] "Sed ego id in eo jure ab ancipiti vindico."   [2] ii. 991.
[3] "Et citra hoc opus homo resistit." The compound word "resistit" is used for the simple *sistit*—stands.

sons from foolish parents, which some persons attribute to fate and the stars. But this is not now the time to discuss the subject of fate. It is sufficient to say this, that even if the stars hold together the efficacy of all things, it is nevertheless certain that all things are done by God, who both made and set in order the stars themselves. They are therefore senseless who detract this power from God, and assign it to His work.

He would have it, therefore, to be in our own power, whether we use or do not use this divine and excellent gift of God. For, having granted this, He bound man himself by the mystery[1] of virtue, by which he might be able to gain life. For great is the power, great the reason, great the mysterious purpose of man; and if any one shall not abandon this, nor betray his fidelity and devotedness, he must be happy: he, in short, to sum up the matter in few words, must of necessity resemble God. For he is in error whosoever judges of[2] man by his flesh. For this worthless body[3] with which we are clothed is the receptacle of man.[4] For man himself can neither be touched, nor looked upon, nor grasped, because he lies hidden within this body, which is seen. And if he shall be more luxurious and delicate in this life than its nature demands, if he shall despise virtue, and give himself to the pursuit of fleshly lusts, he will fall and be pressed down to the earth; but if (as his duty is) he shall readily and constantly maintain his position, which is right for him, and he has rightly obtained,[5]—if he shall not be enslaved to the earth, which he ought to trample upon and overcome, he will gain eternal life.

CHAP. XX.—*Of himself and the truth.*

These things I have written to you, Demetrianus, for the present in few words, and perhaps with more obscurity than was befitting, in accordance with the necessity of circumstances and the time, with which you ought to be content, since you are about to receive more and better things if God shall favour us.

---

[1] "Sacramento."
[2] "Metitur," measures.
[3] "Corpusculum." The diminutive appears to imply contempt.
[4] The expression is too general, since the body as well as the soul is a true part of man's nature.
[5] "Quem rectum rectè sortitus est." In some editions the word "recte" is omitted.

Then, accordingly, I will exhort you with greater clearness and truth to the learning of true philosophy. For I have determined to commit to writing as many things as I shall be able, which have reference to the condition of a happy life; and that indeed against the philosophers, since they are pernicious and weighty for the disturbing of the truth. For the force of their eloquence is incredible, and their subtlety in argument and disputation may easily deceive any one; and these we will refute partly by our own weapons, but partly by weapons borrowed from their mutual wrangling, so that it may be evident that they rather introduced error than removed it.

Perhaps you may wonder that I venture to undertake so great a deed. Shall we then suffer the truth to be extinguished or crushed? I, in truth, would more willingly fail even under this burthen. For if Marcus Tullius, the unparalleled example of eloquence itself, was often vanquished by men void of learning and eloquence,—who, however, were striving for that which was true,—why should we despair that the truth itself will by its own peculiar force and clearness avail against deceitful and captious eloquence? They indeed are wont to profess themselves advocates of the truth; but who can defend that which he has not learned, or make clear to others that which he himself does not know? I seem to promise a great thing; but there is need of the favour of Heaven, that ability and time may be given us for following our purpose. But if life is to be wished for by a wise man, assuredly I should wish to live for no other reason than that I may effect something which may be worthy of life, and which may be useful to my readers, if not for eloquence, because there is in me but a slight stream of eloquence, at any rate for living, which is especially needful. And when I have accomplished this, I shall think that I have lived enough, and that I have discharged the duty of a man, if my labour shall have freed some men from errors, and have directed them to the path which leads to heaven.

THE EPITOME OF THE DIVINE INSTITUTES,

ADDRESSED TO HIS BROTHER PENTADIUS.

THE PREFACE.—*The plan and purport of the whole Epitome, and of the "Institutions."*

ALTHOUGH the books of the *Divine Institutions* which we wrote a long time since to illustrate the truth and religion, may so prepare and mould the minds of the readers, that their length may not produce disgust, nor their copiousness be burthensome; nevertheless you desire, O brother Pentadius, that an epitome of them should be made for you, I suppose for this reason, that I may write something to you, and that your name may be rendered famous by my work, such as it is. I will comply with your desire, although it seems a difficult matter to comprise within the compass of one book those things which have been treated of in seven large volumes. For the whole matter becomes less full when so great a multitude of subjects is to be compressed within a narrow space; and it becomes less clear by its very brevity, especially since many arguments and examples, on which the elucidation of the proofs depends, must of necessity be omitted, since their copiousness is so great, that even by themselves they are enough to make up a book. And when these are removed, what can appear useful, what plain? But I will strive as much as the subject permits, both to contract that which is diffuse and to shorten that which is long; in such a manner, however, that in this work, in which truth is to be brought to light, matter may not seem to be wanting for copiousness, nor clearness for understanding it.

CHAP. I.—*Of the divine providence.*

First a question arises: Whether there is any providence which made or governs the world? That there is, no one doubts, since of almost all the philosophers, except the school of Epicurus, there is but one voice and one opinion, that the world could not have been made without a contriver, and that it cannot exist without a ruler. Therefore Epicurus is refuted not only by the most learned men, but also by the testimonies and perceptions of all mortals. For who can doubt respecting a providence, when he sees that the heavens and the earth have been so arranged, and that all things have been so regulated, that they might be most befittingly adapted, not only to wonderful beauty and adornment, but also to the use of men, and the convenience of the other living creatures? That, therefore, which exists in accordance with a plan, cannot have had its beginning without a plan: thus[1] it is certain that there is a providence.

CHAP. II.—*That there is but one God, and that there cannot be more.*

Another question follows: Whether there be one God or more? And this indeed contains much ambiguity. For not only do individuals differ among themselves, but also peoples and nations. But he who shall follow the guidance of reason will understand that there cannot be a Lord except one, nor a Father except one. For if God, who made all things, is also Lord and Father, He must be one only, so that the same may be the head and source of all things. Nor is it possible for the world[2] to exist unless all things be referred to one person, unless one hold the rudder, unless one guide the reins, and, as it were, one mind direct all the members of the body. If there are many kings in a swarm of bees, they will perish or be scattered abroad, while

"Discord attacks the kings with great commotion."[3]

If there are several leaders in a herd, they will contend until one gains the mastery.[4] If there are many commanders in an army, the soldiers cannot obey, since different commands are

---

[1] "Quoniam." This word appears to be out of place, as its proper meaning is "since." Either it must be taken as above, or, with some editors, the last clause of this chapter may be taken as the beginning of the next chapter—"Since there is a providence," etc.
[2] "Rerum summa."   [3] Virg. *Georg.* iv. 68.   [4] "Obtineat."

given; nor can unity be maintained by themselves, since each consults his own interests according to his humours.[1] Thus, in this commonwealth of the world, unless there were one ruler, who was also its founder, either this mass would be dissolved, or it could not have been put together at all.

Moreover, the whole (authority) could not exist in many (deities), since they separately maintain their own duties and their own prerogatives. No one, therefore, of them can be called omnipotent, which is the true title of God, since he will be able to accomplish that only which depends upon himself, and will not venture to attempt that which depends upon others. Vulcan will not claim for himself water, nor Neptune fire; nor will Ceres claim acquaintance with the arts, nor Minerva with fruits; nor will Mercury lay claim to arms, nor Mars to the lyre; Jupiter will not claim medicine, nor Æsculapius the thunderbolt: he will more easily endure it when thrown by another, than he will brandish it himself. If, therefore, individuals cannot do all things, they have less strength and less power; but he is to be regarded as God who can accomplish the whole, and not he who can only accomplish the smallest part of the whole.

CHAP. III.—*The testimonies of the poets concerning the one God.*

There is, then, one God, perfect, eternal, incorruptible, incapable of suffering, subject to no circumstance or power, Himself possessing all things, ruling all things, whom the human mind can neither estimate in thought nor mortal tongue describe in speech. For He is too elevated and great to be conceived by the thought, or expressed by the language of man. In short, not to speak of the prophets, the preachers of the one God, poets also, and philosophers, and inspired women,[2] utter their testimony to the unity of God. Orpheus speaks of the surpassing God who made the heaven and the sun, with the other heavenly bodies; who made the earth and the seas. Also our own Maro calls the supreme God at one time a spirit, at another time a mind, and says that it, as though infused into limbs, puts in motion the body of the whole world; also, that God permeates the heights of heaven, the tracts of the sea

---

[1] "Pro moribus." Another reading is "pro viribus," with all their power.
[2] "Vates," *i.e.* the Sibyls.

and lands, and that all living creatures derive their life from Him. Even Ovid was not ignorant that the world was prepared by God, whom he sometimes calls the framer of all things, sometimes the fabricator of the world.

CHAP. IV.—*The testimonies of the philosophers to the unity of God.*

But let us come to the philosophers, whose authority is regarded as more certain than that of the poets. Plato asserts His monarchy, saying that there is but one God, by whom the world was prepared and completed with wonderful order. Aristotle, his disciple, admits that there is one mind which presides over the world. Antisthenes says that there is one who is God by nature,[1] the governor of the whole system. It would be a long task to recount the statements which have been made respecting the supreme God, either by Thales, or by Pythagoras and Anaximenes before him, or afterwards by the Stoics Cleanthes and Chrysippus and Zeno, or of our countrymen, by Seneca following the Stoics, and by Tullius himself, since all these attempted to define the being of God,[2] and affirmed that the world is ruled by Him alone, and that He is not subject to any nature, since all nature derives its origin from Him.

Hermes, who, on account of his virtue and his knowledge of many arts, deserved the name of Trismegistus, who preceded the philosophers in the antiquity of his doctrine, and who is reverenced by the Egyptians as a god, in asserting the majesty of the one God with infinite praises, calls Him Lord and Father, and says that He is without a name because He does not stand in need of a proper name, inasmuch as He is alone, and that He has no parents, since He exists of Himself and by Himself. In writing to his son he thus begins: To understand God is difficult, to describe Him in speech is impossible, even for one to whom it is possible to understand Him; for the perfect cannot be comprehended by the imperfect, nor the invisible by the visible.

CHAP. V.—*That the prophetic women—that is, the Sibyls—declare that there is but one God.*

It remains to speak of the prophetic women. Varro relates

[1] "Naturalem."   [2] "Quid sit Deus."

that there were ten Sibyls,—the first of the Persians, the second the Libyan, the third the Delphian, the fourth the Cimmerian, the fifth the Erythræan, the sixth the Samian, the seventh the Cumæan, the eighth the Hellespontian, the ninth the Phrygian, the tenth the Tiburtine, who has the name of Albunea. Of all these, he says that there are three books of the Cumæan alone which contain the fates of the Romans, and are accounted sacred, but that there exist, and are commonly regarded as separate, books of almost all the others, but that they are entitled, as though by one name, Sibylline books, excepting that the Erythræan, who is said to have lived in the times of the Trojan war, placed her name in her book: the writings of the others are mixed together.

All these Sibyls of whom I have spoken, except the Cumæan, whom none but the Quindecemviri[1] are allowed to read, bear witness that there is but one God, the ruler, the maker, the parent, not begotten of any, but sprung from Himself, who was from all ages, and will be to all ages; and therefore is alone worthy of being worshipped, alone of being feared, alone of being reverenced, by all living beings;—whose testimonies I have omitted because I was unable to abridge them; but if you wish to see them, you must have recourse to the books themselves. Now let us follow up the remaining subjects.

CHAP. VI.—*Since God is eternal and immortal, He does not stand in need of sex and succession.*

These testimonies, therefore, so many and so great, clearly teach that there is but one government in the world, and one power, the origin of which cannot be imagined, or its force described. They are foolish, therefore, who imagine that the gods were born of marriage, since the sexes themselves, and the intercourse between them, were given to mortals by God for this reason, that every race might be preserved by a succession of offspring. But what need have the immortals either of sex or succession, since neither pleasure nor death affects them? Those, therefore, who are reckoned as gods, since it is evident that they were born as men, and that they begat others, were

---

[1] The appointed guardians of the Sibylline books. At first there were two; the number was afterwards increased to ten, and subsequently to fifteen, termed Quindecemviri.

plainly mortals: but they were believed to be gods, because, when they were great and powerful kings, on account of the benefits which they had conferred upon men, they deserved to obtain divine honours after death; and temples and statues being erected to them, their memory was retained and celebrated as that of immortals.

CHAP. VII.—*Of the wicked life and death of Hercules.*

But though almost all nations are persuaded that they are gods, yet their actions, as related both by poets and historians, declare that they were men. Who is ignorant of the times in which Hercules lived, since he both sailed with the Argonauts on their expedition, and having stormed Troy, slew Laomedon, the father of Priam, on account of his perjury? From that time rather more than 1500 years are reckoned. He is said not even to have been born honourably, but to have been sprung from Alcmena by adultery, and to have been himself addicted to the vices of his father. He never abstained from women, or males, and traversed the whole world, not so much for the sake of glory as of lust, nor so much for the slaughter of beasts as for the begetting of children. And though he was unvanquished, yet he was triumphed over by Omphale alone, to whom he gave up his club and lion's skin; and being clothed in a woman's garment, and crouching at a woman's feet, he received his task[1] to execute. He afterwards, in a transport of frenzy, killed his little children and his wife Megara. At last, having put on a garment sent by his wife Deianyra, when he was perishing through ulcers, being unable to endure the pain, he constructed for himself a funeral pile on mount Æta, and burnt himself alive. Thus it is effected, that although on account of his excellence[2] he might have been believed to be a god, nevertheless on account of these things he is believed to have been a man.

CHAP. VIII.—*Of Æsculapius, Apollo, Mars, Castor and Pollux, and of Mercurius and Bacchus.*

Tarquitius relates that Æsculapius was born of doubtful parents, and that on this account he was exposed; and being taken up by hunters, and fed by the teats of a hound, was

---

[1] Pensa quæ faceret. "Pensum" properly signifies the wool daily weighed out and given to each servant. [2] Ob virtutem.

given to Chiron for instruction. He lived at Epidaurus, and was buried at Cynosuræ, as Cicero says,[1] when he had been killed by lightning. But Apollo, his father, did not disdain to take charge of another's flock that he might receive a wife;[2] and when he had unintentionally killed a boy whom he loved, he inscribed his own lamentations on a flower. Mars, a man of the greatest bravery, was not free from the charge of adultery, since he was made a spectacle, being bound with a chain together with the adulteress.

Castor and Pollux carried off the brides of others, but not with impunity, to whose death and burial Homer bears witness, not with poetical, but simple faith. Mercurius, who was the father of Androgynus by his intrigue with Venus, deserved to be a god, because he invented the lyre and the palæstra. Father Bacchus, after subduing India as a conqueror, having by chance come to Crete, saw Ariadne on the shore, whom Theseus had forced and deserted. Then, being inflamed by love, he united her in marriage to himself, and placed her crown, as the poets say, conspicuously among the stars. The mother of the gods[3] herself, while she lived in Phrygia after the banishment and death of her husband, though a widow, and aged, was enamoured of a beautiful youth; and because he was not faithful, she mutilated, and rendered him effeminate: on which account even now she delights in the Galli[4] as her priests.

CHAP. IX.—*Of the disgraceful deeds of the gods.*

Whence did Ceres bring forth Proserpine, except from debauchery? Whence did Latona bring forth her twins, except from crime? Venus having been subject to the lusts of gods and men, when she reigned in Cyprus, invented the practice of courtezanship, and commanded women to make traffic of themselves, that she might not alone be infamous. Were the virgins themselves, Minerva and Diana, chaste? Whence, then, did

---

[1] Cicero, *de Nat. Deor.* iii. 22.

[2] When Pelias had promised his daughter Alcestis to Admetus, on condition of his coming to her in a chariot drawn by lions and boars, Apollo enabled Admetus to fulfil this condition.

[3] Rhea, or Cybele.

[4] Galli, the priests of Cybele, were so called: they mutilated themselves, and performed many raving ceremonies.

Erichthonius arise? Did Vulcan shed his seed upon the ground, and was man born from that as a fungus? Or why did Diana banish Hippolytus either to a retired place, or give him up to a woman, where he might pass his life in solitude among unknown groves, and having now changed his name, might be called Virbius? What do these things signify but impurity, which the poets do not venture to confess?

CHAP. X.—*Of Jupiter, and his licentious life.*

But respecting the king and father of all these, Jupiter, whom they believe to possess the chief power in heaven,—what power[1] had he, who banished his father Saturnus from his kingdom, and pursued him with arms when he fled? What self-restraint had he, who indulged every kind of lust? For he made Alcmena and Leda, the wives of great men, infamous through his adultery: he also, captivated with the beauty of a boy, carried him off with violence as he was hunting and meditating manly things, that he might treat him as a woman. Why should I mention his debaucheries of virgins? and how great a multitude of these there was, is shown by the number of his sons. In the case of Thetis alone he was more temperate. For it had been predicted that the son whom she should bring forth would be more powerful than his father. Therefore he struggled with his love, that one might not be born greater than himself. He knew, therefore, that he was not of perfect virtue, greatness, and power, since he feared that which he himself had done to his father. Why, therefore, is he called best and greatest, since he both contaminated himself with faults, which is the part of one who is unjust and bad, and feared a greater than himself, which is the part of one who is weak and inferior?

CHAP. XI.—*The various emblems under which the poets veiled the turpitude of Jupiter.*

But some one will say that these things are feigned by the poets. This is not the usage of the poets, to feign in such a manner that you fabricate the whole, but so that you cover the actions themselves with a figure, and, as it were, with a

---

[1] Quid potestatis. Others read "pietatis," which appears more suitable to the sense of the passage.

variegated veil. Poetic licence has this limit, not that it may invent the whole, which is the part of one who is false and senseless, but that it may change something consistently with reason. They said that Jupiter changed himself into a shower of gold, that he might deceive Danae. What is a shower of gold? Plainly golden coins, by offering a great quantity of which, and pouring them into her bosom, he corrupted the frailty of her virgin soul by this bribe. Thus also they speak of a shower of iron, when they wish to signify a multitude of javelins. He carried off his catamite upon an eagle. What is the eagle? Truly a legion, since the figure of this animal is the standard of the legion. He carried Europa across the sea on a bull. What is the bull? Clearly a ship, which had its tutelary image[1] fashioned in the shape of a bull. So assuredly the daughter of Inachus was not turned into a cow, nor as such did she swim across, but she escaped the anger of Juno in a ship which had the form of a cow. Lastly, when she had been conveyed to Egypt, she became Isis, whose voyage is celebrated on a fixed day, in memory of her flight.

CHAP. XII.—*The poets do not invent all those things which relate to the gods.*

You see, then, that the poets did not invent all things, and that they prefigured some things, that, when they spoke the truth, they might add something like this of divinity to those whom they called gods; as they did also respecting their kingdoms. For when they say that Jupiter had by lot the kingdom of Cœlus, they either mean Mount Olympus, on which ancient stories relate that Saturnus, and afterwards Jupiter, dwelt, or a part of the East, which is, as it were, higher, because the light arises thence; but the region of the West is lower, and therefore they say that Pluto obtained the lower regions; but that the sea was given to Neptune, because he had the maritime coast, with all the islands. Many things are thus coloured by the poets; and they who are ignorant of this, censure them as false, but only in word: for in fact they believe them, since they so fashion the images of the gods, that when they make them male and female, and confess that some are married, some

---

[1] Tutela. The image of some deity, supposed to be the tutelary guardian of the ship, was usually painted on the stern.

parents, and some children, they plainly assent to the poets; for these relations cannot exist without intercourse and the generation of children.

CHAP. XIII.—*The actions of Jupiter are related from the historian Euhemerus.*

But let us leave the poets; let us come to history, which is supported both by the credibility of the facts and by the antiquity of the times. Euhemerus was a Messenian, a very ancient writer, who gave an account of the origin of Jupiter, and his exploits, and all his posterity, gathered from the sacred inscriptions of ancient temples; he also traced out the parents of the other gods, their countries, actions, commands, and deaths, and even their sepulchres. And this history Ennius translated into Latin, whose words are these: "As these things are written, so is the origin and kindred of Jupiter and his brothers; after this manner it is handed down to us in the sacred writing." The same Euhemerus therefore relates that Jupiter, when he had five times gone round the world, and had distributed governments to his friends and relatives, and had given laws to men, and had wrought many other benefits, being endued with immortal glory and everlasting remembrance, ended his life in Crete, and departed to the gods, and that his sepulchre is in Crete, in the town of Gnossus, and that upon it is engraved in ancient Greek letters Zankronou, which is Jupiter the son of Saturnus. It is plain, therefore, from the things which I have related, that he was a man, and reigned on the earth.

CHAP. XIV.—*The actions of Saturnus and Uranus taken from the historians.*

Let us pass on to former things, that we may discover the origin of the whole error. Saturnus is said to have been born of Cœlus and Terra. This is plainly incredible; but there is a certain reason why it is thus related, and he who is ignorant of this rejects it as a fable. That Uranus was the father of Saturnus, both Hermes affirms, and sacred history teaches. When Trismegistus said that there were very few men of perfect learning, he enumerated among them his relatives, Uranus, Saturnus, and Mercurius. Euhemerus relates that the same Uranus was the first who reigned on earth, using these words:

" In the beginning Cœlus first had the chief power on earth: he instituted and prepared that kingdom for himself together with his brothers."[1]

CHAP. XX.—*Of the gods peculiar to the Romans.*

I have spoken of the religious rites which are common to all nations. I will now speak of the gods which the Romans have peculiar to themselves. Who does not know that the wife of Faustulus, the nurse of Romulus and Remus, in honour of whom the Larentinalia were instituted, was a harlot? And for this reason she was called Lupa, and represented in the form of a wild beast. Faula also and Flora were harlots, of whom the one was the mistress of Hercules, as Verrius relates; the other, having acquired great wealth by her person, made the people her heir, and on this account the games called Floralia are celebrated in her honour.

Tatius consecrated the statue of a woman which had been found in the principal sewer, and called it by the name of the goddess Cloacina. The Romans, being besieged by the Gauls, made engines for throwing weapons of the hair of women; and on this account they erected an altar and temple to Venus Calva:[2] also to Jupiter Pistor,[3] because he had advised them in a dream to make all their corn into bread, and to throw it upon the enemy; and when this had been done, the Gauls, despairing of being able to reduce the Romans by famine, had abandoned the siege. Tullus Hostilius made Fear and Pallor gods. Mind is also worshipped; but if they had possessed it, they would never, I believe, have thought that it ought to be worshipped. Marcellus originated Honour and Virtue.

CHAP. XXI.—*Of the sacred rites of the Roman gods.*

But the senate also instituted other false gods of this kind,— Hope, Faith, Concord, Peace, Chastity, Piety; all of which, since they ought truly to be in the minds of men, they have falsely placed within walls. But although these have no substantial existence outside of man, nevertheless I should prefer that they should be worshipped, rather than Blight or Fever, which ought not to be consecrated, but rather to be execrated; than Fornax, together with her sacred ovens; than Stercutus, who first showed

---

[1] From this point the manuscripts are defective to ch. xx.
[2] *i.e.* Venus the bald.   [3] *i.e.* Jupiter the baker.

men to enrich the ground with manure; than the goddess Muta, who brought forth the Lares; than Cumina, who presides over the cradles of infants; than Caca, who gave information to Hercules respecting the stealing of his cattle, that he might slay her brother. How many other monstrous and ludicrous fictions there are, respecting which it is grievous to speak! I do not, however, wish to omit notice of Terminus, since it is related that he did not give way even to Jupiter, though he was an unwrought stone. They suppose that he has the custody of the boundaries, and public prayers are offered to him, that he may keep the stone of the Capitol immoveable, and preserve and extend the boundaries of the Roman empire.

CHAP. XXII.—*Of the sacred rites introduced by Faunus and Numa.*

Faunus was the first in Latium who introduced these follies, who both instituted bloody sacrifices to his grandfather Saturnus, and wished that his father Picus should be worshipped as a god, and placed Fatua Fauna his wife and sister among the gods, and named her the good goddess. Then at Rome, Numa, who burthened those rude and rustic men with new superstitions, instituted priesthoods, and distributed the gods into families and nations, that he might call off the fierce spirits of the people from the pursuits of arms. Therefore Lucilius, in deriding the folly of those who are slaves to vain superstitions, introduced these verses: "Those bugbears[1] the Lamiæ, which Faunus and Numa Pompilius and others instituted, at these he trembles; he places everything in this. As infant boys believe that every statue of bronze is a living man, so these imagine that all things feigned are true: they believe that statues of bronze contain a heart. It is a painter's[2] gallery; nothing is real, everything fictitious." Tullius also, writing of the nature of the gods, complains that false and fictitious gods have been introduced, and that from this source have arisen false opinions, and turbulent errors, and almost old womanly superstitions, which opinion ought in comparison[3] with others to be esteemed more

---

[1] Terriculas. There is another reading, "terricolas." See note at *Institutes*, book i. ch. xxii.
[2] See preceding note and reference.
[3] Comparari. Others read "computari."

weighty, because these things were spoken by one who was both a philosopher and a priest.

CHAP. XXIII.—*Of the gods and sacred rites of the barbarians.*

We have spoken respecting the gods: now we will speak of the rites and practices of their sacred institutions. A human victim used to be immolated to the Cyprian Jupiter, as Teucer had appointed. Thus also the Tauri used to offer strangers to Diana; the Latian Jupiter also was propitiated with human blood. Also before Saturnus, men of sixty years of age, according to the oracle[1] of Apollo, were thrown from a bridge into the Tiber. And the Carthaginians not only offered infants to the same Saturnus; but being conquered by the Sicilians, to make an expiation, they immolated two hundred sons of nobles. And not more mild than these are those offerings which are even now made to the great Mother and to Bellona, in which the priests make an offering, not with the blood of others, but with their own blood; when, mutilating themselves, they cease to be men, and yet do not pass over to the women; or, cutting their shoulders, they sprinkle the loathsome altars with their own blood. But these things are cruel.

Let us come to those which are mild. The sacred rites of Isis show nothing else than the manner in which she lost and found her little son, who is called Osiris. For first her priests and attendants, having shaved all their limbs, and beating their breasts, howl, lament, and search, imitating the manner in which his mother was affected; afterwards the boy is found by Cynocephalus. Thus the mournful rites are ended with gladness. The mystery of Ceres also resembles these, in which torches are lighted, and Proserpine is sought for through the night; and when she has been found, the whole rite is finished with congratulations and the throwing about of torches. The people of Lampsacus offer an ass to Priapus as an appropriate victim.[2] Lindus is a town of Rhodes, where sacred rites in honour of Hercules are celebrated with revilings. For when Hercules had taken away his oxen from a ploughman, and had slain them, he avenged his injury by taunts; and afterwards

---

[1] Ex responso. The common reading is "ex persona."

[2] Ea enim visa est aptior victima, quæ ipsi, cui mactatur, magnitudine virilis obsceni posset æquari.

having been himself appointed priest, it was ordained that he himself, and other priests after him, should celebrate sacrifices with the same revilings. But the mystery of the Cretan Jupiter represents the manner in which he was withdrawn from his father, or brought up. The goat is beside him, by the teats of which Amalthea nourished the boy. The sacred rites of the mother of the gods also show the same thing. For because the Corybantes then drowned the cry of the boy by the tinkling of their helmets and the striking of their shields, a representation of this circumstance is now repeated in the sacred rites; but cymbals are beaten instead of helmets, and drums instead of shields, that Saturnus may not hear the cries of the boy.

CHAP. XXIV.—*Of the origin of sacred rites and superstitions.*

These are the mysteries of the gods. Now let us inquire also into the origin of superstitions, that we may search out by whom and at what times they were instituted. Didymus, in those books which are inscribed *Of the Explanation of Pindar*, relates that Melisseus was king of the Cretans, whose daughters were Amalthea and Melissa, who nourished Jupiter with goats' milk and honey; that he introduced new rites and ceremonies of sacred things, and was the first who sacrificed to gods, that is, to Vesta, who is called Tellus,—whence the poet says:

"And the first of the gods,
Tellus,"—

and afterwards to the mother of the gods. But Euhemerus, in his sacred history, says that Jupiter himself, after that he received the government, erected temples in honour of himself in many places. For in going about the world, as he came to each place, he united the chiefs of the people to himself in friendship and the right of hospitality; and that the remembrance of this might be preserved, he ordered that temples should be built to him, and annual festivals be celebrated by those connected with him in a league of hospitality. Thus he spread the worship of himself through all lands. But at what time they lived can easily be inferred. For Thallus writes in his history, that Belus, the king of the Assyrians, whom the Babylonians worship, and who was the cotemporary and friend of Saturnus, was 322 years before the Trojan war, and it is

1470 years since the taking of Troy. From which it is evident, that it is not more than 1800 years from the time when mankind fell into error by the institution of new forms of divine worship.

CHAP. XXV.—*Of the golden age, of images, and Prometheus, who first fashioned man.*

The poets, therefore, with good reason say that the golden age, which existed in the reign of Saturnus, was changed. For at that time no gods were worshipped, but they knew of one God only. After that they subjected themselves to frail and earthly things, worshipping idols of wood, and brass, and stone, a change took place from the golden age to that of iron. For having lost the knowledge of God, and broken off that one bond of human society, they began to harass one another, to plunder and subdue. But if they would raise their eyes aloft and behold God, who raised them up to the sight of heaven and Himself, they never would bend and prostrate themselves by worshipping earthly things, whose folly Lucretius severely rebukes, saying:[1] "And they abase their souls with fear of the gods, and weigh and press them down to the earth." Wherefore they tremble,[2] and do not understand how foolish it is to fear those things which you have made, or to hope for any protection from those things which are dumb and insensible, and neither see nor hear the suppliant. What majesty, therefore, or deity can they have, which were in the power of a man, that they should not be made, or that they should be made into some other thing, and are so even now? For they are liable to injury and might be carried off by theft, were it not that they are protected by the law and the guardianship of man. Does he therefore appear to be in possession of his senses, who sacrifices to such deities the choicest victims, consecrates gifts, offers costly garments, as if they who are without motion could use them? With reason, then, did Dionysius the tyrant of Sicily plunder and deride the gods of Greece when he had taken possession of it as conqueror; and after the sacrilegious acts which he had committed, he returned to Sicily with a prosperous

---

[1] *De Nat. Deor.* vi. 52.
[2] "Quare tremunt." Another reading is, "qua reddunt," which is unintelligible.

voyage, and held the kingdom even to his old age: nor were the injured gods able to punish him.

How much better is it to despise vanities, and to turn to God, to maintain the condition which you have received from God, to maintain your name! For on this account he is called *anthropos*,[1] because he looks upward. But he looks upward who looks up to the true and living God, who is in heaven; who seeks after the Maker and Parent of his soul, not only with his perception and mind, but also with his countenance and eyes raised aloft. But he who enslaves himself to earthly and humble things, plainly prefers to himself that which is below him. For since he himself is the workmanship of God, whereas an image is the workmanship of man, the human workmanship cannot be preferred to the divine; and as God is the parent of man, so is the man of the statue. Therefore he is foolish and senseless who adores that which he himself has made, of which detestable and foolish handicraft Prometheus was the author, who was born from Iapetus the uncle of Jupiter. For when first of all Jupiter, having obtained supreme dominion, wished to establish himself as a god, and to found temples, and was seeking for some one who was able to imitate the human figure, at that time Prometheus lived, who fashioned the image of a man from thick clay with such close resemblance, that the novelty and cleverness of the art was a wonder. At length the men of his own time, and afterwards the poets, handed him down as the maker of a true and living man; and we, as often as we praise wrought statues, say that they live and breathe. And he indeed was the inventor of earthenware images. But posterity, following him, both carved them out of marble, and moulded them out of bronze; then in process of time ornament was added of gold and ivory, so that not only the likenesses, but also the gleam itself, might dazzle the eyes. Thus ensnared by beauty, and forgetful of true majesty, sensible beings considered that insensible objects, rational beings that irrational objects, living beings that lifeless objects, were to be worshipped and reverenced by them.

[1] ἄνθρωπος, man; said to be compounded of ἄνω, τρίπω, and ὄψ, to turn the face upwards.

CHAP. XXVI.—*Of the worship of the elements and stars.*

Now let us refute those also who regard the elements of the world as gods, that is, the heaven, the sun, and the moon; for being ignorant of the Maker of these things, they admire and adore the works themselves. And this error belongs not to the ignorant only, but also to philosophers; since the Stoics are of opinion that all the heavenly bodies are to be considered as among the number of the gods, since they all have fixed and regular motions, by which they most constantly preserve the vicissitudes of the times which succeed them. They do not then possess voluntary motion, since they obey prescribed laws, and plainly not by their own sense, but by the workmanship of the supreme Creator, who so ordered them that they should complete unerring[1] courses and fixed circuits, by which they might vary the alternations of days and nights, of summer and winter. But if men admire the effects of these, if they admire their courses, their brightness, their regularity, their beauty, they ought to have understood how much more beautiful, more illustrious, and more powerful than these is the maker and contriver Himself, even God. But they estimated the Divinity by objects which fall under the sight of men;[2] not knowing that objects which come within the sight cannot be eternal, and that those which are eternal cannot be discerned by mortal eyes.

CHAP. XXVII.—*Of the creation, sin, and punishment of man; and of angels, both good and bad.*

One subject remains, and that the last: that, since it usually happens, as we read in histories, that the gods appear to have displayed their majesty by auguries, by dreams, by oracles, and also by the punishments of those who had committed sacrilege, I may show what cause produced this effect, so that no one even now may fall into the same snares into which those of old fell. When God, according to His excellent majesty, had framed the world out of nothing, and had decked the heaven with lights, and had filled the earth and the sea with living creatures, then He formed man out of clay, and fashioned him after the resemblance of His own likeness, and breathed into him that he

---

[1] "Inerrabiles." There is another reading, "inenarrabiles," indescribable.
[2] "Humanis visibus."

might live,[1] and placed him in a garden[2] which He had planted with every kind of fruit-bearing tree, and commanded him not to eat of one tree in which He had placed the knowledge of good and evil, warning him that it would come to pass, that if he did so he would lose his life, but that if he observed the command of God he would remain immortal. Then the serpent, who was one of the servants of God, envying man because he was made immortal, enticed him by stratagem to transgress the command and law of God. And in this manner he did indeed receive the knowledge of good and evil, but he lost the life which God had given him to be for ever.

Therefore He drove out the sinner from the sacred place, and banished him into this world, that he might seek sustenance by labour, that he might according to his deserts undergo difficulties and troubles; and He surrounded the garden itself with a fence of fire, that none of men even till the day of judgment might attempt secretly[3] to enter into that place of perpetual blessedness. Then death came upon man according to the sentence of God; and yet his life, though it had begun to be temporary, had as its boundary a thousand years, and that was the extent of human life even to the deluge. For after the flood the life of men was gradually shortened, and was reduced to 120 years. But that serpent, who from his deeds received the name of devil, that is, accuser or informer, did not cease to persecute the seed of man, whom he had deceived from the beginning. At length he urged him who was first born in this world, under the impulse of envy, to the murder of his brother, that of the two men who were first born he might destroy the one, and make the other a parricide.[4] Nor did he cease upon this from infusing the venom of malice into the breasts of men through each generation, from corrupting and depraving them; in short, from overwhelming them with such crimes, that an instance of justice was now rare, but men lived after the manner of the beasts.

But when God saw this, He sent His angels to instruct the race of men, and to protect them from all evil. He gave these a command to abstain from earthly things, lest, being polluted

---

[1] "Inspiravit ad vitam."   [2] "Paradiso."   [3] "Irrepere."
[4] "Parricidam." The word first means the murderer of a parent or near relative; then simply a murderer.

by any taint, they should be deprived of the honour of angels. But that wily accuser, while they tarried among men, allured these also to pleasures, so that they might defile themselves with women. Then, being condemned by the sentence of God, and cast forth on account of their sins, they lost both the name and substance of angels. Thus, having become ministers of the devil, that they might have a solace of their ruin, they betook themselves to the ruining of men, for whose protection they had come.

CHAP. XXVIII.—*Of the demons, and their evil practices.*

These are the demons, of whom the poets often speak in their poems, whom Hesiod calls the guardians of men. For they so persuaded men by their enticements and deceits, that they believed that the same were gods. In fine, Socrates used to give out that he had a demon as the guardian and director of his life from his first childhood, and that he could do nothing without his assent and command. They attach themselves, therefore, to individuals, and occupy houses under the name of Genii or Penates. To these temples are built, to these libations are daily offered as to the Lares, to these honour is paid as to the averters of evils. These from the beginning, that they might turn away men from the knowledge of the true God, introduced new superstitions and worship of gods. These taught that the memory of dead kings should be consecrated, temples be built, and images made, not that they might lessen the honour of God, or increase their own, which they lost by sinning, but that they might take away life from men, deprive them of the hope of true light, lest men should arrive at that heavenly reward of immortality from which they fell. They also brought to light astrology, and augury, and divination; and though these things are in themselves false, yet they themselves, the authors of evils, so govern and regulate them that they are believed to be true. They also invented the tricks of the magic art, to deceive the eyes. By their aid it comes to pass, that that which is appears not to be, and that which is not appears to be. They themselves invented necromancies, responses, and oracles, to delude the minds of men with lying divination by means of ambiguous issues. They are present in the temples and at all sacrifices; and by the exhibition of some deceitful prodigies, to the surprise of those who are present, they so deceive men, that they believe that a divine power is present in images and statues. They even enter secretly into bodies, as being slight spirits; and they excite diseases in the vitiated limbs, which when appeased with sacrifices and vows they may again remove. They send dreams either full of terror,[1] that they themselves may be invoked, or the issues of which may correspond with the truth, that they may increase the veneration paid to themselves. Sometimes also they put forth something of vengeance against the sacrilegious, that whoever sees it may become more timid and superstitious. Thus by their frauds they have drawn darkness over the human race, that truth might be oppressed, and the name of the supreme and matchless God might be forgotten.

CHAP. XXIX.—*Of the patience and providence of God.*

But some one says: Why, then, does the true God permit these things to be done? Why does He not rather remove or destroy the wicked? Why, in truth, did He from the beginning give power[2] to the demon, so that there should be one who might corrupt and destroy all things? I will briefly say why He willed that this should be so. I ask whether virtue is a good or an evil. It cannot be denied that it is a good. If virtue is a good, vice, on the contrary, is an evil. If vice is an evil on this account, because it opposes virtue, and virtue is on this account a good, because it overthrows vice, it follows that virtue cannot exist without vice; and if you take away vice, the merits of virtue will be taken away. For there can be no victory without an enemy. Thus it comes to pass, that good cannot exist without an evil.

Chrysippus, a man of active mind, saw this when discussing the subject of providence, and charges those with folly who think that good is caused by God, but say that evil is not thus caused. Aulus Gellius[3] has interpreted his sentiment in his books of *Attic Nights*; thus saying: "They to whom it does not appear that the world was made for the sake of God and men, and that human affairs are governed by providence, think that they use a weighty argument when they thus speak: If there were a

---

[1] "Plena terroris." Another reading is, "aut plane terrores."
[2] ἀρχήν. Others read δαιμοναρχίαν, "the power of demons."
[3] Lib. vi. 1.

providence, there would be no evils. For they say that nothing is less in agreement with providence, than that in this world, on account of which it is said that God made men,[1] the power of troubles and evils should be so great. In reply to these things, Chrysippus, when he was arguing, in his fourth book respecting providence, said: Nothing can be more foolish than those who think that good things could have existed, if there were not evils in the same place. For since good things are contrary to evil, they must of necessity be opposed to each other, and must stand resting, as it were, on mutual and opposite support.[2] Thus there is no contrary without another contrary. For how could there be any perception of justice, unless there were injuries? or what else is justice, but the removal of injustice? In like manner, the nature of fortitude cannot be understood except by placing[3] beside it cowardice, or the nature of self-control except by intemperance. Likewise, in what manner would there be prudence, unless there were the contrary, imprudence? On the same principle, he says, why do the foolish men not require this also, that there should be truth and not falsehood? For there exist together good and evil things, prosperity and trouble, pleasure and pain. For the one being bound to the other at opposite poles, as Plato says, if you take away one, you take away both." You see, therefore, that which I have often said, that good and evil are so connected with one another, that the one cannot exist without the other. Therefore God acted with the greatest foresight in placing the subject-matter of virtue in evils which He made for this purpose, that He might establish for us a contest, in which He would crown the victorious with the reward of immortality.

CHAP. XXX.—*Of false wisdom.*

I have taught, as I imagine, that the honours paid to gods are not only impious, but also vain, either because they were men whose memory was consecrated after death; or because the images themselves are insensible and deaf, inasmuch as they are formed of earth, and that it is not right for man, who ought

---

[1] "Propter quem homines fecisse dicatur Deus." Others read, "Quem propter homines," etc.
[2] "Quasi mutuo adversoque fulta nisu consistere."
[3] "Appositione." Others read "oppositione."

to look up to heavenly things, to subject himself to earthly things; or because the spirits who claim to themselves those acts of religious service are unholy and impure, and on this account, being condemned by the sentence of God, fell to the earth, and that it is not lawful to submit to the power of those to whom you are superior, if you wish to be a follower of the true God. It remains that, as we have spoken of false religion, we should also discuss the subject of false wisdom, which the philosophers profess,—men endued with the greatest learning and eloquence, but far removed from the truth, because they neither know God nor the wisdom of God. And although they are clever and learned, yet, because their wisdom is human, I shall not fear to contend with them, that it may be evident that falsehood can be easily overcome by truth, and earthly things by heavenly.

They thus define the nature of philosophy. Philosophy is the love or pursuit of wisdom. Therefore it is not wisdom itself; for that which loves must be different from that which is loved. If it is the pursuit of wisdom, not even thus is philosophy (identical with) wisdom. For wisdom is the object itself which is sought, but the pursuit is that which seeks it. Therefore the very definition or meaning of the word plainly shows that philosophy is not wisdom itself. I will say that it (philosophy) is not even the pursuit of wisdom, in which wisdom is not comprised. For who can be said to devote himself to the pursuit of that to which he can by no means attain? He who gives himself to the pursuit of medicine, or grammar, or oratory, may be said to be studious of that art which he is learning; but when he has learned, he is now said to be a physician, a grammarian, or an orator. Thus also those who are studious of wisdom, after they had learned it, ought to have been called wise. But since they are called students of wisdom as long as they live, it is manifest that that is not the pursuit, because it is impossible to arrive at the object itself which is sought for in the pursuit, unless by chance they who pursue wisdom even to the end of life are about to be wise in another world. Now every pursuit is connected with some end. That, therefore, is not a right pursuit which has no end.

CHAP. XXXI.—*Of knowledge and supposition.*

Moreover, there are two things which appear to fall under

the subject of philosophy—knowledge and supposition; and if these are taken away, philosophy altogether falls to the ground. But the chief of the philosophers themselves have taken away both from philosophy. Socrates took away knowledge, Zeno supposition. Let us see whether they were right in doing so. Wisdom is, as Cicero defined it,[1] the knowledge of divine and human things. Now if this definition is true, wisdom does not come within the power of man. For who of mortals can assume this to himself, to profess that he knows divine and human things? I say nothing of human affairs; for although they are connected with divine, yet, since they belong to man, let us grant that it is possible for man to know them. Certainly he cannot know divine things by himself; since he is a man; whereas he who knows them must be divine, and therefore God. But man is neither divine nor God. Man, therefore, cannot thoroughly know divine things by himself. No one, therefore, is wise but God, or certainly that man whom God has taught. But they, because they are neither gods, nor taught by God, cannot be wise, that is, acquainted with divine and human things. Knowledge, therefore, is rightly taken away by Socrates and the Academics. Supposition also does not agree with the wise man. For every one supposes that of which he is ignorant. Now, to suppose that you know that of which you are ignorant, is rashness and folly. Supposition, therefore, was rightly taken away by Zeno. If, therefore, there is no knowledge in man, and there ought to be no supposition, philosophy is cut up by the roots.

CHAP. XXXII.—*Of the sects of philosophers, and their disagreement.*

To this is added, that it[2] is not uniform; but being divided into sects, and scattered into many and discordant opinions, it has no fixed state. For since they all separately attack and harass one another, and there is none of them which is not condemned of folly in the judgment of the rest, while the members are plainly at variance with one another, the whole body of philosophy is brought to destruction. Hence the Academy afterwards originated. For when the leading men of that sect saw that philosophy was altogether overthrown by philosophers mutually

---
[1] *De Offic.* ii. 2.   [2] *i.e* philosophy.

opposing each other, they undertook war against all, that they might destroy all the arguments of all; while they themselves assert nothing except one thing—that nothing can be known. Thus, having taken away knowledge, they overthrew the ancient philosophy. But they did not even themselves retain the name of philosophers, since they admitted their ignorance, because to be ignorant of all things is not only not the part of a philosopher, but not even of a man. Thus the philosophers, because they have no defence, must destroy one another with mutual wounds, and philosophy itself must altogether consume and put an end to itself by its own arms. But they say it is only natural philosophy which thus gives way. How is it with moral? Does that rest on any firm foundation? Let us see whether philosophers are agreed in this part at any rate, which relates to the condition of life.

CHAP. XXXIII.—*What is the chief good to be sought in life.*

What is the chief good must be an object of inquiry, that our whole life and actions may be directed to it. When inquiry is made respecting the chief good of man, it ought to be settled to be of such a kind, first, that it have reference to man alone; in the next place, that it belong peculiarly to the mind; lastly, that it be sought by virtue. Let us see, therefore, whether the chief good which the philosophers mark out be such that it has reference neither to a dumb animal nor to the body, and cannot be attained without virtue.

Aristippus, the founder of the Cyrenaic sect, who thought that bodily pleasure was the chief good, ought to be removed from the number of philosophers, and from the society of men, because he compared himself to a beast. The chief good of Hieronymus is to be without pain, that of Diodorus to cease to be in pain. But the other animals avoid pain; and when they are without pain, or cease to be in pain, are glad. What distinction, then, will be given to man, if his chief good is judged to be common with the beasts? Zeno thought that the chief good was to live agreeably to nature. But this definition is a general one. For all animals live agreeably to nature, and each has its own nature.

Epicurus maintained that it was pleasure of the soul. What is pleasure of the soul but joy, in which the soul for the most part luxuriates, and unbends itself either to sport or to laughter? But this good befalls even dumb animals, which, when they are satisfied with pasture, relax themselves to joy and wantonness. Dinomachus and Callipho approved of honourable pleasure; but they either said the same that Epicurus did, that bodily pleasure is dishonourable; or if they considered bodily pleasures to be partly base and partly honourable, then that is not the chief good which is ascribed to the body. The Peripatetics make up the chief good of goods of the soul, and body, and fortune. The goods of the soul may be approved of; but if they require assistance for the completion of happiness, they are plainly weak. But the goods of the body and of fortune are not in the power of man; nor is that now the chief good which is assigned to the body, or to things placed without us, because this double good extends even to the cattle, which have need of being well, and of a due supply of food. The Stoics are believed to have entertained much better views, who said that virtue was the chief good. But virtue cannot be the chief good, since, if it is the endurance of evils and of labours, it is not happy of itself; but it ought to effect and produce the chief good, because it cannot be attained without the greatest difficulty and labour. But, in truth, Aristotle wandered far from reason, who connected honour with virtue, as though it were possible for virtue at any time to be separated from honour, or to be united with baseness.

Herillus the Pyrrhonist made knowledge the chief good. This indeed belongs to man, and to the soul only, but it may happen to him without virtue. For he is not to be considered happy who has either learnt anything by hearing, or has gained the knowledge of it by a little reading; nor is it a definition of the chief good, because there may be a knowledge either of bad things, or at any rate of things that are useless. And if it is the knowledge of good and useful things which you have acquired by labour, nevertheless it is not the chief good, because knowledge is not sought on its own account, but on account of something else. For the arts are learnt on this account, that they may be to us the means of gaining support, or a source of glory, or even of pleasure; and it is plain that these things cannot be the chief goods. Therefore the philosophers do not observe the rule even in moral philosophy, inasmuch as they are at variance with one another on the main point [1] itself, that is, in that discussion by which the life is moulded. For the precepts cannot be equal, or resembling one another, when some train men to pleasure, others to honour, others indeed to nature, others to knowledge; some to the pursuit, others to the avoiding of riches; some to entire insensibility to pain, others to the endurance of evils: in all which, as I have shown before, they turn aside from reason, because they are ignorant of God.

CHAP. XXXIV.—*That men are born to justice.*

Let us now see what is proposed to the wise man as the chief good.[2] That men are born to justice is not only taught by the sacred writings, but is sometimes acknowledged even by these same philosophers. Thus Cicero says: "But of all things which fall under the discussion of learned men, nothing assuredly is more excellent than that it should be clearly understood that we are born to justice." This is most true. For we are not born to wickedness, since we are a social and sociable animal. The wild beasts are produced to exercise their fierceness; for they are unable to live in any other way than by prey and bloodshed. These, however, although pressed by extreme hunger, nevertheless refrain from animals of their own kind. Birds also do the same, which must feed upon the carcases of others. How much more is it befitting, that man, who is united with man both in the interchange of language and in communion of feeling, should spare man, and love him! For this is justice.

But since wisdom has been given to man alone, that he may understand God, and this alone makes the difference between man and the dumb animals, justice itself is bound up in two duties. He owes the one to God as to a father, the other to man as to a brother; for we are produced by the same God. Therefore it has been deservedly and rightly said, that wisdom is the knowledge of divine and human affairs. For it is right that we should know what we owe to God, and what to man; namely, to God religion, to man affection. But the former belongs to wisdom, the latter to virtue; and justice comprises both. If, therefore, it is evident that man is born to justice, it

---

[1] "In ipso cardine."
[2] Some editions repeat the words "summum bonum," but these words appear to obstruct the sense.

is necessary that the just man should be subject to evils, that he may exercise the virtue with which he is endued. For virtue is the enduring of evils. He will avoid pleasures as an evil: he will despise riches, because they are frail; and if he has them, he will liberally bestow them, to preserve the wretched: he will not be desirous of honours, because they are short and transitory; he will do injury to no one; if he shall suffer, he will not retaliate; and he will not take vengeance upon one who plunders his property. For he will deem it unlawful to injure a man; and if there shall be any one who would compel him to depart from God, he will not refuse tortures nor death. Thus it will come to pass, that he must necessarily live in poverty and lowliness, and in insults, or even tortures.

CHAP. XXXV.—*That immortality is the chief good.*

What, then, will be the advantage of justice and virtue, if they shall have nothing but evil in life? But if virtue, which despises all earthly goods, most wisely endures all evils, and endures death itself in the discharge of duty, cannot be without a reward, what remains but that immortality alone is its reward? For if a happy life falls to the lot of man, as the philosophers will have it, and in this point alone they do not disagree, therefore also immortality falls to him. For that only is happy which is incorruptible; that only is incorruptible which is eternal. Therefore immortality is the chief good, because it belongs both to man, and to the soul, and to virtue. We are only directed to this; we are born to the attainment of this. Therefore God proposes to us virtue and justice, that we may obtain that eternal reward for our labours. But concerning that immortality[1] itself we will speak in the proper place. There remains the philosophy of Logic,[2] which contributes nothing to a happy life. For wisdom does not consist in the arrangement of speech, but in the heart and the feeling. But if natural philosophy is superfluous, and this of logic, and the philosophers have erred in moral philosophy, which alone is necessary, because they have been unable in any way to find

---

[1] "Non mortalitate."
[2] "λογική philosophia." Under this is included everything connected with the system of speaking.

out the chief good; therefore all philosophy is found to be empty and useless, which was unable to comprehend the nature of man, or to fulfil its duty and office.

CHAP. XXXVI.—*Of the philosophers,—namely, Epicurus and Pythagoras.*

Since I have spoken briefly of philosophy, now also I will speak a few things about the philosophers. This is especially the doctrine of Epicurus, that there is no providence. And at the same time he does not deny the existence of gods. In both respects he acts contrary to reason. For if there are gods, it follows that there is a providence. For otherwise we can form no intelligible idea of God, for it is His peculiar province to foresee.[1] But Epicurus says He takes no care about anything. Therefore He disregards not only the affairs of men, but also heavenly things. How, therefore, or from what, do you affirm that He exists? For when you have taken away the divine providence and care, it would naturally follow that you should altogether deny the existence of God; whereas now you have left Him in name, but in reality you have taken Him away. Whence, then, did the world derive its origin, if God takes no care of anything? There are, he says, minute atoms, which can neither be seen nor touched, and from the fortuitous meeting of these all things arose, and are continually arising. If they are neither seen nor perceived by any part of the body, how could you know of their existence? In the next place, if they exist, with what mind do they meet together to effect anything? If they are smooth, they cannot cohere: if they are hooked and angular, then they are divisible; for hooks and angles project, and can be cut off. But these things are senseless and unprofitable. Why should I mention that he also makes souls capable of extinction? who is refuted not only by all philosophers and general persuasion, but also by the answers of bards, by the predictions of the Sibyls, and lastly, by the divine voices of the prophets themselves; so that it is wonderful that Epicurus alone existed, who should place the condition of man on a level with the flocks and beasts.

What of Pythagoras, who was first called a philosopher, who judged that souls were indeed immortal, but that they

[1] "Providere."

passed into other bodies, either of cattle, or of birds, or of beasts? Would it not have been better that they should be destroyed, together with their bodies, than thus to be condemned to pass into the bodies of other animals? Would it not be better not to exist at all, than, after having had the form of a man, to live as a swine or a dog? And the foolish man, to gain credit for his saying, said that he himself had been Euphorbus in the Trojan war, and that, when he had been slain, he passed into other figures of animals, and at last became Pythagoras. O happy man! to whom alone so great a memory was given; or rather unhappy, who, when changed into a sheep, was not permitted to be ignorant of what he was! And would to Heaven that he alone had been thus senseless! He found also some to believe him, and some indeed among the learned,[1] to whom the inheritance of folly passed.

CHAP. XXXVII.—*Of Socrates and his contradiction.*

After him Socrates held the first place in philosophy, who was pronounced most wise even by the oracle, because he confessed that he knew one thing only,—namely, that he knew nothing. And on the authority of this oracle it was right that the natural philosophers should restrain themselves, lest they should either inquire into those things which they could not know, or should think that they knew things which they did not know. Let us, however, see whether Socrates was most wise, as the Pythian god proclaimed. He often made use of this proverb, that that which is above us has also no reference to us. He has now passed beyond the limits of his opinion. For he who said that he knew one thing only, found another thing to speak of, as though he knew it; but that in vain. For God, who is plainly above us, is to be sought for; and religion is to be undertaken, which alone separates us from the brutes, which indeed Socrates not only rejected, but even derided, in swearing by a goose and a dog, as if in truth he could not have sworn by Æsculapius, to whom he had vowed a cock. Behold the sacrifice of a wise man! And because he was unable to offer this in his own person, since he was at the point of death, he entreated his friends to perform the vow after his death, lest forsooth

---

[1] "Inter doctos homines." Others read "indoctos homines," but this does not convey so good a meaning.

he should be detained as a debtor in the lower regions. He assuredly both pronounced that he knew nothing, and made good his statement.

CHAP. XXXVIII.—*Of Plato, whose doctrine approaches more nearly to the truth.*

His disciple Plato, whom Tully speaks of as the god of philosophers, alone of all so studied philosophy that he approached nearer to the truth; and yet, because he was ignorant of God, he so failed in many things, that no one fell into worse errors, especially because in his books respecting the state he wished all things to be common to all. This is endurable concerning property, though it is unjust. For it ought not to be an injury to any one, if he possesses more than another through his own industry; or to be a profit to any one, if through his own fault he possesses less. But, as I have said, this is capable of being endured in some way. Shall there be a community of wives also, and of children? Shall there be no distinction of blood, or certainty of race? Shall there be neither families, nor relationships, nor affinities, but all things confused and indiscriminate, as in herds of cattle? Shall there be no self-restraint in men, no chastity in women? What conjugal affection can there be in these, between whom on either side there is no sure or peculiar[1] love? Who will be dutiful towards a father, when he knows not from whom he was born? Who will love a son, whom he will reckon as not his own?[2] Moreover, he opened[3] the senate house to women, and entrusted to them warfare, magistracies, and commands. But how great will be the calamity of that city, in which women shall discharge the duties of men! But of this more fully at another opportunity.

Zeno, the master of the Stoics, who praises virtue, judged that pity, which is a very great virtue, should be cut away, as though it were a disease of the mind, whereas it is at the same time dear to God and necessary for men. For who is there who, when placed in any evil, would be unwilling to be pitied, and would not desire the assistance of those who might succour them, which is not called forth so as to render aid, except by

---

[1] "Proprius."   [2] "Alienum."
[3] "Reseravit." Others read "reservavit."

the feeling of pity? Although he calls this humanity and piety, he does not change the matter itself, only the name. This is the affection which has been given to man alone, that by mutual assistance we might alleviate our weakness; and he who removes this affection reduces us to the life of the beasts. For his assertion that all faults are equal, proceeds from that inhumanity with which also he assails pity as a disease. For he who makes no difference in faults, either thinks that light offences ought to be visited with severe punishments, which is the part of a cruel judge, or that great offences should be visited with slight punishments, which is the part of a worthless judge. In either case there is injury to the state. For if the greatest crimes are lightly punished, the boldness of the wicked will increase, and go on to deeds of greater daring; and if a punishment of too great severity is inflicted for slight offences, inasmuch as no one can be exempt from fault, many citizens will incur peril, who by correction might become better.

CHAP. XXXIX.—*Of various philosophers, and of the antipodes.*

These things, truly, are of small importance, but they arise from the same falsehood. Xenophanes said that the orb of the moon is eighteen times larger than this earth of ours; and that within its compass is contained another earth, which is inhabited by men and animals of every kind. About the antipodes also one can neither hear nor speak without laughter. It is asserted as something serious, that we should believe that there are men who have their feet opposite to ours. The ravings of Anaxagoras are more tolerable, who said that snow was black. And not only the sayings, but the deeds, of some are ridiculous. Democritus neglected his land which was left to him by his father, and suffered it to become a public pasture. Diogenes with his company of dogs,[1] who professes that great and perfect virtue in the contempt of all things, preferred to beg for his support, rather than to seek it by honest labour, or to have any property. Undoubtedly the life of a wise man ought to be to others an example of living. If all should imitate the wisdom of these, how will states exist? But perhaps the same Cynics were able to afford an example of modesty, who lived

[1] *i.e.* the Cynics.

with their wives in public. I know not how they could defend virtue, who took away modesty.

Nor was Aristippus better than these, who, I believe, that he might please his mistress Lais, instituted the Cyrenaic system, by which he placed the end of the chief good in bodily pleasure, that authority might not be wanting to his faults, or learning to his vices. Are those men of greater fortitude to be more approved, who, that they might be said to have despised death, died by their own hands? Zeno, Empedocles, Chrysippus, Cleanthes, Democritus, and Cato, imitating these, did not know that he who put himself to death is guilty of murder, according to the divine right and law. For it was God who placed us in this abode of flesh: it was He who gave us the temporary habitation of the body, that we should inhabit it as long as He pleased. Therefore it is to be considered impious, to wish to depart from it without the command of God. Therefore violence must not be applied to nature. He knows how to destroy [1] His own work. And if any one shall apply impious hands to that work, and shall tear asunder the bonds of the divine workmanship, he endeavours to flee from God, whose sentence no one will be able to escape, whether alive or dead. Therefore they are accursed and impious, whom I have mentioned above, who even taught what are the befitting reasons for voluntary death; so that it was not enough of guilt that they were self-murderers, unless they instructed others also to this wickedness.

CHAP. XL.—*Of the foolishness of the philosophers.*

There are innumerable sayings and doings of the philosophers, by which their foolishness may be shown. Therefore, since we are unable to enumerate them all, a few will be sufficient. It is enough that it is understood that the philosophers were neither teachers of justice, of which they were ignorant, nor of virtue, of which they falsely boast. For what can they teach, who often confess their own ignorance? I omit to mention Socrates, whose opinion is well known. Anaxagoras proclaims that all things are overspread with darkness. Empedocles says that the paths for finding out the truth of the senses are narrow. Democritus asserts that truth lies sunk in a deep

[1] "Resolvat."

well; and because they nowhere find it, they therefore affirm that no wise man has as yet existed. Since, therefore, human wisdom has no existence (Socrates says in the writings of Plato), let us follow that which is divine, and let us give thanks to God, who has revealed and delivered it to us; and let us congratulate ourselves, that through the divine bounty we possess the truth and wisdom, which, though sought by so many intellects through so many ages, philosophy[1] was not able to discover.

CHAP. XLI.—*Of true religion and wisdom.*

Now, since we have refuted false religion, which is in the worship of the gods, and false wisdom, which is in the philosophers, let us come to true religion and wisdom. And, indeed, we must speak of them both conjointly, because they are closely connected. For to worship the true God, that and nothing else is wisdom. For that God who is supreme and the Maker of all things, who made man as the image of Himself, on this account conferred on him alone of all animals the gift of reason, that he might pay back honour to Him as his Father and his Lord, and by the exercise of this piety and obedience might gain the reward of immortality. This is a true and divine mystery. But among those,[2] because they are not true, there is no agreement. Neither are sacred rites performed in philosophy, nor is philosophy treated of in sacred things; and on this account their religion is false, because it does not possess wisdom; and on this account their wisdom is false, because it does not possess religion. But where both are joined together, there the truth must necessarily be; so that if it is asked what the truth itself is, it may be rightly said to be either wise religion or religious wisdom.

CHAP. XLII.—*Of religious wisdom: the name of Christ known to none, except Himself and His Father.*

I will now say what wise religion, or religious wisdom, is. God, in the beginning, before He made the world, from the fountain of His own eternity, and from the divine and ever-

---

[1] "Philosophia non potuit invenire." Other editions have, "philosophiam nemo potuit invenire."

[2] *i.e.* the philosophers before mentioned.

lasting spirit, begat for Himself a Son incorruptible, faithful, corresponding to His Father's excellence and majesty. He is virtue, He is reason, He is the word of God, He is wisdom. With this artificer, as Hermes says, and counsellor, as the Sibyl says, He contrived the excellent and wondrous fabric of this world. In fine, of all the angels, whom the same God formed from His own breath,[1] He alone was admitted into a participation of His supreme power, He alone was called God. For all things were through Him, and nothing was without Him. In fine, Plato, not altogether as a philosopher, but as a seer, spoke concerning the first and second God, perhaps following Trismegistus in this, whose words I have translated from the Greek, and subjoined: "The Lord and Maker of all things, whom we have thought to be called God, created a second God, who is visible and sensible. But by sensible I mean, not that He Himself receives sensation, but that He causes sensation and sight. When, therefore, He had made this, the first, and one, and only one, He appeared to Him most excellent, and full of all good qualities." The Sibyl also says that God the guide of all was made by God; and another, that " God the Son of God must be known," as those examples which I have brought forward in my books declare. Him the prophets, filled with the inspiration of the Divine Spirit, proclaimed; of whom especially Solomon in the book of Wisdom, and also his father, the writer of divine hymns—both most renowned kings, who preceded the times of the Trojan war by 180 years [2]—testify that He was born of God. His name is known to none, except to Himself and the Father, as John teaches in the Revelation.[3] Hermes says that His name cannot be uttered by mortal mouth. Yet by men He is called by two names—Jesus, which is Saviour, and Christ, which is King. He is called Saviour on this account, because He is the health and safety of all who believe in God through Him. He is called Christ on this account, because He Himself will come from heaven at the end of this dispensation [4] to judge the world, and, having raised the dead, to establish for Himself an everlasting kingdom.

[1] "De suis spiritibus."
[2] This is an error. Both David and Solomon lived after the supposed taking of Troy.
[3] Rev. xix. 12.   [4] "In sæculi hujus consummatione."

CHAP. XLIII.—*Of the name of Jesus Christ, and His twofold nativity.*

But lest by any chance there should be any doubt in your mind why we call Him Jesus Christ, who was born of God before the world, and who was born of man 300 years ago, I will briefly explain to you the reason. The same person is the son of God and of man. For He was twice born: first of God in the spirit before the origin of the world; afterwards in the flesh of man, in the reign of Augustus; and in connection with this fact is an illustrious and great mystery, in which is contained both the salvation of men and the religion of the supreme God, and all truth. For when first the accursed and impious worship of gods crept in through the treachery of the demons, then the religion of God remained with the Hebrews alone, who, not by any law, but after the manner of their fathers, observed the worship handed down to them by successive generations,[1] even until the time when they went forth out of Egypt under the leadership of Moses, the first of all the prophets, through whom the law was given to them from God; and they were afterwards called Jews. Therefore they served God, being bound by the chains of the law. But they also, by degrees going astray to profane rites, undertook the worship of strange gods, and, leaving the worship of their fathers, sacrificed to senseless images. Therefore God sent to them prophets filled with the Divine Spirit, to upbraid them with their sins and proclaim repentance, to threaten them with the vengeance which would follow, and announce that it would come to pass, if they persisted in the same faults, that He would send another as the bearer of a new law; and having removed the ungrateful people from their inheritance, He would assemble to Himself a more faithful people from foreign nations. But they not only persisted in their course, but even slew the messengers themselves. Therefore He condemned them on account of these deeds: nor did He any longer send messengers to a stubborn people; but He sent His own Son, to call all nations to the favour of God. Nor, however, did He shut them out, impious and ungrateful as they were, from the hope of salvation; but He sent Him to them before all others,[2] that if they should by

[1] "Per successiones." [2] "Potissimum."

chance obey, they might not lose that which they had received; but if they should refuse to receive their God, then, the heirs being removed,[1] the Gentiles would come into possession. Therefore the supreme Father ordered Him to descend to the earth, and to put on a human body, that, being subject to the sufferings of the flesh, He might teach virtue and patience not only by words, but also by deeds. Therefore He was born a second time as man, of a virgin, without a father, that, as in His first spiritual birth, being born of God alone, He was made a sacred spirit, so in His second and fleshly birth, being born of a mother only, He might become holy flesh, that through Him the flesh, which had become subject to sin, might be freed from destruction.

CHAP. XLIV.—*The twofold nativity of Christ is proved from the prophets.*

That these things should thus take place as I have set them forth, the prophets had before predicted. In the writings of Solomon it is thus written:[2] "The womb of a virgin was strengthened, and conceived: and a virgin was impregnated, and became a mother in great pity." In Isaiah[3] it is thus written: "Behold, a virgin shall conceive, and bear a son, and ye shall call His name Immanuel;" which, being interpreted, is God with us.[4] For He was with us on the earth, when He assumed flesh; and He was no less God in man, and man in God. That He was both God and man was declared before by the prophets. That He was God, Isaiah[5] thus declares: "They shall fall down unto Thee, they shall make supplication unto Thee; since God is in Thee, and we knew it not, even the God of Israel. They shall be ashamed and confounded, all of them who oppose themselves to Thee, and shall go to confusion." Also Jeremiah:[6] "This is our God, and there shall none other be compared unto Him; He hath found out all the way of knowledge, and hath given it unto Jacob His servant, and to Israel His beloved. Afterward He was seen upon earth, and dwelt among men." Likewise that He was man, the same Jeremiah[7] says: "And He is man, and who knew Him?" Isaiah

---

[1] "Hæredibus abdicatis."   [2] See *Instit.* iv. 12.   [3] Isa. vii. 14.
[4] Matt. i. 23.   [5] Isa. xlv. 14–16.   [6] Baruch iii. 35–37.
[7] xvii. 9. This and the following quotations are from the Septuagint.

also thus speaks:[1] "And the Lord shall send them a man who shall save them, and with judgment shall He heal them." Also Moses himself in the book of Numbers:[2] "There shall come a star out of Jacob, and a man shall arise out of Israel." For this cause, therefore, being God, He took upon Him flesh, that, becoming a mediator[3] between God and man, having overcome death, He might by His guidance lead man to God.

CHAP. XLV.—*The power and works of Christ are proved from the Scriptures.*

We have spoken of His nativity; now let us speak of His power and works, which, when He wrought them among men, the Jews, seeing them to be great and wonderful, supposed that they were done by the influence of magic, not knowing that all those things which were done by Him had been foretold by the prophets. He gave strength to the sick, and to those languishing under various diseases, not by any healing remedy, but instantaneously, by the force and power of His word; He restored the weak, He made the lame to walk, He gave sight to the blind, He made the dumb to speak, the deaf to hear; He cleansed the polluted and unclean, He restored their right mind to those who were maddened with the attack of demons, He recalled to life and light those who were dead or now buried. He also fed and satisfied[4] five thousand men with five loaves and two fishes. He also walked upon the sea. He also in a tempest commanded the wind to be still, and immediately there was a calm; all which things we find predicted both in the books of the prophets and in the verses of the Sibyls.

When a great multitude resorted to Him on account of these miracles, and, as He truly was, believed Him to be the Son of God, and sent from God, the priests and rulers of the Jews, filled with envy, and at the same time excited with anger, because He reproved their sins and injustice, conspired to put Him to death; and that this would happen, Solomon had foretold a little more than a thousand years before, in the book of Wisdom, using these words:[5] "Let us defraud the righteous, for he is unpleasant to us, and upbraideth us with our offences

---

[1] Isa. xix. 20.   [2] Num. xxiv. 17. The prophecy of Balaam.
[3] "Inter deum et hominem medius factus."
[4] "Saturavit."   [5] Wisd. ii. 12-22. See *Instit.* iv. 16.

against the law. He maketh his boast that he has the knowledge of God, and he calleth himself the Son of God. He is made to reprove our thoughts: it grieveth us even to look upon him; for his life is not like the life of others, his ways are of another fashion. We are counted by him as triflers; he withdraweth himself from our ways, as from filthiness; he commendeth greatly the latter end of the just, and boasteth that he has God for his father. Let us see, therefore, if his words be true; let us prove what end he shall have; let us examine him with rebukes and torments, that we may know his meekness and prove his patience; let us condemn him to a shameful death. Such things have they imagined, and have gone astray; for their own folly hath blinded them, and they do not understand the mysteries of God."

Therefore, being unmindful of these writings which they read, they incited the people as though against an impious man, so that they seized and led Him to trial, and with impious words demanded His death. But they alleged against Him as a crime this very thing, that He said that He was the Son of God, and that by healing on the Sabbath He broke the law, which He said that He did not break, but fulfilled. And when Pontius Pilate, who then as legate had authority in Syria, perceived that the cause did not belong to the office of the Roman judge, he sent Him to Herod the Tetrarch, and permitted the Jews themselves to be the judges of their own law: who, having received the power of punishing His guilt, sentenced [1] Him to the cross, but first scourged and struck Him with their hands, put on Him a crown of thorns, spat upon His face, gave Him gall and vinegar to eat and drink; and amidst these things no word was heard to fall from His lips. Then the executioners, having cast lots over His tunic and mantle, suspended Him on the cross, and affixed Him to it, though on the next day they were about to celebrate the Passover, that is, their festival. Which crime was followed by prodigies, that they might understand the impiety which they had committed; for at the same moment in which He expired, there was a great earthquake, and a withdrawing [2] of the sun, so that the day was turned into night.

[1] "Addixerunt." Some read "affixerunt," affixed Him to the cross.
[2] "Deliquium solis."

CHAP. XLVI.—*It is proved from the prophets that the passion and death of Christ had been foretold.*

And the prophets had predicted that all these things would thus come to pass. Isaiah thus speaks:[1] "I am not rebellious, nor do I oppose: I gave my back to the scourge, and my cheeks to the hand: I turned not away my face from the foulness of spitting." The same prophet says respecting His silence:[2] "I was brought as a sheep to the slaughter, and as a lamb before its shearers is dumb, so He opened not His mouth." David also, in the 34th Psalm:[3] "The abjects were gathered together against me, and they knew me not: they were scattered, yet felt no remorse: they tempted me, and gnashed upon me with their teeth." The same also says respecting food and drink in the 68th Psalm:[4] "They gave me also gall for my meat, and in my thirst they gave me vinegar to drink." Also respecting the cross of Christ:[5] "And they pierced my hands and my feet, they numbered all my bones: they themselves have looked and stared upon me; they parted my garments among them, and cast lots upon my vesture." Moses also says in Deuteronomy:[6] "And thy life shall hang in doubt before thine eyes, and thou shalt fear day and night, and shalt have none assurance of thy life." Also in Numbers:[7] "God is not in doubt as a man, nor does He suffer threats as the son of man." Also Zechariah says:[8] "And they shall look on me whom they pierced." Amos[9] thus speaks of the obscuring of the sun: "In that day, saith the Lord, the sun shall go down at noon, and the clear day shall be dark; and I will turn your feasts into mourning, and your songs into lamentation." Jeremiah[10] also speaks of the city of Jerusalem, in which He suffered: "Her sun is gone down while it was yet day; she hath been confounded and reviled, and the residue of them will I deliver to the sword." Nor were these things spoken in vain. For after a short time the Emperor Vespasian subdued the Jews, and laid waste their lands with the sword and fire, besieged and reduced them by

[1] Isa. l. 5.
[2] Isa. liii. 7.
[3] Ps. xxxv. 15, 16. See *Instit.* iv. 18.
[4] Ps. lxix. 21.
[5] Ps. xxii. 16-18.
[6] Deut. xxviii. 66.
[7] Num. xxiii. 19.
[8] Zech. xii. 10.
[9] Amos viii. 9, 10.
[10] Jer. xv. 9.

famine, overthrew Jerusalem, led the captives in triumph, and prohibited the others who were left from ever returning to their native land. And these things were done by God on account of that crucifixion of Christ, as He before declared this to Solomon in their Scriptures, saying,[1] "And Israel shall be for perdition and a reproach[2] to the people, and this house shall be desolate; and every one that shall pass by shall be astonished, and shall say, Why hath God done these evils to this land, and to this house? And they shall say, Because they forsook the Lord their God, and persecuted their King, who was dearly beloved by God, and crucified Him with great degradation, therefore hath God brought upon them these evils." For what would they not deserve who put to death their Lord, who had come for their salvation?

CHAP. XLVII.—*Of the resurrection of Jesus Christ, the sending of the apostles, and the ascension of the Saviour into heaven.*

After these things they took His body down from the cross, and buried it in a tomb. But on the third day, before daybreak, there was an earthquake, and the stone with which they had closed the sepulchre was removed, and He arose. But nothing was found in the sepulchre except the clothes in which the body had been wrapped.[3] But that He would rise again on the third day, the prophets had long ago foretold. David, in the 15th Psalm:[4] "Thou wilt not leave my soul in hell, neither wilt Thou suffer Thine Holy One to see corruption." Likewise Hosea:[5] "This my Son is wise, therefore He shall not stay long in the anguish of His sons: and I will ransom Him from the hand of the grave. Where is thy judgment, O death, where is thy sting?" The same again says:[6] "After two days He will revive us on the third day."

Therefore, after His resurrection He went into Galilee, and again assembled His disciples, who had fled through fear; and having given them commands which He wished to be observed, and having arranged for the preaching of the gospel throughout the whole world, He breathed into them the Holy Spirit, and gave them the power of working miracles, that they might act

---

[1] 1 Kings ix. 7-9.   [2] See *Instit.* iv. 18.   [3] "Exuviæ corporis."
[4] Ps. xvi. 10.   [5] Hos. xiii. 13, Septuagint version.
[6] Hos. vi. 2.

for the welfare of men as well by deeds as words; and then at length, on the fortieth day, He returned to His Father, being carried up into a cloud. The prophet Daniel[1] had long before shown this, saying, "I saw in the night vision, and, behold, one like the Son of man came with the clouds of heaven, and came to the Ancient of days; and they who stood beside Him brought Him near before Him. And there was given Him a kingdom, and glory, and dominion, and all people, tribes, and languages shall serve Him; and His power is an everlasting one, which shall not pass away, and His kingdom that which shall not be destroyed." Also David in the 109th Psalm:[2] "The Lord said unto my Lord, Sit Thou at my right hand, until I make Thine enemies Thy footstool."

CHAP. XLVIII.—*Of the disinheriting of the Jews, and the adoption of the Gentiles.*

Since, therefore, He sits at the right hand of God, about to tread down His enemies, who tortured Him, when He shall come to judge the world, it is evident that no hope remains to the Jews, unless, turning themselves to repentance, and being cleansed from the blood with which they polluted themselves, they shall begin to hope in Him whom they denied.[3] Therefore Esdras thus speaks:[4] "This passover is our Saviour and our refuge. Consider and let it come into your heart, that we have to abase Him in a figure: and after these things we have hoped[5] in Him."

Now that the Jews were disinherited, because thay rejected Christ, and that we, who are of the Gentiles, were adopted into their place, is proved by the Scriptures. Jeremiah[6] thus speaks: "I have forsaken mine house, I have given mine heritage into the hands of her enemies. Mine heritage is become unto me as a lion in the forest; it hath given forth its voice against me: therefore have I hated it." Also Malachi:[7] "I have no pleasure in you, saith the Lord, neither will I accept an offering at your hand. For from the rising of the sun even unto the going down thereof, my name shall be great among the

---

[1] Dan. vii. 13.
[2] Ps. cx. 1.
[3] "Negaverunt;" others read "necaverunt," killed.
[4] See *Instit.* iv. 18.
[5] "Speravimus;" others " sperabimus."
[6] Jer. xii. 7, 8.
[7] Mal. i. 10, 11.

Gentiles." Isaiah also thus speaks:[1] "I come to gather all nations and tongues: and they shall come and see my glory." The same says in another place,[2] speaking in the person of the Father to the Son: "I the Lord have called Thee in righteousness, and will hold Thine hand, and will keep Thee, and give Thee for a covenant of my people, for a light of the Gentiles; to open the eyes of the blind, to bring out the prisoners from the prison, and them that sit in darkness out of the prison-house."

CHAP. XLIX.—*That God is one only.*

If therefore the Jews have been rejected by God, as the faith due to the sacred writings shows, and the Gentiles, as we see, brought in, and freed from the darkness of this present life and from the chains of demons, it follows that no other hope is proposed to man, unless he shall follow true religion and true wisdom, which is in Christ, and he who is ignorant of Him is always estranged from the truth and from God. Nor let the Jews, or philosophers, flatter themselves respecting the supreme God. He who has not acknowledged the Son has been unable to acknowledge the Father. This is wisdom, and this is the mystery of the supreme God. God willed that He should be acknowledged and worshipped through Him. On this account He sent the prophets beforehand to announce His coming, that when the things which had been foretold were fulfilled in Him, then He might be believed by men to be both the Son of God and God.

Nor, however, must the opinion be entertained that there are two Gods, for the Father and the Son are one. For since the Father loves the Son, and gives all things to Him, and the Son faithfully obeys the Father, and wills nothing except that which the Father does, it is plain that so close a relationship cannot be separated, so that they should be said to be two in whom there is but one substance, and will, and faith. Therefore the Son is through the Father, and the Father through the Son. One honour is to be given to both, as to one God, and is to be so divided through the worship of the two, that the division itself may be bound by an inseparable bond of union. He will leave nothing to himself, who separates either the Father from the Son, or the Son from the Father.

[1] Isa. lxvi. 18.   [2] Isa. xlii. 6, 7.

CHAP. L.—*Why God assumed a mortal body, and suffered death.*

It remains to answer those also, who deem that it was unbecoming and unreasonable that God should be clothed with a mortal body; that He should be in subjection to men; that He should endure insults; that He should even suffer tortures and death. I will speak my sentiments, and I will sum up, as I shall be able, an immense subject in few words. He who teaches anything, ought, as I think, himself to practise what he teaches, that he may compel men to obey. For if he shall not practise them, he will detract from the faith due to his precepts. Therefore there is need of examples, that the precepts which are given may have firmness, and if any one shall prove contumacious, and shall say that they cannot be carried out in practice, the instructor may refute him by actual fact.[1] Therefore a system of teaching cannot be perfect, when it is delivered by words only; but it then becomes perfect, when it is completed by deeds.

Since therefore Christ was sent to men as a teacher of virtue, for the perfection of His teaching it was plainly befitting that He should act as well as teach. But if He had not assumed a human body, He would not have been able to practise what He taught,—that is, not to be angry, not to desire riches, not to be inflamed with lust, not to fear pain, to despise death. These things are plainly virtues, but they cannot be done without flesh. Therefore He assumed a body on this account, that, since He taught that the desires of the flesh must be overcome, He might in person first practise it, that no one might allege the frailty of the flesh as an excuse.

CHAP. LI.—*Of the death of Christ on the cross.*

I will now speak of the mystery of the cross, lest any one should happen to say, If death must be endured by Him, it should have been not one that was manifestly infamous and dishonourable, but one which had some honour. I know, indeed, that many, while they dislike the name of the cross, shrink from the truth, though there is in it great reasonableness and power. For since He was sent for this purpose, that He might open to the lowest men the way to salvation, He

[1] "Præsenti opere convincat."

made Himself humble that He might free them. Therefore He underwent that kind of death which is usually inflicted on the humble, that an opportunity of imitation might be given to all. Moreover, since He was about to rise again, it was not allowable that His body should be in any way mutilated, or a bone broken, which happens to those who are beheaded. Therefore the cross was preferred, which reserved the body with the bones uninjured for the resurrection.

To these grounds it was also added, that having undertaken to suffer and to die, it was befitting that He should be lifted up. Thus the cross exalted Him both in fact and in emblem,[1] so that His majesty and power became known to all, together with His passion. For in that He extended His hands on the cross, He plainly stretched out His wings towards the east and the west, under which all nations from either side of the world might assemble and repose. But of what great weight this sign is, and what power it has, is evident, since all the host of demons is expelled and put to flight by this sign. And as He Himself before His passion put to confusion demons by His word and command, so now, by the name and sign of the same passion, unclean spirits, having insinuated themselves into the bodies of men, are driven out, when racked and tormented, and confessing themselves to be demons, they yield themselves to God, who harasses them. What therefore can the Greeks expect from their superstitions and with their wisdom, when they see that their gods, whom they do not deny to be demons also, are subdued by men through the cross?

CHAP. LII.—*The hope of the salvation of men consists in the knowledge of the true God, and of the hatred of the heathens against the Christians.*

There is therefore but one hope of life for men, one harbour of safety, one refuge of liberty, if, laying aside the errors by which they were held, they open the eyes of their mind and recognise God, in whom alone is the abode of truth; despise earthly things, and those made from the ground; esteem as nothing philosophy, which is foolishness with God; and having undertaken true wisdom, that is, religion, become heirs of immortality. But indeed they are not so much opposed to

[1] "Significatione."

the truth as to their own safety; and when they hear these things, they abominate them as some inexpiable wickedness. But they do not even endure[1] to hear: they think that their ears are polluted with impiety[2] if they hear; nor do they now refrain from reproaches, but assail them with the most insulting words; and also, if they have obtained the power, persecute them as public enemies, yea, even as worse than enemies; for enemies, when they have been vanquished, are punished with death or slavery; nor is there any torturing after the laying down of arms, although those deserved to suffer all things who wished so to act, that piety might have place among swords.

Cruelty, combined with innocence, is unheard of, nor is it worthy of the condition of victorious enemies. What is the so powerful cause of this fury? Doubtless, because they cannot contend on the ground of reason, they urge forward their cause by means of violence; and, with the subject not understood, they condemn those as most pernicious persons who have declined to make a stand respecting the fact of their innocence. Nor do they deem it sufficient that those whom they unreasonably hate should die by a speedy and simple death; but they lacerate them with refined tortures, that they may satisfy their hatred, which is not produced by any fault, but by the truth, which is hateful to those who live wickedly, because they take it ill that there are some whom their deeds cannot please. They desire in every way to destroy these, that they may be able to sin without restraint in the absence of any witness.

CHAP. LIII.—*The reasons of the hatred against the Christians are examined and refuted.*

But they say that they do these things for the defence of their gods. In the first place, if they are gods, and have any power and influence, they have no need of the defence and protection of men, but they manifestly defend themselves. Or how is man able to hope for aid from them, if they are unable to avenge even their own injuries? Therefore it is a vain and foolish thing to wish to be avengers of the gods, except that their distrust is more apparent from this. For he who undertakes the protection of the god whom he worships, admits the

---

[1] "Ne audire quidem patiuntur;" others read "patienter."
[2] "Sacrilegio."

worthlessness of that god; but if he worships him on this account, because he thinks him powerful, he ought not to wish to defend him, by whom he himself ought to be defended. We therefore act rightly. For when those defenders of false gods, who are rebellious against the true God, persecute His name in us, we resist not either in deed or in word, but with meekness, and silence, and patience, we endure whatever cruelty is able to contrive against us. For we have confidence in God, from whom we expect that retribution will hereafter follow. Nor is this confidence ungrounded, since we have in some cases heard, and in other cases seen, the miserable ends of all those who have dared to commit this crime. Nor has any one had it in his power to insult God with impunity; but he who has been unwilling to learn by word has learned by his own punishment who is the true God.

I should wish to know, when they compel men to sacrifice against their will, what reasoning they have with themselves, or to whom they make that offering. If it is made to the gods, that is not worship, nor an acceptable sacrifice, which is made by those who are displeasing to them, which is extorted by injury, which is enforced by pain. But if it is done to those whom they compel, it is plainly not a benefit, which any one would not receive, he even prefers rather to die. If it is a good to which you call me, why do you invite me with evil? why with blows, and not with words? why not by argument, but by bodily tortures? Whence it is manifest that that is an evil, to which you do not allure me willing, but drag me refusing. What folly is it to wish to consult the good of any one against his will! If any one, under the pressure of evils, attempts to have recourse to death, can you, if you either wrest the sword from his hand, or cut the halter, or drag him away from the precipice, or pour out the poison, boast yourself as the preserver of the man, when he, whom you think that you have preserved, does not thank you, and thinks that you have acted ill towards him, in averting from him the death which he desired, and in not permitting him to reach the end and rest from his labours? For a benefit ought not to be weighed according to the quality of the action, but according to the feelings of him who receives it. Why should you reckon as a benefit that which is an injury to me? Do you wish me to worship your gods, which I consider deadly to myself? If it is a good, I do not envy it. Enjoy your good by yourself. There is no reason why you should wish to succour my error, which I have undertaken by my judgment and inclination. If it is evil, why do you drag me to a participation in evil? Use your own fortune. I prefer to die in the practice of that which is good, than to live in evil.

CHAP. LIV.—*Of the freedom of religion in the worship of God.*

These things may indeed be said with justice. But who will hear, when men of furious and unbridled spirit think that their authority is diminished if there is any freedom in the affairs of men? But it is religion alone in which freedom has placed its dwelling. For it is a matter which is voluntary above all others, nor can necessity be imposed upon any, so as to worship that which he does not wish to worship. Some one may perhaps pretend, he cannot wish it. In short, some, through fear of torments, or overcome by tortures, have assented to detestable sacrifices: they never do that voluntarily which they did from necessity; but when the opportunity is again given to them, and liberty restored, they again betake themselves to God, and appease Him with prayers and tears, repenting not of the will, which they had not, but of the necessity which they endured; and pardon is not denied to those who make satisfaction. What then does he accomplish who pollutes the body, since he cannot change the will?

But, in fact, men of weak understanding, if they have induced any man of spirit[1] to sacrifice to their gods, with incredible alacrity insolently exult, and rejoice, as though they had sent an enemy under the yoke. But if any one, neither frightened by threats nor by tortures, shall have chosen to prefer his faith to his life, cruelty puts forth all its ingenuity against him, plans dreadful and intolerable things; and because they know that death for the cause of God is glorious, and that this is a victory on our side, if, having overcome the torturers, we lay down our life in behalf of the faith and religion, they also themselves strive to conquer us. They do not put us to death, but they search out new and unheard-of tortures, that the frailty of the flesh may yield to pains, and if it does not yield, they put off further punishment, and apply diligent care to the wounds, that while

[1] "Fortem;" some read "forte," by chance.

the scars are yet fresh, a repetition of the torture may inflict more pain; and while they practise this torture[1] upon the innocent, they evidently consider themselves pious, and just, and religious (for they are delighted with such sacrifices to their gods), but they term the others impious and desperate. What perversity is this, that he who is punished, though innocent, should be called desperate and impious, and that the torturer, on the other hand, should be called just and pious!

CHAP. LV.—*The heathens charge justice with impiety in following God.*

But they say that those are rightly and deservedly punished, who dislike the public rites of religion handed down to them by their ancestors. What if those ancestors were foolish in undertaking vain religious rites, as we have shown before, shall we be prohibited from following true and better things? Why do we deprive ourselves of liberty, and become enslaved to the errors of others, as though bound[2] to them? Let it be permitted us to be wise, let it be permitted us to inquire into the truth. But, however, if it pleases them to defend (the folly)[3] of their ancestors, why are the Egyptians suffered to escape, who worship cattle and beasts of every kind as deities? Why are the gods themselves made the subjects of comic[4] representations? and why is he honoured who derides them most wittily? Why are philosophers attended to, who either say that there are no gods, or that, if there are any, they take no interest in, and do not regard the affairs of men, or argue that there is no providence at all, which rules the world?

But they alone of all are judged impious who follow God and the truth. And since this is at once justice, and wisdom, they lay to its charge either impiety or folly, and do not perceive what it is which deceives them, when they call evil good, and good evil. Many indeed of the philosophers, and especially Plato and Aristotle, spoke many things about justice, asserting and extolling that virtue with the greatest praise, because it gives to each its due, because it maintains equity in all things;

---

[1] "Carnificinam."   [2] "Addicti."
[3] "Stultitiam." This word is wanting in the MSS., but this or some such word is necessary to complete the sense.
[4] "Mimi;" wanting in some editions.

and whereas the other virtues are as it were silent, and shut up within, that it is justice alone which is neither concerned[1] for itself only, nor hidden, but altogether shows itself[2] abroad, and is ready for conferring a benefit, so as to assist as many as possible: as though in truth justice ought to be in judges only, and those placed in any post of authority, and not in all men.

And yet there is no one of men, not even of the lowest and of beggars, who is not capable of justice. But because they did not know what it was, from what source it proceeded, and what was its mode of operation, they assigned to a few only that highest virtue, that is, the common good of all, and said that it aimed at[3] no advantages peculiar to itself, but only the interests of others. And not without reason was Carneades raised up, a man of the greatest talent and penetration, to refute their speech, and overthrow the justice, which had no firm foundation; not because he thought that justice was to be blamed, but that he might show that its defenders brought forward no firm or certain argument respecting justice.

CHAP. LVI.—*Of justice, which is the worship of the true God.*

For if justice is the worship of the true God (for what is so just with respect to equity, so pious with respect to honour, so necessary with respect to safety, as to acknowledge God as a parent, to reverence Him as Lord, and to obey His law or precepts?), it follows that the philosophers were ignorant of justice, for they neither acknowledged God Himself, nor observed His worship and law; and on this account they might have been refuted by Carneades, whose disputation was to this effect, that there is no natural justice, and therefore that all animals defended their own interests by the guidance of nature itself, and therefore that justice, if it promotes the advantages of others and neglects its own, is to be called foolishness. But if all people who are possessed of power, and the Romans themselves, who are masters of the whole world, were willing to follow justice, and to restore to every one his property which they have seized by force and arms, they will return to cottages and a condition of want. And if they did this, they might indeed be just, but they must of necessity be considered foolish,

[1] "Sibi tantum conciliata sit."   [2] "Foras tota promineat."
[3] "Aucupari."

who proceed to injure themselves for the advantage of others. Then, if any one should find a man who was through a mistake offering for sale gold as mountain-brass, or silver as lead, and necessity should compel him to buy it, will he conceal his knowledge and buy it for a small sum, or will he rather inform the seller of its value? If he shall inform him, he will manifestly be called just; but he will also be foolish, for conferring an advantage upon another, and injuring himself. But it is easy (to judge) in a case of injury. What if he shall incur danger of his life, so that it shall be necessary for him either to kill another or to die, what will he do? It may happen that, having suffered shipwreck, he may find some feeble person clinging to a plank; or, his army having been defeated, in his flight he may find a wounded man on horseback: will he thrust the one from the plank, the other from his horse, that he himself may be able to escape? If he shall wish to be just, he will not do it; but he will also be judged foolish, who in sparing the life of another shall lose his own. If he shall do it, he will indeed appear wise, because he will provide for his own interests; but he will also be wicked, because he will commit a wrong.

Chap. LVII.—*Of wisdom and foolishness.*

These things indeed are said with acuteness; but we are able very readily to reply to them. For the imitation of names causes it thus to appear. For justice bears a resemblance to foolishness, and yet it is not foolishness; and at the same time malice bears a resemblance to wisdom, and yet it is not wisdom. But as that malice is intelligent and shrewd in preserving its own interests, it is not wisdom, but cunning and craftiness; so likewise justice ought not to be called foolishness, but innocence, because the just man must be wise, and the foolish man unjust. For neither reason nor nature itself permits that he who is just should not be wise, since it is plain that the just man does nothing except that which is right and good, and always avoids that which is perverted[1] and evil. But who will be able to distinguish between good and evil, depravity and rectitude, but he who shall be wise? But the fool acts badly, because he is ignorant of what is good and evil. Therefore he

---

[1] "Pravum."

does wrong, because he is unable to distinguish between things which are perverted and those which are right. Therefore justice cannot be befitting to the foolish man, nor wisdom to the unjust. He is not then a foolish person who has not thrust off a shipwrecked man from a plank, nor a wounded man from his horse, because he has abstained from injury, which is a sin; and it is the part of the wise man to avoid sin.

But that he should appear foolish at first sight is caused by this, that they suppose the soul to be extinguished together with the body; and for this reason they refer all advantage to this life. For if there is no existence after death, it is plain that he acts foolishly who spares the life of another to his own loss, or who consults the gain of another more than his own. If death destroys the soul, we must use our endeavours to live for a longer time, and more to our own advantage; but if there remains after death a life of immortality and blessedness, the just and wise man will certainly despise this corporeal existence, with all earthly goods, because he will know what kind of a reward he is about to receive from God. Therefore let us maintain innocency, let us maintain justice, let us undergo the appearance of foolishness, that we may be able to maintain true wisdom. And if it appears to men senseless and foolish to prefer torture and death rather than to sacrifice to gods, and to escape without harm, let us however strive to exhibit faithfulness towards God by all virtue and by all patience. Let not death terrify us, nor pain subdue us, so as to prevent the vigour of our mind and constancy from being preserved unshaken. Let them call us foolish, whilst they themselves are most foolish, and blind and dull, and like sheep; who do not understand that it is a deadly thing to leave the living God, and prostrate themselves in the adoration of earthly objects; who do not know that eternal punishment awaits those who have worshipped senseless images; and that those who have neither refused tortures nor death for the worship and honour of the true God will obtain eternal life. This is the highest faith; this is true wisdom; this is perfect justice. It matters nothing to us what fools may judge, what trifling men may think. We ought to await the judgment of God, that we may hereafter judge those who have passed judgment on us.

CHAP. LVIII.—*Of the true worship of God, and sacrifice.*

I have spoken of justice, what was its nature. It follows that I show what is true sacrifice to God, what is the most just manner of worshipping Him, lest any one should think that victims, or odours, or precious gifts, are desired by God, who, if He is not subject to hunger, and thirst, and cold, and desire of all earthly things, does not therefore make use of all these things which are presented in temples and to gods of earth; but as corporeal offerings are necessary for corporeal beings, so manifestly an incorporeal sacrifice is necessary for an incorporeal being. But God has no need of those things which He has given to man for his use, since all the earth is under His power: He needs not a temple, since the world is His dwelling; He needs not an image, since He is incomprehensible both to the eyes and to the mind; He needs not earthly lights, for He was able to kindle the light of the sun, with the other stars, for the use of man. What then does God require from man but worship of the mind, which is pure and holy? For those things which are made by the hands, or are outside of man, are senseless, frail, and displeasing. This is true sacrifice, which is brought forth not from the chest but from the heart; not that which is offered by the hand, but by the mind. This is the acceptable victim, which the mind sacrifices of itself. For what do victims bestow? what does incense? what do garments? what does silver? what gold? what precious stones,—if there is not a pure mind on the part of the worshipper? Therefore it is justice only which God requires. In this is sacrifice; in this the worship of God, respecting which I must now speak, and show in what works justice must necessarily be contained.

CHAP. LIX.—*Of the ways of life, and the first times of the world.*

That there are two ways of human life was unknown neither to philosophers nor to poets, but both introduced them in a different manner. The philosophers wished the one to be the way of industry, the other of idleness; but in this respect they were less correct in their statements, that they referred them to the advantages of this life only. The poets spoke better who said that one of them was the way of the just, the other of the unjust; but they err in this, that they say that they are not in this life, but in the shades below. We manifestly speak more correctly, who say that the one is the way of life, the other that of death. And here, however, we say that there are two ways; but the one on the right hand, in which the just walk, does not lead to Elysium, but to heaven, for they become immortal; the other on the left leads to Tartarus, for the unjust are sentenced to eternal tortures. Therefore the way of justice, which leads to life, is to be held by us. Now the first duty of justice is to acknowledge God as a parent, and to fear Him as a master, to love Him as a father. For the same Being who begat us, who animated us with vital breath, who nourishes and preserves us, has over us, not only as a father but also as a master, authority to correct us, and the power of life and death; wherefore twofold honour is due to Him from man, that is, love combined with fear. The second duty of justice is to acknowledge man as a brother. For if the same God made us, and produced all men on equal terms to justice and eternal life, it is manifest that we are united by the relationship of brotherhood; and he who does not acknowledge this is unjust. But the origin of this evil, by which the mutual society of men, by which the bond of relationship has been torn asunder, arises from ignorance of the true God. For he who is ignorant of that fountain of bounty can by no means be good. Hence it is that, from the time when a multitude of gods began to be consecrated and worshipped by men, justice, as the poets relate, being put to flight, every compact was destroyed, the fellowship of human justice was destroyed. Then every one, consulting his own interest, reckoned might to be right, injured another, attacked by frauds, deceived[1] by treachery, increased his own advantages by the inconvenience of others, did not spare relatives, or children, or parents, prepared poisoned cups for the destruction of men, beset the ways with the sword, infested the seas, gave the rein to his lust, wherever passion led him, — in short, esteemed nothing sacred which his dreadful desire did not violate. When these things were done, then men instituted laws for themselves to promote the public advantage, that they might meanwhile protect themselves from injuries. But the fear of laws did not suppress crimes, but it checked licentious-

[1] "Circumscribere."

ness. For laws were able to punish offences, they were unable to punish the conscience. Therefore the things which before were done openly began to be done secretly. Justice also was evaded by stealth, since they who themselves presided over the administration of the laws, corrupted by gifts and rewards, made a traffic of their sentences, either to the escape[1] of the evil or to the destruction of the good. To these things were added dissensions, and wars, and mutual depredations; and the laws being crushed, the power of acting with violence was assumed without restraint.

Chap. LX.—*Of the duties of justice.*

When the affairs of men were in this condition, God pitied us, revealed and displayed Himself to us, that in Himself we might learn religion, faith, purity, and mercy; that having laid aside the error of our former life, together with God Himself we might know ourselves, whom impiety had disunited from Him, and we might choose[2] the divine law, which unites human affairs with heavenly, the Lord Himself delivering it to us; by which law all the errors with which we have been ensnared, together with vain and impious superstitions, might be taken away. What we owe to man, therefore, is prescribed by that same divine law which teaches that whatever you render to man is rendered to God. But the root of justice, and the entire foundation of equity, is that you should not do that which you would be unwilling to suffer, but should measure the feelings of another by your own. If it is an unpleasant thing to bear an injury, and he who has done it appears unjust, transfer to the person of another that which you feel respecting yourself, and to your own person that which you judge respecting another, and you will understand that you act as unjustly if you injure another as another would if he should injure you. If we consider these things, we shall maintain innocence, in which the first step of justice is, as it were, contained. For the first thing is, not to injure; the next is, to be of service. And as in uncultivated lands, before you begin to sow, the fields must be cleansed by tearing up the thorns and cutting off all the roots of trunks, so vices must first be thrust out from our souls, and then

---

[1] "In remissionem."
[2] "Sumere," to take by selection and choice.

at length virtues must be implanted, from which the fruits of immortality, being engendered by the word of God, may spring up.

CHAP. LXI.—*Of the passions.*

There are three passions, or, so to speak, three furies, which excite such great perturbations in the souls of men, and sometimes compel them to offend in such a manner, as to permit them to have regard neither for their reputation nor for their personal safety: these are anger, which desires vengeance; love of gain, which longs for riches; lust, which seeks for pleasures. We must above all things resist these vices: these trunks must be rooted up, that virtues may be implanted. The Stoics are of opinion that these passions must be cut off; the Peripatetics think that they must be restrained. Neither of them judge rightly, because they cannot entirely be taken away, since they are implanted by nature, and have a sure and great influence; nor can they be diminished, since, if they are evil, we ought to be without them, even though restrained and used with moderation; if they are good, we ought to use them in their completeness.[1] But we say that they ought not to be taken away nor lessened. For they are not evil of themselves, since God has reasonably implanted them in us; but inasmuch as they are plainly good by nature,—for they are given us for the protection of life,—they become evil by their evil use. And as bravery, if you fight in defence of your country, is a good, if against your country, is an evil, so the passions, if you employ them to good purposes, will be virtues, if to evil uses, they will be called vices. Anger therefore has been given by God for the restraining of offences, that is, for controlling the discipline of subjects, that fear may suppress licentiousness and restrain audacity. But they who are ignorant of its limits are angry with their equals, or even with their superiors. Hence they rush to deeds of cruelty, hence they rise to slaughters, hence to wars. The love of gain also has been given that we may desire and seek for the necessaries of life. But they who are unacquainted with its boundaries strive insatiably to heap up riches. Hence poisoning, hence defraudings,[2] hence false

---

[1] "Integris abutendum est." Lactantius sometimes uses "abuti" for "uti."

[2] "Circumscriptiones."

wills, hence all kinds of frauds have burst forth. Moreover, the passion of lust is implanted and innate in us for the procreation of children; but they who do not fix its limits in the mind use it for pleasure only. Thence arise unlawful loves, thence adulteries and debaucheries, thence all kinds of corruption. These passions, therefore, must be kept within their boundaries and directed into their right course, in which, even though they should be vehement, they cannot incur blame.

CHAP. LXII.—*Of restraining the pleasures of the senses.*

Anger is to be restrained when we suffer an injury, that the evil may be suppressed which is imminent from a contest, and that we may retain two of the greatest virtues, harmlessness and patience. Let the desire of gain be broken when we have that which is enough. For what madness is it to labour in heaping up those things which must pass to others, either by robbery, or theft, or by proscription, or by death? Let lust not go beyond the marriage bed, but be subservient to the procreation of children. For a too great eagerness for pleasure both produces danger and generates disgrace, and that which is especially to be avoided, leads to eternal death. Nothing is so hateful to God as an unchaste mind and an impure soul. Nor let any one think that he must abstain from this pleasure only, quæ capitur ex fœminei corporis copulatione, but also from the other pleasures which arise from the rest of the senses, because they also are of themselves vicious, and it is the part of the same virtue to despise them. The pleasure of the eyes is derived from the beauty of objects, that of the ears from harmonious and pleasant sounds, that of the nostrils from pleasant odour, that of taste from sweet food,—all of which virtue ought strongly to resist, lest, ensnared by these attractions, the soul should be depressed from heavenly to earthly things, from things eternal to things temporal, from life immortal to perpetual punishment. In pleasures of the taste and smell there is this danger, that they are able to draw us to luxury. For he who shall be given up to these things, either will have no property, or, if he shall have any, he will expend it, and afterwards live a life to be abominated. But he who is carried away by hearing (to say nothing respecting songs, which often so charm the inmost senses that they even disturb with madness a settled state of the mind by certain elaborately composed speeches and harmonious poems, or skilful disputations) is easily led aside to impious worship. Hence it is that they who are either themselves eloquent, or prefer to read eloquent writings, do not readily believe the sacred writings, because they appear unpolished; they do not seek things that are true, but things that are pleasant; nay, to them those things appear to be most true which soothe the ears. Thus they reject the truth, while they are captivated by the sweetness of the discourse. But the pleasure which has reference to the sight is manifold. For that which is derived from the beauty of precious objects excites avarice, which ought to be far removed from a wise and just man; but that which is received from the appearance of woman hurries a man to another pleasure, of which we have already spoken above.

CHAP. LXIII.—*That shows are most powerful to corrupt the minds.*

It remains to speak of public shows, which, since they have a more powerful influence on the corruption of the mind, ought to be avoided by the wise, and to be altogether guarded against, because it is said that they were instituted in celebration of the honours of the gods. For the exhibitions of shows are festivals of Saturnus. The stage belongs to Father Liber; but the Circensian games are supposed to be dedicated to Neptunus: so that now he who takes part in these shows appears to have left the worship of God, and to have passed over to profane rites. But I prefer to speak of the matter itself rather than of its origin. What is so dreadful, what so foul, as the slaughter of man? Therefore our life is protected by the most severe laws; therefore wars are detestable. Yet custom finds how a man may commit homicide without war, and without laws; and this is a pleasure to him, that he has avenged guilt. But if to be present at homicide implies a consciousness of guilt, and the spectator is involved in the same guilt as the perpetrator, then in these slaughters of gladiators, he who is a spectator is no less sprinkled with blood than he who sheds it; nor can he be free from the guilt of bloodshed who wished it to be poured out, or appear not to have slain, who both favoured the slayer and asked a reward for him. What of the stage? Is it more holy,

—on which comedy converses on the subject of debaucheries and amours, tragedy of incest and parricide? The immodest gestures also of players, with which they imitate disreputable women, teach the lusts, which they express by dancing. For the pantomime is a school of corruption,[1] in which things which are shameful are acted by a figurative representation,[2] that the things which are true may be done without shame. These spectacles are viewed by youths, whose dangerous age, which ought to be curbed and governed, is trained by these representations to vices and sins. The circus, in truth, is considered more innocent, but there is greater madness in this, since the minds of the spectators are transported with such great madness, that they not only break out into revilings, but often rise to strifes, and battles, and contentions. Therefore all shows are to be avoided, that we may be able to maintain a tranquil state of mind. We must renounce hurtful pleasures, lest, charmed by pestilential sweetness, we fall into the snares of death.

CHAP. LXIV.—*The passions are to be subdued, and we must abstain from forbidden things.*

Let virtue alone please us, whose reward is immortal when it has conquered pleasure. But when the passions have been overcome and pleasures subdued, labour in suppressing other things is easy to him who is a follower of God and of truth: he will never revile, who shall hope for a blessing from God; he will not commit perjury, lest he should mock God; but he will not even swear, lest at any time, either by necessity or through habit, he should fall into perjury. He will speak nothing deceitfully, nothing with dissimulation; he will not refuse that which he has promised, nor will he promise that which he is unable to perform; he will envy no one, since he is content with himself and with his own possessions; nor will he take away from, or wish ill to another, upon whom, perhaps, the benefits of God are more plenteously[3] bestowed. He will not steal, nor will he covet anything at all belonging to another. He will not give his money to usury, for that is to seek after gain from the evils of others; nor, however, will he refuse to

---

[1] "Mimus corruptelarum disciplina est."   [2] "Per imaginem."
[3] "Proniora sunt."

lend, if necessity shall compel any one to borrow. He must not be harsh towards a son, nor towards a slave: he must remember that he himself has a Father and a Master. He will so act towards these as he will wish that others should act towards him. He will not receive excessive gifts from those who have less resources than himself; for it is not just that the estates of the wealthy should be increased by the losses of the wretched.

It is an old precept not to kill, which ought not to be taken in this light, as though we are commanded to abstain only from homicide, which is punished even by public laws. But by the intervention of this command, it will not be permitted us to apply peril of death by word, nor to put to death or expose an infant, nor to condemn one's self by a voluntary death. We are likewise commanded not to commit adultery; but by this precept we are not only prohibited from polluting the marriage of another, which is condemned even by the common law of nations, but even to abstain from those who prostitute their persons. For the law of God is above all laws; it forbids even those things which are esteemed lawful, that it may fulfil justice. It is a part of the same law not to utter false witness, and this also itself has a wider meaning. For if false witness by falsehood is injurious to him against whom it is spoken, and deceives him in whose presence it is spoken, we must therefore never speak falsely, because falsehood always deceives or injures. Therefore he is not a just man who, even without inflicting injury, speaks in idle discourse. Nor indeed is it lawful for him to flatter, for flattery is pernicious and deceitful; but he will everywhere guard the truth. And although this may for the present be unpleasant, nevertheless, when its advantage and usefulness shall appear, it will not produce hatred, as the poet says,[1] but gratitude.

CHAP. LXV.—*Precepts about those things which are commanded, and of pity.*

I have spoken of those things which are forbidden; I will now briefly say what things are commanded. Closely connected with harmlessness is pity. For the former does not inflict injury, the latter works good; the former begins justice, the latter completes it. For since the nature of men is more

[1] Terent. *And.* i. 1.

feeble than that of the other animals, which God has provided with means of inflicting violence, and with defences for repelling it, He has given to us the affection of pity, that we might place the whole protection of our life in mutual aid. For if we are created by one God, and descended from one man, and are thus connected by the law of consanguinity, we ought on this account to love every man; and therefore we are bound not only to abstain from the infliction of injury, but not even to avenge it when inflicted on us, that there may be in us complete harmlessness. And on this account God commands us to pray always even for our enemies. Therefore we ought to be an animal fitted for companionship and society, that we may mutually protect ourselves by giving and receiving assistance. For our frailty is liable to many accidents and inconveniences. Expect that that which you see has happened to another may happen to you also. Thus you will at length be excited to render aid, if you shall assume the mind of him who, being placed in evils, implores your aid. If any one is in need of food, let us bestow it; if any one meets us who is naked, let us clothe him; if any one suffers injury from one who is more powerful than himself, let us rescue him. Let our house be open to strangers, or to those who are in need of shelter. Let our defence not be wanting to wards, or our protection to the defenceless.[1] To ransom captives is a great work of pity, and also to visit and comfort the sick who are in poverty. If the helpless or strangers die, we should not permit them to lie unburied. These are the works, these the duties, of pity; and if any one undertakes these, he will offer unto God a true and acceptable sacrifice. This victim is more adapted for an offering to God, who is not appeased with the blood of a sheep, but with the piety of man, whom God, because He is just, follows up with His own law, and with His own condition. He shows mercy to him whom He sees to be merciful; He is inexorable to him whom He sees to be harsh to those who entreat him. Therefore, that we may be able to do all these things, which are pleasing to God, money is to be despised, and to be transferred to heavenly treasures, where neither thief can break through, nor rust corrupt, nor tyrant take away, but it may be preserved for us under the guardianship of God to our eternal wealth.

[1] "Viduis."

Chap. LXVI.—*Of faith in religion, and of fortitude.*

Faith also is a great part of justice; and this ought especially to be preserved by us, who bear the name of faith, especially in religion, because God is before and to be preferred to man. And if it is a glorious thing to undergo death in behalf of friends, of parents, and of children, that is, in behalf of man, and if he who has done this obtains lasting memory and praise, how much more so in behalf of God, who is able to bestow eternal life in return for temporal death? Therefore, when a necessity of this kind happens, that we are compelled to turn aside from God, and to pass over to the rites of the heathens, no fear, no terror should turn us aside from guarding the faith delivered to us. Let God be before our eyes, in our heart, by whose inward help we may overcome the pain of our flesh, and the torments applied to our body. Then let us think of nothing else but the rewards of an immortal life. And thus, even though our limbs should be torn in pieces, or burnt, we shall easily endure all things which the madness of tyrannical cruelty shall contrive against us. Lastly, let us strive to undergo death itself, not unwillingly or timidly, but willingly and undauntedly, as those who know what glory we are about to have in the presence of God, having triumphed over the world and coming to the things promised us; with what good things and how great blessedness we shall be compensated for these brief evils of punishments, and the injuries of this life. But if the opportunity of this glory shall be wanting, faith will have its reward even in peace.

Therefore let it be observed in all the duties of life, let it be observed in marriage. For it is not sufficient if you abstain from another's bed, or from the brothel. Let him who has a wife seek nothing further, but, content with her alone, let him guard the mysteries of the marriage bed chaste and undefiled. For he is equally an adulterer in the sight of God and impure, who, having thrown off the yoke, wantons in strange pleasure either with a free woman or a slave. But as a woman is bound by the bonds of chastity not to desire any other man, so let the husband be bound by the same law, since God has joined together the husband and the wife in the union of one body. On this account He has commanded that the wife shall not be put away unless convicted of adultery, and that the bond of the conjugal compact shall never be dissolved, unless unfaithfulness have broken it. This also is added for the completion of chastity, that there should be an absence not only of the offence, but even of the thought. For it is evident that the mind is polluted by the desire, though unaccomplished; and so that a just man ought neither to do, nor to wish to do, that which is unjust. Therefore the conscience must be cleansed; for God, who cannot be deceived, inspects it. The breast must be cleared from every stain, that it may be a temple of God, which is enlightened not by the gleam of gold or ivory, but by the brightness of faith and purity.

CHAP. LXVII.—*Of repentance, the immortality of the soul, and of providence.*

But it is true all these things are difficult to man, nor does the condition of his frailty permit that any one should be without blemish. Therefore the last remedy is this, that we have recourse to repentance, which has not the least place among the virtues, because it is a correction of oneself; that when we have happened to fail either in deed or in word, we may immediately come to a better mind, and confess that we have offended, and entreat pardon from God, which according to His mercy He will not deny, except to those who persist in their error. Great is the aid, great the solace of repentance. That is the healing of wounds and offences, that hope, that the harbour of safety; and he who takes away this cuts off from himself the way of salvation, because no one can be so just that repentance is never necessary for him. But we, even though there is no offence of ours, yet ought to confess to God, and to entreat pardon for our faults, and to give thanks even in evils. Let us always offer this obedience to our Lord. For humility is dear and lovely in the sight of God; for since He rather receives the sinner who confesses his fault, than the just man who is haughty, how much more will He receive the just man who confesses, and exalt him in His heavenly kingdom in proportion to his humility! These are the things which the worshipper of God ought to hold forth; these are the victims, this the sacrifice, which is acceptable; this is true worship, when a man offers upon the altar of God the pledges of his own mind. That supreme Majesty rejoices in such a worshipper as this, as it takes him as a son and bestows upon him the befitting reward of immortality, concerning which I must now speak, and refute the persuasion of those who think that the soul is destroyed together with the body. For inasmuch as they neither knew God nor were able to perceive the mystery of the world, they did not even comprehend the nature of man and of the soul. For how could they see the consequences, who did not hold the main point?[1] Therefore, in denying the existence of a providence, they plainly denied the existence of God, who is the fountain and source of all things. It followed that they should either affirm that those things which exist have always existed, or were produced of their own accord, or arose from a meeting together of minute seeds.

It cannot be said that that which exists, and is visible, always existed; for it cannot exist of itself without some beginning. But nothing can be produced of its own accord, because there is no nature without one who generates it. But how could there be original[2] seeds, since both the seeds arise from objects,[3] and, in their turn, objects from seeds? Therefore there is no seed which has not an origin. Thus it came to pass, that when they supposed that the world was produced by no providence, they did not suppose that even man was produced by any plan.[4] But if no plan was made use of in the creation of man, therefore the soul cannot be immortal. But others, on the other hand, thought there was but one God, and that the world was made by Him, and made for the sake of men, and that souls are immortal. But though they entertained true sentiments, nevertheless they did not perceive the causes, or reasons, or issues of this divine work and design, so as to complete the whole mystery of the truth, and to comprise it within some limit. But that which they were not able to do, because they did not hold the truth in its integrity,[5] must be done by us, who know it on the announcement of God.

[1] "Summam." Lactantius uses this word to express a compendious summary of divine mysteries.
[2] "Semina principalia."   [3] "Ex rebus."
[4] "Aliquâ ratione."   [5] "Perpetuo," i.e. without intermission.

CHAP. LXVIII.—*Of the world, man, and the providence of God.*

Let us therefore consider what was the plan of making this so great and so immense a work. God made the world, as Plato thought, but he does not show why He made it. Because He is good, he says, and envying no one, He made the things which are good. But we see that there are both good and evil things in the system of nature. Some perverse person may stand forth, such as that atheist Theodorus was, and answer Plato: Nay, because He is evil, He made the things which are evil. How will he refute him? If God made the things which are good, whence have such great evils burst forth, which, for the most part, even prevail over those which are good? They were contained, he says, in the matter. If there were evil, therefore there were also good things; so that either God made nothing, or if He made only good things, the evil things which were not made are more eternal than the good things which had a beginning. Therefore the things which at one time began will have an end, and those which always existed will be permanent. Therefore evils are preferable. But if they cannot be preferable, they cannot indeed be more eternal. Therefore they either always existed, and God has been inactive,[1] or they both flowed from one source. For it is more in accordance with reason that God made all things, than that He made nothing.

Therefore, according to the sentiments of Plato, the same God is both good, because He made good things, and evil, because He made evil things. And if this cannot be so, it is evident that the world was not made by God on this account, because He is good. For He comprised all things, both good and evil; nor did He make anything for its own sake, but on account of something else. A house is built not for this purpose only, that there may be a house, but that it may receive and shelter an inhabitant. Likewise a ship is built not for this purpose, that it may appear only to be a ship, but that men may be able to sail in it. Vessels also are made, not only that the vessels may exist, but that they may receive things which are necessary for use. Thus also God must have made the world for some use. The Stoics say that it was made for the

[1] "Otiosus."

sake of men; and rightly so. For men enjoy all these good things which the world contains in itself. But they do not explain why men themselves were made, or what advantage Providence, the Maker of all things, has in them.

Plato also affirms that souls are immortal, but why, or in what manner, or at what time, or by whose instrumentality they attain to immortality, or what is the nature of that great mystery, why those who are about to become immortal are previously born mortal, and then, having completed the course [1] of their temporal life, and having laid aside the covering [2] of their frail bodies, are transferred to that eternal blessedness,—of all this he has no comprehension. Finally, he did not explain the judgment of God, nor the distinction between the just and the unjust, but supposed that the souls which have plunged themselves into crimes are condemned thus far, that they may be reproduced in the lower animals, and thus atone for their offences, until they again return to the forms of men, and that this is always taking place, and that there is no end of this transmigration. In my opinion, he introduces some sport resembling a dream, in which there appears to be neither plan, nor government of God, nor any design.

CHAP. LXIX.—*That the world was made on account of man, and man on account of God.*

I will now say what is that chief [3] point which not even those who spoke the truth were able to connect together, bringing into one view causes and reasons. The world was made by God, that men might be born; again, men are born, that they may acknowledge God as a Father, in whom is wisdom; they acknowledge Him, that they may worship Him, in whom is justice; they worship Him, that they may receive the reward of immortality; they receive immortality, that they may serve God for ever. Do you see how closely connected the first are with the middle, and the middle with the last? Let us look into them separately, and see whether they are consistent [4] with each other. God made the world on account of man. He who does not see this, does not differ much from

---

[1] "Decurso . . . spatio." The expression is borrowed from a chariot race.
[2] "Corporum exuviis." [3] "Summa."
[4] "Utrumne illis ratio subsistat."

a beast. Who but man looks up to the heaven? who views with admiration the sun, who the stars, who all the works of God? Who inhabits the earth? who receives the fruit from it? Who has in his power the fishes, who the winged creatures, who the quadrupeds, except man? Therefore God made all things on account of man, because all things have turned out for the use of man.

The philosophers saw this, but they did not see the consequence, that He made man himself on His own account. For it was befitting, and pious, and necessary, that since He contrived such great works for the sake of man, when He gave him so much honour, and so much power, that he should bear rule in the world, man should both acknowledge God, the Author of such great benefits, who made the world itself on his account, and should pay Him the worship and honour due to Him. Here Plato erred; here he lost the truth which he had at first laid hold of, when he was silent concerning the worship of that God whom he confessed to be the framer and parent of all things, and did not understand that man is bound to God by the ties of piety, whence religion itself receives its name, and that this is the only thing on account of which souls become immortal. He perceived, however, that they are eternal, but he did not descend by the regular gradations to that opinion. For the middle arguments being taken away, he rather fell into the truth, as though by some abrupt precipice; nor did he advance further, since he had found the truth by accident, and not by reason. Therefore God is to be worshipped, that by means of religion, which is also justice, man may receive from God immortality, nor is there any other reward of a pious mind; and if this is invisible, it cannot be presented by the invisible God with any reward but that which is invisible.

CHAP. LXX.—*The immortality of the soul is confirmed.*

It may in truth be collected from many arguments that souls are eternal. Plato says that that which always moves by itself, and has no beginning of motion, also has no end; but that the soul of man always moves by itself, and because it is flexible for reflection, subtle for discovery, easy of perception, adapted to learning, and because it retains the past, comprehends the present, foresees the future, and embraces the knowledge of many subjects and arts, that it is immortal, since it contains nothing which is mixed with the contagion of earthly weight. Moreover, the eternity of the soul is understood from virtue and pleasure. Pleasure is common to all animals, virtue belongs only to man; the former is vicious, the latter is honourable; the former is in accordance with nature, the latter is opposed to nature, unless the soul is immortal. For in defence of faith and justice, virtue neither fears want, nor is alarmed at exile, nor dreads imprisonment, nor shrinks from pain, nor refuses death; and because these things are contrary to nature, either virtue is foolishness, if it stands in the way of advantages, and is injurious to life; or if it is not foolishness, then the soul is immortal, and despises present goods, because other things are preferable which it attains after the dissolution of the body. But that is the greatest proof of immortality, that man alone has the knowledge of God. In the dumb animals there is no notion[1] of religion, because they are earthly and bent down to the earth. Man is upright, and beholds the heaven for this purpose, that he may seek God. Therefore he cannot be other than immortal, who longs for the immortal. He cannot be liable to dissolution, who is connected[2] with God both in countenance and mind. Finally, man alone makes use of the heavenly element, which is fire. For if light is through fire, and life through light, it is evident that he who has the use of fire is not mortal, since this is closely connected, this is intimately related to Him without whom neither light nor life can exist.

But why do we infer from arguments that souls are eternal, when we have divine testimonies? For the sacred writings and the voices of the prophets teach this. And if this appears to any one insufficient, let him read the poems of the Sibyls, let him also weigh the answers of the Milesian Apollo, that he may understand that Democritus, and Epicurus, and Dicæarchus raved, who alone of all mortals denied that which is evident. Having proved the immortality of the soul, it remains to teach by whom, and to whom, and in what manner, and at what time, it is given. Since fixed and divinely appointed times have begun to be filled up, a destruction and consummation of

[1] "Suspicio."   [2] "Cum Deo communis est."

all things must of necessity take place, that the world may be renewed by God. But that time is at hand, as far as may be collected from the number of years, and from the signs which are foretold by the prophets. But since the things which have been spoken concerning the end of the world and the conclusion of the times are innumerable, those very things which are spoken are to be laid down without adornment, since it would be a boundless task to bring forward the testimonies. If any one wishes for them, or does not place full confidence in us, let him approach to the very shrine of the heavenly letters, and being more fully instructed through their trustworthiness, let him perceive that the philosophers have erred, who thought either that this world was eternal, or that there would be numberless thousands of years from the time when it was prepared. For six thousand years have not yet been completed, and when this number shall be made up, then at length all evil will be taken away, that justice alone may reign. And how this will come to pass, I will explain in few words.

CHAP. LXXI.—*Of the last times.*

These things are said by the prophets, but as seers, to be about to happen. When the last end shall begin to approach to the world, wickedness will increase; all kinds of vices and frauds will become frequent; justice will perish; faith, peace, mercy, modesty, truth, will have no existence; violence and daring will abound; no one will have anything, unless it is acquired by the hand, and defended by the hand. If there shall be any good men, they will be esteemed as a prey and a laughing-stock. No one will exhibit filial affection to parents, no one will pity an infant or an old man; avarice and lust will corrupt all things. There will be slaughter and bloodshed. There will be wars, and those not only between foreign and neighbouring states, but also intestine wars. States will carry on wars among themselves, every sex and age will handle arms. The dignity of government will not be preserved, nor military discipline; but after the manner of robbery, there will be depredation and devastation. Kingly power will be multiplied, and ten men will occupy, portion out, and devour the world. There will arise another by far more powerful and wicked, who, having destroyed three, will obtain Asia, and having reduced and subdued the others under his own power, will harass all the earth. He will appoint new laws, abrogate old ones; he will make the state his own, and will change the name and seat of the government.

Then there will be a dreadful and detestable time, in which no one would choose to live. In fine, such will be the condition of things, that lamentation will follow the living, and congratulation the dead. Cities and towns will be destroyed, at one time by fire and the sword, at another by repeated earthquakes; now by inundation of waters, now by pestilence and famine. The earth will produce nothing, being barren either through excessive cold or heat. All water will be partly changed into blood, partly vitiated by bitterness, so that none of it can be useful for food, or wholesome for drinking. To these evils will also be added prodigies from heaven, that nothing may be wanting to men for causing fear. Comets will frequently appear. The sun will be overshadowed with perpetual paleness. The moon will be stained with blood, nor will it repair the losses of its light taken away. All the stars will fall, nor will the seasons preserve their regularity, winter and summer being confused. Then both the year, and the month, and the day will be shortened. And Trismegistus has declared that this is the old age and decline of the world. And when this shall have come, it must be known that the time is at hand in which God will return to change the world. But in the midst of these evils there will arise an impious king, hostile not only to mankind, but also to God. He will trample upon, torment, harass and put to death those who have been spared by that former tyrant. Then there will be ever-flowing tears, perpetual wailings and lamentations, and useless prayers to God; there will be no rest from fear, no sleep for a respite. The day will always increase disaster, the night alarm. Thus the world will be reduced almost to solitude, certainly to fewness of men. Then also the impious man will persecute the just and those who are dedicated to God, and will give orders that he himself shall be worshipped as God. For he will say that he is Christ, though he will be His adversary. That he may be believed, he will receive the power of doing wonders, so that fire may descend from heaven, the sun retire from his course, and the image which he shall have set up may speak. And by these prodigies he shall entice many to worship him, and to receive his sign in their hand or forehead. And he who shall not worship him and receive his sign will die with refined tortures. Thus he will destroy nearly two parts, the third will flee into desolate solitudes. But he, frantic and raging with implacable anger, will lead an army and besiege the mountain to which the righteous shall have fled. And when they shall see themselves besieged, they will implore the aid of God with a loud voice, and God shall hear them, and shall send to them a deliverer.

CHAP. LXXII.—*Of Christ descending from heaven to the general judgment, and of the millenarian reign.*

Then the heaven shall be opened in a tempest,[1] and Christ shall descend with great power, and there shall go before Him a fiery brightness and a countless host of angels, and all that multitude of the wicked shall be destroyed, and torrents of blood shall flow, and the leader himself shall escape, and having often renewed his army, shall for the fourth time engage in battle, in which, being taken, with all the other tyrants, he shall be delivered up to be burnt. But the prince also of the demons himself, the author and contriver of evils, being bound with fiery chains, shall be imprisoned, that the world may receive peace, and the earth, harassed through so many years, may rest. Therefore peace being made, and every evil suppressed, that righteous King and Conqueror will institute a great judgment on the earth respecting the living and the dead, and will deliver all the nations into subjection to the righteous who are alive, and will raise the (righteous) dead to eternal life, and will Himself reign with them on the earth, and will build the holy city, and this kingdom of the righteous shall be for a thousand years. Throughout that time the stars shall be more brilliant, and the brightness of the sun shall be increased, and the moon shall not be subject to decrease. Then the rain of blessing shall descend from God at morning and evening, and the earth shall bring forth all her fruit without the labour of men. Honey shall drop from rocks, fountains of milk and wine shall abound. The beasts shall lay aside their ferocity and become mild, the wolf shall roam among the

[1] "In tempestate;" others read "intempestâ nocte."

flocks without doing harm, the calf shall feed with the lion, the dove shall be united with the hawk, the serpent shall have no poison; no animal shall live by bloodshed. For God shall supply to all abundant and harmless[1] food. But when the thousand years shall be fulfilled, and the prince of the demons loosed, the nations will rebel against the righteous, and an innumerable multitude will come to storm the city of the saints. Then the last judgment of God will come to pass against the nations. For He will shake the earth from its foundations, and the cities shall be overthrown, and He shall rain upon the wicked fire with brimstone and hail, and they shall be on fire, and slay each other. But the righteous shall for a little space be concealed under the earth, until the destruction of the nations is accomplished, and after the third day they shall come forth, and see the plains covered with carcases. Then there shall be an earthquake, and the mountains shall be rent, and valleys shall sink down to a profound depth, and into this the bodies of the dead shall be heaped together, and its name shall be called Polyandrion.[2] After these things God will renew the world, and transform the righteous into the forms of angels, that, being presented with the garment of immortality, they may serve God for ever; and this will be the kingdom of God, which shall have no end. Then also the wicked shall rise again, not to life but to punishment; for God shall raise these also, when the second resurrection takes place, that, being condemned to eternal torments and delivered to eternal fires, they may suffer the punishments which they deserve for their crimes.

CHAP. LXXIII.—*The hope of safety is in the religion and worship of God.*

Wherefore, since all these things are true and certain, in harmony with the predicted announcement of the prophets, since Trismegistus and Hystaspes and the Sibyls have foretold the same things, it cannot be doubted that all hope of life and salvation is placed in the religion of God alone. Therefore, unless a man shall have received Christ, whom God has sent, and is

---

[1] "Innocentem," without injury to any.

[2] A name sometimes given to cemeteries, because many men (πολλοί ἄνδρες) are borne thither.

about to send for our redemption, unless he shall have known the supreme God through Christ, unless he shall have kept His commandments and law, he will fall into those punishments of which we have spoken. Therefore frail things must be despised, that we may gain those which are substantial; earthly things must be scorned, that we may be honoured with heavenly things; temporal things must be shunned, that we may reach those which are eternal. Let every one train himself to justice, mould himself to self-restraint, prepare himself for the contest, equip himself for virtue, that if by any chance an adversary shall wage war, he may be driven from that which is upright and good by no force, no terror, and no tortures, may give [1] himself up to no senseless fictions, but in his uprightness acknowledge the true and only God, may cast away pleasures, by the attractions of which the lofty soul is depressed to the earth, may hold fast innocency, may be of service to as many as possible, may gain for himself incorruptible treasures by good works, that he may be able, with God for his judge, to gain for the merits of his virtue either the crown of faith, or the reward of immortality.

[1] "Se substernet."

OF THE MANNER IN WHICH THE PERSECUTORS DIED.

Chapter i.

THE Lord has heard those supplications which you, my best beloved Donatus, pour forth in His presence all the day long, and the supplications of the rest of our brethren, who by a glorious confession have obtained an everlasting crown, the reward of their faith. Behold, all the adversaries are destroyed, and tranquillity having been re-established throughout the Roman empire, the late oppressed Church arises again, and the temple of God, overthrown by the hands of the wicked, is built with more glory than before. For God has raised up princes to rescind the impious and sanguinary edicts of the tyrants and provide for the welfare of mankind; so that now the cloud of past times is dispelled, and peace and serenity gladden all hearts. And after the furious whirlwind and black tempest, the heavens are now become calm, and the wished-for light has shone forth; and now God, the hearer of prayer, by His divine aid has lifted His prostrate and afflicted servants from the ground, has brought to an end the united devices of the wicked, and wiped off the tears from the faces of those who mourned. They who insulted over the Divinity, lie low; they who cast down the holy temple, are fallen with more tremendous ruin; and the tormentors of just men have poured out their guilty souls amidst plagues inflicted by Heaven, and amidst deserved tortures. For God delayed to punish them, that, by great and marvellous examples, He might teach posterity that He alone is God, and that with fit vengeance He executes judgment on the proud, the impious, and the persecutors.

Of the end of those men I have thought good to publish a narrative, that all who are afar off, and all who shall arise hereafter, may learn how the Almighty manifested His power and sovereign greatness in rooting out and utterly destroying the enemies of His name. And this will become evident, when I relate *who* were the persecutors of the Church from the time of its first constitution, and *what* were the punishments by which the divine Judge, in His severity, took vengeance on them.

Chapter II.

In the latter days of the Emperor Tiberius, in the consulship of Ruberius Geminus and Fufius Geminus, and on the tenth of the kalends of April (23d of March), as I find it written, Jesus Christ was crucified by the Jews. After He had risen again on the third day, He gathered together His apostles, whom fear, at the time of His being laid hold on, had put to flight; and while He sojourned with them forty days, He opened their hearts, interpreted to them the Scripture, which hitherto had been wrapped up in obscurity, ordained and fitted them for the preaching of His word and doctrine, and regulated all things concerning the institutions of the New Testament; and this having been accomplished, a cloud and whirlwind enveloped Him, and caught Him up from the sight of men unto heaven.

His apostles were at that time eleven in number, to whom were added Matthias, in the room of the traitor Judas, and afterwards Paul. Then were they dispersed throughout all the earth to preach the gospel, as the Lord their Master had commanded them; and during twenty-five years, and until the beginning of the reign of the Emperor Nero, they occupied themselves in laying the foundations of the Church in every province and city. And while Nero reigned, the Apostle Peter came to Rome, and, through the power of God committed unto him, wrought certain miracles, and, by turning many to the true religion, built up a faithful and stedfast temple unto the Lord. When Nero heard of those things, and observed that not only in Rome, but in every other place, a great multitude revolted daily from the worship of idols, and, condemning their old ways, went over to the new religion, he, an execrable and pernicious tyrant, sprung forward to raze the heavenly temple and destroy the true faith. He it was who first persecuted the servants of God; he crucified Peter, and slew Paul: nor did he escape with impunity; for God looked on the affliction of His people; and therefore the tyrant, bereaved of authority, and precipitated from the height of empire, suddenly disappeared, and even the burial-place of that noxious wild beast was nowhere to be seen. This has led some persons of extravagant imagination to suppose that, having been conveyed to a distant region, he is still reserved alive; and to him they apply the Sibylline verses concerning "the fugitive, who slew his own mother, being to come from the uttermost boundaries of the earth;" as if he who was the first should also be the last persecutor, and thus prove the forerunner of Antichrist! But we ought not to believe those who, affirming that the two prophets Enoch and Elias have been translated into some remote place that they might attend our Lord when He shall come to judgment, also fancy that Nero is to appear hereafter as the forerunner of the devil, when he shall come to lay waste the earth and overthrow mankind.

Chapter III.

After an interval of some years from the death of Nero, there arose another tyrant no less wicked (Domitian), who, although his government was exceedingly odious, for a very long time oppressed his subjects, and reigned in security, until at length he stretched forth his impious hands against the Lord. Having been instigated by evil demons to persecute the righteous people, he was then delivered into the power of his enemies, and suffered due punishment. To be murdered in his own palace was not vengeance ample enough: the very memory of his name was erased. For although he had erected many admirable edifices, and rebuilt the Capitol, and left other distinguished marks of his magnificence, yet the senate did so persecute his name, as to leave no remains of his statues, or traces of the inscriptions put up in honour of him; and by most solemn and severe decrees it branded him, even after death, with perpetual infamy. Thus, the commands of the tyrant having been rescinded, the Church was not only restored to her former state, but she shone forth with additional splendour, and became more and more flourishing. And in the times that followed, while many well-deserving princes guided the helm of the Roman empire, the Church suffered no violent assaults from her enemies, and she extended her hands unto the east and unto the west, insomuch that now there was not any the most remote corner of the earth to which the divine religion had not penetrated, or any nation of manners so barbarous that did not, by being converted to the worship of God, become mild and gentle.

CHAPTER IV.

This long peace, however, was afterwards interrupted. Decius appeared in the world, an accursed wild beast, to afflict the Church,—and *who* but a bad man would persecute religion? It seems as if he had been raised to sovereign eminence, at once to rage against God, and at once to fall; for, having undertaken an expedition against the Carpi, who had then possessed themselves of Dacia and Moefia, he was suddenly surrounded by the barbarians, and slain, together with great part of his army; nor could he be honoured with the rites of sepulture, but, stripped and naked, he lay to be devoured by wild beasts and birds,—a fit end for the enemy of God!

CHAPTER V.

And presently Valerian also, in a mood alike frantic, lifted up his impious hands to assault God, and, although his time was short, shed much righteous blood. But God punished him in a new and extraordinary manner, that it might be a lesson to future ages that the adversaries of Heaven always receive the just recompense of their iniquities. He, having been made prisoner by the Persians, lost not only that power which he had exercised without moderation, but also the liberty of which he had deprived others; and he wasted the remainder of his days in the vilest condition of slavery: for Sapores, the king of the Persians, who had made him prisoner, whenever he chose to get into his carriage or to mount on horseback, commanded the Roman to stoop and present his back; then, setting his foot on the shoulders of Valerian, he said, with a smile of reproach, "*This* is true, and not what the Romans delineate on board or plaster." Valerian lived for a considerable time under the well-merited insults of his conqueror; so that the Roman name remained long the scoff and derision of the barbarians: and this also was added to the severity of his punishment, that although he had an emperor for his son, he found no one to revenge his captivity and most abject and servile state; neither indeed was he ever demanded back. Afterward, when he had finished this shameful life under so great dishonour, he was flayed, and his skin, stripped from the flesh, was dyed with vermilion, and placed in the temple of the gods of the barbarians, that the remembrance of a triumph so signal might be perpetuated, and that this spectacle might always be exhibited to our ambassadors, as an admonition to the Romans, that, beholding the spoils of their captived emperor in a Persian temple, they should not place too great confidence in their own strength.

Now since God so punished the sacrilegious, is it not strange that any one should afterward have dared to do, or even to devise, aught against the majesty of the one God, who governs and supports all things?

Chapter VI.

Aurelian might have recollected the fate of the captived emperor, yet, being of a nature outrageous and headstrong, he forgot both *his* sin and its punishment, and by deeds of cruelty irritated the divine wrath. He was not, however, permitted to accomplish what he had devised; for just as he began to give a loose to his rage, he was slain. His bloody edicts had not yet reached the more distant provinces, when he himself lay all bloody on the earth at Cænophrurium in Thrace, assassinated by his familiar friends, who had taken up groundless suspicions against him.

Examples of such a nature, and so numerous, ought to have deterred succeeding tyrants; nevertheless they were not only not dismayed, but, in their misdeeds against God, became more bold and presumptuous.

Chapter VII.

While Diocletian, that author of ill, and deviser of misery, was ruining all things, he could not withhold his insults, not even against God. This man, by avarice partly, and partly by timid counsels, overturned the Roman empire: for he made choice of three persons to share the government with him; and thus, the empire having been quartered, armies were multiplied, and each of the four princes strove to maintain a much more considerable military force than any sole emperor had done in times past. There began to be fewer men who paid taxes than there were who received wages; so that the means of the husbandmen being exhausted by enormous impositions, the farms were abandoned, cultivated grounds became woodland, and universal dismay prevailed. Besides, the provinces were divided into minute portions, and many presidents and a multitude of inferior officers lay heavy on each territory, and almost on each city. There were also many stewards of different degrees, and deputies of presidents. Very few civil causes came before them: but there were condemnations daily, and forfeitures frequently inflicted; taxes on numberless commodities, and those not only often repeated, but perpetual, and, in exacting them, intolerable wrongs.

Whatever was laid on for the maintenance of the soldiery might have been endured; but Diocletian, through his insatiable avarice, would never allow the sums of money in his treasury to be diminished: he was constantly heaping together extraordinary aids and free gifts, that his original hoards might remain untouched and inviolable. He also, when by various extortions he had made all things exceedingly dear, attempted by an ordinance to limit their prices. Then much blood was shed for the veriest trifles; men were afraid to expose aught to sale, and the scarcity became more excessive and grievous than ever, until, in the end, the ordinance, after having proved destructive to multitudes, was from mere necessity abrogated. To this there were added a certain endless passion for building, and, on that account, endless exactions from the provinces for furnishing wages to labourers and artificers, and supplying carriages and whatever else was requisite to the works which he projected. *Here* public halls, *there* a circus, *here* a mint, and *there* a workhouse for making implements of war; in one place an habitation for his empress, and in another for his daughter. Presently great part of the city was quitted, and all men removed with their wives and children, as from a town taken by enemies; and when those buildings were completed, to the destruction of whole provinces, he said, " They are not right, let them be done on another plan." Then they were to be pulled down, or altered, to undergo perhaps a future demolition. By such folly was he continually endeavouring to equal Nicomedia with the city Rome in magnificence.

I omit mentioning how many perished on account of their possessions or wealth; for such evils were exceedingly frequent, and through their frequency appeared almost lawful. But this was peculiar to him, that whenever he saw a field remarkably well cultivated, or a house of uncommon elegance, a false accusation and a capital punishment were straightway prepared against the proprietor; so that it seemed as if Diocletian could not be guilty of rapine without also shedding blood.

CHAPTER VIII.

What was the character of his brother in empire, Maximian, called *Herculius?* Not unlike to that of Diocletian; and, indeed, to render their friendship so close and faithful as it was, there must have been in them a sameness of inclinations and purposes, a corresponding will and unanimity in judgment. Herein alone they were different, that Diocletian was more avaricious and less resolute, and that Maximian, with less avarice, had a bolder spirit, prone not to good, but to evil. For while he possessed Italy, itself the chief seat of empire, and while other very opulent provinces, such as Africa and Spain, were near at hand, he took little care to preserve those treasures which he had such fair opportunities of amassing. Whenever he stood in need of more, the richest senators were presently charged, by suborned evidences, as guilty of aspiring to the empire; so that the chief luminaries of the senate were daily extinguished. And thus the treasury, delighting in blood, overflowed with ill-gotten wealth.

Add to all this the incontinency of that pestilent wretch, not only in debauching males, which is hateful and abominable, but also in the violation of the daughters of the principal men of the state; for wherever he journeyed, virgins were suddenly torn from the presence of their parents. In such enormities he placed his supreme delight, and to indulge to the utmost his lust and flagitious desires was in his judgment the felicity of his reign.

I pass over Constantius, a prince unlike the others, and worthy to have had the sole government of the empire.

CHAPTER IX.

But the other Maximian (Galerius), chosen by Diocletian for his son-in-law, was worse, not only than those two princes whom our own times have experienced, but worse than all the bad princes of former days. In this wild beast there dwelt a native barbarity and a savageness foreign to Roman blood; and no wonder, for his mother was born beyond the Danube, and it was an inroad of the Carpi that obliged her to cross over and take refuge in New Dacia. The form of Galerius corresponded with his manners. Of stature tall, full of flesh, and swollen to a horrible bulk of corpulency; by his speech, gestures, and looks, he made himself a terror to all that came near him. His father-in-law, too, dreaded him excessively. The cause was this. Narseus, king of the Persians, emulating the example set him by his grandfather Sapores, assembled a great army, and aimed at becoming master of the eastern provinces of the Roman empire. Diocletian, apt to be low-spirited and timorous in every commotion, and fearing a fate like that of Valerian, would not in person encounter Narseus; but he sent Galerius by the way of Armenia, while he himself halted in the eastern provinces, and anxiously watched the event. It is a custom amongst the barbarians to take everything that belongs to them into the field. Galerius laid an ambush for them, and easily overthrew men embarrassed with the multitude of their followers and with their baggage. Having put Narseus to flight, and returned with much spoil, his own pride and Diocletian's fears were greatly increased. For after this victory he rose to such a pitch of haughtiness as to reject the appellation of Cæsar; and when he heard that appellation in letters addressed to him, he cried out, with a stern look and terrible voice, "How long am I to be *Cæsar?*" Then he began to act extravagantly, insomuch that, as if he had been a second Romulus, he wished to pass for and to be called the offspring of Mars; and that he might appear the issue of a divinity, he was willing that his mother Romula should be dishonoured with the name of adulteress. But, not to confound the chronological order of events, I delay the recital of his actions; for indeed afterwards, when Galerius got the title of emperor, his father-in-law having been divested of the imperial purple, he became altogether outrageous, and of unbounded arrogance.

While by such a conduct, and with such associates, Diocles— for *that* was the name of Diocletian before he attained sovereignty—occupied himself in subverting the commonweal, there was no evil which his crimes did not deserve: nevertheless he reigned most prosperously, as long as he forbore to defile his hands with the blood of the just; and what cause he had for persecuting them, I come now to explain.

CHAPTER X.

Diocletian, as being of a timorous disposition, was a searcher into futurity, and during his abode in the East he began to slay victims, that from their livers he might obtain a prognostic of events; and while he sacrificed, some attendants of his, who were Christians, stood by, and they put the *immortal sign* on their foreheads. At this the demons were chased away, and the holy rites interrupted. The soothsayers trembled, unable to investigate the wonted marks on the entrails of the victims. They frequently repeated the sacrifices, as if the former had been unpropitious; but the victims, slain from time to time, afforded no tokens for divination. At length Tages, the chief of the soothsayers, either from guess or from his own observation, said, "There are profane persons here, who obstruct the rites." Then Diocletian, in furious passion, ordered not only all who were assisting at the holy ceremonies, but also all who resided within the palace, to sacrifice, and, in case of their refusal, to be scourged. And further, by letters to the commanding officers, he enjoined that all soldiers should be forced to the like impiety, under pain of being dismissed the service. Thus far his rage proceeded; but at that season he did nothing more against the law and religion of God. After an interval of some time he went to winter in Bithynia; and presently Galerius Cæsar came thither, inflamed with furious resentment, and purposing to excite the inconsiderate old man to carry on that persecution which he had begun against the

Christians. I have learned that the cause of his fury was as follows.

CHAPTER XI.

The mother of Galerius, a woman exceedingly superstitious, was a votary of the gods of the mountains. Being of such a character, she made sacrifices almost every day, and she feasted her servants on the meat offered to idols: but the Christians of her family would not partake of those entertainments; and while she feasted with the Gentiles, they continued in fasting and prayer. On this account she conceived ill-will against the Christians, and by woman-like complaints instigated her son, no less superstitious than herself, to destroy them. So, during the whole winter, Diocletian and Galerius held councils together, at which no one else assisted; and it was the universal opinion that their conferences respected the most momentous affairs of the empire. The old man long opposed the fury of Galerius, and showed how pernicious it would be to raise disturbances throughout the world and to shed so much blood; that the Christians were wont with eagerness to meet death; and that it would be enough for him to exclude persons of that religion from the court and the army. Yet he could not restrain the madness of that obstinate man. He resolved, therefore, to take the opinion of his friends. Now this was a circumstance in the bad disposition of Diocletian, that whenever he determined to do good, he did it without advice, that the praise might be all his own; but whenever he determined to do ill, which he was sensible would be blamed, he called in many advisers, that his own fault might be imputed to other men: and therefore a few civil magistrates, and a few military commanders, were admitted to give their counsel; and the question was put to them according to priority of rank. Some, through personal ill-will towards the Christians, were of opinion that they ought to be cut off, as enemies of the gods and adversaries of the established religious ceremonies. Others thought differently, but, having understood the will of Galerius, they, either from dread of displeasing or from a desire of gratifying him, concurred in the opinion given against the Christians. Yet not even then could the emperor be prevailed upon to yield his assent. He determined above all to consult his gods; and to that end he despatched a soothsayer to inquire of Apollo at Miletus, whose answer was such as might be expected from an enemy of the divine religion. So Diocletian was drawn over from his purpose. But although he could struggle no longer against his friends, and against Cæsar and Apollo, yet still he attempted to observe such moderation as to command the business to be carried through without bloodshed; whereas Galerius would have had all persons burnt alive who refused to sacrifice.

CHAPTER XII.

A fit and auspicious day was sought out for the accomplishment of this undertaking; and the festival of the god Terminus, celebrated on the seventh of the kalends of March (23d February), was chosen, in preference to all others, to terminate, as it were, the Christian religion.

> "That day, the harbinger of death, arose,
> First cause of ill, and long enduring woes;"

of woes which befell not only the Christians, but the whole earth. When that day dawned, in the eighth consulship of Diocletian and seventh of Maximian, suddenly, while it was yet hardly light, the prefect, together with chief commanders, tribunes, and officers of the treasury, came to the church in Nicomedia, and the gates having been forced open, they searched everywhere for an image of the Divinity. The books of the Holy Scriptures were found, and they were committed to the flames; the utensils and furniture of the church were abandoned to pillage: all was rapine, confusion, tumult. That church, situated on rising ground, was within view of the palace; and Diocletian and Galerius stood, as if on a watchtower, disputing long whether it ought to be set on fire. The sentiment of Diocletian prevailed, who dreaded lest, so great a fire being once kindled, some part of the city might be burnt; for there were many and large buildings that surrounded the church. Then the Pretorian Guards came in battle array, with axes and other iron instruments, and having been let loose everywhere, they in a few hours levelled that very lofty edifice with the ground.

CHAPTER XIII.

Next day an edict was published, depriving the Christians of all honours and dignities; ordaining also that, without any distinction of rank or degree, they should be subjected to tortures, and that every suit at law should be received against them; while, on the other hand, they were debarred from being plaintiffs in questions of wrong, adultery, or theft; and, finally, that they should neither be capable of freedom, nor have right of suffrage. A certain person tore down this edict, and cut it in pieces, improperly indeed, but with high spirit, saying in scorn, "These are the triumphs of Goths and Sarmatians." Having been instantly seized and brought to judgment, he was not only tortured, but burnt alive, in the forms of law; and having displayed admirable patience under sufferings, he was consumed to ashes.

Chapter XIV.

But Galerius, not satisfied with the tenor of the edict, sought in another way to gain on the emperor. That he might urge him to excess of cruelty in persecution, he employed private emissaries to set the palace on fire; and some part of it having been burnt, the blame was laid on the Christians as public enemies; and the very appellation of *Christian* grew odious on account of that fire. It was said that the Christians, in concert with the eunuchs, had plotted to destroy the princes; and that both of the princes had well-nigh been burnt alive in their own palace. Diocletian, shrewd and intelligent as he always chose to appear, suspected nothing of the contrivance, but, inflamed with anger, immediately commanded that all his own domestics should be tortured to force a confession of the plot. He sat on his tribunal, and saw innocent men tormented by fire to make discovery. All magistrates, and all who had superintendency in the imperial place, obtained special commissions to administer the torture; and they strove with each other *who* should be first in bringing to light the conspiracy. No circumstances, however, of the fact were detected anywhere; for no one applied the torture to any domestics of Galerius. He himself was ever with Diocletian, constantly urging him, and never allowing the passions of the inconsiderate old man to cool. Then, after an interval of fifteen days, he attempted a second fire; but that was perceived quickly, and extinguished.

Still, however, its author remained unknown. On that very day, Galerius, who in the middle of winter had prepared for his departure, suddenly hurried out of the city, protesting that he fled to escape being burnt alive.

CHAPTER XV.

And now Diocletian raged, not only against his own domestics, but indiscriminately against all; and he began by forcing his daughter Valeria and his wife Prisca to be polluted by sacrificing. Eunuchs, once the most powerful, and who had chief authority at court and with the emperor, were slain. Presbyters and other officers of the Church were seized, without evidence by witnesses or confession, condemned, and together with their families led to execution. In burning alive, no distinction of sex or age was regarded; and because of their great multitude, they were not burnt one after another, but a herd of them were encircled with the same fire; and servants, having millstones tied about their necks, were cast into the sea. Nor was the persecution less grievous on the rest of the people of God; for the judges, dispersed through all the temples, sought to compel every one to sacrifice. The prisons were crowded; tortures, hitherto unheard of, were invented; and lest justice should be inadvertently administered to a Christian, altars were placed in the courts of justice, hard by the tribunal, that every litigant might offer incense before his cause could be heard. Thus judges were no otherwise approached than divinities. Mandates also had gone to Maximian Herculius and Constantius, requiring their concurrence in the execution of the edicts; for in matters even of such mighty importance their opinion was never once asked. Herculius, a person of no merciful temper, yielded ready obedience, and enforced the edicts throughout his dominions of Italy. Constantius, on the other hand, lest he should have seemed to dissent from the injunctions of his superiors, permitted the demolition of churches,—mere walls, and capable of being built up again,— but he preserved entire that true temple of God, which is the human body.

CHAPTER XVI.

Thus was all the earth afflicted; and from east to west,

except in the territories of Gaul, three ravenous wild beasts continued to rage.

> "Had I a hundred mouths, a hundred tongues,
> A voice of brass, and adamantine lungs,
> Not half the dreadful scene could I disclose,"

or recount the punishments inflicted by the rulers in every province on religious and innocent men.

But what need of a particular recital of those things, especially to you, my best beloved Donatus, who above all others was exposed to the storm of that violent persecution? For when you had fallen into the hands of the prefect Flaccinian, no puny murderer, and afterwards of Hierocles, who from a deputy became president of Bithynia, the author and adviser of the persecution, and last of all into the hands of his successor Priscillian, you displayed to mankind a pattern of invincible magnanimity. Having been nine times exposed to racks and diversified torments, nine times by a glorious profession of your faith you foiled the adversary; in nine combats you subdued the devil and his chosen soldiers; and by nine victories you triumphed over this world and its terrors. How pleasing the spectacle to God, when He beheld you a conqueror, yoking in your chariot not white horses, or enormous elephants, but those very men who had led captive the nations! After this sort to lord it over the lords of the earth is triumph indeed! Now, by your valour were they conquered, when you set at defiance their flagitious edicts, and, through stedfast faith and the fortitude of your soul, you routed all the vain terrors of tyrannical authority. Against you neither scourges, nor iron claws, nor fire, nor sword, nor various kinds of torture, availed aught; and no violence could bereave you of your fidelity and persevering resolution. This it is to be a disciple of God, and this it is to be a soldier of Christ; a soldier whom no enemy can dislodge, or wolf snatch, from the heavenly camp; no artifice ensnare, or pain of body subdue, or torments overthrow. At length, after those nine glorious combats, in which the devil was vanquished by you, he dared not to enter the lists again with one whom, by repeated trials, he had found unconquerable; and he abstained from challenging you any more, lest you should have laid hold on the garland of victory already stretched out to you; an unfading garland, which, although you have not at present received it, is laid up in the kingdom of the Lord for your virtue and deserts. But let us now return to the course of our narrative.

CHAPTER XVII.

The wicked plan having been carried into execution, Diocletian, whom prosperity had now abandoned, set out instantly for Rome, *there* to celebrate the commencement of the twentieth year of his reign. That solemnity was performed on the twelfth of the kalends of December (20th November); and suddenly the emperor, unable to bear the Roman freedom of speech, peevishly and impatiently burst away from the city. The kalends of January (1st of January) approached, at which day the consulship, for the ninth time, was to be offered to him; yet, rather than continue thirteen days longer in Rome, he chose that his first appearance as consul should be at Ravenna. Having, however, begun his journey in winter, amidst intense cold and incessant rains, he contracted a slight but lingering disease: it harassed him without intermission, so that he was obliged for the most part to be carried in a litter. Then, at the close of summer, he made a circuit along the banks of the Danube, and so came to Nicomedia. His disease had now become more grievous and oppressing; yet he caused himself to be brought out, in order to dedicate that circus which, at the conclusion of the twentieth year of his reign, he had erected. Immediately he grew so languid and feeble, that prayers for his life were put up to all the gods. Then suddenly, on the ides of December (13th December), there was heard in the palace sorrow, and weeping, and lamentation, and the courtiers ran to and fro; there was silence throughout the city, and a report went of the death, and even of the burial, of Diocletian: but early on the morrow it was suddenly rumoured that he still lived. At this the countenance of his domestics and courtiers changed from melancholy to gay. Nevertheless there were who suspected his death to be kept secret until the arrival of Galerius Cæsar, lest in the meanwhile the soldiery should attempt some change in the government; and this suspicion grew so universal, that no one would believe the emperor alive, until, on the kalends of March (1st March), he appeared in public, but so wan, his illness having lasted almost a year, as hardly to be known again. The fit of stupor, resembling death, happened on the ides of December; and although he in some measure recovered, yet he never attained to perfect health again, for he became disordered in his judgment, being at certain times insane and at others of sound mind.

Chapter XVIII.

Within a few days Galerius Cæsar arrived, not to congratulate his father-in-law on the re-establishment of his health, but to force him to resign the empire. Already he had urged Maximian Herculius to the like purpose, and by the alarm of civil wars terrified the old man into compliance; and he now assailed Diocletian. At first, in gentle and friendly terms, he said that age and growing infirmities disabled Diocletian for the charge of the commonweal, and that he had need to give himself some repose after his labours. Galerius, in confirmation of his argument, produced the example of Nerva, who laid the weight of empire on Trajan.

But Diocletian made answer, that it was unfit for one who had held a rank, eminent above all others and conspicuous, to sink into the obscurity of a low station; neither indeed was it safe, because in the course of so long a reign he must unavoidably have made many enemies. That the case of Nerva was very different: he, after having reigned a single year, felt himself, either from age or from inexperience in business, unequal to affairs so momentous, and therefore threw aside the helm of government, and returned to that private life in which he had already grown old. But Diocletian added, that if Galerius wished for the title of emperor, there was nothing to hinder its being conferred on him and Constantius, as well as on Maximian Herculius.

Galerius, whose imagination already grasped at the whole empire, saw that little but an unsubstantial name would accrue to him from this proposal, and therefore replied that the settlement made by Diocletian himself ought to be inviolable; a settlement which provided that there should be two of higher rank vested with supreme power, and two others of inferior, to assist them. Easily might concord be preserved between *two* equals, never amongst *four;* that he, if Diocletian would not resign, must consult his own interests, so as to remain no longer in an inferior rank, and the last of that rank; that for fifteen years past he had been confined, as an exile, to Illyricum and the banks of the Danube, perpetually struggling against barbarous nations, while others, at their ease, governed dominions more extensive than his, and better civilised.

Diocletian already knew, by letters from Maximian Herculius, all that Galerius had spoken at their conference, and also that he was augmenting his army; and now, on hearing his discourse, the spiritless old man burst into tears, and said, "Be it as you will."

It remained to choose *Cæsars* by common consent. "But," said Galerius, "why ask the advice of Maximian and Constantius, since they must needs acquiesce in whatever we do?"—"Certainly they will," replied Diocletian, "for we must elect their sons."

Now Maximian Herculius had a son, Maxentius, married to the daughter of Galerius, a man of bad and mischievous dispositions, and so proud and stubborn withal, that he would never pay the wonted obeisance either to his father or father-in-law, and on that account he was hated by them both. Constantius also had a son, Constantine, a young man of very great worth, and well meriting the high station of *Cæsar*. The distinguished comeliness of his figure, his strict attention to all military duties, his virtuous demeanour and singular affability, had endeared him to the troops, and made him the choice of every individual. He was then at court, having long before been created by Diocletian a tribune of the first order.

"What is to be done?" said Galerius, "for *that* Maxentius deserves not the office. He who, while yet a private man, has treated me with contumely, how will he act when once he obtains power?"—"But Constantine is amiable, and will so rule as hereafter, in the opinion of mankind, to surpass the mild virtues of his father."—"Be it so, if my inclinations and judgment are to be disregarded. Men ought to be appointed who are at my disposal, who will dread me, and never do anything unless by my orders."—"Whom then shall we appoint?" —"Severus."—"How! that dancer, that habitual drunkard, who turns night into day, and day into night?"—"He deserves the office, for he has approved himself a faithful paymaster and purveyor of the army; and, indeed, I have already despatched him to receive the purple from the hands of Maximian."—"Well, I consent; but whom else do you suggest?"— "Him," said Galerius, pointing out Daia, a young man, half-barbarian. Now Galerius had lately bestowed part of his own name on that youth, and called him *Maximin*, in like manner as Diocletian formerly bestowed on Galerius the name of *Maximian*, for the omen's sake, because Maximian Herculius had served him with unshaken fidelity.—"Who is that you present?"—"A kinsman of mine."—"Alas!" said Diocletian, heaving a deep sigh, "you do not propose men fit for the charge of public affairs!"—"I have tried them."—"Then do *you* look to it, who are about to assume the administration of the empire: as for *me*, while I continued emperor, long and diligent have been my labours in providing for the security of the commonweal; and now, should anything disastrous ensue, the blame will not be mine."

Chapter XIX.

Matters having been thus concerted, Diocletian and Galerius went in procession to publish the nomination of *Cæsars*. Every one looked at Constantine; for there was no doubt that the choice would fall on him. The troops present, as well as the chief soldiers of the other legions, who had been summoned to the solemnity, fixed their eyes on Constantine, exulted in the hope of his approaching election, and occupied themselves in prayers for his prosperity. Near three miles from Nicomedia there is an eminence, on the summit of which Galerius formerly received the purple; and *there* a pillar, with the statue of Jupiter, was placed. Thither the procession went. An assembly of the soldiers was called. Diocletian, with tears, harangued them, and said that he was become infirm, that he needed repose after his fatigues, and that he would resign the empire into hands more vigorous and able, and at the same time appoint new *Cæsars*. The spectators, with the utmost earnestness, waited for the nomination. Suddenly he declared that the *Cæsars* were Severus and Maximin. The amazement was universal. Constantine stood near in public view, and men began to question amongst themselves whether his name too had not been changed into *Maximin;* when, in the sight of all, Galerius, stretching back his hand, put Constantine aside, and drew Daia forward, and, having divested him of the garb of a private person, set him in the most conspicuous place. All men wondered who he could be, and from whence he came; but none ventured to interpose or move objections, so confounded were their minds at the strange and unlooked-for event. Diocletian took off his purple robe, put it on Daia, and resumed his own original name of Diocles. He descended from the tribunal, and passed through Nicomedia in a chariot; and then this old emperor, like a veteran soldier freed from military service, was dismissed into his own country: while Daia, lately taken from the tending of cattle in forests to serve as a common soldier, immediately made one of the life-guard, presently a tribune, and next day *Cæsar*, obtained authority to trample under foot and oppress the empire of the East; a person ignorant alike of war and of civil affairs, and from a herdsman become the leader of armies.

CHAPTER XX.

Galerius having effected the expulsion of the two old men, began to consider himself alone as the sovereign of the Roman empire. Necessity had required the appointment of Constantius to the first rank; but Galerius made small account of one who was of an easy temper, and of health declining and precarious. He looked for the speedy death of Constantius. And although that prince should recover, it seemed not difficult to force him to put off the imperial purple; for what else could he do, if pressed by his three colleagues to abdicate? Galerius had Licinius ever about his person, his old and intimate acquaintance, and his earliest companion in arms, whose counsels he used in the management of all affairs; yet he would not nominate Licinius to the dignity of *Cæsar*, with the title of *son*, for he purposed to nominate him, in the room of Constantius, to the dignity of *emperor*, with the title of *brother*, while he himself might hold sovereign authority, and rule over the whole globe with unbounded licence. After that, he meant to have solemnized the *vicennial* festival; to have conferred on his son Candidianus, then a boy of nine years of age, the office of *Cæsar;* and, in conclusion, to have resigned, as Diocletian had done. And thus, Licinius and Severus being emperors, and Maximin and Candidianus in the next station of *Cæsars*, he fancied that, environed as it were by an impregnable wall, he should lead an old age of security and peace. Such were his projects; but God, whom he had made his adversary, frustrated all those imaginations.

Chapter XXI.

Having thus attained to the highest power, he bent his mind to afflict that empire into which he had opened his way. It is the manner and practice of the Persians for the people to yield themselves slaves to their kings, and for the kings to treat their people as slaves. This flagitious man, from the time of his victories over the Persians, was not ashamed incessantly to extol such an institution, and he resolved to establish it in the Roman dominions; and because he could not do this by an express law, he so acted, in imitation of the Persian kings, as to bereave men of their liberties. He first of all degraded those whom he meant to punish; and then not only were inferior magistrates put to the torture by him, but also the chief men in cities, and persons of the most eminent rank, and this too in matters of little moment, and in civil questions. Crucifixion was the punishment ready prepared in capital cases; and for lesser crimes, fetters. Matrons of honourable station were dragged into workhouses; and when any man was to be scourged, there were four posts fixed in the ground, and to them he was tied, after a manner unknown in the chastisement of slaves. What shall I say of his apartment for sport, and of his favourite diversions? He kept bears, most resembling himself in fierceness and bulk, whom he had collected together during the course of his reign. As often as he chose to indulge his humour, he ordered some particular bear to be brought in, and men were thrown to that savage animal, rather to be swallowed up than devoured; and when their limbs were torn asunder, he laughed with excessive complacency: nor did he ever sup without being spectator of the effusion of human blood. Men of private station were condemned to be burnt alive; and he began this mode of execution by edicts against the Christians, commanding that, after torture and condemnation, they should be burnt at a slow fire. They were fixed to a stake, and first a moderate flame was applied to the soles of their feet, until the muscles, contracted by burning, were torn from the bones; then torches, lighted and put out again, were directed to all the members of their bodies, so that no part had any exemption. Meanwhile cold water was continually poured on their faces, and their mouths moistened, lest, by reason of their jaws being parched, they should expire. At length they did expire, when, after many hours, the violent heat had consumed their skin and penetrated into their intestines. The dead carcases were laid on a funeral pile, and wholly burnt; their bones were gathered, ground to powder, and thrown into the river, or into the sea.

CHAPTER XXII.

And now *that* cruelty, which he had learned in torturing the Christians, became habitual, and he exercised it against all men indiscriminately. He was not wont to inflict the slighter sorts of punishment, as to banish, to imprison, or to send criminals to work in the mines; but to burn, to crucify, to expose to wild beasts, were things done daily, and without hesitation. For smaller offences, those of his own household and his stewards were chastised with lances, instead of rods; and, in great offences, to be beheaded was an indulgence shown to very few; and it seemed as a favour, on account of old services, when one was permitted to die in the easiest manner. But these were slight evils in the government of Galerius, when compared with what follows. For eloquence was extinguished, pleaders cut off, and the learned in the laws either exiled or slain. Useful letters came to be viewed in the same light as magical and forbidden arts; and all who possessed them were trampled upon and execrated, as if they had been hostile to government, and public enemies. Law was dissolved, and unbounded licence permitted to judges,—to judges chosen from amongst the soldiery, rude and illiterate men, and let loose upon the provinces, without assessors to guide or control them.

CHAPTER XXIII.

But that which gave rise to public and universal calamity, was the tax imposed at once on each province and city. Surveyors having been spread abroad, and occupied in a general and severe scrutiny, horrible scenes were exhibited, like the outrages of victorious enemies, and the wretched state of captives. Each spot of ground was measured, vines and fruit-trees numbered, lists taken of animals of every kind, and a capitation-roll made up. In cities, the common people, whether residing within or without the walls, were assembled, the market-places filled with crowds of families, all attended with their children and slaves, the noise of torture and scourges resounded, sons were hung on the rack to force discovery of the effects of their fathers, the most trusty slaves compelled by pain to bear witness against their masters, and wives to bear witness against their husbands. In default of all other evidence, men were tortured to speak against themselves; and no sooner did agony oblige them to acknowledge what they had not, but those imaginary effects were noted down in the lists. Neither youth, nor old age, nor sickness, afforded any exemption. The diseased and the infirm were carried in; the age of each was estimated; and, that the capitation-tax might be enlarged, years were added to the young and struck off from the old. General lamentation and sorrow prevailed. Whatever, by the laws of war, conquerors had done to the conquered, the like did this man presume to perpetrate against Romans and the subjects of Rome, because his forefathers had been made liable to a like tax imposed by the victorious Trajan, as a penalty on the Dacians for their frequent rebellions. After this, money was levied for each head, as if a price had been paid for liberty to exist; yet full trust was not reposed on the same set of surveyors, but others and others still were sent round to make further discoveries; and thus the tributes were redoubled, not because the new surveyors made any fresh discoveries, but because they added at pleasure to the former rates, lest they should seem to have been employed to no purpose. Meanwhile the number of animals decreased, and men died; nevertheless taxes were paid even for the dead, so that no one could either live or cease to live without being subject to impositions. There remained mendicants alone, from whom nothing could be exacted, and whom their misery and wretchedness secured from ill-treatment. But this pious man had compassion on them, and determining that they should remain no longer in indigence, he caused them all to be assembled, put on board vessels, and sunk in the sea. So merciful was he in making provision that under his administration no man should want! And thus, while he took effectual measures that none, under the feigned pretext of poverty, should elude the tax, he put to death a multitude of real wretches, in violation of every law of humanity.

Chapter XXIV.

Already the judgment of God approached him, and that season ensued in which his fortunes began to droop and to waste away. While occupied in the manner that I have described above, he did not set himself to subvert or expel Constantius, but waited for his death, not imagining, however, that it was so nigh. Constantius, having become exceedingly ill, wrote to Galerius, and requested that his son Constantine might be sent to see him. He had made a like request long before, but in vain; for Galerius meant nothing less than to grant it; on the contrary, he laid repeated snares for the life of that young man, because he durst not use open violence, lest he should stir up civil wars against himself, and incur that which he most dreaded, the hate and resentment of the army. Under pretence of manly exercise and recreation, he made him combat with wild beasts: but this device was frustrated; for the power of God protected Constantine, and in the very moment of jeopardy rescued him from the hands of Galerius. At length, Galerius, when he could no longer avoid complying with the request of Constantius, one evening gave Constantine a warrant to depart, and commanded him to set out next morning with the imperial despatches. Galerius meant either to find some pretext for detaining Constantine, or to forward orders to Severus for arresting him on the road. Constantine discerned his purpose; and therefore, after supper, when the emperor was gone to rest, he hasted away, carried off from the principal stages all the horses maintained at the public expense, and escaped. Next day the emperor, having purposely remained in his bed-chamber until noon, ordered Constantine to be called into his presence; but he learnt that Constantine had set out immediately after supper. Outrageous with passion, he ordered horses to be made ready, that Constantine might be pursued and dragged back; and hearing that all the horses had been carried off from the great road, he could hardly refrain from tears. Meanwhile Constantine, journeying with incredible rapidity, reached his father, who was already about to expire. Constantius recommended his son to the soldiers, delivered the sovereign authority into his hands, and then died, as his wish had long been, in peace and quiet.

Constantine Augustus, having assumed the government, made it his first care to restore the Christians to the exercise of their worship and to their God; and so began his administration by re-establishing the holy religion.

CHAPTER XXV.

Some few days after, the portrait of Constantine, adorned with laurels, was brought to the pernicious wild beast (that, by receiving that symbol, he might acknowledge Constantine in the quality of *emperor*). He hesitated long whether to receive it or not, and he was about to commit both the portrait and its bearer to the flames, but his confidants dissuaded him from a resolution so frantic: they admonished him of the danger, and they represented that, if Constantine came with an armed force, all the soldiers, against whose inclination obscure or unknown *Cæsars* had been created, would acknowledge him, and crowd eagerly to his standard. So Galerius, although with the utmost unwillingness, accepted the portrait, and sent the imperial purple to Constantine, that he might seem of his own accord to have received that prince into partnership of power with him. And now his plans were deranged, and he could not, as he intended formerly, admit Licinius, without exceeding the limited number of emperors. But *this* he devised, that Severus, who was more advanced in life, should be named *emperor*, and that Constantine, instead of the title of *emperor*, to which he had been named, should receive that of *Cæsar* in common with Maximin Daia, and so be degraded from the second place to the fourth.

CHAPTER XXVI.

Things seemed to be arranged in some measure to the satisfaction of Galerius, when another alarm was brought, that his son-in-law Maxentius had been declared *emperor* at Rome. The cause was this: Galerius having resolved by permanent taxes to devour the empire, soared to such extravagance in folly, as not to allow an exemption from that thraldom even to the Roman people. Tax-gatherers therefore were appointed to go to Rome, and make out lists of the citizens. Much about the same time Galerius had reduced the Pretorian Guards. There remained at Rome a few soldiers of that body, who, profiting of the opportunity, put some magistrates to death, and, with the acquiescence of the tumultuary populace, clothed Maxentius in the imperial purple. Galerius, on receiving this news, was disturbed at the strangeness of the event, but not much dismayed. He hated Maxentius, and he could not bestow on him the dignity of *Cæsar*, already enjoyed by two (Daia and Constantine); besides, he thought it enough for him to have once bestowed that dignity against his inclination. So he sent for Severus, exhorted him to regain his dominion and sovereignty, and he put under his command that army which Maximian Herculius had formerly commanded, that he might attack Maxentius at Rome. *There* the soldiers of Maximian had been oftentimes received with every sort of luxurious accommodation, so that they were not only interested to preserve the city, but they also longed to fix their residence in it.

Maxentius well knew the enormity of his own offences; and although he had as it were an hereditary claim to the services of his father's army, and might have hoped to draw it over to himself, yet he reflected that this consideration might occur to Galerius also, and induce him to leave Severus in Illyricum, and march in person with his own army against Rome. Under such apprehensions, Maxentius sought to protect himself from the danger that hung over him. To his father, who since his abdication resided in Campania, he sent the purple, and saluted him again *Augustus*. Maximian, given to change, eagerly resumed that purple of which he had unwillingly divested himself. Meanwhile Severus marched on, and with his troops approached the walls of the city. Presently the soldiers raised up their ensigns, abandoned Severus, and yielded themselves to Maxentius, against whom they had come. What remained but flight for Severus, thus deserted? He was encountered by Maximian, who had resumed the imperial dignity. On this he took refuge in Ravenna, and shut himself up *there* with a few soldiers. But perceiving that he was about to be delivered up, he voluntarily surrendered himself, and restored the purple to him from whom he had received it; and after this he obtained no other grace but that of an easy death, for he was compelled to open his veins, and in that gentle manner expired.

Chapter XXVII.

But Maximian, who knew the outrageous temper of Galerius, began to consider that, fired with rage on hearing of the death of Severus, he would march into Italy, and that possibly he might be joined by Daia, and so bring into the field forces too powerful to be resisted. Having therefore fortified Rome, and made diligent provision for a defensive war, Maximian went into Gaul, that he might give his younger daughter Fausta in marriage to Constantine, and thus win over that prince to his interest. Meantime Galerius assembled his troops, invaded Italy, and advanced towards Rome, resolving to extinguish the senate and put the whole people to the sword. But he found everything shut and fortified against him. There was no hope of carrying the place by storm, and to besiege it was an arduous undertaking; for Galerius had not brought with him an army sufficient to invest the walls. Probably, having never seen Rome, he imagined it to be little superior in size to those cities with which he was acquainted. But some of his legions, detesting the wicked enterprise of a father against his son-in-law, and of Romans against Rome, renounced his authority, and carried over their ensigns to the enemy. Already had his remaining soldiers begun to waver, when Galerius, dreading a fate like that of Severus, and having his haughty spirit broken and humiliated, threw himself at the feet of his soldiers, and continued to beseech them that he might not be delivered to the foe, until, by the promise of mighty largesses, he prevailed on them. Then he retreated from Rome, and fled in great disorder. Easily might he have been cut off in his flight, had any one pursued him even with a small body of troops. He was aware of his danger, and allowed his soldiers to disperse themselves, and to plunder and destroy far and wide, that, if there were any pursuers, they might be deprived of all means of subsistence in a ruined country. So the parts of Italy through which that pestilent band took its course were wasted, all things pillaged, matrons forced, virgins violated, parents and husbands compelled by torture to disclose where they had concealed their goods, and their wives and daughters; flocks and herds of cattle were driven off like spoils taken from barbarians. And thus did he, once a Roman emperor, but now the ravager of Italy, retire into his own territories, after having afflicted all men indiscriminately with the calamities of war. Long ago, indeed, and at the very time of his obtaining sovereign power, he had avowed himself the enemy of the Roman name; and he proposed that the empire should be called, not the *Roman*, but the *Dacian* empire.

CHAPTER XXVIII.

After the flight of Galerius, Maximian, having returned from Gaul, held authority in common with his son; but more obedience was yielded to the young man than to the old: for Maxentius had most power, and had been longest in possession of it; and it was to him that Maximian owed on this occasion the imperial dignity. The old man was impatient at being denied the exercise of uncontrolled sovereignty, and envied his son with a childish spirit of rivalry; and therefore he began to consider how he might expel Maxentius and resume his ancient dominion. This appeared easy, because the soldiers who deserted Severus had originally served in his own army. He called an assembly of the people of Rome, and of the soldiers, as if he had been to make an harangue on the calamitous situation of public affairs. After having spoken much on that subject, he stretched his hands towards his son, charged him as author of all ills and prime cause of the calamities of the state, and then tore the purple from his shoulders. Maxentius, thus stripped, leaped headlong from the tribunal, and was received into the arms of the soldiers. Their rage and clamour confounded the unnatural old man, and, like another Tarquin the Proud, he was driven from Rome.

CHAPTER XXIX.

Then Maximian returned into Gaul; and after having made some stay in those quarters, he went to Galerius, the enemy of his son, that they might confer together, as he pretended, about the settlement of the commonweal; but his true purpose was, under colour of reconciliation, to find an opportunity of murdering Galerius, and of seizing his share of the empire, instead of his own, from which he had been everywhere excluded.

Diocles was at the court of Galerius when Maximian arrived; for Galerius, meaning now to invest Licinius with the ensigns of supreme power in the room of Severus, had lately sent for Diocles to be present at the solemnity. So it was performed in presence both of him and of Maximian; and thus there were six who ruled the empire at one and the same time.

Now the designs of Maximian having been frustrated, he took flight, as he had done twice before, and returned into Gaul, with a heart full of wickedness, and intending by treacherous devices to overreach Constantine, who was not only his own son-in-law, but also the child of his son-in-law; and that he might the more successfully deceive, he laid aside the imperial purple. The Franks had taken up arms. Maximian advised the unsuspecting Constantine not to lead all his troops against them, and he said that a few soldiers would suffice to subdue those barbarians. He gave this advice that an army might be left for him to win over to himself, and that Constantine, by reason of his scanty forces, might be overpowered. The young prince believed the advice to be judicious, because given by an aged and experienced commander; and he followed it, because given by a father-in-law. He marched, leaving the most considerable part of his forces behind. Maximian waited a few days; and as soon as, by his calculation, Constantine had entered the territory of the barbarians, he suddenly resumed the imperial purple, seized the public treasures, after his wont made ample donatives to the soldiery, and feigned that such disasters had befallen Constantine as soon after befell himself. Constantine was presently informed of those events, and, by marches astonishingly rapid, he flew back with his army. Maximian, not yet prepared to oppose him, was overpowered at unawares, and the soldiers returned to their duty. Maximian had possessed himself of Marseilles (he fled thither), and shut the gates. Constantine drew nigh, and seeing Maximian on the walls, addressed him in no harsh or hostile language, and demanded what he meant, and what it was that he wanted, and why he had acted in a way so peculiarly unbecoming him. But Maximian from the walls incessantly uttered abuse and curses against Constantine. Then, of a sudden, the gates on the opposite side having been unbarred, the besiegers were admitted into the city. The rebel emperor, an unnatural parent and a perfidious father-in-law, was dragged into the presence of Constantine, heard a recital made of his crimes, was divested of his imperial robe, and, after this reprimand, obtained his life.

CHAPTER XXX.

Maximian, having thus forfeited the respect due to an emperor and a father-in-law, grew impatient at his abased condition, and, emboldened by impunity, formed new plots against Constantine. He addressed himself to his daughter Fausta, and, as well by entreaties as by the soothing of flattery, solicited her to betray her husband. He promised to obtain for her a more honourable alliance than that with Constantine; and he requested her to allow the bed-chamber of the emperor to be left open, and to be slightly guarded. Fausta undertook to do whatever he asked, and instantly revealed the whole to her husband. A plan was laid for detecting Maximian in the very execution of his crime. They placed a base eunuch to be murdered instead of the emperor. At the dead of night Maximian arose, and perceived all things to be favourable for his insidious purpose. There were few soldiers on guard, and these too at some distance from the bed-chamber. However, to prevent suspicion, he accosted them, and said that he had had a dream which he wished to communicate to his son-in-law. He went in armed, slew the eunuch, sprung forth exultingly, and avowed the murder. At that moment Constantine showed himself on the opposite side with a band of soldiers; the dead body was brought out of the bed-chamber; the murderer, taken in the fact, all aghast,

"Stood like a stone, silent and motionless;"

while Constantine upbraided him for his impiety and enormous guilt. At last Maximian obtained leave that the manner of his death should be at his own choice, and he strangled himself.

Thus that mightiest sovereign of Rome, who ruled so long with exceeding glory, and who celebrated his twentieth anniversary, thus that most haughty man had his neck broken, and ended his detestable life by a death base and ignominious.

CHAPTER XXXI.

From Maximian, God, the avenger of religion and of His people, turned his eyes to Galerius, the author of the accursed persecution, that in his punishment also He might manifest the power of His majesty. Galerius, too, was purposing to celebrate his twentieth anniversary; and as, under that pretext, he had, by new taxes payable in gold and silver, oppressed the provinces, so now, that he might recompense them by celebrating the promised festival, he used the like pretext for repeating his oppressions. Who can relate in fit terms the methods used to harass mankind in levying the tax, and especially with regard to corn and the other fruits of the earth? The officers, or rather the executioners, of all the different magistrates, seized on each individual, and would never let go their hold. No man knew to whom he ought to make payment first. There was no dispensation given to those who had nothing; and they were required, under pain of being variously tortured, instantly to pay, notwithstanding their inability. Many guards were set round, no breathing time was granted, or, at any season of the year, the least respite from exactions. Different magistrates, or the officers of different magistrates, frequently contended for the right of levying the tax from the same persons. No threshing-floor without a tax-gatherer, no vintage without a watch, and nought left for the sustenance of the husbandman! That food should be snatched from the mouths of those who had earned it by toil, was grievous: the hope, however, of being afterwards relieved, might have made that grievance supportable; but it was necessary for every one who appeared at the anniversary festival to provide robes of various kinds, and gold and silver besides. And "how (might one have said) shall I furnish myself with those things, O tyrant void of understanding, if you carry off the whole fruits of my ground, and violently seize its expected produce?" Thus, throughout the dominions of Galerius, men were spoiled of their goods, and all was raked together into the imperial treasury, that the emperor might be enabled to perform his vow of celebrating a festival which he was doomed never to celebrate.

CHAPTER XXXII.

Maximin Daia was incensed at the nomination of Licinius to the dignity of *emperor*, and he would no longer be called *Cæsar*, or allow himself to be ranked as third in authority. Galerius, by repeated messages, besought Daia to yield, and to acquiesce in *his* arrangement, to give place to age, and to reverence the grey hairs of Licinius. But Daia became more and more insolent: he urged that, as it was he who first assumed the purple, so, by possession, he had right to priority in rank; and he set at nought the entreaties and the injunctions of Galerius. That brute animal was stung to the quick, and bellowed when the mean creature whom he had made *Cæsar*, in expectation of his thorough obsequiousness, forgot the great favour conferred on him, and impiously withstood the requests and will of his benefactor. Galerius at length, overcome by the obstinacy of Daia, abolished the subordinate title of *Cæsar*, gave to himself and Licinius that of *the Augusti*, and to Daia and Constantine that of *sons of the Augusti*. Daia, some time after, in a letter to Galerius, took occasion to observe, that at the last general muster he had been saluted by his army under the title of *Augustus*. Galerius, vexed and grieved at this, commanded that all the four should have the appellation of *emperor*.

Chapter XXXIII.

And now, when Galerius was in the eighteenth year of his reign, God struck him with an incurable plague. A malignant ulcer formed itself low down in his secret parts, and spread by degrees. The physicians attempted to eradicate it, and healed up the place affected. But the sore, after having been skinned over, broke out again; a vein burst, and the blood flowed in such quantity as to endanger his life. The blood, however, was stopped, although with difficulty. The physicians had to undertake their operations anew, and at length they cicatrized the wound. In consequence of some slight motion of his body, Galerius received a hurt, and the blood streamed more abundantly than before. He grew emaciated, pallid, and feeble, and the bleeding then stanched. The ulcer began to be insensible to the remedies applied, and a gangrene seized all the neighbouring parts. It diffused itself the wider the more the corrupted flesh was cut away, and everything employed as the means of cure served but to aggravate the disease.

"The masters of the healing art withdrew."

Then famous physicians were brought in from all quarters;

but no human means had any success. Apollo and Æsculapius were besought importunately for remedies: Apollo did prescribe, and the distemper augmented. Already approaching to its deadly crisis, it had occupied the lower regions of his body: his bowels came out, and his whole seat putrefied. The luckless physicians, although without hope of overcoming the malady, ceased not to apply fomentations and administer medicines. The humours having been repelled, the distemper attacked his intestines, and worms were generated in his body. The stench was so foul as to pervade not only the palace, but even the whole city; and no wonder, for by that time the passages from his bladder and bowels, having been devoured by the worms, became indiscriminate, and his body, with intolerable anguish, was dissolved into one mass of corruption.

"Stung to the soul, he bellowed with the pain,
So roars the wounded bull."—PITT.

They applied warm flesh of animals to the chief seat of the disease, that the warmth might draw out those minute worms; and accordingly, when the dressings were removed, there issued forth an innumerable swarm: nevertheless the prolific disease had hatched swarms much more abundant to prey upon and consume his intestines. Already, through a complication of distempers, the different parts of his body had lost their natural form: the superior part was dry, meagre, and haggard, and his ghastly-looking skin had settled itself deep amongst his bones; while the inferior, distended like bladders, retained no appearance of joints. These things happened in the course of a complete year; and at length, overcome by calamities, he was obliged to acknowledge God, and he cried aloud, in the intervals of raging pain, that he would re-edify the Church which he had demolished, and make atonement for his misdeeds; and when he was near his end, he published an edict of the tenor following:

CHAPTER XXXIV.

"Amongst our other regulations for the permanent advantage of the commonweal, we have hitherto studied to reduce all things to a conformity with the ancient laws and public discipline of the Romans.

"It has been our aim in an especial manner, that the Christians also, who had abandoned the religion of their forefathers, should return to right opinions. For such wilfulness and folly had, we know not how, taken possession of them, that instead of observing those ancient institutions, which possibly their own forefathers had established, they, through caprice, made laws to themselves, and drew together into different societies many men of widely different persuasions.

"After the publication of our edict, ordaining the Christians to betake themselves to the observance of the ancient institutions, many of them were subdued through the fear of danger, and moreover many of them were exposed to jeopardy; nevertheless, because great numbers still persist in their opinions, and because we have perceived that at present they neither pay reverence and due adoration to the gods, nor yet worship their own God, therefore we, from our wonted clemency in bestowing pardon on all, have judged it fit to extend our indulgence to those men, and to permit them again to be Christians, and to establish the places of their religious assemblies; yet so as that they offend not against good order.

"By another mandate we purpose to signify unto magistrates how they ought herein to demean themselves.

"Wherefore it will be the duty of the Christians, in consequence of this our toleration, to pray to their God for our welfare, and for that of the public, and for their own; that the commonweal may continue safe in every quarter, and that they themselves may live securely in their habitations."

CHAPTER XXXV.

This edict was promulgated at Nicomedia on the day preceding the kalends of May (30th of April), in the eighth consulship of Galerius, and the second of Maximin Daia. Then the prison-gates having been thrown open, you, my best beloved Donatus, together with the other confessors for the faith, were set at liberty from a jail, which had been your residence for six years. Galerius, however, did not, by publication of this edict, obtain the divine forgiveness. In a few days after he was consumed by the horrible disease that had brought on an universal putrefaction. Dying, he recommended his wife and son to Licinius, and delivered them over into his hands. This event was known at Nicomedia before the end of the month (May). His vicennial anniversary was to have been celebrated on the ensuing kalends of March (1st March following).

CHAPTER XXXVI.

Daia, on receiving this news, hasted with relays of horses from the East, to seize the dominions of Galerius, and, while Licinius lingered in Europe, to arrogate to himself all the country as far as the narrow seas of Calcedon. On his entry into Bithynia, he, with the view of acquiring immediate popularity, abolished Galerius' tax, to the great joy of all. Dissension arose between the two emperors, and almost an open war. They stood on the opposite shores with their armies. Peace, however, and amity were established under certain conditions. Licinius and Daia met on the narrow seas, concluded a treaty, and in token of friendship joined hands. Then Daia, believing all things to be in security, returned (to Nicomedia), and was in his new dominions what he had been in Syria and Egypt. First of all, he took away the toleration and general protection granted by Galerius to the Christians, and, for this end, he secretly procured addresses from different cities, requesting that no Christian church might be built within their walls; and thus he meant to make that which was his own choice appear as if extorted from him by importunity. In compliance with those addresses, he introduced a new mode of government in things respecting religion, and for each city he created a high priest, chosen from among the persons of most distinction. The office of those men was to make daily sacrifices to all their gods, and, with the aid of the former priests, to prevent the Christians from erecting churches, or from worshipping God either publicly or in private; and he authorized them to compel the Christians to sacrifice to idols, and, on their refusal, to bring them before the civil magistrate; and, as if this had not been enough, in every province he established a superintendent priest, one of chief eminence in the state; and he commanded that all those priests newly instituted should appear in white habits (that being the most honourable distinction of dress). And as to the Christians, he purposed to follow the course that he had followed in the East, and, affecting the show of clemency, he forbade the slaying of God's servants, but he gave command that they should be mutilated. So the confessors for the faith had their ears and nostrils slit, their hands and feet lopped off, and their eyes dug out of the sockets.

CHAPTER XXXVII.

While occupied in this plan, he received letters from Constantine which deterred him from proceeding in its execution, so for a time he dissembled his purpose; nevertheless any Christian that fell within his power was privily thrown into the sea. Neither did he cease from his custom of sacrificing every day in the palace. It was also an invention of his to cause all animals used for food to be slaughtered, not by cooks, but by priests at the altars; so that nothing was ever served up, unless foretasted, consecrated, and sprinkled with wine, according to the rites of paganism; and whoever was invited to an entertainment must needs have returned from it impure and defiled. In all things else he resembled his preceptor Galerius. For if aught chanced to have been left untouched by Diocles and Maximian, *that* did Daia greedily and shamelessly carry off. And now the granaries of each individual were shut, and all warehouses sealed up, and taxes, not yet due, were levied by anticipation. Hence famine, from neglect of cultivation, and the prices of all things enhanced beyond measure. Herds and flocks were driven from their pasture for the daily sacrifice. By gorging his soldiers with the flesh of sacrifices, he so corrupted them, that they disdained their wonted pittance in corn, and wantonly threw it away. Meanwhile Daia recompensed his body-guards, who were very numerous, with costly raiment and gold medals, made donatives in silver to the common soldiers and recruits, and bestowed every sort of largess on the barbarians who served in his army. As to grants of the property of living persons, which he made to his favourites whenever they chose to ask what belonged to another, I know not whether the same thanks might not be due to him that are given to merciful robbers, who spoil without murdering.

CHAPTER XXXVIII.

But *that* which distinguished his character, and in which he transcended all former emperors, was his desire of debauching women. What else can I call it but a blind and headstrong passion? Yet such epithets feebly express my indignation in reciting his enormities. The magnitude of the guilt overpowers my tongue, and makes it unequal to its office. Eunuchs and panders made search everywhere, and no sooner was any comely face discovered, than husbands and parents were obliged to withdraw. Matrons of quality and virgins were stripped of their robes, and all their limbs were inspected, lest any part should be unworthy of the bed of the emperor. Whenever a woman resisted, death by drowning was inflicted on her; as if, under the reign of this adulterer, chastity had been treason. Some men there were, who, beholding the violation of wives whom for virtue and fidelity they affectionately loved, could not endure their anguish of mind, and so killed themselves. While this monster ruled, it was singular deformity alone which could shield the honour of any female from his savage desires. At length he introduced a custom prohibiting marriage unless with the imperial permission; and he made this an instrument to serve the purposes of his lewdness. After having debauched freeborn maidens, he gave them for wives to his slaves. His courtiers also imitated the example of the emperor, and violated with impunity the beds of their dependants. For who was there to punish such offences? As for the daughters of men of middle rank, any who were inclined took them by force. Ladies of quality, who could not be taken by force, were petitioned for, and obtained from the emperor by way of free gift. Nor could a father oppose this; for the imperial warrant having been once signed, he had no alternative but to die, or to receive some barbarian as his son-in-law. For hardly was there any person in the life-guard except of those people, who, having been driven from their habitations by the Goths in the twentieth year of Diocletian, yielded themselves to Galerius, and entered into his service. It was ill for humankind, that men who had fled from the bondage of barbarians should thus come to lord it over the Romans. Environed by such guards, Daia oppressed and insulted the Eastern empire.

CHAPTER XXXIX.

Now Daia, in gratifying his libidinous desires, made his own will the standard of right; and therefore he would not refrain from soliciting the widow of Galerius, the Empress Valeria, to whom he had lately given the appellation of mother. After the death of her husband, she had repaired to Daia, because she imagined that she might live with more security in his dominions than elsewhere, especially as he was a married man; but the flagitious creature became instantly inflamed with a passion for her. Valeria was still in weeds, the time of her mourning not being yet expired. He sent a message to her proposing marriage, and offering, on her compliance, to put away his wife. She frankly returned an answer such as she alone could dare to do: first, that she would not treat of marriage while she was in weeds, and while the ashes of Galerius, *her* husband, and, by adoption, the father of Daia, were yet warm; next, that he acted impiously, in proposing to divorce a faithful wife to make room for another, whom in her turn he would also cast off; and, lastly, that it was indecent, unexampled, and unlawful for a woman of her title and dignity to engage a second time in wedlock. This bold answer having been reported to Daia, presently his desires changed into rage and furious resentment. He pronounced sentence of forfeiture against the princess, seized her goods, removed her attendants, tortured her eunuchs to death, and banished her and her mother Prisca: but he appointed no particular place for her residence while in banishment; and hence he insultingly expelled her from every abode that she took in the course of her wanderings; and, to complete all, he condemned the ladies who enjoyed most of her friendship and confidence to die on a false accusation of adultery.

Chapter XL.

There was a certain matron of high rank who already had grandchildren by more than one son. Her Valeria loved like a second mother, and Daia suspected that her advice had produced that refusal which Valeria gave to his matrimonial offers; and therefore he charged the president Eratineus to have her put to death in a way that might injure her fame. To her two others, equally noble, were added. One of them, who had a daughter a Vestal virgin at Rome, maintained an intercourse by stealth with the banished Valeria. The other, married to a senator, was intimately connected with the empress. Excellent beauty and virtue proved the cause of their death. They were dragged to the tribunal, not of an upright judge, but of a robber. Neither indeed was there any accuser, until a certain Jew, one charged with other offences, was induced, through hope of pardon, to give false evidence against the innocent. The equitable and vigilant magistrate conducted him out of the city under a guard, lest the populace should have stoned him. This tragedy was acted at Nicæa. The Jew was ordered to the torture till he should speak as he had been instructed, while the torturers by blows prevented the women from speaking in their own defence. The innocent were condemned to die. Then there arose wailing and lamentation, not only of the senator, who attended on his well-deserving consort, but amongst the spectators also, whom this proceeding, scandalous and unheard of, had brought together; and, to prevent the multitude from violently rescuing the condemned persons out of the hands of the executioners, military commanders followed with light infantry and archers. And thus, under a guard of armed soldiers, they were led to punishment. Their domestics having been forced to flee, they would have remained without burial, had not the compassion of friends interred them by stealth. Nor was the promise of pardon made good to the feigned adulterer, for he was fixed to a gibbet, and then he disclosed the whole secret contrivance; and with his last breath he protested to all the beholders that the women died innocent.

Chapter XLI.

But the empress, an exile in some desert region of Syria, secretly informed her father Diocletian of the calamity that had befallen her. He despatched messengers to Daia, requesting that his daughter might be sent to him. He could not prevail. Again and again he entreated; yet she was not sent. At length he employed a relation of his, a military man high in power and authority, to implore Daia by the remembrance of past favours. This messenger, equally unsuccessful in his negotiation as the others, reported to Diocletian that his prayers were vain.

Chapter XLII.

At this time, by command of Constantine, the statues of

Maximian Herculius were thrown down, and his portraits removed; and, as the two old emperors were generally delineated in one piece, the portraits of both were removed at the same time. Thus Diocletian lived to see a disgrace which no former emperor had ever seen, and, under the double load of vexation of spirit and bodily maladies, he resolved to die. Tossing to and fro, with his soul agitated by grief, he could neither eat nor take rest. He sighed, groaned, and wept often, and incessantly threw himself into various postures, now on his couch, and now on the ground. So he, who for twenty years was the most prosperous of emperors, having been cast down into the obscurity of a private station, treated in the most contumelious manner, and compelled to abhor life, became incapable of receiving nourishment, and, worn out with anguish of mind, expired.

CHAPTER XLIII.

Of the adversaries of God there still remained one, whose overthrow and end I am now to relate.

Daia had entertained jealousy and ill-will against Licinius from the time that the preference was given to him by Galerius; and those sentiments still subsisted, notwithstanding the treaty of peace lately concluded between them. When Daia heard that the sister of Constantine was betrothed to Licinius, he apprehended that the two emperors, by contracting this affinity, meant to league against him; so he privily sent ambassadors to Rome, desiring a friendly alliance with Maxentius: he also wrote to him in terms of cordiality. The ambassadors were received courteously, friendship established, and in token of it the effigies of Maxentius and Daia were placed together in public view. Maxentius willingly embraced this, as if it had been an aid from heaven; for he had already declared war against Constantine, as if to revenge the death of his father Maximian. From this appearance of filial piety a suspicion arose, that the detestable old man had but feigned a quarrel with his son that he might have an opportunity to destroy his rivals in power, and so make way for himself and his son to possess the whole empire. This conjecture, however, had no foundation; for his true purpose was to have destroyed his son and the others, and then to have reinstated himself and Diocletian in sovereign authority.

Chapter XLIV.

And now a civil war broke out between Constantine and Maxentius. Although Maxentius kept himself within Rome, because the soothsayers had foretold that if he went out of it he should perish, yet he conducted the military operations by able generals. In forces he exceeded his adversary; for he had not only his father's army, which deserted from Severus, but also his own, which he had lately drawn together out of Mauritania and Italy. They fought, and the troops of Maxentius prevailed. At length Constantine, with steady courage and a mind prepared for every event, led his whole forces to the neighbourhood of Rome, and encamped them opposite to the Milvian bridge. The anniversary of the reign of Maxentius approached, that is, the sixth of the kalends of November (27th October), and the fifth year of his reign was drawing to an end.

Constantine was directed in a dream to cause *the heavenly sign* to be delineated on the shields of his soldiers, and so to proceed to battle. He did as he had been commanded, and he marked on their shields the letter X, with a perpendicular line drawn through it and turned round at the top, thus ☧, being the cipher of CHRIST. Having this sign, his troops stood to arms. The enemies advanced, but without their emperor, and they crossed the bridge. The armies met, and fought with the utmost exertions of valour, and firmly maintained their ground. In the meantime a sedition arose at Rome, and Maxentius was reviled as one who had abandoned all concern for the safety of the commonweal; and suddenly, while he exhibited the Circensian games on the anniversary of his reign, the people cried with one voice, "Constantine cannot be overcome!" Dismayed at this, Maxentius burst from the assembly, and having called some senators together, ordered the Sibylline books to be searched. In them it was found that "on the same day the enemy of the Romans should perish." Led by this response to the hopes of victory, he went to the field. The bridge in his rear was broken down. At sight of that the battle grew hotter. The hand of the Lord prevailed, and the forces of Maxentius were routed. He fled towards the broken bridge; but the multitude pressing on him, he was driven headlong into the Tiber.

This destructive war being ended, Constantine was acknowledged as emperor, with great rejoicings, by the senate and people of Rome. And now he came to know the perfidy of Daia; for he found the letters written to Maxentius, and saw the statues and portraits of the two associates which had been set up together. The senate, in reward of the valour of Constantine, decreed to him the title of *Maximus* (the Greatest), a title which Daia had always arrogated to himself. Daia, when he heard that Constantine was victorious and Rome freed, expressed as much sorrow as if he himself had been vanquished; but afterwards, when he heard of the decree of the senate, he grew outrageous, avowed enmity towards Constantine, and made his title of *the Greatest* a theme of abuse and raillery.

CHAPTER XLV.

Constantine having settled all things at Rome, went to Milan about the beginning of winter. Thither also Licinius came to receive his wife Constantia. When Daia understood that they were busied in solemnizing the nuptials, he moved out of Syria in the depth of a severe winter, and by forced marches he came into Bithynia with an army much impaired; for he lost all his beasts of burden, of whatever kind, in consequence of excessive rains and snow, miry ways, cold and fatigue. Their carcases, scattered about the roads, seemed an emblem of the calamities of the impending war, and the presage of a like destruction that awaited the soldiers. Daia did not halt in his own territories; but immediately crossed the Thracian Bosphorus, and in a hostile manner approached the gates of Byzantium. There was a garrison in the city, established by Licinius to check any invasion that Daia might make. At first Daia attempted to entice the soldiers by the promise of donatives, and then to intimidate them by assault and storm. Yet neither promises nor force availed aught. After eleven days had elapsed, within which time Licinius might have learned the state of the garrison, the soldiers surrendered, not through treachery, but because they were too weak to make a longer resistance. Then Daia moved on to Heraclea (otherwise called Perinthus), and by delays of the like nature before that place lost some days. And now Licinius by expeditious marches had reached Adrianople, but with forces not numerous. Then

Daia, having taken Perinthus by capitulation, and remained there for a short space, moved forwards eighteen miles to the first station. Here his progress was stopped; for Licinius had already occupied the second station, at the distance also of eighteen miles. Licinius, having assembled what forces he could from the neighbouring quarters, advanced towards Daia, rather indeed to retard his operations than with any purpose of fighting, or hope of victory: for Daia had an army of seventy thousand men, while he himself had scarce thirty thousand; for his soldiers being dispersed in various regions, there was not time, on that sudden emergency, to collect all of them together.

CHAPTER XLVI.

The armies thus approaching each other, seemed on the eve of a battle. Then Daia made this vow to Jupiter, that if he obtained victory he would extinguish and utterly efface the name of the Christians. And on the following night an angel of the Lord seemed to stand before Licinius while he was asleep, admonishing him to arise immediately, and with his whole army to put up a prayer to the supreme God, and assuring him that by so doing he should obtain victory. Licinius fancied that, hearing this, he arose, and that his monitor, who was nigh him, directed how he should pray, and in what words. Awaking from sleep, he sent for one of his secretaries, and dictated these words exactly as he had heard them: "Supreme God, we beseech Thee; Holy God, we beseech Thee; unto Thee we commend all right; unto Thee we commend our safety; unto Thee we commend our empire. By Thee we live, by Thee we are victorious and happy. Supreme Holy God, hear our prayers; to Thee we stretch forth our arms. Hear, Holy Supreme God." Many copies were made of these words, and distributed amongst the principal commanders, who were to teach them to the soldiers under their charge. At this all men took fresh courage, in the confidence that victory had been announced to them from heaven. Licinius resolved to give battle on the kalends of May (1st May); for precisely eight years before Daia had received the dignity of *Cæsar*, and Licinius chose that day in hopes that Daia might be vanquished on the anniversary of *his* reign, as Maxentius had been on *his*. Daia, however, purposed to give battle earlier, to fight on the day before those kalends (30th April), and to triumph on the anniversary of his reign. Accounts came that Daia was in motion; the soldiers of Licinius armed themselves, and advanced. A barren and open plain, called *Campus Serenus*, lay beween the two armies. They were now in sight of one another. The soldiers of Licinius placed their shields on the ground, took off their helmets, and, following the example of their leaders, stretched forth their hands towards heaven. Then the emperor uttered the prayer, and they all repeated it after him. The host, doomed to speedy destruction, heard the murmur of the prayers of their adversaries. And now, the ceremony having been thrice performed, the soldiers of Licinius became full of courage, buckled on their helmets again, and resumed their shields. The two emperors advanced to a conference: but Daia could not be brought to peace; for he held Licinius in contempt, and imagined that the soldiers would presently abandon an emperor parsimonious in his donatives, and enter into the service of one liberal even to profusion. And indeed it was on this notion that he began the war. He looked for the voluntary surrender of the armies of Licinius; and, thus reinforced, he meant forthwith to have attacked Constantine.

Chapter XLVII.

So the two armies drew nigh; the trumpets gave the signal; the military ensigns advanced; the troops of Licinius charged. But the enemies, panic-struck, could neither draw their swords nor yet throw their javelins. Daia went about, and, alternately by entreaties and promises, attempted to seduce the soldiers of Licinius. But he was not hearkened to in any quarter, and they drove him back. Then were the troops of Daia slaughtered, none making resistance; and such numerous legions, and forces so mighty, were mowed down by an inferior enemy. No one called to mind his reputation, or former valour, or the honourable rewards which had been conferred on him. The supreme God did so place their necks under the sword of their foes, that they seemed to have entered the field, not as combatants, but as men devoted to death. After great numbers had fallen, Daia perceived that everything went contrary to his hopes; and therefore he threw aside the purple, and having put on the habit of a slave, hasted across the Thracian Bosphorus. One half of his army perished in battle, and the rest either surrendered to the victor or fled; for now that the emperor himself had deserted, there seemed to be no shame in desertion. Before the expiration of the kalends of May, Daia arrived at Nicomedia, although distant one hundred and sixty miles from the field of battle. So in the space of one day and two nights he performed that journey. Having hurried away with his children and wife, and a few officers of his court, he went towards Syria; but having been joined by some troops from those quarters, and having collected together a part of his fugitive forces, he halted in Cappadocia, and then he resumed the imperial garb.

CHAPTER XLVIII.

Not many days after the victory, Licinius, having received part of the soldiers of Daia into his service, and properly distributed them, transported his army into Bithynia, and having made his entry into Nicomedia, he returned thanks to God, through whose aid he had overcome; and on the ides of June (13th June), while he and Constantine were consuls for the third time, he commanded the following edict for the restoration of the Church, directed to the president of the province, to be promulgated:—

"When we, Constantine and Licinius, emperors, had an interview at Milan, and conferred together with respect to the good and security of the commonweal, it seemed to us that, amongst those things that are profitable to mankind in general, the reverence paid to the Divinity merited our first and chief attention, and that it was proper that the Christians and all others should have liberty to follow that mode of religion which to each of them appeared best; so that that God, who is seated in heaven, might be benign and propitious to us, and to every one under our government: and therefore we judged it a salutary measure, and one highly consonant to right reason, that no man should be denied leave of attaching himself to the rites of the Christians, or to whatever other religion his mind directed him, that thus the supreme Divinity, to whose worship we freely devote ourselves, might continue to vouchsafe His favour and beneficence to us. And accordingly we give you to know that, without regard to any provisos in our former orders to you concerning the Christians, all who choose that religion are to be permitted, freely and absolutely, to remain in it, and not to be disturbed any ways, or molested. And we thought fit to be thus special in the things committed to your charge, that you might understand that the indulgence which we have granted in matters of religion to the Christians is ample and unconditional; and perceive at the same time that the open and free exercise of their respective religions is granted to all others, as well as to the Christians: for it befits the well-ordered state and the tranquillity of our times that each individual be allowed, according to his own choice, to worship the Divinity; and we mean not to derogate aught from the honour due to any religion or its votaries. Moreover, with respect to the Christians, we formerly gave certain orders concerning the places appropriated for their religious assemblies; but now we will that all persons who have purchased such places, either from our exchequer or from any one else, do restore them to the Christians, without money demanded or price claimed, and that this be performed peremptorily and unambiguously; and we will also, that they who have obtained any right to such places by form of gift do forthwith restore them to the Christians: reserving always to such persons, who have either purchased for a price, or gratuitously acquired them, to make application to the judge of the district, if they look on themselves as entitled to any equivalent from our beneficence.—All those places are, by your intervention, to be immediately restored to the Christians. And because it appears that, besides the places appropriated to religious worship, the Christians did possess other places, which belonged not to individuals, but to their society in general, that is, to their churches, we comprehend all such within the regulation aforesaid, and we will that you cause them all to be restored to the society or churches, and *that* without hesitation or controversy: Provided always, that the persons making restitution without a price paid shall be at liberty to seek indemnification from our bounty. In furthering all which things for the behoof of the Christians, you are to use your utmost diligence, to the end that our orders be speedily obeyed, and our gracious purpose in securing the public tranquillity promoted. So shall that divine favour which, in affairs of the mightiest importance, we have already experienced, continue to give success to us, and in our successes make the commonweal happy. And that the tenor of this our gracious ordinance may be made known unto all, we will that you cause it by your authority to be published everywhere."

Licinius having issued this ordinance, made an harangue, in which he exhorted the Christians to rebuild their religious edifices.

And thus, from the overthrow of the Church until its restoration, there was a space of ten years and about four months.

Chapter XLIX.

While Licinius pursued with his army, the fugitive tyrant retreated, and again occupied the passes of mount Taurus; and there, by erecting parapets and towers, attempted to stop the march of Licinius. But the victorious troops, by an attack made on the right, broke through all obstacles, and Daia at length fled to Tarsus. *There*, being hard pressed both by sea and land, he despaired of finding any place for refuge; and in the anguish and dismay of his mind, he sought death as the only remedy of those calamities that God had heaped on him. But first he gorged himself with food, and large draughts of wine, as those are wont who believe that they eat and drink for the last time; and so he swallowed poison. However, the force of the poison, repelled by his full stomach, could not immediately operate, but it produced a grievous disease, resembling the pestilence; and his life was prolonged only that his sufferings might be more severe. And now the poison began to rage, and to burn up everything within him, so that he was driven to distraction with the intolerable pain; and during a fit of frenzy, which lasted four days, he gathered handfuls of earth, and greedily devoured it. Having undergone various and excruciating torments, he dashed his forehead against the wall, and his eyes started out of their sockets. And now, become blind, he imagined that he saw God, with His servants arrayed in white robes, sitting in judgment on him. He roared out as men on the rack are wont, and exclaimed that not he, but others, were guilty. In the end, as if he had been racked into confession, he acknowledged his own guilt, and lamentably implored Christ to have mercy upon him. Then, amidst groans, like those of one burnt alive, did he breathe out his guilty soul in the most horrible kind of death.

CHAPTER L.

Thus did God subdue all those who persecuted His name, so that neither root nor branch of them remained; for Licinius, as soon as he was established in sovereign authority, commanded that Valeria should be put to death. Daia, although exasperated against her, never ventured to do this, not even after his discomfiture and flight, and when he knew that his end approached. Licinius commanded that Candidianus also should be put to death. He was the son of Galerius by a concubine, and Valeria, having no children, had adopted him. On the news of the death of Daia, she came in disguise to the court of Licinius, anxious to observe what might befall Candidianus. The youth, presenting himself at Nicomedia, had an outward show of honour paid to him, and, while he suspected no harm, was killed. Hearing of this catastrophe, Valeria immediately fled. The Emperor Severus left a son, Severianus, arrived at man's estate, who accompanied Daia in his flight from the field of battle. Licinius caused him to be condemned and executed, under the pretence that, on the death of Daia, he had intentions of assuming the imperial purple. Long before this time, Candidianus and Severianus, apprehending evil from Licinius, had chosen to remain with Daia; while Valeria favoured Licinius, and was willing to bestow on him that which she had denied to Daia, all rights accruing to her as the widow of Galerius. Licinius also put to death Maximus, the son of Daia, a boy eight years old, and a daughter of Daia, who was seven years old, and had been betrothed to Candidianus. But before their death, their mother had been thrown into the Orontes, in which river she herself had frequently commanded chaste women to be drowned. So, by the unerring and just judgment of God, all the impious received according to the deeds that they had done.

CHAPTER LI.

Valeria, too, who for fifteen months had wandered under a mean garb from province to province, was at length discovered in Thessalonica, was apprehended, together with her mother Prisca, and suffered capital punishment. Both the ladies were conducted to execution; a fall from grandeur which moved the pity of the multitude of beholders that the strange sight had gathered together. They were beheaded, and their bodies cast into the sea. Thus the chaste demeanour of Valeria, and the high rank of her and her mother, proved fatal to both of them.

Chapter LII.

I relate all those things on the authority of well-informed persons; and I thought it proper to commit them to writing exactly as they happened, lest the memory of events so important should perish, and lest any future historian of the persecutors should corrupt the truth, either by suppressing their offences against God, or the judgment of God against them. To His everlasting mercy ought we to render thanks, that, having at length looked on the earth, He deigned to collect again and to restore His flock, partly laid waste by ravenous wolves, and partly scattered abroad, and to extirpate those noxious wild beasts who had trod down its pastures, and destroyed its resting-places. Where now are the surnames of the *Jovii* and the *Herculii*, once so glorious and renowned amongst the nations; surnames insolently assumed at first by Diocles and Maximian, and afterwards transferred to their successors? The Lord has blotted them out and erased them from the earth. Let us therefore with exultation celebrate the triumphs of God, and oftentimes with praises make mention of His victory; let us in our prayers, by night and by day, beseech Him to confirm for ever that peace which, after a warfare of ten years, He has bestowed on His own: and do you, above all others, my best beloved Donatus, who so well deserve to be heard, implore the Lord that it would please Him propitiously and mercifully to continue His pity towards His servants, to protect His people from the machinations and assaults of the devil, and to guard the now flourishing churches in perpetual felicity!

FRAGMENTS

OF

LACTANTIUS FIRMIANUS.

I. FEAR, love, joy, sadness, lust, eager desire, anger, pity, emulation, admiration,—these motions or affections of the mind exist from the beginning of man's creation by the Lord; and they were usefully and advantageously introduced into human nature, that by governing himself by these with method, and in accordance with reason, man may be able, by acting manfully, to exercise those good qualities by means of which he would justly have deserved to receive from the Lord eternal life. For these affections of the mind being restrained within their proper limits, that is, being rightly employed, produce at present good qualities, and in the future eternal rewards. But when they advance[1] beyond their boundaries, that is, when they turn aside to an evil course, then vices and iniquities come forth, and produce everlasting punishments.

Muratorii Antiquit. Ital. med. æv.

II. Within our memory, also, Lactantius speaks of metres,—the pentameter (he says) and the tetrameter.

Maxim. Victorin. de carmine heroico. (Cf. Hieron. *Catal.* c. 80. We have also another treatise, which is entitled "On Grammar.")

III. Firmianus, writing to Probus on the metres of comedies, thus speaks: "For as to the question which you proposed concerning the metres of comedies, I also know that many are of opinion that the plays of Terence in particular have not the metre of Greek comedy,—that is, of Menander, Philemon, and

[1] "Affluentes."

Diphilus, which consist of trimeter verses; for our ancient writers of comedies, in the modulation of their plays, preferred to follow Eupolis, Cratinus, and Aristophanes, as has been before said." That there is a measure—that is, metre[1]—in the plays of Terence and Plautus, and of the other comic and tragic writers, let these declare: Cicero, Scaurus, and Firmianus.

Rufinus, the grammarian, on *Comic Metres*, p. 2712.

IV. We will bring forward the sentiments of our Lactantius, which he expressed in words in his third volume to Probus on this subject. The Gauls, he says, were from ancient times called Galatians, from the whiteness of their body; and thus the Sibyl terms them. And this is what the poet intended to signify when he said, "Gold collars deck their milk-white necks,"[2] when he might have used the word "white." It is plain that from this the province was called Galatia, in which, on their arrival in it, the Gauls united themselves with Greeks, from which circumstance that region was called Gallogræcia, and afterwards Galatia. And it is no wonder if he said this concerning the Galatians, and related that a people of the West, having passed over so great a distance in the middle of the earth, settled in a region of the East.

Hieron. *Commentar. in ep. ad Gal.* l. ii., opp. ed. Vallars. viii. 1, p. 426. (Hieron. *De Viris Illus.* c. 80: we have "four books of epistles to Probus.")

---

[1] μέτρον.   [2] Virg. Æn. viii. 660.

THE PHŒNIX.

BY AN UNCERTAIN AUTHOR.

ATTRIBUTED TO LANCTANTIUS.

THERE is a happy spot, retired[1] in the first East, where the great gate of the eternal pole lies open. It is not, however, situated near to his rising in summer or in winter, but where the sun pours the day from his vernal chariot. There a plain spreads its open tracts; nor does any mound rise, nor hollow valley open[2] itself. But through twice six ells that place rises above the mountains, whose tops are thought to be lofty among us. Here is the grove of the sun; a wood stands planted with many a tree, blooming with the honour of perpetual foliage. When the pole had blazed with the fires of Phaethon, that place was uninjured by the flames; and when the deluge had immersed the world in waves, it rose above the waters of Deucalion. No enfeebling diseases, no sickly old age, nor cruel death, nor harsh fear, approaches hither, nor dreadful crime, nor mad desire of riches, nor Mars, nor fury, burning with the love of slaughter.[3] Bitter grief is absent, and want clothed in rags, and sleepless cares, and violent hunger. No tempest rages there, nor dreadful violence of the wind; nor does the hoar-frost cover the earth with cold dew. No cloud extends its fleecy[4] covering above the plains, nor does the turbid moisture of water fall from on high; but

---

[1] "Remotus." The reference is supposed to be to Arabia, though some think that India is pointed out as the abode of the phœnix.

[2] "Hiat."

[3] "Cædis amore furor." There is another reading, "cedit."

[4] "Vellera," thin fleecy clouds. So Virg. *Georg.* i. 397: "Tenuia nec lanæ per cœlum vellera ferri."

there is a fountain in the middle, which they call by the name of "living;"[1] it is clear, gentle, and abounding with sweet waters, which, bursting forth once during the space of each[2] month, twelve times irrigates all the grove with waters. Here a species of tree, rising with lofty stem, bears mellow fruits not about to fall on the ground. This grove, these woods, a single[3] bird, the phœnix, inhabits,—single, but it lives reproduced by its own death. It obeys and submits[4] to Phœbus, a remarkable attendant. Its parent nature has given it to possess this office. When at its first rising the saffron morn grows red, when it puts to flight the stars with its rosy light, thrice and four times she plunges her body into the sacred waves, thrice and four times she sips water from the living stream.[5] She is raised aloft, and takes her seat on the highest top of the lofty tree, which alone looks down upon the whole grove; and turning herself to the fresh risings of the nascent Phœbus, she awaits his rays and rising beam. And when the sun has thrown back the threshold of the shining gate, and the light gleam[6] of the first light has shone forth, she begins to pour strains of sacred song, and to hail[7] the new light with wondrous voice, which neither the notes of the nightingale[8] nor the flute of the Muses can equal with Cyrrhæan[9] strains. But neither is it thought that the dying swan can imitate it, nor the tuneful strings of the lyre of Mercury. After that Phœbus has brought back his horses to the open heaven,[10] and continually advancing, has displayed[11] his whole orb; she applauds with thrice-repeated flapping of her wings, and having thrice adored

[1] "Vivum."
[2] "Per singula tempora mensum."
[3] "Unica," the only one. It was supposed that only one phœnix lived at one time. So the proverb, "Phœnice rarior."
[4] Birds were considered sacred to peculiar gods; thus the phœnix was held sacred to Phœbus.
[5] "Gurgite."
[6] "Aura." So Virg. Æneid, vi. 204: "Discolor unde auri per ramos aura refulsit."
[7] "Ciere."
[8] "Aëdoniæ voces." The common reading is "Ædoniæ," contrary to the metre.
[9] i.e. strains of Apollo and the Muses, for Cyrrha is at the foot of Parnassus, their favourite haunt.
[10] "Aperta Olympi," when he has mounted above the horizon.
[11] "Protulit."

the fire-bearing head, is silent. And she also distinguishes the
swift hours by sounds not liable to error by day and night: an
overseer[1] of the groves, a venerable priestess of the wood, and
alone admitted to thy secrets, O Phœbus. And when she
has now accomplished the thousand years of her life, and length
of days has rendered her burdensome,[2] in order that she may
renew the age which has glided by, the fates pressing[3] her, she
flees from the beloved couch of the accustomed grove. And
when she has left the sacred places, through a desire of being
born[4] again, then she seeks this world, where death reigns.
Full of years, she directs her swift flight into Syria, to which
Venus herself has given the name of Phœnice;[5] and through
trackless deserts she seeks the retired groves in the place, where
a remote wood lies concealed through the glens. Then she
chooses a lofty palm, with top reaching to the heavens, which
has the pleasing[6] name of phœnix from the bird, and where[7] no
hurtful living creature can break through, or slimy serpent, or
any bird of prey. Then Æolus shuts in the winds in hanging
caverns, lest they should injure the bright[8] air with their blasts,
or lest a cloud collected by the south wind through the empty
sky should remove the rays of the sun, and be a hindrance[9] to
the bird. Afterwards she builds for herself either a nest or a
tomb, for she perishes that she may live; yet she produces
herself. Hence she collects juices and odours, which the
Assyrian gathers from the rich wood, which the wealthy
Arabian gathers; which either the Pygmæan[10] nations, or India
crops, or the Sabæan land produces from its soft bosom. Hence
she heaps together cinnamon and the odour of the far-scented
amomum, and balsams with mixed leaves. Neither the twig of
the mild casia nor of the fragrant acanthus is absent, nor the
tears and rich drop of frankincense. To these she adds tender

[1] "Antistes." [2] "Gravem," *i.e.* a burden to herself.
[3] "Fatis urgentibus;" others read "spatiis vergentibus."
[4] "Studio renascendi."
[5] Venus was worshipped in Syro-Phœnice.
[6] "Gratum;" others read "Graium," Grecian.
[7] "Quâ;" another reading is "quam," that which.
[8] "Purpureum." There may be a reference to the early dawn.
[9] "Obsit."
[10] Some ancient writers place these fabulous people in India, others beyond Arabia.

ears[1] of flourishing spikenard, and joins the too pleasing pastures[2] of myrrh. Immediately she places her body about to be changed on the strewed nest, and her quiet limbs on such[3] a couch. Then with her mouth she scatters juices around and upon her limbs, about to die with her own funeral rites. Then amidst various odours she yields up[4] her life, nor fears the faith of so great a deposit. In the meantime, her body, destroyed by death, which proves the source of life,[5] is hot, and the heat itself produces a flame; and it conceives fire afar off from the light of heaven: it blazes, and is dissolved into burnt ashes. And these ashes collected in death it fuses,[6] as it were, into a mass, and has an effect[7] resembling seed. From this an animal is said to arise without limbs, but the worm is said to be of a milky colour. And it suddenly increases vastly with an imperfectly formed[8] body, and collects itself into the appearance of a well-rounded egg. After this it is formed again, such as its figure was before, and the phœnix, having burst her shell,[9] shoots forth, even as caterpillars[10] in the fields, when they are fastened by a thread to a stone, are wont to be changed into a butterfly. No food is appointed for her in our world, nor does any one make it his business to feed her while unfledged. She sips the delicate[11] ambrosial dews of heavenly nectar which have fallen from the star-bearing pole. She gathers these; with these the bird is nourished in the midst of odours, until she bears a natural form. But when she begins to flourish with early youth, she flies forth now about to return to her native abode. Previously, however, she encloses in an ointment of balsam, and in myrrh and dissolved[12] frankincense, all the remains of her own body, and the bones or ashes, and

---

[1] "Aristas." The word is sometimes applied, as here, to spikenard.

[2] "Et sociat myrrhæ pascua grata nimis;" another reading is, "et sociam myrrhæ vim, Panachaia tuæ."

[3] "In talique toro;" others, "vitalique toro," *i.e.* on a death-bed.

[4] "Commendat." [5] "Genitali," productive; observe the antithesis.

[6] "Conflat."

[7] "Effectum;" others read, "ad fœtum seminis instar habent."

[8] "Cum corpore curto;" others read, "cum tempore certo."

[9] "Ruptis exuviis." The same word is used by Virgil to describe the serpent slipping its skin—"positis exuviis."

[10] "Tineæ."   [11] "Tenues;" others read "teneri."

[12] "Thure soluto."

relics[1] of herself, and with pious mouth brings it into a round form,[2] and carrying this with her feet, she goes to the rising of the sun, and tarrying at the altar, she draws it forth in the sacred temple. She shows and presents herself an object of admiration to the beholder; such great beauty is there, such great honour abounds. In the first place, her colour is like the brilliancy[3] of that which the seeds of the pomegranate when ripe take under the smooth rind;[4] such colour as is contained in the leaves which the poppy produces in the fields, when Flora spreads her garments beneath the blushing sky. Her shoulders and beautiful breasts shine with this covering; with this her head, with this her neck, and the upper parts of her back shine. And her tail is extended, varied with yellow metal, in the spots of which mingled purple blushes. Between her wings there is a bright[5] mark above, as[6] Iris on high is wont to paint a cloud from above. She gleams resplendent with a mingling of the green emerald, and a shining beak[7] of pure horn opens itself. Her eyes are large;[8] you might believe that they were two jacinths;[9] from the middle of which a bright flame shines. An irradiated crown is fitted[10] to the whole of her head, resembling on high the glory of the head of Phœbus.[11] Scales cover her thighs spangled with yellow metal, but a rosy[12] colour paints her claws with honour. Her form is seen to blend the figure of the peacock with that of the painted bird of Phasis.[13] The winged creature which is produced in the lands of the Arabians, whether it be beast or bird, can scarcely equal her magnitude.[14] She is not, however, slow, as birds which

[1] "Exuvias suas." [2] "In formam conglobat."
[3] "Quem croceum." The word is properly used to denote the colour of saffron; it is also applied to other bright colours.
[4] "Sub cortice lævi;" the common reading is "sub sidere cæli."
[5] "Clarum insigne;" others read, "aurum . . . insigneque."
[6] "Ceu;" others read, "seu."
[7] "Gemmea cuspis." Her beak is of horn, but bright and transparent as a gem.
[8] "Ingentes oculi;" others read, "oculos."
[9] "Hyacinthos;" gems of this colour.
[10] "Æquatur." [11] i.e. the rays of the sun.
[12] "Roseus;" others read, "roseo honore."
[13] The pheasant.
[14] "Magniciem." Some take this as denoting the name of a bird, but no such bird is known.

through the greatness of their body have sluggish motions, and a very heavy[1] weight. But she is light and swift, full of royal beauty. Such she always shows herself [2] in the sight of men. Egypt comes hither to such a wondrous[3] sight, and the exulting crowd salutes the rare bird. Immediately they carve her image on the consecrated marble, and mark both the occurrence and the day with a new title. Birds of every kind assemble together; none is mindful of prey, none of fear. Attended by a chorus of birds, she flies through the heaven, and a crowd accompanies her, exulting in the pious duty. But when she has arrived at the regions of pure ether, she presently returns;[4] afterwards she is concealed in her own regions. But oh, bird of happy lot and fate,[5] to whom the god himself granted to be born from herself! Whether it be female, or male, or neither, or both, happy she, who enters into[6] no compacts of Venus. Death is Venus to her; her only pleasure is in death: that she may be born, she desires previously to die. She is an offspring to herself, her own father and heir, her own nurse, and always a foster-child to herself. She is herself indeed, but not the same, since she is herself, and not herself, having gained eternal life by the blessing of death.

[1] "Pergrave pondus;" others read, "per grave pondus," "by reason of the heavy weight."
[2] "Se exhibet;" others read, "se probat."
[3] "Tanti ad miracula visus."
[4] "Inde;" others read, "ille," but the allusion is very obscure.
[5] "Fili," the thread, *i.e.* of fate. [6] "Colit."

A POEM,

BY AN UNCERTAIN AUTHOR,

ON THE PASSION OF THE LORD.

———

WHOEVER you are who approach, and are entering the precincts[1] of the middle of the temple, stop a little and look upon me, who, though innocent, suffered for your crime; lay me up in your mind, keep me in your breast. I am He who, pitying the bitter misfortunes of men, came hither as a messenger[2] of offered peace, and as a full atonement[3] for the fault of men.[4] Here the brightest light from above is restored to the earth; here is the merciful image of safety; here I am a rest to you, the right way, the true redemption, the banner[5] of God, and a memorable sign of fate. It was on account of you and your life that I entered the virgin's womb, was made man, and suffered a dreadful death; nor did I find rest anywhere in the regions of the earth, but everywhere threats, everywhere labours. First of all a wretched dwelling[6] in the land of Judæa was a shelter for me at my birth, and for my mother with me: here first, amidst the outstretched sluggish cattle, dry grass gave me a bed in a narrow stall. I passed my earliest years in the Pharian[7] regions, being an exile in the reign of Herod; and after my return to Judæa I spent the rest of my years, always engaged[8] in fastings, and the extremity of poverty itself, and the lowest circumstances; always by healthful admonitions applying the minds of men to the pursuit of genial upright-

[1] "Limina," the threshold.
[2] "Interpres."
[3] "Venia," remission.
[4] "Communis culpæ."
[5] "Vexillum."
[6] "Magalia."
[7] *i.e.* Egypt.
[8] "Secutus."

ness, uniting with wholesome teaching many evident miracles: on which account impious Jerusalem, harassed by the raging cares of envy and cruel hatred, and blinded by madness, dared to seek for me, though innocent, by deadly punishment, a cruel death on the dreadful cross. And if you yourself wish to discriminate these things more fully,[1] and if it delights you to go through all my groans, and to experience griefs with me, put together[2] the designs and plots, and the impious price of my innocent blood, and the pretended kisses of a disciple,[3] and the insults and strivings of the cruel multitude; and, moreover, the blows, and tongues prepared[4] for accusations. Picture to your mind both the witnesses, and the accursed[5] judgment of the blinded Pilate, and the immense cross pressing my shoulders and wearied back, and my painful steps to a dreadful death. Now survey me from head to foot, deserted as I am, and lifted up afar from my beloved mother. Behold and see my locks clotted with blood, and my blood-stained neck under my very hair, and my head drained[6] with cruel thorns, and pouring down like rain[7] from all sides a stream[8] of blood over my divine face. Survey my compressed and sightless eyes, and my afflicted cheeks; see my parched tongue poisoned with gall, and my countenance pale with death. Behold my hands pierced with nails, and my arms drawn out, and the great wound in my side; see the blood streaming from it, and my perforated[9] feet, and blood-stained limbs. Bend your knee, and with lamentation adore the venerable wood of the cross, and with lowly countenance stooping[10] to the earth, which is wet with innocent blood, sprinkle it with rising tears, and at times[11] bear me and my admonitions in your devoted heart. Follow the footsteps of my life, and while you look upon my torments and cruel death, remembering my innumerable pangs of body and soul, learn to endure hardships,[12] and to watch

---

[1] "Latius," more widely, in greater detail.
[2] "Collige."
[3] "Clientis." The "cliens" is one who puts himself under the protection of a "patronus." Here it is used of a follower.
[4] "Promptas." [5] "Infanda," unspeakable, wicked.
[6] "Haustum." [7] "Pluens." [8] "Vivum cruorem."
[9] "Fossos." [10] "Terram petens."
[11] "Nonnunquam;" others read, "nunquam non," always.
[12] "Adversa."

over your own safety. These memorials,[1] if at any time you find pleasure in thinking over them, if in your mind there is any confidence to bear (anything) like my (sufferings),[2] if the piety due, and gratitude worthy of my labours shall arise, will be incitements[3] to true virtue, and they will be shields against the snares of an enemy, aroused[4] by which you will be safe, and as a conqueror bear off the palm in every contest. If these memorials shall turn away your senses, which are devoted to a perishable[5] world, from the fleeting shadow of earthly beauty, the result will be, that you will not venture,[6] enticed by empty hope, to trust the frail[7] enjoyments of fickle fortune, and to place your hope in the fleeting years of life. But, truly, if you thus regard this perishable world,[8] and through your love of a better country deprive yourself[9] of earthly riches and the enjoyment of present things,[10] the prayers of the pious will bring you up[11] in sacred habits, and in the hope of a happy life, amidst severe punishments, will cherish you with heavenly dew, and feed you with the sweetness of the promised good. Until the great favour of God shall recall your happy[12] soul to the heavenly regions,[13] your body being left after the fates of death. Then freed from all labour, then joyfully beholding the angelic choirs, and the blessed companies of saints in perpetual bliss, it shall reign with me in the happy abode of perpetual peace.

[1] "Monumenta."
[2] "Meorum."
[3] "Stimuli."
[4] "Acer."
[5] "Labilis orbis amicos sensus."
[6] "Auseris," an unusual form.
[7] "Occiduis rebus."
[8] "Ista caduca sæcula."
[9] "Exutum."
[10] "Rerum usus."
[11] "Extollent." The reading is uncertain; some editions have "expolient."
[12] "Purpuream," bright, or shining.
[13] "Sublimes ad auras."

POEM

OF

VENANTIUS HONORIUS[1] CLEMENTIANUS FORTUNATUS,

ON EASTER.

The seasons blush varied with the flowery, fair weather,[2] and the gate of the pole lies open with greater light. His path in the heaven raises the fire-breathing[3] sun higher, who goes forth on his course,[4] and enters the waters of the ocean. Armed with rays traversing the liquid elements, in this[5] brief night he stretches out the day in a circle. The brilliant firmament[6] puts forth its clear countenance, and the bright stars show their joy. The fruitful earth pours forth its gifts with varied increase,[7] when the year has well returned its vernal riches.[8] Soft beds of violets paint the purple plain; the meadows are green with plants,[9] and the plant shines with its leaves. By degrees gleaming brightness of the flowers[10] comes forth; all the herbs smile with their blossoms.[11] The seed being deposited, the corn springs up far and wide[12] in the fields, promising to be able to overcome the hunger of the husbandman. Having deserted its stem, the vine-shoot bewails its joys; the vine gives

---

[1] Venantius Honorius, to whom this poem is ascribed, was an Italian presbyter and poet. In some editions the title is *De Resurrectione*. It was addressed to the bishop Felix.
[2] "Florigero sereno."   [3] "Ignivomus."   [4] "Vagus."
[5] "Hac in nocte brevi." Other editions read, "adhuc nocte brevi."
[6] "Æthera," an unusual form.   [7] "Fœtu;" others read "cultu."
[8] "Cum bene vernales reddidit annus opes." Another reading is, "cum bene vernarit; reddit et annus opes."
[9] "Herbis."   [10] "Stellantia lumina florum."
[11] "Floribus;" another reading is, "arridentque oculis."
[12] "Late;" others read, "lactens," juicy.

water only from the source from which it is wont to give wine. The swelling bud, rising with tender down from the back of its mother, prepares its bosom for bringing forth. Its foliage[1] having been torn off in the wintry season, the verdant grove now renews its leafy shelter. Mingled together, the willow, the fir, the hazel, the osier,[2] the elm, the maple, the walnut, each tree applauds, delightful with its leaves. Hence the bee, about to construct its comb, leaving the hive, humming over the flowers, carries off honey with its leg. The bird which, having closed its song, was dumb, sluggish with the wintry cold, returns to its strains. Hence Philomela attunes her notes with her own instruments,[3] and the air becomes sweeter with the re-echoed melody. Behold, the favour of the reviving world bears witness that all gifts have returned together with its Lord. For in honour of Christ rising triumphant after (His descent to) the gloomy Tartarus, the grove on every side with its leaves (expresses approval), the plants with their flowers express approval.[4] The light, the heaven, the fields, and the sea duly praise the God ascending above the stars, having crushed the laws of hell. Behold, He who was crucified reigns as God over all things, and all created objects offer prayer to their Creator. Hail, festive day, to be reverenced throughout the world,[5] on which God has conquered hell, and gains the stars! The changes of the year and of the months, the bounteous light of the days, the splendour of the hours, all things with voice applaud.[6] Hence, in honour of you, the wood with its foliage applauds; hence the vine, with its silent shoot, gives thanks. Hence the thickets now resound with the whisper of birds; amidst these the sparrow sings with exuberant[7] love.

[1] "Foliorum crine revulso;" others read, "refuso."
[2] "Siler," supposed to be the osier, but the notices of the tree are too scanty to enable us to identify it. See Conington, *Virg. Georg.* ii. 12.
[3] "Suis attemperat organa cannis." "Canna" seems to be used for "gutturis canna," the windpipe; "organum," often used for a musical instrument.
[4] "Favent." [5] "Toto venerabilis ævo."
[6] "Mobilitas anni, mensum, lux alma dierum
Horarum splendor, stridula cuncta favent."
There are great variations in the readings of this passage. Some read
"Nobilitas anni, mensum decus, alma dierum,
Horarum splendor, scriptula, puncta fovent."
[7] "Nimio;" another reading is, "minimus."

O Christ, Thou Saviour of the world, merciful Creator and Redeemer, the only offspring from the Godhead of the Father, flowing in an indescribable[1] manner from the heart of Thy Parent, Thou self-existing Word, and powerful from the mouth of Thy Father, equal to Him, of one mind with Him, His fellow, coeval with the Father, from whom at first[2] the world derived its origin! Thou dost suspend the firmament,[3] Thou heapest together the soil, Thou dost pour forth the seas, by whose[4] government all things which are fixed in their places flourish. Who seeing that the human race was plunged in the depth[5] (of misery), that Thou mightest rescue man, didst Thyself also become man: nor wert Thou willing only to be born with a body,[6] but Thou becamest flesh, which endured to be born and to die. Thou dost undergo[7] funeral obsequies, Thyself the author of life and (framer) of the world, Thou dost enter[8] the path of death, in giving the aid of salvation. The gloomy chains of the infernal law yielded, and chaos feared to be pressed by the presence[9] of the light. Darkness perishes, put to flight by the brightness of Christ; the thick pall of eternal[10] night falls. But restore the promised[11] pledge, I pray Thee, O power benign! The third day has returned; arise, my buried One; it is not becoming that Thy limbs should lie in the lowly sepulchre, nor that worthless stones should press (that which is) the ransom[12] of the world. It is unworthy that a stone should shut in with a confining[13] rock, and cover Him in whose fist[14] all things are enclosed. Take away the linen clothes, I pray; leave the napkins in the tomb: Thou art sufficient for us, and without Thee there is nothing. Release the chained shades of the infernal prison, and recall to the upper regions[15] whatever

---

[1] "Irrecitabiliter." [2] "Principe." [3] "Æthera."
[4] "Quo moderante;" others read, "quæ moderata."
[5] "Profundo."
[6] "Cum corpore;" others read, "nostro e corpore nasci."
[7] "Pateris vitæ auctor;" others have "patris novus auctor."
[8] "Intras;" others, "intra." [9] "Luminis ore."
[10] "Æternæ;" another reading is, "et tetræ."
[11] "Pollicitam;" others have "sollicitam." [12] "Pretium mundi."
[13] "Rupe vetante."
[14] "Pugillo." Thus Prov. xxx. 4: "Who hath gathered the wind in His fists?"
[15] "Revoca sursum."

sinks to the lowest depths. Give back Thy face, that the world may see the light; give back the day which flees from us at Thy death. But returning, O holy conqueror! Thou didst altogether fill the heaven![1] Tartarus lies depressed, nor retains its rights. The ruler of the lower regions, insatiably opening his hollow jaws, who has always been a spoiler, becomes[2] a prey to Thee. Thou rescuest an innumerable people from the prison of death, and they follow in freedom to the place whither their leader[3] approaches. The fierce monster in alarm vomits forth the multitude whom he had swallowed up, and the Lamb[4] withdraws the sheep from the jaw of the wolf. Hence re-seeking the tomb from the lower regions,[5] having resumed Thy flesh, as a warrior Thou carriest back ample trophies to the heavens. Those whom chaos held in punishment[6] he[7] has now restored; and those whom death might seek, a new life holds. Oh, sacred King, behold a great part of Thy triumph shines forth, when the sacred laver blesses pure souls! A host, clad in white,[8] come forth from the bright waves, and cleanse their old[9] fault in a new stream. The white garment also designates bright souls, and the shepherd has enjoyments from the snow-white flock. The priest Felix is added sharing[10] in this reward, who wishes to give double talents to his Lord. Drawing those who wander in Gentile error to better things, that a beast of prey may not carry them away, He guards the fold of God. Those whom guilty Eve had before infected, He now restores, fed[11] with abundant milk at the bosom of the Church. By cultivating rustic hearts with mild conversations, a crop is produced from a briar by the bounty of Felix. The Saxon, a fierce nation, living as it were after the manner of wild beasts, when you, O sacred One! apply a remedy, the beast of prey resembles[12] the sheep. About to remain with you through an age with the return[13] of a hundred-

---

[1] "Olympum;" others read, "in orbem," returning to the world.
[2] "Fit;" others read, "sit."   [3] "Auctor."
[4] *i. e.* "the Lamb of God."   [5] "Post tartara."
[6] "Pœnale."   [7] "Iste;" another reading is, "in te."
[8] An allusion to the white garments in which the newly baptized were arrayed.
[9] "Vetus vitium," original sin; as it was termed, "peccatum originis."
[10] "Consors;" others read "concors," harmonious.
[11] "Pastos;" others, "pastor."   [12] "Reddit."   [13] "Centeno reditu."

fold, you fill the barns with the produce of an abundant harvest. May this people, free from stain, be strengthened[1] in your arms, and may you bear to the stars a pure pledge to God. May one crown be bestowed on you from on high (gained) from yourself,[2] may another flourish gained from your people.

[1] "Vegetetur;" another reading is, "agitetur."
[2] "De te;" others read, "detur et," with injury to the metre.

INDEXES.

I.—INDEX OF TEXTS OF SCRIPTURE.

OLD TESTAMENT.

GENESIS.
	VOL.	PAGE
xiv. 13,	i.	229

EXODUS.
xxiii. 20,	i. 226

NUMBERS.
xi. 31,	i. 228
xiii. 8,	i. 252
xxiv. 17,	i. 238

DEUTERONOMY.
xviii. 17-19,	i. 252
xviii. 66,	i. 259
xxx. 6,	i. 253

JOSHUA.
v. 2,	i. 253

1 SAMUEL.
xvi. 7,	i. 254

2 SAMUEL.
ii. 35,	i. 241
vii. 4, 5, 12, 14, 16,	i. 240

1 KINGS.
ix. 6-9,	i. 260
xix. 10,	i. 231

2 KINGS.
xxv.,	i. 220

1 CHRONICLES.
vii. 19-22,	i. 260

NEHEMIAH.
ix. 26,	i. 231

PSALMS.
	VOL.	PAGE
i. 1,	i.	249
i. 5,	i.	471
ii. 7,	i.	244
iii. 5,	i.	262
xvi. 10,	i.	262
xviii. 43,	i.	231
xxii. 16-18,	i.	260
xxviii. 4, 5,	i.	239
xxxiii. 6,	i.	225
xxxv. 15, 16,	i.	257
xlv. 1,	i.	226
xlv. 6, 7,	i.	238
lxix. 21,	i.	258
lxxii. 6, 7,	i.	250
lxxviii. 24,	i.	228
lxxxv. 12,	i.	234
xc. 2,	i.	235
xc. 4,	i.	460
xciv. 21, 22,	i.	259
xcv. 5,	i.	84
civ. 4,	i.	224
cix. 6,	i.	241
cx. 1,	i.	235
cx. 3, 4,	i.	241
cxxxvii. 1,	i.	240
cxlviii. 6,	i.	88

PROVERBS.
viii. 22-31,	i. 221

ISAIAH.
i. 2, 3,	i. 232
vii. 14,	i. 233
ix. 6,	i. 234
xi. 1, 2,	i. 239
xi. 10,	i. 239
xix. 20,	i. 238
xxxv. 3-6,	i. 245
xlii. 6, 7,	i. 264
xlv. 1-3,	i. 236
xlv. 6,	i. 285
xlv. 8,	i. 234
xlv. 14,	i. 285
xlv. 14-16,	i. 237
l. 5, 6,	i. 257
liii. 1-6,	i. 250
liii. 7,	i. 258
liii. 8,	i. 224
liii. 8-10, 12,	i. 259
lv. 4,	i. 214
lxiii. 10,	i. 233, 234
lxvi. 18, 19,	i. 231

JEREMIAH.
i. 5,	i. 223
ii. 13,	i. 286
iv. 3, 4,	i. 253
viii. 7-19,	i. 232
xi. 18, 19,	i. 259
xii. 7, 8,	i. 263
xv. 9,	i. 261
xvii. 9,	i. 238
xxv. 4-6,	i. 231
xxix., lii.,	i. 220
xxxi. 31, 32,	i. 263

EZEKIEL.
xli.,	i. 232

DANIEL.
vii.,	i. 468
vii. 13,	i. 265
vii. 13, 14,	i. 234
xii.,	i. 186

HOSEA.
vi. 2,	i. 262
xiii. 13, 14,	i. 262
xiii. 14,	i. 286

AMOS.
viii. 9, 10,	i. 261

INDEX OF SUBJECTS.

MICAH.
	VOL. PAGE
iv. 2, 3,	i. 252

ZECHARIAH.
iii. 1-8,	i. 241
xii. 10,	i. 260

MALACHI.
i. 6,	i. 217
i. 10, 11,	i. 231

APOCRYPHA.

ECCLESIASTICUS.
xxiv. 5-7,	i. 226

WISDOM.
ii. 2-22,	i. 249

BARUCH.
iii. 35-37,	i. 338

NEW TESTAMENT.

MATTHEW.
iii. 15,	i. 244
iii. 17,	i. 244
v. 44,	i. 399
viii.,	i. 247
ix. 33,	i. 274
xiv. 24,	i. 246
xviii. 7,	i. 287

MARK.
iv.,	i. 247
vii. 37,	i. 274

LUKE.
	VOL. PAGE
vi. 28,	i. 399
viii.,	i. 247
xiv. 11,	i. 328
xvii. 1,	i. 287
xxii. 15,	i. 231

JOHN.
i. 1-3,	i. 226
i. 9,	i. 201
ii. 19, 20,	i. 256
iii. 29,	i. 231
v. 29,	i. 121
ix. 9,	i. 245
xii. 25,	i. 439
xvii. 3,	i. 282

ACTS.
i. 9,	i. 235
xv. 10,	i. 229
xxiv. 15,	i. 121
xxvi. 6,	i. 311

ROMANS.
i. 22,	i. 81
v. 9, 10,	i. 233
vii. 15-21,	i. 276
xii. 14,	i. 399
xii. 19,	i. 400
xvi. 25,	i. 225

1 CORINTHIANS.
i. 20, 22,	i. 213
ii. 7,	i. 81
ii. 9,	i. 211
ii. 14,	i. 81
xi. 19,	i. 287

2 CORINTHIANS.
iv. 6,	i. 114

EPHESIANS.
	VOL. PAGE
i. 9, 10,	i. 214
ii. 12,	i. 231
iv. 24,	i. 114
iv. 26,	i. 403

COLOSSIANS.
i. 18,	i. 231
i. 26, 27,	i. 214
iii. 2,	i. 203
iii. 10,	i. 114

1 THESSALONIANS.
iv. 14,	i. 121

1 TIMOTHY.
ii. 5,	i. 272

HEBREWS.
i. 2,	i. 214
i. 3,	i. 285
i. 7,	i. 224
iv. 8,	i. 241
vii. 3,	i. 237
viii. 2,	i. 272
viii. 13,	i. 264
x. 30,	i. 400
xi. 37,	i. 232

1 PETER.
ii. 5,	i. 246

2 PETER.
ii. 1,	i. 287
ii. 22,	i. 254
iii. 8,	i. 491

REVELATION.
ii.,	i. 468
xi.,	i. 232

II.—INDEX OF PRINCIPAL SUBJECTS.

ACADEMICS, the, i. 142.
Accius Nævius and Tarquinius Priscus, i. 97.
Advent of Christ, the, to judgment, i. 469, etc., ii. 161.
Adversary, the, i. 207, 208.
Æsculapius, i. 23, 24.
Affections, the, i. 389, 390, ii. 212; refutation of the views of the Peripatetics respecting, i. 293; use of, 394, etc., 403, etc.
Africanus, i. 51.
Amalthea, the goat of, i. 63.

Anaxagoras, his testimony to the existence of God, i. 13; refutation of his answer to the question why he was born, 156, 157.
Anaximenes, his view of God, i. 13.
Ancestors, the authority of, i. 95, 96, 97.
Angels, assigned the care of the earth, the corruption of, i. 126, 127, ii. 110.
Anger, i. 401, ii. 35; and desire, and lust, i. 403, 404; forbidden in men, ii. 41, etc.

INDEX OF SUBJECTS.

Anger of God, the, ii. 1, etc., 31, etc., 35, etc.
Aniceris ransoms Plato, i. 199.
Animals, the lower, their uses, ii. 26; use of noxious, 26, 27; the figure and limbs of, 59, 60; the folly and error of Epicurus in his views respecting, 62, 63.
Anointing, i. 222, 223.
Anthropians, the, i. 288, note.
Ἄνθρωπος, meaning of the term, i. 74.
Antichrist, i. 467, 468, 470, 471, ii. 160.
Antipodes, the folly of believing that there are, i. 169; the idea of, ridiculous, ii. 122.
Antisthenes, his testimony to the unity of God, i. 13.
Apollo, his testimony at Colophon to the unity of God, i. 18; his disgraceful conduct, 24; his utterance respecting Jesus, 239.
Apollonius of Tyana, i. 298 and note.
Apologists, the first Christian, i. 293.
Apuleius, i. 298 and note.
Aratus quoted, i. 63, 303, 304.
Arcesilas, i. 145, 146, 147.
Archimedes, the orrery constructed by, i. 90.
Archytas, ii. 37, 38.
Aristippus and Lais, i. 173.
Aristotle, the testimony of, to the unity of God, i. 13; believed the world to be eternal, 423.
Aristoxenus quoted, i. 459.
Ascension, the, of Jesus, i. 264.
Asclepiades, i. 434.
Ass, an, sacrificed to Priapus, i. 61.
Astrology, etc., invented by demons, i. 130.
Asystaton, the fallacy so called, i. 148.
Atoms, the world not formed by the meeting together of, ii. 14-21.
Augury, i. 97.
Augustus Cæsar, a remarkable dream of, i. 100.
Aurelian, a persecutor, ii. 168.
Avarice and idolatry, i. 94.

Bald Venus, the, i. 56.
Beasts and men, the production of, ii. 51, 52; the condition of, 53; the figures of, 59, 60.
Beginning, the, i. 116, 117.
Bellona, i. 60.
Beneficence, various kinds of, i. 382, etc.
Bibaculus, Furius, i. 64.
Body, the parts of, ii. 64, 70-74.
Body and soul, the conflict between, i. 161.

Born, why men are, according to Cicero, i. 185.
Bounty, or liberality, i. 379, 380.
Brutes and men, their similarity and dissimilarity, ii. 9-11.
Burial of the dead, the duty of, i. 385, 386.

Cæsar, Julius, made a god, i. 44; Augustus, a remarkable dream of, 100.
Cæsars, nominated by Diocletian and Maximian, ii. 181-184.
Cancer, the two stars of, i. 62.
Candidianus, ii. 210.
Candles and lights, the vanity of offering them to God, i. 353.
Captives, the duty of ransoming, i. 384.
Carneades, the Athenian ambassador to Rome, disputes for and against justice, i. 324, 325; the substance of his disputation, 328, 329; reply to the argument of, 330, etc., 334, etc.; epitome of his argument and the reply, ii. 140-142.
Carthaginians, the, offer human sacrifices, i. 60.
Castor and Pollux, i. 24; alleged appearances of, 98.
Catholic Church, the, i. 288.
Cato commits suicide, i. 184.
Chananites, the, i. 125.
Chaos, i. 100.
Chastity, ii. 152.
Children, the exposing of, condemned, i. 407.
Chloris and Zephyrus, i. 54.
Christ, meaning of the name, i. 223; reason of the incarnation of, 230, etc. [see Jesus]; lie of Hierocles respecting, 297; not a magician, 298, 299; why believed to be God, 299, 300; advent of, to judgment, 469, etc., ii. 161; the name of, known to Himself and the Father, 125; twofold nativity of, 126, 127; the power and works of, 128; the death of, foretold, 130; the resurrection and ascension of, 131; the death of, on the cross, 134, 135; poem on the passion of, 220-222.
Christian religion, the, contrasted with heathenism, i. 341; the beginning of, ii. 165.
Christian truth, assailed by rash men, i. 294, etc.; the harmony of, 297.
Christians, the causeless hatred of, i. 291; tortures inflicted on, by the heathen, 310-312; refinements of cruelty practised on, by the heathen,

316-319; the increase and punishment of, 321, etc.; the fortitude of, 323; equality of, 327; equity and wisdom of, 328; the irrationality and cruelty of the persecution of, exposed, 337-344; the unresisting submission of, to suffering, 343; why their God, being almighty, does not protect them, 345, etc., 347, etc.; the justice and patience of, 346; the divine vengeance inflicted on the persecutors of, 349, ii. 164-211. [See Persecutors.]
Chronos, i. 36.
Chrysippus, his testimony to the unity of God, i. 13; who he was, 83, note; quoted, ii. 19.
Church, the Catholic, i. 288, 289.
Cicero, testimony of, to the unity of God, i. 13, 14; quoted respecting Jupiter, 32; his *De Natura Deorum* quoted, 35, 36, 41; cited to prove the gods to be mere men, 42, 43, 44; quoted again respecting the gods, 47; saw the folly of idolatry, but lacked courage to declare the truth, 78, 79; a memorable saying of, 82; against Verres, 86, 87; on the regularity of nature, 88, 89; on reason and the authority of ancestors, 95; on creation, 101, 102; on philosophy, 167; refuted in his views respecting wisdom, 169-171; on the character of philosophers, 172, 174; opinion of, as to why men were born, 185; how he teaches the immortality of the soul, 185, 186, etc.; on the future of the righteous and the wicked, 186; of life and death, 187; holds that philosophy is adverse to the multitude, 198, 199; on fortune, 204; on the meaning of religion, 282; on the cause of discord among men, 309; prefers death rather than to be changed into a beast, 317; cited respecting the good man tortured and the bad man honoured, 319, 320; on justice, 367; sets forth the invaluableness of the true law, 370; on liberality, 379, 380; on hospitality, 382, 383; on ransoming captives, 384; on injuries, and the forgetting of, 400-403; the death of, 402; on the hostility of the lower pleasures to virtue, 405; on the impossibility of repentance, 415; on conscience, 417, 418; answer to his question, why God made snakes, etc., 433; respecting God, ii. 12; on the origin of souls, 20; otherwise cited, i. 420, ii. 34, 50, 51.

Cimon, i. 372.
Circensian games, the, i. 409.
Circumcision, the abolition of, prophesied, i. 253; a sign, 254.
Claudia miraculously moves a vessel which had struck on shoals, i. 98.
Cleanthes, the testimony of, to the unity of God, i. 13; mode of living and death of, 182, note.
Cleombrutus, i. 184.
Cloacina, i. 54.
Cœlus, i. 36.
Comedies, metres of, ii. 212, 213.
Commands of God, i. 393, etc., ii. 150, 151.
Conflict, the, between body and soul, i. 161.
Conjecture, its unsatisfactory nature illustrated—repudiated by Zeno, i. 144.
Conscience, i. 417, 418.
Constancy, i. 397, 398.
Constantine, an address to, i. 483; sent for by his father Constantius, ii. 186; escapes from Galerius, 186; acknowledged as emperor by Galerius, 187; marries Fausta, a daughter of Maximian, 189; plotted against by Maximian, 191, 192; commands the statues of Maximian to be thrown down, 202; plot of Daia against, 202; his dream and the heavenly SIGN shown to; wages war against and defeats Maxentius, 203; edict of, for the restoration of the church of Nicomedia, 207-209.
Creation, not made out of previously existing materials, i. 101, 102, etc.; the use for which it was intended, 432, etc.; of pernicious animals, 433; of man, 434, etc., ii. 108.
Cross of Jesus, the meaning of,—why Jesus suffered the death of, i. 276-278; wonders effected by, a terror to demons, 279; the virtue of the sign of, 280; shown to Constantine in a dream, ii. 203.
Cupid, represented by a poet as the most powerful of the gods, i. 26.
Curetes, the, nourishers of Jupiter, i. 64.
Cynics, the, i. 173, 174.
Cyprian, i. 293.

DAIA made *Cæsar* by Galerius, ii. 181, 182; made emperor, 193, 194; takes from the Christians the toleration and protection granted by Galerius, 197; his superstition and oppression of the people, 198; his unbridled licentiousness, 198, 199; solicits

INDEX OF SUBJECTS.

Valeria, widow of Galerius, in marriage, and refused, banishes her, 199, 200; cruel and barbarous treatment of two ladies of high rank, 200, 201; unites with Maxentius against Constantine, 202; marches against Licinius and Constantine, 204, 205; his battle with Licinius, defeat, and flight, 205-207; his miserable end, 209, 210.
Danae, i. 28.
Death and life, how to be regarded, i. 188, 189; according to Cicero, 451, 452.
Death, the first and second, i. 121, 122.
Decius, a persecutor, ii. 167.
Demetrianus, i. 301.
Democritus, i. 194; what he says of truth, 205.
Demons, their origin, i. 127; meaning of the name, 127 and note; the influence of, 128-130; the inventors of astrology, soothsaying, and divination, 130; the connection of, with oracles, 132; the connection of, with the religious rites of the heathen, 135; the cross of Jesus a terror to, 279, 280; the gods are nothing else than, 280-282; the rage of, against Christians, 344, 345; evil practices of, ii. 110.
Desire, lust, and anger, i. 403, 404.
Deucalion, i. 115.
Devil, the origin and fall of, i. 100, 101; tempted and deceived angels, but has no power over believers, 127; his wiles and enmity, 207, 208; bound, 478; loosed, 481, ii. 161.
Diabolus, i. 101.
Didymus the grammarian, quoted, i. 67, 68.
Diocletian, a persecutor, ii. 168; his avarice, 169; a searcher into futurity, 172; is stirred up to persecute the Christians, 173; the plans of Galerius to excite him against the Christians, 175; rages against all Christians indiscriminately, 176; his sickness, 178; forced by Galerius to nominate as Cæsars men whom he deemed unfit, 179-181; obliged by Galerius to resign, 181-184; his death, 202.
Dionysius of Sicily, despoils the images of the gods, i. 84, 85.
Divination and soothsaying invented by demons, i. 130, etc.
Dolls, presented to Venus, — the images of the gods only large, i. 84.
Domitian, a persecutor, ii. 166.

Donatus, ii. 1, 164; the tortures inflicted on, his heroic endurance, 177.
Dreams, remarkable, i. 99, 100, ii. 88.

EARS, the, the pleasures derived from, i. 409, etc.; and eyes of men, ii. 67, 68.
Earth, animals not produced by, but by God, i. 105; made by God, 105, etc.; made for man, 429, 434-437; the renewal of the, 479, 480.
East, the, and west, i. 111.
Easter, a poem on, ii. 223-227.
Egeria and Numa, i. 65.
Egyptians, the first astronomers, i. 126.
Elements, the, not to be worshipped, i. 88, 91, ii. 108; the four, i. 121.
Eloquence, and truth, compared, i. 138-140; how esteemed, 292, 293.
Empedocles, i. 183, note.
End, the, i. 479-483.
Ennius, quoted respecting Jupiter, i. 34; respecting the gods, 39, etc.; respecting Romulus, 44; respecting Africanus, 51.
Epicurus, i. 107; the adaptation of his teaching, 177; held there is no providence, 178, ii. 13, 119; what he says of the wise man, i. 201, 202; and the Stoics, their views of God and nature censured, 427, etc.; his view of the production of the world, 431; his inquiry why God should be supposed to have made man for Himself, answered, 435; his views of God erroneous, ii. 4, 5, 12; the folly of, 62.
Error, the origin of, expounded, i. 71, etc.; and truth, the way of, 368.
Euhemerus, i. 35 and note; his teaching, 177; held there is no teaching respecting the gods, 39, etc.; respecting Jupiter, ii. 101, 105.
Evil things, why permitted in the world, ii. 26, 27; necessary, 30.
Example must sustain the precepts of a teacher, i. 267, 270.
Eyes and ears, the, of men, ii. 67.

FALL, the, of man, i. 123.
Falsehood and deceit, i. 399.
False prophet, the, his miracles and murders, i. 468.
Father, God our, i. 216.
Father, the, and the Son, one God, i. 284-286.
Faunus and Fatua Fauna, i. 66, 67.
Fear, i. 395.
Fear of God, the, ii. 24.
Festus Pescenius quoted, i. 60.

Fire, the divine, which shall burn wicked souls, i. 474.
Fire and water, i. 112; forbidden to the exiled, 113.
Flora and *Floralia*, i. 54.
Folly, i. 324; why justice sometimes appears as, 330, etc.; why Christians are charged with, 336.
Forbidden things, to be shunned, ii. 149, 150.
Fortitude in religion, ii. 152.
Fortune, i. 204, 206, 207, 208.
Fortune, the statue of, speaks, i. 98.
Freedom of religion, the, in the worship of God, ii. 138.
Furies, the three, i. 403.
Furius and Lælius, the discussion between, in Cicero, respecting justice, i. 330, etc.

GALERIUS, ii. 171, 172; the mother of, stirs him up to destroy the Christians, 173; destroys the church of Nicomedia, 174; edict of, against the Christians, 174, 175; his plans to inflame Diocletian against the Christians, 175; gets rid of Diocletian and Maximian, 179-182; barbarous and oppressive proceedings of, 183, 184, 185; Constantine escapes from, 186; compelled to send the imperial purple to Constantine, 187; his son-in-law Maxentius declared emperor at Rome, 187, 188; invades Italy, but deserted by his troops, is obliged to retreat, 189; his oppressions, 192, 193; stricken with an incurable plague, 194, 195; his remorse, and edict in favour of the Christians, 195, 196; his death, 196, 197.
Games, the Circensian, their evil influence, i. 409.
Ganymede, i. 28, 29.
Gauls, or Galatians, the, ii. 213.
Gentiles, the calling of the, ii. 132, 133.
Germanicus Cæsar, his translation of a poem of Aratus cited, i. 63, 302, 303.
Goat, the, of Amalthea, i. 63.
God, the universe the work of one, i. 6, etc.; the one, foretold by the prophets, 10; testified to by the poets, 11, ii. 94; borne witness to by the philosophers, i. 13, ii. 95; testimony of Hermes Trismegistus to, 14, 15; the Sibyls quoted respecting, i. 15, 16-18, ii. 96; testimony of Apollo to, i. 18, 19, 20; without a body and without sex, i. 20, 21, ii. 96; cannot be worshipped along with false deities, i. 52; men's forgetfulness, yet recognition of, 72, 73; the Creator, and alone to be worshipped, 87, etc.; the Son of, 100, 101; the Creator of matter, 101-109; the Creator of the world, 101-110; the Creator of animals, 117-120; the governor of the world, 130, 131; the patience of, 133, ii. 11; begets the Son, i. 220; the Father and the Son one, 284-286; the happy results of worshipping Him alone, 309; bestows His gifts bountifully on all, 326; man's highest duty to worship, 351; the worship of, and of other gods contrasted, 353; the first head of the true law is to worship and obey Him, 371; the world and, not to be confounded, 427, 428, etc.; the anger of, ii. 1, etc., 31, etc., 35, etc.; wrong views of the Epicureans respecting, 4, 5; views of the Stoics respecting, 6; Epicurus and Cicero quoted respecting, 11, 12; the providence of, 13, 14, etc., 111, etc.; the love and hatred of, 39; the mercy of, 40; but one, 93; the only, 133; assumed a mortal body and died, why? 134.
Gods, the, the physical interpretation which the Stoics give of, 35, 36, etc.; teaching of Ennius and Euhemerus respecting, 39; how men obtained the name of, 40, etc.; those who possess sex proved not to be, 45, etc.; the hardships and lewdness of, 48; an account of the consecration of, the bloodshed and crimes committed by, 49-51; Ceres and Liber made, on account of the benefits bestowed by them, 51; those peculiar to the Romans, and their sacred rites, 53, etc., ii. 102; kinds of sacrifice offered to, i. 58; who first introduced the worship of, 65, etc., 67, etc.; the elements and stars regarded as, 88, 89; the rites of, vain, 134, etc.; of the heathens, demons, 280-282; the depraving influence of the worship of, 316, 353; the religion of, 341; the vanity of the worship of, 443; the vicious actions of, ii. 97, 98; the poets do not invent all they relate of, 100; those peculiar to the barbarians, 104.
Golden age, the, ii. 106.
Good, the chief, various opinions of the philosophers respecting, i. 150, ii. 115; views of the philosophers respecting, refuted, i. 150-155; the nature of, determined, and Anaxa-

INDEX OF SUBJECTS.

goras refuted, 155-157, 158, etc.; is found in immortality alone, 163; and virtue, 364, etc.; not contained in bodily life, 437, 438; cannot exist without evil—objection answered, 439, 440, 441.
Good man, the, and the bad, the supposed treatment of, respectively in the world, i. 319.

HARLOTS made deities, i. 53, 54.
Heat and cold, i. 111.
Heathens, the, their persecution of Christians reproved, 337, etc., 342, 343; challenged to convict Christians of error, 338; character of, 352; their worship, 353.
Hebrews, the, i. 125, 126; sketch of the history of, 227-230.
Hercules, his life and death, i. 22, 23, 50, ii. 97; sacred rites in honour of, at Lindus, in Rhodes, 62.
Heresies, foretold, i. 286; and heretics, 287, 288.
Hermes Trismegistus, his testimony to the unity of God, i. 14, 15; on the immortality of the soul, 458; his *Complete Treatise* quoted, 469.
Hesiod, on the generation of the gods, i. 12; of demons, 127.
Hierocles, writes against Christianity, i. 296, 297.
Horace, quoted about the image of Priapus, i. 82; as to the safety of the innocent man, 332; on virtue and vice, 363.
Homer, i. 12.
Hospitality, i. 382.
Hydaspes, king of Media, i. 465.

IGNORANCE, human, ii. 1, 2.
Images, the cause of their first being made, and the folly of making, i. 74-78; the folly of trusting in, 82, etc.; treated with contempt by their worshippers, 84; speaking, 98; of the worship of, 136, etc.
Immortality, the reward of virtue, i. 162; the chief good found in, 163, ii. 118; belongs to the soul, i. 165; how taught by Cicero, 185, etc.; sad effects of taking away the hope of, 373; upheld by Plato and others, 446, 447; arguments in support of, 447, etc., 458, ii. 157-159.
Incarnation of Christ, the, reason of, i. 230, etc.; arguments of unbelievers against, 265, 266.
Infanticide condemned, i. 407.
Infants immolated to Saturn, i. 59.
Inquisitiveness, culpable, i. 189.

Intestines of the human body, the, display the wisdom of God, ii. 74, etc.; unknown use of some, 80, 81.
Isis, the sacred rites of, i. 60.

JESUS, the birth of, i. 223; the advent of, foretold by the prophets, 227; born of a virgin according to prophecy, 233; Son of God and Son of man, God-man, 236-238; the priesthood of, 241; the life and miracles of, 244, etc.; the passion of, foretold, 248, 255; hated by the Jews, 255, etc.; death, burial, and resurrection of, 261, etc.; departure of, into Galilee after His resurrection, 262; the ascension of, 264; arguments of unbelievers against the resurrection of, 265; His advent in the flesh to be a Mediator, 272, etc.; meaning of the miracles of, 273-275; meaning of the passion of, 275, 276; meaning of His cross, 276-278; the spotless paschal lamb, a type of, 278; a poem on the passion of, ii. 220, etc.; a poem on the resurrection of, 223, etc.
Jews, the, the disinheriting of, ii. 132, 133.
Judgment, the, i. 469, etc., 471, etc., 481, etc., ii. 161.
Juno, explanation of the name, i. 31.
Juno Monita, the statue of, speaks, i. 98.
Jupiter, the father of the gods, his character and conduct, i. 25; the origin, life, name, and death of, 26; Cicero's explanation of the name of, 31; the tomb of, 32; three of the name, 32; the father of, 33; the Cretan, 63; nursed on Mount Ida by the Curetes, 63, 64; various temples built in various places in honour of, 68; the bad state of things which existed when he banished his father, 303, 304-306; the licentious life of, ii. 99; emblems under which poets veiled the turpitude of, 99; the actions of, related by Euhemerus, 101.
Justice, banished by Jupiter, but restored by Christ, i. 303, 304; made known to all, but embraced by few, 308; Carneades argues for and against, 324, 325; what, 325, 326; answer to objection, 327; of the Christians, 327, 328; violated in the persecution of the Christians, ii. 139; the duties of, 145.
Juvenal quoted, i. 208.

KING, the impious, ii. 160.
Kings, the ten, i. 465.
Knowledge, discarded by Socrates and the Academics, i. 42; of many things necessary, 145, etc.; and virtue, 362; human, its imperfections, ii. 1, etc.; and supposition, 113, 114.

LÆLIUS and Furius, the disputation between, in Cicero respecting justice, i. 330, etc.
Lamb, the paschal, a type of Christ, i. 278.
Larentina and *Larentinialia*, i. 53.
Last things, the, i. 452-456.
Last times, the, ii. 159, etc.
Laughter peculiar to man, i. 10.
Law, the true, as described by Cicero, i. 370; the first precept of, 371.
Leæna, i. 53.
Liber, i. 24, 25, 62; the rites of, introduced into Greece by Orpheus, 67.
Liberality or bounty, i. 379, 380, etc.
Licinius, Daia incensed at his being made emperor, ii. 193, 194; Daia concludes a treaty with, 197; attacked by Daia, 204; his dream, defeats Daia, 205-207; puts to death many, among the rest Valeria, 210, 211.
Limbs of men, the, their use, ii. 270.
Lindus of Rhodes, peculiar religious rites in honour of Hercules at, i. 62, 63.
Lucilius, quoted, 67, 88, 89; respecting the depravity of the people, 313, 361, 399.
Lucretius, quoted, i. 65, 80, 168, 178, 179, 180, 283, 284, 399.
Lust, the source of all evils, i. 304, etc.; and desire, and anger, the three furies, 403, etc.; the evils flowing from, 412.

MAGICIAN, Christ not a, i. 298, 299.
Man, the creation of, by God, i. 114, 121; the fable of the creation of, by Prometheus, 114, 115; why of two sexes, 120, etc.; the compound nature of, 122; the transgression and fall of, 123; the peculiar property of, to know and worship God, 158; the upright form of, 449; why God made, ii. 29; how or whence sin came to attach to, 30; placed in Eden, and expelled thence, 109; made on account of God, 157.
Marcionites, the, i. 288, note.
Mars, i. 24.

Matter, not uncreated, i. 101-105; created by God, 105-108.
Maxentius, made emperor at Rome, ii. 187, 188; rules along with Maximian, 190; defeat of, by Constantine, and death, 203.
Maximian, Herculius, his character, ii. 170, 171; resumes the purple, 188; goes into Gaul to give his daughter Fausta in marriage to Constantine, 189; rules with Maxentius, 190; plots against Galerius, 190; plots against Constantine, 191; divested of the purple, 191, 192; new plots of, against Constantine, and death, 192.
Maximin, Daia, so named by Galerius when made Cæsar, ii. 181.
Mediator, the, Jesus Christ sent to be, i. 272.
Melissa, priestess of Jupiter, i. 68.
Melisseus, king of the Cretans, i. 68.
Men, the deification of, among the heathen, i. 40-45; the original state of, according to some writers, 376, 377; the duties of, to each other, 378; created by God for Himself, 433, 434; the production of, and of beasts, ii. 51, 52; the weakness of, 56; the bodies of, 64; other parts of, 66, 67; the senses of, 69, etc.; the limbs of, 70-74; the intestines of, 74, etc.; the lower parts of, 77, etc.; unknown use of some of the intestines of, 80, 81; born to justice, 117, etc.
Mercury, the character of, i. 24.
Mercy, towards men, i. 374; works of, 382.
Μετάνοια, i. 416.
Mind, the, and the seat of, ii. 82-85.
Millennium, the, ii. 161.
Minerva and Vulcan, i. 48, 49.
Minucius Felix, quoted respecting Saturn, i. 33; eulogized, 293.
Miracles, the, of Jesus, i. 244, 245, 246; the meaning of, 273-275.
Miracles, pagan, i. 98, 99.
Mother of the gods, the, the sacred rites of, i. 60.

NARSEUS, king of Persia, conquered by Galerius, ii. 171.
Nativity, the twofold, of Christ, ii. 126, 127.
Nature, the use of the word, by the heathen, i. 204, 206, 208, 427, 428.
Neighbour, who is our? i. 378, etc.
Nepos, Cornelius, quoted as to the character of philosophers, i. 172.
Nero, the first persecutor, his death, ii. 166.

INDEX OF SUBJECTS. 237

Nicomedia, the church of, destroyed by Diocletian and Galerius, ii. 174; edict of Licinius and Constantine for the restoration of the church of, 207-209.
Noah, makes and is saved in an ark, invents wine, and gets drunk, i. 124, 125.
Novatians, the, 288 and note.
Noxious animals, why permitted in the world, ii. 26, 27.
Numa Pompilius, introduces new gods and their worship, i. 65, ii. 103; the books of, found and burned, i. 66.

OFFERINGS, such as are acceptable to God, i. 419, etc.
Ops, i. 37.
Orphans and widows, the duty of protecting and defending, i. 384.
Orpheus, his testimony to the unity of God, i. 11; respecting Saturn, 38; first introduced the rites of Father Liber into Greece, 67.
Osiris, i. 60, 61.
Ovid, his testimony to the unity of the Creator, i. 12; quoted as to Vesta, 35, 36; his *Fasti* quoted respecting the wanderings of Saturn, 37, 38; respecting human sacrifices, 59; respecting Vesta and Priapus, 61; respecting the nursing of Jupiter on Mount Ida, 63, 64; on creation, 88; on the creation of man, 109; on the production of all things, 112.

PANTHEISM, exposed, i. 427-429.
Paradise, man driven from, i. 123.
Parcæ, the three, i. 116, 117.
Paschal lamb, the, a type of Christ, i. 278.
Passions, the, ii. 146; to be subdued, 149.
Patience, i. 401-403.
Patience of God, the, i. 133, 134.
Perillus, i. 200.
Peripatetics, refutation of their views respecting the affections, i. 393.
Persecution, reproved, and its cruelty and irrationality exposed, i. 337-344, ii. 139.
Persecutors of the Christians, Roman emperors who were, and their punishment, ii. 164-211.
Persius quoted, i. 77, 83, 84, 354.
Peter and Paul put to death at Rome, ii. 165, 166.
Phædo, i. 199.
Phalaris, i. 200.

Philosophers, the testimony of, to the unity of God, i. 11, etc.; their lives at variance with their precepts, 172, etc.; the folly of certain, 194; the precepts of, contributed little to true wisdom, 201; resemble disinherited sons or runaway slaves, 216; the errors of, 369, etc., 426; the variety of, and of their opinions, 444, ii. 114, 119, 122; the foolishness of, 123.
Philosophy, the vanity of, i. 140, etc.; the subjects of, 142; and the chief good, 149, etc.; moral, 149; not the mistress of life, 169.
Phœnix, the, a descriptive and historical poem on, ii. 214-219.
Phrygians, the heretics so called, i. 288, note.
Piety, false, i. 314; true, 325.
Plato, his testimony to the unity of God, i. 13; what he thanks God for, 187-188; the hurtful and vile doctrine taught by, of a community of goods and wives, 191, 192; his theory would overthrow all virtue and make vice universal, 193; ransomed from slavery, 199; his teaching makes the nearest approach of all philosophers to the truth, 121; affirms the immortality of the soul, 156, 157.
Plautus, quoted, i. 379.
Pleasures of the senses, the, i. 404, etc.
Poets and philosophers, the testimony of, to the one God, i. 11, etc.
Polites, his question to Apollo respecting the soul, i. 459.
Pontius Pilate, Jesus brought before, i. 255, 256.
Poverty, i. 286, 287.
Precept to be backed by example, i. 267, 270.
Predictions respecting the birth of Jesus, i. 233-238, 241, etc., 249, 250, 251, 257, 261, etc.
Priapus, the sacrifice of an ass to, i. 61; his contest with Liber, 62; the image of, 82, 83.
Priesthood, the, of Jesus, i. 241, etc.
Private judgment, i. 96.
Prodigies, strange, i. 98.
Prometheus, the fable of the creation of man by, i. 114, 115, ii. 107.
Propertius, quoted, i. 96.
Prophet, the false, i. 467, etc.
Prophets, the, i. 219.
Protagoras doubts the existence of a Deity, ii. 13.
Providence, divine, i. 5, 6, ii. 13, 14, 15, 92, 154, 155.

Punishment, ii. 36, 37.
Pythagoras, the testimony of, to the unity of God, i. 13; pretended to have been once Euphorbus, 185; and Plato, why they did not approach the Jews in their search for wisdom, 213, 214; held that the soul is immortal, ii. 119, 120.
Pythagoreans, the, persuade to suicide, i. 182.

QUINTILLIAN, his *Fanatic* quoted, i. 60, 307.
Quirinus, or Romulus, deified by the Romans, i. 44.

RANSOMING captives, an exercise of justice, i. 384.
Reason, and the authority of ancestors, i. 95, 96; use of, in religion, 96, 97.
Religion, meaning of the term, i. 282.
Religion, and wisdom, i. 3-5, ii. 124; reason in, i. 96; the chief good, 158; errors respecting, 159; and wisdom cannot be separated, 214, 215, 217; and superstition, 282, 284; false and true, 314, etc.; and mercy towards men, 374; Epicurus and Cicero quoted respecting, ii. 11, 12; the freedom of, 138; safety in, at the last, 163.
Repentance, i. 388, 416, ii. 153; the possibility of, i. 415.
Resurrection, the, of Christ, i. 261; a poem on, ii. 223-227.
Resurrection, the, of men, i. 477; the second, 482.
Revenge, i. 400.
Rites, sacred, of the Roman gods, ii. 102; introduced by Numa and Faunus, 103; of the barbarians, 104; and superstition, 105.
Rome, the ages of, i. 464.
Romulus deified by the Romans, i. 42.

SACRED things forbidden to be looked at under a penalty, i. 189.
Sacrifice, the, worthy of God, i. 419, ii. 143.
Sacrifices offered to the gods, human and other sorts, i. 58, etc.
Sacrilege, the punishment of, yet committed with impunity by Dionysius of Sicily, and Verres, 85-87; instances of the miraculous punishment of, 98, 99.
Sallust, quoted, i. 122.
Salvation, the hope of, ii. 135.
Samos, i. 48.

Sapor, king of Persia, his treatment of the captive Emperor Valerian, ii. 167, 168.
Saturn, father of Jupiter, i. 33-35, 36, 37; infants immolated to, 59; happy state of things under the reign of, 302, 303; actions of, ii. 101.
Scriptures, the simplicity of the style of, i. 139, 140; why despised by the wise and learned, 292.
Seasons, the use and advantages of the, ii. 24, etc.
Seneca, Annæus, his testimony to the unity of God, i. 14, 19, 20; respecting Jupiter, 46; respecting the images of the gods, 76; respecting God and nature, 103; the error of, in philosophy, 171; quoted as to the character of philosophers, 172, 173; censures Aniceris for paying so small a ransom for Plato, 199, 200; on the prosperity of the bad and the sufferings of the good, 347; on living to God, 417; on the worship of God, 419.
Senses, the, and the pleasures of, i. 404, etc., 409, 410, 411; and their power, ii. 69; the pleasures of, to be restrained, 147.
Severianus, ii. 210.
Severus, nominated Caesar, ii. 180, 181; defeated by Maxentius, his death, 188.
Sex, cannot be attributed to God, i. 21; beings distinguished by, cannot be gods, 45-47.
Sextus Claudius, quoted respecting Fatua Fauna, i. 66.
Shield, the sacred, i. 64, 65.
Sibylline books, the, i. 16.
Sibyls, the, who? their number, i. 15, 16, 17; the testimony of, respecting God, 18; rebuke the worshipping of men as gods, 42; the Erythrean, quoted, 123; the Erythrean, proclaims the Son of God, 221; respecting the works of Christ, 245, 246, 247, 248; respecting the portents at the death of Christ, 261; other quotations from, 459, 465, 466, 467, 469, 471, 477, 478, ii. 44, 45, 96.
Sight, the pleasures of, i. 405, 406.
Sign, the heavenly, shown to Constantine, ii. 203.
Sign of the cross, the, its efficacy, i. 280.
Sins, how they extended to man, ii. 30.
Snakes and vipers, why made by God, i. 433.
Socrates, and the Academics take

INDEX OF SUBJECTS. 239

away human knowledge, i. 142, ii. 1, 2; his wisdom, 189; deserving of censure, 190; his contradiction, ii. 120.

Solomon and David, prophets, i. 225.

Son of God, the, produced by the Father, and set over His works, i. 100, 101; begotten, 220; the name of, 222; the Word of God, 224, 225, 226; and the Father, one God, 284-286.

Soothsaying invented by demons, i. 130.

Soul, the, the immortality of, i. 446, etc., ii. 156, 157; and body, i. 452, etc., 454, etc.; testimonies respecting the eternity of, 458, etc.; Virgil quoted respecting, 472; the torment and punishment of, 473, 474; the seat of—opinions of philosophers, ii. 85; and the mind, 87; given by God, 89.

Sound man, the, i. 418.

Sparti, the, i. 145.

Spectacles, the polluting influence of, i. 406, ii. 148.

Speech peculiar to man, ii. 10.

Stage, the, the evil influence of, i. 408.

Stars, the, regarded as gods, i. 88, 89; ordered by God, 89, 90, 91.

Statues that spoke, i. 98.

Stoics, the, gave a physical interpretation to the mythology of the ancients, i. 35, etc., 36-39; reckon the elements in the number of the gods, 88; conclude that the world is God, 92; take away all the affections from man, 390, 391; their view and that of Epicurus respecting God and nature censured, 427, etc.; their views of God further stated, ii. 6, etc.

Straton, his view of the origin of the world, ii. 14.

Suicide, the Pythagoreans and Stoics persuade to, i. 182, etc.

Superstition and religion, i. 282-284.

Swine, the flesh of, forbidden, why, i. 254.

TACTUS voluptate et libidine, de, i. 411, etc.

Tages the soothsayer, ii. 172.

Tarquitius, quoted respecting Æsculapius, i. 24.

Taste and smell, the pleasures of the senses of, i. 410.

Teacher, a, and his precepts, i. 267; the divine, perfect, 268, 269; the true, must be human and divine, 270, 271.

Temple of God, the true, i. 308.

Terence, quoted, i. 184.

Terminus, 57, 58.

Tertullian, characterized, i. 293; his *Apology* referred to, 301.

Testaments, the two, i. 268.

Thales of Miletus, his testimony to the unity of the Creator, i. 13.

Themiste, i. 199 and note.

Theophilus of Antioch, quoted, i. 69, note.

Thoth, i. 15.

Times, the first and the last, of the world, i. 460, 462, etc.; the last, 480, ii. 159.

Titan, i. 40.

Transmigration of souls, i. 185, 188.

Trismegistus, quoted, i. 226, 420, 421.

Truth, the great value of the knowledge of, i. 1, 2; and eloquence, compared, i. 138-140; the philosophers ignorant of,—saying of Democritus respecting, 205; and error, the way of, 368; steps to the abode of, ii. 2, 3.

Tuditanus, i. 194, note.

UNITY of God, the, asserted, i. 6, etc.; testimonies of poets and philosophers to, 11, etc.; testimony of Hermes Trismegistus to, 14, 15; testimony of the Sibyls to, 18; testimony of Apollo to, 18, 19.

Universe, whether it is governed by the power of one God, i. 6, etc.; not God, 91.

Usury, i. 399.

Utero et conceptione atque sexibus, de, ii. 77.

VALENTINIANS, the, i. 288 and note.

Valeria the empress solicited in marriage by Daia,—refusing is banished, 200, 201; put to death by order of Licinius, 210, 211.

Valerian, a persecutor, his punishment, ii. 167.

Varro, quoted respecting the Sibyls, i. 15, 16; respecting human sacrifices, 59; respecting Fatua Fauna, 66; respecting the length of human life, 124.

Venantius, Honorius, a poem of, on Easter, ii. 223-227.

Venus, the lewdness of, i. 48; the Bald, 56; the Armed, 57.

Verres, Caius, plunders the gods of Sicily, i. 86, 87.

Vesta, the chastity of, preserved by the braying of an ass, i. 61.

Vices, the, and the virtues, i. 355-357, 450-452.

Virgil, quoted on the unity of God, i. 12; respecting Saturn, 38, 42; respecting the concealment of Virbius, or Hippolytus, 49; respecting the image of Priapus, 82, 83; respecting men springing from the earth, 116; on superstition, 284; as to the exile of Saturn by Jupiter, 303, 304; of wicked men, 11; respecting the piety of Æneas, 314, 315; as to war, 317; as to the left way, 358; respecting the ascent from Hades, 416; as to the soul of the world, 428; on the soul, and its purification, 472, 475, 476.

Virtue, i. 160; the reward of, 162, 163; the influence of, 201-203; persecuted, 319, etc.; never loses its reward, 335; the way of, 358; false and true, 361; and knowledge, 362; and the chief good, 364; no true, without the acknowledgment of God, 372, etc.; the first steps of, 388; never without evil, 439.

Virtues, the, and the vices, i. 355-357; neither to be deified, 54, 55, 56.

Virtus, offerings to, i. 60.
Voice, the, ii. 82.
Vulcan and Minerva, i. 48, 49.

WARFARE, the Christian, i. 359, 360.
Ways, the two, of virtue and vice, of life and death, i. 355, etc., 358-361; of error and of truth, 368, etc., ii. 143-145.
Wicked men, the crimes of, i. 310, 311, 312, 313, 352.
Widows and orphans, the duty of protecting and defending, i. 384, 385.
Wisdom, and religion, i. 3-5; human and divine, 81, 82; error of Lucretius and Cicero in fixing the origin of, 168, etc.; where to be found, 213; and religion cannot be separated, 214, 217; and folly, 330, etc., 336, ii. 141; false, 112.
Wise man, the, of Epicurus, i. 201, 202.
Wise men, the seven, i. 212.
Word of God, the, its marvellous efficacy, i. 200.
WORD OF GOD, the personal, i. 224, 225; called the LOGOS, 226.
World, the, made by God, i. 101-110; the parts and elements of, 110, etc.; and God, to be distinguished, 427-429; made for man, 429, 432, 435; Epicurus' view of its production, 431; the first and last times of, 460, etc.; the devastation of, 462, etc., 465; the fortunes of, at the last day, 468, 469; the renewed, 478, etc.; the end of, at hand, 481; the origin of, ii. 14, etc.; the advantages and use of, 24, etc.; why made, 155, 157.
Worship of God, the true, ii. 143.

XENOPHANES, his foolish belief about the moon, i. 195.

ZENO, his testimony to the unity of God, i. 13; repudiates conjecture, 144; the death of, 183; places *pity* among the vices, 195.

THE TESTAMENTS OF

THE TWELVE PATRIARCHS,

AND

FRAGMENTS OF THE

SECOND AND THIRD CENTURIES.

EDINBURGH:
T. & T. CLARK, 38, GEORGE STREET.
MDCCCLXXI.

CONTENTS.

THE TESTAMENTS OF THE TWELVE PATRIARCHS.

	PAGE
INTRODUCTORY NOTICE,	7
The Testament of Reuben concerning Thoughts,	13
The Testament of Simeon concerning Envy,	17
The Testament of Levi concerning the Priesthood and Arrogance,	21
The Testament of Judah concerning Fortitude, and Love of Money, and Fornication,	31
The Testament of Issachar concerning Simplicity,	42
The Testament of Zebulun concerning Compassion and Mercy,	45
The Testament of Dan concerning Anger and Lying,	50
The Testament of Naphtali concerning Natural Goodness,	54
The Testament of Gad concerning Hatred,	58
The Testament of Asher concerning Two Faces of Vice and Virtue,	62
The Testament of Joseph concerning Sobriety,	65
The Testament of Benjamin concerning a Pure Mind,	74

FRAGMENTS OF THE SECOND AND THIRD CENTURIES.

INTRODUCTORY NOTICE,	83
Bardesan,	85
Melito,	112
Quadratus, Bishop of Athens,	139
Aristo of Pella,	139
Claudius Apollinaris, Bishop of Hierapolis,	140
Hegesippus,	142
Pantænus,	147
Rhodo,	149
Maximus, Bishop of Jerusalem,	150
Polycrates, Bishop of Ephesus,	162

	PAGE
Theophilus, Bishop of Cæsarea,	163
Serapion, Bishop of Antioch,	164
Apollonius,	165
Dionysius, Bishop of Corinth,	167
Letter of the Churches of Vienna and Lugdunum to the Churches of Asia and Phrygia,	168

CLEMENS ALEXANDRINUS ON THE SALVATION OF THE RICH MAN, ... 185

THE TESTAMENTS OF
THE TWELVE PATRIARCHS.

TRANSLATED BY

REV. ROBERT SINKER, M.A.
TRIN. COLL. CAMBRIDGE.

INTRODUCTORY NOTICE.

THE apocryphal work known as the *Testaments of the Twelve Patriarchs* professes to be, as its name implies, the utterances of the dying patriarchs, the sons of Jacob. In these they give some account of their lives, embodying particulars not found in the scriptural account, and build thereupon various moral precepts for the guidance of their descendants. The book partakes also of the nature of an Apocalypse: the patriarchs see in the future their children doing wickedly, stained with the sins of every nation; and thus they foretell the troubles impending on their race. Still at last God will put an end to their woe, and comfort is found in the promise of a Messiah.

There can be little or no doubt that the author was a Jew, who, having been converted to Christianity, sought to win over his countrymen to the same faith, and thus employed the names of the patriarchs as a vehicle for conveying instruction to their descendants, as winning by this means for his teaching at any rate a *prima facie* welcome in the eyes of the Jewish people.

It does not seem hard to settle approximately the limits of time within which the book was probably written. It cannot be placed very late in the second century, seeing that it is almost certainly quoted by Tertullian (*adv. Marcionem*, v. 1; *Scorpiace*, 13; cf. *Benj.* 11), and that Origen (*Hom. in Josuam*, xv. 6; cf. *Reub.* 2, 3) cites the *Testaments* by name, apparently indeed holding it in considerable respect. We can, however, approximate much more nearly than this; for the allusions to the destruction of Jerusalem assign to the *Testaments* a date subsequent to that event. This will harmonize perfectly with what is the natural inference from several passages,—namely, that the Gentiles now were a majority in the church,—as well as with the presence of the many formulæ to express the incarnation, and with the apparent collection of the books of the New Testament into a volume (*Benj.* 11).

On the other hand, important evidence as to the posterior limit of the date of writing may be derived from the language used with reference to the priesthood. Christ is both High Priest and King, and His former office is higher than the latter, and to Him the old priesthood must resign its rights. Now such language as this would be almost meaningless after Hadrian's destruction of Jerusalem consequent on the revolt of Bar-Cochba (A.D. 135), after which all power of Judaism for acting directly upon Christianity ceased; and, indeed, on the hypothesis of a later date, we should doubtless find allusions to the revolt and its suppression. On the above grounds, we infer that the writing of the *Testaments* is to be placed in a period ranging from late in the first century to the revolt of Bar-Cochba; closer than this it is perhaps not safe to draw our limits.

The language in which the *Testaments* were written was no doubt the Hellenistic Greek in which we now possess them; presenting as they do none of the peculiar marks which characterize a version. Whether there were a Hebrew work on which the present was modelled—a supposition by no means improbable in itself—we cannot tell, nor is it a matter of much importance. The phenomena of the book itself may be cited in support of this conclusion: for instance, the use of the word διαθήκη in its ordinary classical meaning of "testament," not "covenant" as in Hellenistic Greek, for which former meaning there would be no strictly equivalent word in Hebrew; the numerous instances of paronomasia, such as ἀθετεῖν, νουθετεῖν (*Benj.* 4), ἀφαίρεσις, ἀναίρεσις (*Judah* 23), λιμός, λοιμός (*ib.*), ἐν τάξει, ἄτακτον (*Naph.* 2), τάξις, ἀταξία (*Naph.* 3); the frequent use of the genitive absolute, and of the verb μέλλειν; the use of various expressions pertaining to the Greek philosophy, as διάθεσις, αἴσθησις, φύσις, τέλος.

It seems doubtful how far we can attempt with safety to determine accurately the religious standpoint of the writer beyond the obvious fact of his Jewish origin, though some have attempted to show that he was a Nazarene, and others a Jewish Christian of Pauline tendencies. We shall therefore content ourselves with referring those who seek for more specific information on this point to the works mentioned below.

To refer now briefly to the external history of our document, we meet with nothing definite, after its citation by Origen, for many centuries: there are possible allusions in Jerome (*adv. Vigilantium*, c. 6) and in Procopius Gazæus (*Comm. in Genesin*, c. 38); there is also a mention of πατριάρχαι in the *Synopsis Sacræ Scripturæ* found among the writings of Athanasius, as well as in the *Stichometria* of Nicephorus of Constantinople, on which it is probably based. Again, in the Canons of the Council of Rome (494 A.D.) under Gelasius, and of the Council of Bracara (563 A.D.), are possible references, though it is far from improbable that in some of the foregoing passages the reference may be to a writing τῶν τριῶν Πατριαρχῶν alluded to in the *Apostolic Constitutions* (vi. 16), or is even of somewhat loose application.

After this a blank ensues until the middle of the thirteenth century, when it was brought to the knowledge of Western Europe by Robert Grosseteste, Bishop of Lincoln, the earliest of the great English reformers. We cite here the account of the matter given by Matthew Paris, although of course we need not accept all the opinions of the old chronicler respecting the document in question: "At this same time, Robert, Bishop of Lincoln, a man most deeply versed in Latin and Greek, accurately translated the *Testaments of the XII Patriarchs* from Greek into Latin. These had been for a long time unknown and hidden through the jealousy of the Jews, on account of the prophecies of the Saviour contained in them. The Greeks, however, the most unwearied investigators of all writings, were the first to come to a knowledge of this document, and translated it from Hebrew into Greek, and have kept it to themselves till our times. And neither in the time of the blessed Jerome nor of any other holy interpreter could the Christians gain an acquaintance with it, through the malice of the ancient Jews. This glorious treatise, then, the aforesaid bishop (with the help of Master Nicolaus, a Greek, and a clerk of the Abbey of St. Alban's) translated fully and clearly, and word for word, from Greek into Latin, to the strengthening of the Christian faith, and to the greater confusion of the Jews." (*Historia Anglorum*, A.D. 1242, p. 801, ed. London 1571.)

Again, after speaking of the death of "Master John de Basingstokes, Archdeacon of Leicester," a man of very great learning in Latin and Greek, he proceeds: "This Master John had mentioned to Robert, Bishop of Lincoln, that when he was studying at Athens he had seen and heard from learned Greek doctors certain things unknown to the Latins. Among these he found the *Testaments of the XII Patriarchs*, that is to say, of the sons of Jacob. Now it is plain that these really form part of the sacred volume, but have been long hidden through the jealousy of the Jews, on account of the evident prophecies about Christ which are clearly seen in them. Consequently this same bishop sent into Greece; and when he obtained them, he translated them from Greek into Latin, as well as certain other things." (*Op. cit.* A.D. 1252, p. 1112.)

After this it would seem as though the same fate still pursued our document, for the entire Greek text was not printed until the eve of the eighteenth century, when it was published for the first time by Grabe, whose edition has been several times reprinted. (*Vide infra.*)

Four Greek MSS. of the *Testaments* are known to exist:—

1. The MS. [Ff. i. 24] in the University Library of Cambridge, to which it was given by Archbishop Parker, whose autograph it bears on its first page. It is a quarto on parchment, of 261 leaves (in which the *Testaments* occupy ff. 203a–261b), double columns, 20 lines in a column, handwriting of the tenth century. It is furnished with accents and breathings, and a fairly full punctuation. There are very strong grounds for believing that it was from this MS. that Grosseteste's version was made, exhibiting as it does a very large amount of curious verbal coincidence with it.[1] The text of this MS. has been that given in the various editions mentioned below.

2. The MS. [Barocci 133] in the Bodleian Library at Oxford, where it came with the rest of the Barocci collection from Venice, and was presented to the University by its Chancellor, the Earl of Pembroke. It is a quarto volume; and except a leaf or two of parchment, containing writing of an older period, consists of a number of treatises on paper, apparently by several

---

[1] See, *e.g.*, the curious reading in *Levi* 18, καὶ στήσει, where the Latin MSS. are unanimous in giving *stare faciet*; also the mistake of 'Ιακώβ for 'Ρουβήμ in *Issachar* 1.

different hands, in the writing of the latter part of the fourteenth century. The *Testaments* occupy ff. 179a–203b. The amount of difference between this MS. and the preceding is considerable, and is sufficient to show that it has had no direct communication with the latter. A large number of omissions occur in it, in some instances amounting to entire chapters. The variations of this MS. are given more or less fully in the various editions.

3. A MS. in the Vatican Library at Rome, not yet edited. It is said to be a small quarto on paper, written in a very distinct hand, though unfortunately some leaves are damaged. It bears a subscription with the date 1235. I owe my knowledge of this MS. to an article by Dr. Vorstman in the *Godgeleerde Bijdragen* for 1866, p. 953 sqq.

4. A MS. discovered by Tischendorf in the island of Patmos, of which no details have yet been published. (See Tischendorf, *Aus dem heiligen Lande*, p. 341.)

The entire Greek text of the *Testaments* was first printed by Grabe in his *Spicilegium Patrum et Hæreticorum* (Oxford 1698), professedly from the Cambridge MS., but in reality from some very inaccurate transcript of it, very possibly from one made by Abednego Seller, also in the Cambridge University Library [Oo. vi. 91]. Grabe also gave a few of the variations of the Oxford MS. Fabricius, in his *Codex Pseudepigraphus Veteris Testamenti* (Hamburgh 1713), gives little more than a reprint from Grabe. In the second edition of the latter (1714) the true text has been restored in several passages; but in many places Grosseteste's Latin version, which witnessed to the true reading, was altered to suit Grabe's incorrect text. Fabricius' second edition (1722) is perhaps, on the whole, less accurate than his first. Since then the text and notes, as given in Grabe's second edition, have been reprinted, with but few additions, by Gallandi, in his *Bibliotheca Veterum Patrum*, vol. i. p. 193 sqq. (Venice 1765), and in Migne's *Patrologia Græca*, vol. ii. (Paris 1857). The text of the Cambridge MS., with a full statement of the variations of the Oxford MS., has recently been edited directly from the MSS. by myself (Cambridge 1869); from this edition the present translation has been made.

The MSS. of Grosseteste's Latin version are numerous, there

being no less than twelve in Cambridge alone; and it has been frequently printed, both with the editions of the Greek text and independently (*e.g.* 1483, Hagenau 1532, Paris 1549, and often).

Besides the Latin version, the *Testaments* have also been translated into several European languages, in all cases apparently from the Latin. The English translation made by Arthur Golding was first printed by John Daye in Aldersgate in 1581, and has since been frequently reproduced; the British Museum, which does not possess all the editions, having no less than eleven.[1]

The author of the French translation ("Monsieur Macé, Chefcier, curé de Saint Opportune," Paris 1713) appears to believe, as the English translator had done, that we have here really the last words of the sons of Jacob. A German translation has also several times been published (*e.g.* Vienna 1544, Strasburgh 1596, Hamburgh 1637), and a German translation in MS. is to be found in the British Museum (MSS. Harl. 1252). We may further mention a Dutch translation (Antwerp 1570), a Danish translation (1601), and a MS. Icelandic translation of the eighteenth century in the British Museum (add. MSS. 11,068).

For further information on the subject of the *Testaments*, reference may be made, in addition to works already mentioned, to the following:—Nitzsch, *Commentatio Critica de Testamentis XII Patriarcharum, libro V. T. Pseudepigrapho* (Wittenberg 1810); Ritschl, *Die Entstehung der Altkatholischen Kirche* (Bonn 1850; ed. 2, 1857), p. 171 sqq.; Vorstman, *Disquisitio de Testamentorum XII Patriarcharum origine et pretio* (Rotterdam 1857); Kayser in Reuss and Cunitz's *Beiträge zu den theol. Wissenschaften* for 1851, pp. 107–140; Lücke, *Einleitung in die Offenbarung des Joh.* vol. i. p. 334 sqq., ed. 2.

R. S.

TRINITY COLLEGE, CAMBRIDGE.
February 21, 1871.

---

[1] This English translation having been made from the Latin, the printed editions of which swarm with inaccuracies (Grosseteste's Latin version itself being a most exact translation), I have been able to make much less use of it than I could have desired. It has, however, been compared throughout.

THE TESTAMENTS OF
THE TWELVE PATRIARCHS.

THE TESTAMENT OF REUBEN CONCERNING THOUGHTS.

1. THE copy of the Testament of Reuben, what things he charged his sons before he died in the hundred and twenty-fifth year of his life. When he was sick two years after the death of Joseph, his sons and his sons' sons were gathered together to visit him. And he said to them, My children, I am dying, and go the way of my fathers. And when he saw there Judah and Gad and Asher, his brethren, he said to them, Raise me up, my brethren, that I may tell to my brethren and to my children what things I have hidden in my heart, for from henceforth my strength faileth me. And he arose and kissed them, and said, weeping: Hear, my brethren, give ear to Reuben your father, what things I command you. And, behold, I call to witness against you this day the God of heaven, that ye walk not in the ignorance of youth and fornication wherein I ran greedily, and I defiled the bed of Jacob my father. For I tell you that He smote me with a sore plague in my loins for seven months; and had not Jacob our father prayed for me to the Lord, surely the Lord would have destroyed me. For I was thirty years old when I did this evil in the sight of the Lord, and for seven months I was sick even unto death; and I repented for seven years in the set purpose of my soul before the Lord. Wine and strong drink I drank not, and flesh entered not into my mouth, and I tasted not pleasant food,[1] mourning over my sin, for it was great. And it shall not so be done in Israel.

2. And now hear me, my children, what things I saw in my repentance concerning the seven spirits of error. Seven spirits

[1] There seems a reminiscence here of the words of Dan. x. 3, LXX.

are given against man from Beliar, and they are chief of the works of youth; and seven spirits are given to him at his creation, that in them should be done every work of man.[1] The first spirit is of life, with which man's whole being is created. The second spirit is of sight, with which ariseth desire. The third spirit is of hearing, with which cometh teaching. The fourth spirit is of smelling, with which taste is given to draw air and breath. The fifth spirit is of speech, with which cometh knowledge. The sixth spirit is of taste, with which cometh the eating of meats and drinks; and by them strength is produced, for in food is the foundation of strength. The seventh spirit is of begetting and sexual intercourse, with which through love of pleasure sin also entereth in: wherefore it is the last in order of creation, and the first of youth, because it is filled with ignorance, which leadeth the young as a blind man to a pit, and as cattle to a precipice.

3. Besides all these, there is an eighth spirit of sleep, with which is created entrancement of man's nature, and the image of death. With these spirits are mingled the spirits of error. The first, the spirit of fornication, dwelleth in the nature and in the senses; the second spirit of insatiateness in the belly; the third spirit of fighting in the liver and the gall. The fourth is the spirit of fawning and trickery, that through over-officiousness a man may be fair in seeming. The fifth is the spirit of arrogance, that a man may be stirred up and become high-minded. The sixth is the spirit of lying, in perdition and in jealousy to feign words, and to conceal[2] words from kindred and friends. The seventh is the spirit of injustice, with which are theft and pilferings, that a man may work the desire of his heart; for injustice worketh together with the other spirits by means of craft. Besides all these, the spirit of sleep, the eighth spirit, is conjoined with error and fantasy. And so perisheth every young man, darkening his mind from the truth, and not understanding the law of God, nor obeying the admonitions of his

---

[1] For this use of πνεύματα as applied to the senses, we may cite Plutarch (*De placitis philosophorum*, iv. 21), who, speaking with reference to the Stoic philosophy, says, ἡ μὲν ὅρασις ἐστὶ πνεῦμα διατεῖνον ἀπὸ τοῦ ἡγεμονικοῦ μέχρις ὀφθαλμῶν.

[2] This clause is only found in Cd. Oxon.; it seems demanded by the following ἀπό.

fathers, as befell me also in my youth. And now, children, love the truth, and it shall preserve you. I counsel you, hear ye Reuben your father. Pay no heed to the sight of a woman, nor yet associate privately with a female under the authority of a husband, nor meddle with affairs of womankind. For had I not seen Bilhah bathing in a covered place, I had not fallen into this great iniquity.[1] For my mind, dwelling on the woman's nakedness, suffered me not to sleep until I had done the abominable deed. For while Jacob our father was absent with Isaac his father, when we were in Gader, near to Ephratha in Bethlehem, Bilhah was drunk, and lay asleep uncovered in her chamber; and when I went in and beheld her nakedness, I wrought that impiety, and leaving her sleeping I departed. And forthwith an angel of God revealed to my father Jacob concerning my impiety, and he came and mourned over me, and touched her no more.

4. Pay no heed, therefore, to the beauty of women, and muse not upon their doings; but walk in singleness of heart in the fear of the Lord, and be labouring in works, and roaming in study and among your flocks, until the Lord give to you a wife whom He will, that ye suffer not as I did. Until my father's death I had not boldness to look stedfastly into the face of Jacob, or to speak to any of my brethren, because of my reproach; and even until now my conscience afflicteth me by reason of my sin. And my father comforted me; for he prayed for me unto the Lord, that the anger of the Lord might pass away from me, even as the Lord showed me. From henceforth, then, I was protected, and I sinned not. Therefore, my children, observe all things whatsoever I command you, and ye shall not sin. For fornication is the destruction of the soul, separating it from God, and bringing it near to idols, because it deceiveth the mind and understanding, and bringeth down young men into hell before their time. For many hath fornication destroyed; because, though a man be old or noble, it maketh him a reproach and a laughing-stock with Beliar and the sons of men. For in that Joseph kept himself from every woman, and purged his thoughts from all fornication, he found favour before the Lord and men. For the Egyptian woman

[1] Cf. Gen. xxxv. 22. The Gader mentioned below is the Edar of ver. 21, the Hebrew ע being reproduced, as often, by γ.

did many things unto him, and called for magicians, and offered him love potions, and the purpose of his soul admitted no evil desire. Therefore the God of my fathers delivered him from every visible and hidden death. For if fornication overcome not the mind, neither shall Beliar overcome you.

5. Hurtful are women, my children; because, since they have no power or strength over the man, they act subtilly through outward guise how they may draw him to themselves; and whom they cannot overcome by strength, him they overcome by craft. For moreover the angel of God told me concerning them, and taught me that women are overcome by the spirit of fornication more than men, and they devise in their heart against men; and by means of their adornment they deceive first their minds, and instil the poison by the glance of their eye, and then they take them captive by their doings, for a woman cannot overcome a man by force. Flee therefore fornication, my children, and command your wives and your daughters that they adorn not their heads and their faces; because every woman who acteth deceitfully in these things hath been reserved to everlasting punishment. For thus they allured the Watchers[1] before the flood; and as these continually beheld them, they fell into desire each of the other, and they conceived the act in their mind, and changed themselves into the shape of men, and appeared to them in their congress with their husbands; and the women, having in their minds desire towards their apparitions, gave birth to giants, for the Watchers appeared to them as reaching even unto heaven.

6. Beware, therefore, of fornication; and if you wish to be pure in your mind, guard your senses against every woman. And command them likewise not to company with men, that they also be pure in their mind. For constant meetings, even though the ungodly deed be not wrought, are to them an irre-

---

[1] This name, occurring once again in the *Testaments* (*Naph.* 3), is one frequently found applied to the angels as the custodians of the world and of men. Thus, in the Chaldee of Daniel (iv. 10, 14, 20: 13, 17, 23, Eng. Ver.), we find the expression עִיר, which Aquila and Symmachus render ἐγρήγορος. The corresponding Ethiopic term is of frequent occurrence in the book of Enoch, not only of the fallen angels (*e.g.* x. 9, 15, xvi. 1, etc.), but of the good (xii. 2, 3, etc., ed. Dillmann). See also Gesenius, *Thesaurus, s.v.* עִיר.

mediable disease, and to us an everlasting reproach of Beliar; for fornication hath neither understanding nor godliness in itself, and all jealousy dwelleth in the desire thereof. Therefore ye will be jealous against the sons of Levi, and will seek to be exalted over them; but ye shall not be able, for God will work their avenging, and ye shall die by an evil death. For to Levi the Lord gave the sovereignty, and to Judah, and to me also with them,[1] and to Dan and Joseph, that we should be for rulers. Therefore I command you to hearken to Levi, because he shall know the law of the Lord, and shall give ordinances for judgment and sacrifice for all Israel until the completion of the times of Christ, the High Priest whom the Lord hath declared. I adjure you by the God of heaven to work truth each one with his neighbour; and draw ye near to Levi in humbleness of heart, that ye may receive a blessing from his mouth. For he shall bless Israel and Judah, because him hath the Lord chosen to rule over all the peoples. And worship ye his seed, because he shall die for us in wars visible and invisible, and shall be among you an everlasting king.

7. And Reuben died after that he had given command to his sons; and they placed him in a coffin until they bore him up from Egypt, and buried him in Hebron in the double[2] cave where his fathers were.

THE TESTAMENT OF SIMEON CONCERNING ENVY.

1. The copy of the words of Simeon, what things he spake to his sons before he died, in the hundred and twentieth year of his life, in the year in which Joseph died. For they came to visit him when he was sick, and he strengthened himself and sat up and kissed them, and said to them:—

2. Hear, O my children, hear Simeon your father, what things I have in my heart. I was born of Jacob my father, his second son; and my mother Leah called me Simeon, because the Lord heard her prayer.[3] I became strong exceed-

---

[1] The reading of Cd. Oxon., μετ' αὐτόν, is doubtless to be preferred.
[2] i.e. Machpelah, which in Hebrew means double, and is so rendered by the LXX., e.g. Gen. xxiii. 9.
[3] Gen. xxix. 33.

B

ingly; I shrank from no deed, nor was I afraid of anything. For my heart was hard, and my mind was unmoveable, and my bowels unfeeling: because valour also has been given from the Most High to men in soul and in body. And at that time I was jealous of Joseph because our father loved him;[1] and I set my mind against him to destroy him, because the prince of deceit sent forth the spirit of jealousy and blinded my mind, that I regarded him not as a brother, and spared not Jacob my father. But his God and the God of his fathers sent forth His angel, and delivered him out of my hands. For when I went into Shechem to bring ointment for the flocks, and Reuben to Dotham, where were our necessaries and all our stores, Judah our brother sold him to the Ishmaelites. And when Reuben came he was grieved, for he wished to have restored him safe to his father. But I was wroth against Judah in that he let him go away alive, and for five months I continued wrathful against him; but God restrained me, and withheld from me all working of my hands, for my right hand was half withered for seven days. And I knew, my children, that because of Joseph this happened to me, and I repented and wept; and I besought the Lord that He would restore my hand unto me, and that I might be kept from all pollution and envy, and from all folly. For I knew that I had devised an evil deed before the Lord and Jacob my father, on account of Joseph my brother, in that I envied him.

3. And now, children, take heed of the spirit of deceit and of envy. For envy ruleth over the whole mind of a man, and suffereth him neither to eat, nor to drink, nor to do any good thing: it ever suggesteth to him to destroy him that he envieth; and he that is envied ever flourisheth, but he that envieth fades away. Two years of days I afflicted my soul with fasting in the fear of the Lord, and I learnt that deliverance from envy cometh by the fear of God. If a man flee to the Lord, the evil

---

[1] That Simeon was prominent in the hostility to Joseph, is perhaps implied by his detention in Egypt as a surety for the return of the others; and Jewish tradition generally accords with this view. Cf. the Targum of the Pseudo-Jonathan on Gen. xxxvii. 19: "Simeon and Levi, who were brothers in counsel, said one to another, Let us kill him." Also this same Targum on Gen. xlii. 24: "And he took from them Simeon, who had counselled to kill him." Cf. also *Breshith Rabba*, § 91.

spirit runneth away from him, and his mind becometh easy. And henceforward he sympathizeth with him whom he envied, and condemneth not those who love him, and so ceaseth from his envy.

4. And my father asked concerning me, because he saw that I was sad; and I said, I am pained in my liver. For I mourned more than they all, because I was guilty of the selling of Joseph. And when we went down into Egypt, and he bound me as a spy, I knew that I was suffering justly, and I grieved not. Now Joseph was a good man, and had the Spirit of God within him: compassionate and pitiful, he bore not malice against me; nay, he loved me even as the rest of his brothers. Take heed, therefore, my children, of all jealousy and envy, and walk in singleness of soul and with good heart, keeping in mind the brother of your father, that God may give to you also grace and glory, and blessing upon your heads, even as ye saw in him. All his days he reproached us not concerning this thing, but loved us as his own soul, and beyond his own sons; and he glorified us, and gave riches, and cattle, and fruits freely to us all. Do ye then also, my beloved children, love each one his brother with a good heart, and remove from you the spirit of envy, for this maketh savage the soul and destroyeth the body; it turneth his purposes into anger and war, and stirreth up unto blood, and leadeth the mind into frenzy, and suffereth not prudence to act in men: moreover, it taketh away sleep, and causeth tumult to the soul and trembling to the body. For even in sleep some malicious jealousy, deluding him, gnaweth at his soul, and with wicked spirits disturbeth it, and causeth the body to be troubled, and the mind to awake from sleep in confusion; and as though having a wicked and poisonous spirit, so appeareth it to men.

5. Therefore was Joseph fair in appearance, and goodly to look upon, because there dwelt not in him any wickedness; for in trouble of the spirit the face declareth it. And now, my children, make your hearts good before the Lord, and your ways straight before men, and ye shall find grace before God and men. And take heed not to commit fornication, for fornication is mother of all evils, separating from God, and bringing near to Beliar. For I have seen it inscribed in the writing of Enoch that your sons shall with you be corrupted in fornication, and shall do wrong against Levi with the sword. But they

shall not prevail against Levi, for he shall wage the war of the Lord, and shall conquer all your hosts; and there shall be a few divided in Levi and Judah, and there shall be none[1] of you for sovereignty, even as also my father Jacob prophesied in his blessings.

6. Behold, I have foretold you all things, that I may be clear from the sin of your souls. Now, if ye remove from you your envy, and all your stiffneckedness, as a rose shall my bones flourish in Israel, and as a lily my flesh in Jacob, and my odour shall be as the odour of Libanus; and as cedars shall holy ones be multiplied from me for ever, and their branches shall stretch afar off. Then shall perish the seed of Canaan, and a remnant shall not be to Amalek, and all the Cappadocians[2] shall perish, and all the Hittites shall be utterly destroyed. Then shall fail the land of Ham, and every people shall perish. Then shall all the earth rest from trouble, and all the world under heaven from war. Then shall Shem be glorified, because the Lord God, the Mighty One of Israel, shall appear upon earth as man, and save by Him Adam.[3] Then shall all the spirits of deceit be given to be trampled under foot, and men shall rule over the wicked spirits. Then will I arise in joy, and will bless the Most High because of His marvellous works, because God hath taken a body and eaten with men and saved men.

7. And now, my children, obey Levi, and in Judah shall ye be redeemed: and be not lifted up against these two tribes, for from them shall arise to you the salvation of God. For the Lord shall raise up from Levi as it were a Priest, and from Judah as it were a King, God and man. So shall He save all the Gentiles and the race of Israel. Therefore I command you all things, in order that ye also may command your children, that they may observe them throughout their generations.

8. And Simeon made an end of commanding his sons, and slept with his fathers, being an hundred and twenty years old.

---

[1] The Cam. MS. seems wrongly to omit the negative here. The reference is doubtless to Gen. xlix. 7.

[2] The reference seems to be to the Philistines. Cf. Deut. ii. 23, Amos ix. 7, where the LXX. reads Καππαδοκία.

[3] The construction here is awkward of the participles after ὅτι: possibly a clause may have dropped out after 'Ἀδάμ.

And they laid him in a coffin of incorruptible wood, to take up his bones to Hebron. And they carried them up in a war of the Egyptians secretly: for the bones of Joseph the Egyptians guarded in the treasure-house of the palace; for the sorcerers told them that at the departure of the bones of Joseph there should be throughout the whole of Egypt darkness and gloom, and an exceeding great plague to the Egyptians, so that even with a lamp a man should not recognise his brother.

9. And the sons of Simeon bewailed their father according to the law of mourning, and they were in Egypt until the day of their departure from Egypt by the hand of Moses.

THE TESTAMENT OF LEVI CONCERNING THE PRIESTHOOD AND ARROGANCE.

1. The copy of the words of Levi, what things he appointed to his sons, according to all that they should do, and what things should befall them until the day of judgment. He was in sound health when he called them to him, for it had been shown to him that he should die. And when they were gathered together he said to them:—

2. I Levi was conceived in Haran and born there, and after that I came with my father to Shechem. And I was young, about twenty years of age, when with Simeon I wrought the vengeance on Hamor for our sister Dinah. And when we were feeding our flocks in Abel-Maul, a spirit of understanding of the Lord came upon me, and I saw all men corrupting their way, and that unrighteousness had built to itself walls, and iniquity sat upon towers; and I grieved for the race of men, and I prayed to the Lord that I might be saved. Then there fell upon me a sleep, and I beheld a high mountain: this is the mountain of Aspis[1] in Abel-Maul. And behold, the heavens were opened, and an angel of God said to me, Levi, enter. And I entered from the first heaven into the second, and I saw there water hanging between the one and the other. And I saw a third heaven far brighter than those two, for there was in it a height without bounds. And I said to the angel, Where-

[1] See below, c. 6.

fore is this? And the angel said to me, Marvel not at these, for thou shalt see four other heavens brighter than these, and without comparison, when thou shalt have ascended thither: because thou shalt stand near the Lord, and shalt be His minister, and shalt declare His mysteries to men, and shalt proclaim concerning Him who shall redeem Israel;[1] and by thee and Judah shall the Lord appear among men, saving in them every race of men; and of the portion of the Lord shall be thy life, and He shall be thy field and vineyard, fruits, gold, silver.

3. Hear, then, concerning the seven[2] heavens. The lowest is for this cause more gloomy, in that it is near all the iniquities of men. The second hath fire, snow, ice, ready for the day of the ordinance of the Lord, in the righteous judgment of God: in it are all the spirits of the retributions for vengeance on the wicked. In the third are the hosts of the armies which are ordained for the day of judgment, to work vengeance on the spirits of deceit and of Beliar. And the heavens up to the fourth above these are holy, for in the highest of all dwelleth the Great Glory, in the holy of holies, far above all holiness. In the heaven next to it are the angels of the presence of the Lord, who minister and make propitiation to the Lord for all the ignorances of the righteous; and they offer to the Lord a reasonable sweet-smelling savour, and a bloodless offering. And in the heaven below this are the angels who bear the answers to the angels of the presence of the Lord. And in the heaven next to this are thrones, dominions, in which hymns are ever offered to God. Therefore, whenever the Lord looketh upon us, all of us are shaken; yea, the heavens, and the earth, and the abysses, are shaken at the presence of His majesty; but the sons of men, regarding not these things, sin, and provoke the Most High.

4. Now, therefore, know that the Lord will execute judgment upon the sons of men; because when the rocks are rent, and the sun quenched, and the waters dried up, and the fire trembling, and all creation troubled, and the invisible spirits melting away, and the grave spoiled in the suffering of the

---

[1] Cf. Luke xxiv. 21.

[2] For the Jewish idea of seven heavens, cf. Clement of Alexandria, *Strom.* iv. 7; and Wetstein's note on 2 Cor. xii. 2.

Most High, men unbelieving will abide in their iniquity, therefore with punishment shall they be judged. Therefore the Most High hath heard thy prayer, to separate thee from iniquity, and that thou shouldest become to Him a son, and a servant, and a minister of His presence. A shining light of knowledge shalt thou shine in Jacob, and as the sun shalt thou be to all the seed of Israel. And a blessing shall be given to thee, and to all thy seed, until the Lord shall visit all the heathen in the tender mercies of His Son, even for ever. Nevertheless thy sons shall lay hands upon Him to crucify Him; and therefore have counsel and understanding been given thee, that thou mightest instruct thy sons concerning Him, because he that blesseth Him shall be blessed, but they that curse Him shall perish.

5. And the angel opened to me the gates of heaven, and I saw the holy temple, and the Most High upon a throne of glory. And He said to me, Levi, I have given thee the blessings of the priesthood until that I shall come and sojourn in the midst of Israel. Then the angel brought me to the earth, and gave me a shield and a sword, and said, Work vengeance on Shechem because of Dinah, and I will be with thee, because the Lord hath sent me. And I destroyed at that time the sons of Hamor, as it is written in the heavenly tablets.[1] And I said to him, I pray Thee, O Lord, tell me Thy name, that I may call upon Thee in a day of tribulation. And He said, I am the angel who intercedeth for the race of Israel, that He smite them not utterly, because every evil spirit attacketh it. And after these things I was as it were awaked, and blessed the Most High, and the angel that intercedeth for the race of Israel, and for all the righteous.

---

[1] This document, the idea of which is that of a book containing what is fore-ordained in heaven as to the course of the future, is one often appealed to in Apocalyptic literature, when some oracular declaration of weighty import is needed. Thus, in the book of Enoch, the angel Uriel tells Enoch that the tablets contain all wisdom, the dying Enoch tells his children that the tablets are the source of all understanding, etc. (see, *e.g.*, cc. 81. 1; 93. 2; 106. 19, ed. Dillmann). In the book of Jubilees, again, it is said that inscribed on the tablets are, *e.g.*, the punishment of the angels who sinned with mortal women, the plan of the division of weeks, the name of Abraham as the friend of God, etc. (cc. 5, 6, 19). See also *Test. Asher* 2, 7.

6. And when I came to my father I found a brazen shield [1] (ἀσπίς); wherefore also the name of the mountain is Aspis, which is near Gebal, on the right side of Abila; and I kept these words in my heart. I took counsel with my father, and with Reuben my brother, that he should bid the sons of Hamor that they should be circumcised; for I was jealous because of the abomination which they had wrought in Israel. And I slew Shechem at the first, and Simeon slew Hamor. And after this our brethren came and smote the city with the edge of the sword; and our father heard it and was wroth, and he was grieved in that they had received the circumcision, and after that had been put to death, and in his blessings he dealt otherwise [with us]. For we sinned because we had done this thing against his will, and he was sick upon that day. But I knew that the sentence of God was for evil upon Shechem; for they sought to do to Sarah as they did to Dinah our sister, and the Lord hindered them. And so they persecuted Abraham our father when he was a stranger, and they harried his flocks when they were multiplied upon him; and Jeblae his servant, born in his house, they shamefully handled. And thus they did to all strangers, taking away their wives by force, and the men themselves driving into exile. But the wrath of the Lord came suddenly upon them to the uttermost.[2]

7. And I said to my father, Be not angry, sir, because by thee will the Lord bring to nought the Canaanites, and will give their land to thee, and to thy seed after thee. For from this day forward shall Shechem be called a city of them that are without understanding; for as a man mocketh at a fool, so did we mock them, because they wrought folly in Israel to defile our sister. And we took our sister from thence, and departed, and came to Bethel.

8. And there I saw a thing again even as the former, after we had passed seventy days. And I saw seven men in white raiment saying to me, Arise, put on the robe of the priesthood,

---

[1] The Latin version gives the other meaning to ἀσπίς here, of asp or viper. The epithet χαλκῆν, however, renders "shield" much more probable, as there seems nothing in the context pointing to the "brazen serpent."

[2] A quotation from 1 Thess. ii. 16, where the context also is similar to the present.

and the crown of righteousness, and the breastplate of understanding, and the garment of truth, and the diadem of faith, and the tiara of miracle, and the ephod of prophecy.[1] And each one of them bearing each of these things put them on me, and said, From henceforth become a priest of the Lord, thou and thy seed for ever. And the first anointed me with holy oil, and gave to me the rod of judgment. The second washed me with pure water, and fed me with bread and wine, the most holy things,[2] and clad me with a holy and glorious robe. The third clothed me with a linen vestment like to an ephod. The fourth put round me a girdle like unto purple. The fifth gave to me a branch of rich olive. The sixth placed a crown on my head. The seventh placed on my head a diadem of priesthood, and filled my hands with incense, so that I served as a priest to the Lord. And they said to me, Levi, thy seed shall be divided into three branches,[3] for a sign of the glory of the Lord who is to come; and he that hath been faithful shall be first: no portion shall be greater than his. The second shall be in the priesthood. The third—a new name shall be called over Him, because He shall arise as King from Judah, and shall establish a new priesthood, after the fashion of the Gentiles, to all the Gentiles. And His appearing shall be unutterable, as of an exalted[4] prophet of the seed of Abraham our father. Every desirable thing in Israel shall be for thee and for thy seed, and everything fair to look upon shall ye eat, and the table of the Lord shall thy seed apportion, and some of them shall be high priests, and judges, and scribes; for by their mouth shall the holy place be guarded. And when I awoke, I understood that

---

[1] With the whole of this passage we may compare the description of the vestments of Aaron. See especially Ex. xxix. 5, 6 (LXX.). The πίταλον is the translation of ץיצ, the plate of gold on the forehead of the high priest over the mitre. The λογίον, or λογεῖον, is the breastplate, with the Urim and Thummim. For the ποδήρης, see Ex. xxviii. 27 (LXX.).

[2] On the possible reference here to the elements of the Eucharist, see Grabe's note, *Spicilegium*, in loc.

[3] Nitzsch (p. 19, n. 37) explains this division into three ἀρχαί, as referring to the three orders of the Christian priesthood. This, however, seems improbable. Cf. Kayser, p. 119; Vorstman, p. 41. It is far more probable that the reference is to Moses, Aaron, and Christ. Thus with πιστεύσας we may compare Num. xii. 7. For this use of ἀρχή, cf. Gen. ii. 10.

[4] Or, if we follow the reading of Cd. Oxon., "Prophet of the Most High."

this thing was like unto the former. And I hid this also in my heart, and told it not to any man upon the earth.

9. And after two days I and Judah went up to Isaac after[1] our father; and the father of my father blessed me according to all the words of the visions which I had seen: and he would not come with us to Bethel. And when we came to Bethel, my father Jacob saw in a vision concerning me, that I should be to them for a priest unto the Lord; and he rose up early in the morning, and paid tithes of all to the Lord through me. And we came to Hebron to dwell there, and Isaac called me continually to put me in remembrance of the law of the Lord, even as the angel of God showed to me. And he taught me the law of the priesthood, of sacrifices, whole burnt-offerings, first-fruits, free-will offerings, thank-offerings. And each day he was instructing me, and was busied for me before the Lord. And he said to me, Take heed, my child, of the spirit of fornication; for this shall continue, and shall by thy seed pollute the holy things. Take therefore to thyself, while yet thou art young, a wife, not having blemish, nor yet polluted, nor of the race of the Philistines or Gentiles. And before entering into the holy place, bathe;[2] and when thou offerest the sacrifice, wash; and again when thou finishest the sacrifice, wash. Of twelve trees ever having leaves, offer up [the fruits] to the Lord, as also Abraham taught me; and of every clean beast and clean bird offer a sacrifice to the Lord, and of every firstling and of wine offer first-fruits; and every sacrifice thou shalt salt with salt.[3]

10. Now, therefore, observe whatsoever I command you, children; for whatsoever things I have heard from my fathers I have made known to you. I am clear from all your ungodliness and transgression which ye will do in the end of the ages against the Saviour of the world, acting ungodly, deceiving Israel, and raising up against it great evils from the Lord. And ye will deal lawlessly with Israel, so that Jerusalem shall not endure your wickedness; but the veil of the temple shall

---

[1] Or rather, with Cd. Oxon., "with our father."

[2] We constantly find Peter, in the *Clementine Homilies* and *Recognitions*, combining with the Agapæ the practice of bathing. Cf. *e.g. Recog.* iv. 3, v. 36.

[3] Cf. *Hom.* xiv. 1.

be rent, so as not to cover your shame. And ye shall be scattered as captives among the heathen, and shall be for a reproach and for a curse, and for a trampling under foot. For the house which the Lord shall choose shall be called Jerusalem, as is contained in the book of Enoch the righteous.[1]

11. Therefore, when I took a wife I was twenty-eight years old, and her name was Melcha. And she conceived and bare a son, and she called his name Gersham, for we were sojourners in our land: for Gersham is interpreted sojourning. And I saw concerning him that he would not be in the first rank. And Kohath was born in my thirty-fifth year, towards the east. And I saw in a vision that he was standing on high in the midst of all the congregation. Therefore I called his name Kohath, which meaneth, beginning of majesty and instruction. And thirdly, she bare to me Merari, in the fortieth year of my life; and since his mother bare him with difficulty, she called him Merari, which meaneth my bitterness, because he also died. And Jochebed was born in my sixty-fourth year, in Egypt, for I was renowned then in the midst of my brethren.

12. And Gersham took a wife, and she bare to him Lomni and Semei. And the sons of Kohath, Ambram, Isaar, Chebro, and Ozel. And the sons of Merari, Mooli and Homusi. And in my ninety-fourth year Ambram took Jochebed my daughter to him to wife, for they were born in one day, he and my daughter. Eight years old was I when I went into the land of Canaan, and eighteen years when I slew Shechem, and at nineteen years I became priest, and at twenty-eight years I took a wife, and at forty years I went into Egypt. And behold, ye are my children, my children even a third generation. In my hundred and eighteenth year Joseph died.

13. And now, my children, I command you that ye fear our Lord with your whole heart, and walk in simplicity according to all His[2] law. And do ye also teach your children

---

[1] This document is frequently quoted in the *Testaments*: cf. *Sim.* 5; *Levi* 14, 16; *Judah* 18; *Dan* 5; *Naph.* 4; *Benj.* 9. Most of these citations, however, are not to be found in the work as it has come down to us. We must therefore either assume the reference to some other books of Enoch not now extant, or rather perhaps that they are general appeals to the spirit of the book, regarded as a great fount of prophecy.

[2] Read αὐτοῦ with Cd. Oxon.

learning, that they may have understanding in all their life, reading unceasingly the law of God; for every one who shall know the law of God shall be honoured, and shall not be a stranger wheresoever he goeth. Yea, many friends shall he gain more than his forefathers; and many men shall desire to serve him, and to hear the law from his mouth. Work righteousness, my children, upon the earth, that ye may find [treasure] in the heavens, and sow good things in your souls, that ye may find them in your life. For if ye sow evil things, ye shall reap all trouble and affliction. Get wisdom in the fear of God with diligence; for though there shall be a leading into captivity, and cities be destroyed, and lands and gold and silver and every possession shall perish, the wisdom of the wise none can take away, save the blindness of ungodliness and the palsy of sin: for even among his enemies shall it be to him glorious, and in a strange country a home, and in the midst of foes shall it be found a friend. If a man teach these things and do them, he shall be enthroned with kings, as was also Joseph our brother.

14. And now, my children, I have learnt from the writing of Enoch that at the last ye will deal ungodly, laying your hands upon the Lord in all malice; and your brethren shall be ashamed because of you, and to all the Gentiles shall it become a mocking. For our father Israel shall be pure from the ungodliness of the chief priests who shall lay their hands upon the Saviour of the world. Pure is the heaven above the earth, and ye are the lights of the heaven as the sun and the moon. What shall all the Gentiles do if ye be darkened in ungodliness? So shall ye bring a curse upon our race for whom came the light of the world, which was given among you for the lighting up of every man. Him will ye desire to slay, teaching commandments contrary to the ordinances of God. The offerings of the Lord will ye rob, and from His portion will ye steal; and before ye sacrifice to the Lord, ye will take the choicest parts, in despitefulness eating them with harlots. Amid excesses[1] will ye teach the commandments of

---

[1] The word πλεονεξία, like the English "excess," has not unfrequently special reference to sins of sensuality. Cf. 1 Cor. v. 11, Eph. iv. 19, v. 3, 5, Col. iii. 5, 1 Thess. iv. 6, the context in all of which passages points strongly to this conclusion. See Suicer's *Thesaurus, s.v.*

the Lord, the women that have husbands will ye pollute, and
the virgins of Jerusalem will ye defile; and with harlots and
adulteresses will ye be joined. The daughters of the Gentiles
will ye take for wives, purifying them with an unlawful
purification; and your union shall be like unto Sodom and
Gomorrah in ungodliness. And ye will be puffed up because
of the priesthood lifting yourselves up against men. And not
only so, but being puffed up also against the commands of God,
ye will scoff at the holy things, mocking in despitefulness.

15. Therefore the temple which the Lord shall choose shall
be desolate in uncleanness, and ye shall be captives throughout
all nations, and ye shall be an abomination among them, and
ye shall receive reproach and everlasting shame from the
righteous judgment of God; and all who see you shall flee
from you. And were it not for Abraham, Isaac, and Jacob our
fathers, not one from my seed should be left upon the earth.

16. And now I have learnt in the book of Enoch that for
seventy weeks will ye go astray, and will profane the priesthood, and pollute the sacrifices, and corrupt the law, and set
at nought the words of the prophets. In perverseness ye will
persecute righteous men, and hate the godly; the words of
the faithful will ye abhor, and the man who reneweth the law
in the power of the Most High will ye call a deceiver;[1]
and at last, as ye suppose, ye will slay Him, not understanding
His resurrection, wickedly taking upon your own heads the
innocent blood. Because of Him shall your holy places be
desolate, polluted even to the ground, and ye shall have no
place that is clean; but ye shall be among the Gentiles a curse
and a dispersion, until He shall again look upon you, and in
pity shall take you to Himself through faith and water.

17. And because ye have heard concerning the seventy
weeks, hear also concerning the priesthood; for in each jubilee
there shall be a priesthood. In the first jubilee, the first who
is anointed into the priesthood shall be great, and shall speak
to God as to a Father; and his priesthood shall be filled with
the fear of the Lord, and in the day of his gladness shall he
arise for the salvation of the world. In the second jubilee, he
that is anointed shall be conceived in the sorrow of beloved
ones; and his priesthood shall be honoured, and shall be glorified

---

[1] Cf. Matt. xxvii. 63, where ἐκεῖνος ὁ πλάνος is said of our Lord.

among all. And the third priest shall be held fast in sorrow; and the fourth shall be in grief, because unrighteousness shall be laid upon him exceedingly, and all Israel shall hate each one his neighbour. The fifth shall be held fast in darkness, likewise also the sixth and the seventh. And in the seventh there shall be such pollution as I am not able to express, before the Lord and men, for they shall know it who do these things. Therefore shall they be in captivity and for a prey, and their land and their substance shall be destroyed. And in the fifth week they shall return into their desolate country, and shall renew the house of the Lord. And in the seventh week shall come the priests, worshippers of idols, contentious, lovers of money, proud, lawless, lascivious, abusers of children and beasts.

18. And after their punishment shall have come from the Lord, then will the Lord raise up to the priesthood a new Priest, to whom all the words of the Lord shall be revealed; and He shall execute a judgment of truth upon the earth, in the fulness of days. And His star shall arise in heaven, as a king shedding forth the light of knowledge in the sunshine of day, and He shall be magnified in the world until His ascension. He shall shine forth as the sun in the earth, and shall drive away all darkness from the world under heaven, and there shall be peace in all the earth. The heavens shall rejoice in His days, and the earth shall be glad, and the clouds shall be joyful, and the knowledge of the Lord shall be poured forth upon the earth, as the water of seas; and the angels of the glory of the presence of the Lord shall be glad in Him. The heavens shall be opened, and from the temple of glory shall the sanctification come upon Him with the Father's voice, as from Abraham the father of Isaac. And the glory of the Most High shall be uttered over Him, and the spirit of understanding and of sanctification shall rest upon Him in the water. He shall give the majesty of the Lord to His sons in truth for evermore; and there shall none succeed Him for all generations, even for ever.[1] And in His priesthood shall all sin come to an end, and the lawless shall rest from evil, and the just shall rest in Him. And He shall open the gates of paradise,

---

[1] An additional clause occurs here in Cd. Oxon., which generally has a tendency to omit; the copyist of Cd. Cam. having possibly looked on to the same initial words in the next clause: "And in His priesthood shall

and shall remove¹ the threatening sword against Adam; and He shall give to His saints to eat from the tree of life, and the spirit of holiness shall be on them. And Beliar shall be bound by Him, and He shall give power to His children to tread upon the evil spirits. And the Lord shall rejoice in His children, and the Lord shall be well pleased in His beloved for ever. Then shall Abraham and Isaac and Jacob be joyful, and I will be glad, and all the saints shall put on gladness.

19. And now, my children, ye have heard all; choose therefore for yourselves either the darkness or the light, either the law of the Lord or the works of Beliar. And we answered our father, saying, Before the Lord will we walk according to His law. And our father said, The Lord is witness, and His angels are witnesses, and I am witness, and ye are witnesses, concerning the word of your mouth. And we said, We are witnesses. And thus Levi ceased giving charge to his sons; and he stretched out his feet, and was gathered to his fathers, after he had lived a hundred and thirty-seven years. And they laid him in a coffin, and afterwards they buried him in Hebron, by the side of Abraham, and Isaac, and Jacob.

THE TESTAMENT OF JUDAH CONCERNING FORTITUDE, AND LOVE OF MONEY, AND FORNICATION.

1. The copy of the words of Judah, what things he spake to his sons before he died. They gathered themselves together, and came to him, and he said to them: I was the fourth son born to my father, and my mother called me Judah, saying, I give thanks to the Lord, because He hath given to me even a fourth son.² I was swift and active in my youth, and obedient

the Gentiles be multiplied in knowledge on the earth, and shall be enlightened through the grace of the Lord; but Israel shall be minished in ignorance, and be darkened in sorrow."

¹ The reading of Cd. Oxon. here, ἀποστήσει, is to be preferred to Cd. Cam., στήσει. Grosseteste's Latin version, in all probability made from the latter, has *stare faciet*.
² Gen. xxix. 35.

to my father in everything. And I honoured my mother and my mother's sister. And it came to pass, when I became a man, that my father Jacob prayed over me, saying, Thou shalt be a king, and prosperous in all things.

2. And the Lord showed me favour in all my works both in the field and at home. When I saw that I could run with the hind, then I caught it, and prepared meat for my father. I seized upon the roes in the chase, and all that was in the plains I outran. A wild mare I outran, and I caught it and tamed it; and I slew a lion, and plucked a kid out of its mouth. I took a bear by its paw, and rolled it over a cliff; and if any beast turned upon me, I rent it like a dog. I encountered the wild boar, and overtaking it in the chase, I tore it. A leopard in Hebron leaped upon the dog, and I caught it by the tail, and flung it from me, and it was dashed to pieces in the coasts of Gaza. A wild ox feeding in the field I seized by the horns; and whirling it round and stunning it, I cast it from me, and slew it.

3. And when the two kings of the Canaanites came in warlike array against our flocks, and much people with them, I by myself rushed upon King Sur and seized him; and I beat him upon the legs, and dragged him down, and so I slew him. And the other king, Taphue,[1] I slew as he sat upon his horse, and so I scattered all the people. Achor the king, a man of giant stature, hurling darts before and behind as he sat on horseback, I slew; for I hurled a stone of sixty pounds weight, and cast it upon his horse, and killed him. And I fought with Achor for two hours, and I killed him; and I clave his shield into two parts, and I chopped off his feet. And as I stripped off his breastplate, behold, eight men his companions began to fight with me. I wound round therefore my garment in my hand; and I slang stones at them, and killed four of them, and the rest fled. And Jacob my father slew Beelisa, king of all the kings, a giant in strength, twelve cubits high; and fear fell upon them, and they ceased from making war with us. Therefore

---

[1] In c. 5 we find this name, with a slight variety of spelling, as that of a place over which this king may have ruled. It is doubtless equivalent to the Hebrew Tappuah, a name of several cities mentioned in the Old Testament. See Josh. xv. 34, xvi. 8. xvii. 8, 1 Chron. ii. 43. Cf. Thapha, *Jubilees*, 34.

my father had no care in the wars when I was among my brethren. For he saw in a vision concerning me, that an angel of might followed me everywhere, that I should not be overcome.

4. And in the south there befell us a greater war than that in Shechem; and I joined in battle array with my brethren, and pursued a thousand men, and slew of them two hundred men and four kings. And I went up against them upon the wall, and two other kings I slew; and so we freed Hebron, and took all the captives of the kings.

5. On the next day we departed to Areta,[1] a city strong and walled and inaccessible, threatening us with death. Therefore I and Gad approached on the east side of the city, and Reuben and Levi on the west and south. And they that were upon the wall, thinking that we were alone, charged down upon us; and so our brethren secretly climbed up the wall on both sides by ladders, and entered into the city, while the men knew it not. And we took it with the edge of the sword; and those who had taken refuge in the tower,—we set fire to the tower, and took both it and them. And as we were departing the men of Thaffu set upon our captives, and we took it with our sons, and fought with them even to Thaffu; and we slew them, and burnt their city, and spoiled all the things that were therein.

6. And when I was at the waters of Chuzeba,[2] the men of Jobel came against us to battle, and we fought with them; and their allies from Selom[3] we slew, and we allowed them no means of escaping, and of coming against us. And the men of Machir[4] came upon us on the fifth day, to carry away our captives; and we attacked them, and overcame them in fierce battle: for they were a host and mighty in themselves, and we slew them before they had gone up the ascent of the hill. And when we came to their city, their women rolled upon us stones from the brow of the hill on which the city stood. And I and Simeon hid ourselves behind the town, and seized upon the heights, and utterly destroyed the whole city.

---

[1] Cd. Oxon. reads ἐτέραν; but cf. Aresa, *Jubilees*, 34.

[2] Cf. c. 12; also Chezib (Gen. xxxviii. 5), Chozeba (1 Chron. iv. 22), and Achzib (Josh. xv. 44; Mic. i. 14), all of which are probably different names for the same place, and all connected with Judah.

[3] Cf. Selo, *Jubilees*, l.c.   [4] Cf. 1 Chron. xi. 36 [?].

7. And the next day it was told us that the cities[1] of the two kings with a great host were coming against us. I therefore and Dan feigned ourselves to be Amorites, and went as allies into their city. And in the depth of night our brethren came, and we opened to them the gates; and we destroyed all the men and their substance, and we took for a prey all that was theirs, and their three walls we cast down. And we drew near to Thamna,[2] where was all the refuge of the hostile kings. Then having received hurt I was wroth, and charged upon them to the brow of the hill; and they slang at me with stones and darts; and had not Dan my brother aided me, they would have been able to slay me. We came upon them therefore with wrath, and they all fled; and passing by another way, they besought my father, and he made peace with them, and we did to them no hurt, but made a truce with them, and restored to them all the captives. And I built Thamna, and my father built Rhambael.[3] I was twenty years old when this war befell, and the Canaanites feared me and my brethren.

8. Moreover, I had much cattle, and I had for the chief of my herdsmen Iran[4] the Adullamite. And when I went to him I saw Barsan king of Adullam, and he made us a feast; and he entreated me, and gave me his daughter Bathshua to wife. She bare me Er, and Onan, and Shelah; and the two of them the Lord smote that they died childless: for Shelah lived, and his children are ye.

9. Eighteen years we abode at peace, our father and we, with his brother Esau, and his sons with us, after that we came from Mesopotamia, from Laban. And when eighteen years were fulfilled, in the fortieth year of my life, Esau, the brother of my father, came upon us with much people and strong; and

---

[1] Cd. Oxon. reads Γαᾶς πόλις βασιλέων. Cf. Josh. xxiv. 30; Judg. ii. 9; 2 Sam. xxiii. 30. Cf. also "Gaiz," *Jubilees*, l.c.

[2] The Timnah of the Old Testament, which name is, however, borne by several places. Most probably it is the Timnah near Bethshemesh, on the north frontier of Judah, in the neighbourhood, that is, of many of the other localities mentioned in the *Testaments*. This may be the same as the Timnathah on the Danite frontier (Josh. xix. 43), and with the Timnathah where Samson's wife dwelt (Judg. xiv. 1 sqq.). The geographical position of Timnath-serah is against the allusion being to it here. Cf., however, *Jubilees*, c. 34, where *Thamnathares* is one of the hostile towns.

[3] Cf. Robel, *Jubilees*, l.c.   [4] Cf. Gen. xxxviii. 1.

he fell by the bow of Jacob, and was taken up dead in Mount Seir: even as he went above Iramna[1] was he slain. And we pursued after the sons of Esau. Now they had a city with walls of iron and gates of brass; and we could not enter into it, and we encamped around, and besieged them. And when they opened not to us after twenty days, I set up a ladder in the sight of all, and with my shield upon my head I climbed up, assailed with stones of three talents' weight; and I climbed up, and slew four who were mighty among them. And the next day Reuben and Gad entered in and slew sixty others. Then they asked from us terms of peace; and being aware of our father's purpose, we received them as tributaries. And they gave us two hundred cors of wheat, five hundred baths of oil, fifteen hundred measures of wine, until we went down into Egypt.

10. After these things, my son Er took to wife Tamar, from Mesopotamia, a daughter of Aram.[2] Now Er was wicked, and he doubted concerning Tamar, because she was not of the land of Canaan. And on the third day an angel of the Lord smote him in the night, and he had not known her, according to the evil craftiness of his mother, for he did not wish to have children from her. In the days of the wedding-feast I espoused Onan to her; and he also in wickedness knew her not, though he lived with her a year. And when I threatened him, he lay with her, διέφθειρε δὲ τὸ σπέρμα ἐπὶ τὴν γῆν, according to the command of his mother, and he also died in his wickedness. And I wished to give Shelah also to her, but my wife Bathshua suffered it not; for she bore a spite against Tamar, because she was not of the daughters of Canaan, as she herself was.

11. And I knew that the race of Canaan was wicked, but the thoughts of youth blinded my heart. And when I saw her pouring out wine, in the drunkenness of wine was I deceived, and I fell before her. And while I was away, she went and took for Shelah a wife from the land of Canaan. And when I knew what she had done, I cursed her in the anguish of my soul, and she also died in the wickedness of her sons.

---

[1] Cd. Oxon. ἐν 'Ασονιράμ, probably per incuriam scribæ, for ἐπάνω 'Ιράμ.

[2] This seems to arise from the wish to disconnect Israel as far as possible from non-Shemite associations. Cf. the Targum of Onkelos on Gen. xxxviii. 6. "Judah took a wife for Er, his first-born, *a daughter of the great Shem*, whose name was Tamar."

12. And after these things, while Tamar was a widow, she heard after two years that I was going up to shear my sheep; then she decked herself in bridal array, and sat over against the city by the gate. For it is a law of the Amorites, that she who is about to marry sit in fornication seven days by the gate. I therefore being drunk at the waters of Chozeb, recognised her not by reason of wine; and her beauty deceived me, through the fashion of her adorning. And I turned aside to her, and said, I would enter in to thee. And she said to me, What wilt thou give me? And I gave her my staff, and my girdle, and my royal crown; and I lay with her, and she conceived. I then, not knowing what she had done, wished to slay her; but she privily sent my pledges, and put me to shame. And when I called her, I heard also the secret words which I spoke when lying with her in my drunkenness; and I could not slay her, because it was from the Lord. For I said, Lest haply she did it in subtlety, and received the pledge from another woman: but I came near her no more till my death, because I had done this abomination in all Israel. Moreover, they who were in the city said that there was no bride in the city, because she came from another place, and sat for awhile in the gate, and she thought that no one knew that I had gone in to her. And after this we came into Egypt to Joseph, because of the famine. Forty and six years old was I, and seventy and three years lived I there.

13. And now, my children, in what things soever I command you hearken to your father, and keep all my sayings to perform the ordinances of the Lord, and to obey the command of the Lord God. And walk not after your lusts, nor in the thoughts of your imaginations in the haughtiness of your heart; and glory not in the works of the strength of youth, for this also is evil in the eyes of the Lord. For since I also gloried that in wars the face of no woman of goodly form ever deceived me, and upbraided Reuben my brother concerning Bilhah, the wife of my father, the spirits of jealousy and of fornication arrayed themselves within me, until I fell before Bathshua the Canaanite, and Tamar who was espoused to my sons. And I said to my father-in-law, I will counsel with my father, and so will I take thy daughter. And he showed me a boundless store of gold in his daughter's behalf, for he was a king. And he

decked her with gold and pearls, and caused her to pour out wine for us at the feast in womanly beauty. And the wine led my eyes astray, and pleasure blinded my heart; and I loved her, and I fell, and transgressed the commandment of the Lord and the commandment of my fathers, and I took her to wife. And the Lord rewarded me according to the thought of my heart, insomuch that I had no joy in her children.

14. And now, my children, be not drunk with wine; for wine turneth the mind away from the truth, and kindleth in it the passion of lust, and leadeth the eyes into error. For the spirit of fornication hath wine as a minister to give pleasures to the mind; for these two take away the power from a man. For if a man drink wine to drunkenness, he disturbeth his mind with filthy thoughts to fornicaion, and exciteth his body to carnal union; and if the cause of the desire be present, he worketh the sin, and is not ashamed. Such is wine, my children; for he who is drunken reverenceth no man. For, lo, it made me also to err, so that I was not ashamed of the multitude in the city, because before the eyes of all I turned aside unto Tamar, and I worked a great sin, and I uncovered the covering of the shame of my sons. After that I drank wine I reverenced not the commandment of God, and I took a woman of Canaan to wife. Wherefore, my children, he who drinketh wine needeth discretion; and herein is discretion in drinking wine, that a man should drink as long as he keepeth decency; but if he go beyond this bound, the spirit of deceit attacketh his mind and worketh his will; and it maketh the drunkard to talk filthily, and to transgress and not to be ashamed, but even to exult in his dishonour, accounting himself to do well.

15. He that committeth fornication, and[1] uncovereth his nakedness, hath become the servant of fornication, and escapeth not[2] from the power thereof, even as I also was uncovered. For I gave my staff, that is, the stay of my tribe; and my girdle, that is, my power; and my diadem, that is, the glory of my kingdom. Then I repented for these things, and

[1] Cd. Oxon. here reads the additional clause, ζημιούμενος οὐκ αἰσθάνεται καὶ ἄδοξον οὐκ αἰσχύνεται. Κἂν γάρ τις βασιλεύσῃ, πορνεύων,—perhaps omitted from Cd. Cant. through the homœoteleuton.

[2] Cd. Oxon. omits the negative. The βασιλεία will then be that from which the man falls by his sin.

took no wine or flesh until my old age, nor did I behold any joy. And the angel of God showed me that for ever do women bear rule over king and beggar alike; and from the king they take away his glory, and from the valiant man his strength, and from the beggar even that little which is the stay of his poverty.

16. Observe therefore, my children, moderation in wine; for there are in it four evil spirits—of lust, of wrath, of riot, of filthy lucre. If ye drink wine in gladness, with shamefacedness, with the fear of God, ye shall live. For if ye drink not with shamefacedness, and the fear of God departeth from you, then cometh drunkenness, and shamelessness stealeth in. But[1] if ye drink not at all, take heed lest ye sin in words of outrage, and fighting, and slander, and transgression of the commandments of God; so shall ye perish before your time. Moreover, wine revealeth the mysteries of God and men to aliens, even as I also revealed the commandments of God and the mysteries of Jacob my father to the Canaanitish Bathshua, to whom God forbade to declare them. And wine also is a cause of war and confusion.

17. I charge you, therefore, my children, not to love money, nor to gaze upon the beauty of women; because for the sake of money and beauty I was led astray to Bathshua the Canaanite. For I know that because of these two things shall ye who are my race fall into wickedness; for even wise men among my sons shall they mar, and shall cause the kingdom of Judah to be diminished, which the Lord gave me because of my obedience to my father. For I never disobeyed a word of Jacob my father, for all things whatsoever he commanded I did. And Abraham, the father of my father, blessed me that I should be king in Israel, and Isaac further blessed me in like manner. And I know that from me shall the kingdom be established.

18. For I have read also in the books of Enoch the righteous what evils ye shall do in the last days. Take heed, therefore, my children, of fornication and the love of money; hearken to Judah your father, for these things do withdraw you from the law of God, and blind the understanding of the soul, and teach

---

[1] Cd. Oxon. reads τί δὲ λέγω; μηδ' ὅλως πίνετε, which seems much more suitable to the context.

arrogance, and suffer not a man to have compassion upon his neighbour: they rob his soul of all goodness, and bind him in toils and troubles, and take away his sleep and devour his flesh, and hinder the sacrifices of God; and he remembereth not blessing, and he hearkeneth not to a prophet when he speaketh, and is vexed at the word of godliness. For one who serveth two passions contrary to the commandments of God cannot obey God, because they have blinded his soul, and he walketh in the day-time as in the night.

19. My children, the love of money leadeth to idols; because, when led astray through money, men make mention of those who are no gods, and it causeth him who hath it to fall into madness. For the sake of money I lost my children, and but for the repentance of my flesh, and the humbling of my soul, and the prayers of Jacob my father, I should have died childless. But the God of my fathers, who is pitiful and merciful, pardoned me, because I did it in ignorance. For the prince of deceit blinded me, and I was ignorant as a man and as flesh, being corrupted in sins; and I learnt my own weakness while thinking myself unconquerable.

20. [1] Learn therefore, my children, that two spirits wait upon man—the spirit of truth and the spirit of error; and in the midst is the spirit of the understanding of the mind, to which it belongeth to turn whithersoever it will. And the works of truth and the works of error are written upon the breast of men, and each one of them the Lord knoweth. And there is no time at which the works of men can be hid from Him; for on the bones of his breast hath he been written down before the Lord. And the spirit of truth testifieth all things, and accuseth all; and he who sinneth is burnt up by his own heart, and cannot raise his face unto the Judge.

21. And now, my children, love Levi, that ye may abide, and exalt not yourselves against him, lest ye be utterly destroyed. For to me the Lord gave the kingdom, and to him the priesthood, and He set the kingdom beneath the priesthood. To me He gave the things upon the earth; to him the things in the heavens. As the heaven is higher than the earth, so is the priesthood of God higher than the kingdom upon the earth. For the Lord chose him above thee, to draw near to Him, and

[1] Cd. Oxon. omits the whole of this chapter.

to eat of His table and first-fruits, even the choice things of the sons of Israel, and thou shalt be to them as a sea. For as, on the sea, just and unjust are tossed about, some taken into captivity while others are enriched, so also shall every race of men be in thee, some are in jeopardy and taken captive, and others shall grow rich by means of plunder. For they who rule will be as great sea-monsters, swallowing up men like fishes: free sons and daughters do they enslave; houses, lands, flocks, money, will they plunder; and with the flesh of many will they wrongfully feed the ravens and the cranes; and they will go on further in evil, advancing on still in covetousness. And there shall be false prophets like tempests, and they shall persecute all righteous men.

22. And the Lord shall bring upon them divisions one against another, and there shall be continual wars in Israel; and among men of other race shall my kingdom be brought to an end, until the salvation of Israel shall come, until the appearing of the God of righteousness, that Jacob and all the Gentiles may rest in peace. And he shall guard the might of my kingdom for ever: for the Lord sware to me with an oath that the kingdom should never fail from me, and from my seed for all days, even for ever.

23. Now I have much grief, my children, because of your lewdness, and witchcrafts, and idolatries, which ye will work against the kingdom, following them that have familiar spirits; ye[1] will make your daughters singing girls and harlots for divinations and demons of error, and ye will be mingled in the pollutions of the Gentiles: for which things' sake the Lord shall bring upon you famine and pestilence, death and the sword, avenging siege, and dogs for the rending in pieces of enemies, and revilings of friends, destruction and blighting of eyes, children slaughtered, wives carried off, possessions plundered, temple of God in flames, your land desolated, your own selves enslaved among the Gentiles, and they shall make some of you eunuchs for their wives; and whenever ye will return to the Lord with humility of heart, repenting and walking in all the commandments of God, then will the Lord visit you in mercy and in love, bringing you from out of the bondage of your enemies.

---

[1] The reading of Cd. Oxon. is doubtless to be preferred, which joins κλήδοσι καὶ δαίμοσι πλάνης to what precedes.

24. And after these things shall a star arise to you from Jacob in peace, and a man shall rise from my seed, like the Sun of righteousness, walking with the sons of men in meekness and righteousness, and no sin shall be found in Him. And the heavens shall be opened above Him, to shed forth the blessing of the Spirit from the Holy Father; and He shall shed forth a spirit of grace upon you, and ye shall be unto Him sons in truth, and ye shall walk in His commandments, the first and the last. This is the Branch of God Most High, and this the well-spring unto life for all flesh. [1]Then shall the sceptre of my kingdom shine forth, and from your root shall arise a stem; and in it shall arise a rod of righteousness to the Gentiles, to judge and to save all that call upon the Lord.

25. And after these things shall Abraham and Isaac and Jacob arise unto life, and I and my brethren will be chiefs, even your sceptre in Israel: Levi first, I the second, Joseph third, Benjamin fourth, Simeon fifth, Issachar sixth, and so all in order. And the Lord blessed Levi; the Angel of the Presence, me; the powers of glory, Simeon; the heaven, Reuben; the earth, Issachar; the sea, Zebulun; the mountains, Joseph; the tabernacle, Benjamin; the lights of heaven, Dan; the fatness of earth, Naphtali; the sun, Gad; the olive, Asher: and there shall be one people of the Lord, and one tongue; and there shall no more be a spirit of deceit of Beliar, for he shall be cast into the fire for ever. And they who have died in grief shall arise in joy, and they who have lived in poverty for the Lord's sake shall be made rich, and they who have been in want shall be filled, and they who have been weak shall be made strong, and they who have been put to death for the Lord's sake shall awake in life. And the harts of Jacob shall run in joyfulness, and the eagles of Israel shall fly in gladness; but the ungodly shall lament, and sinners shall weep, and all the people shall glorify the Lord for ever.

26. Observe, therefore, my children, all the law of the Lord, for there is hope for all them who follow His way aright. And he said to them: I die before your eyes this day, a hundred and nineteen years old. Let no one bury me in costly apparel, nor tear open my bowels,[2] for this shall they who are kings

---

[1] Cd. Oxon. omits from here to end of c. 25.
[2] *i.e.* for the purpose of embalmment.

do: and carry me up to Hebron with you. And Judah, when he had said these things, fell asleep; and his sons did according to all whatsoever he commanded them, and they buried him in Hebron with his fathers.

THE TESTAMENT OF ISSACHAR CONCERNING SIMPLICITY.

1. The record of the words of Issachar. He called his sons, and said to them: Hearken, my children, to Issachar your father; give ear to my words, ye who are beloved of the Lord. I was the fifth son born to Jacob, even the hire of the mandrakes.[1] For Reuben[2] brought in mandrakes from the field, and Rachel met him and took them. And Reuben wept, and at his voice Leah my mother came forth. Now these mandrakes were sweet-smelling apples which the land of Aram produced on high ground below a ravine of water. And Rachel said, I will not give them to thee, for they shall be to me instead of children. Now there were two apples; and Leah said, Let it suffice thee that thou hast taken the husband of my virginity: wilt thou also take these? And she said, Behold, let Jacob be to thee this night instead of the mandrakes of thy son. And Leah said to her, Boast not, and vaunt not thyself; for Jacob is mine, and I am the wife of his youth. But Rachel said, How so? for to me was he first espoused, and for my sake he served our father fourteen years. What shall I do to thee, because the craft and the subtlety of men are increased, and craft prospereth upon the earth. And were it not so, thou wouldest not now see the face of Jacob. For thou art not his wife, but in craft wert taken to him in my stead. And my father deceived me, and removed me on that night, and suffered me not to see him; for had I been there, it had not happened thus. And Rachel said, Take one mandrake, and for the other thou shalt hire him from me for one night. And Jacob knew Leah, and she conceived and bare me, and on account of the hire (*sachar*) I was called Issachar.

2. Then appeared to Jacob an angel of the Lord, saying,

---

[1] See Gen. xxx. 14 sqq.
[2] The Cam. MS. reads 'Ιακώβ by an obvious error.

Two children shall Rachel bear; for she hath refused company with her husband, and hath chosen continency. And had not Leah my mother given up the two apples for the sake of his company, she would have borne eight sons; and for this thing she bare six, and Rachel two: because on account of the mandrakes the Lord visited her. For He knew that for the sake of children she wished to company with Jacob, and not for lust of pleasure. For she went further, and on the morrow too gave up Jacob that she might receive also the other mandrake. Therefore the Lord hearkened to Rachel because of the mandrakes: for though she desired them, she ate them not, but brought them to the priest of the Most High who was at that time, and offered them up in the house of the Lord.

3. When, therefore, I grew up, my children, I walked in uprightness of heart, and I became a husbandman for my parents and my brethren, and I brought in fruits from the field according to their season; and my father blessed me, for he saw that I walked in simplicity. And I was not a busybody in my doings, nor malicious and slanderous against my neighbour. I never spoke against any one, nor did I censure the life of any man, but walked in the simplicity of my eyes. Therefore when I was thirty years old I took to myself a wife, for my labour wore away my strength, and I never thought upon pleasure with women; but through my labour my sleep sufficed me, and my father always rejoiced in my simplicity. For on whatever I laboured I offered first to the Lord, by the hands of the priests, of all my produce and all first-fruits; then to my father, and then took for myself. And the Lord increased twofold His benefits in my hands; and Jacob also knew that God aided my simplicity, for on every poor man and every one in distress I bestowed the good things of the earth in simplicity of heart.

4. And now hearken to me, my children, and walk in simplicity of heart, for I have seen in it all that is well-pleasing to the Lord. The simple coveteth not gold, defraudeth not his neighbour, longeth not after manifold dainties, delighteth not in varied apparel, doth not picture to himself to live a long life, but only waiteth for the will of God, and the spirits of error have no power against him. For he cannot allow within his mind a thought of female beauty, that he should not pollute his mind in corruption. No envy can enter into his thoughts,

no jealousy melteth away his soul, nor doth he brood over gain with insatiate desire; for he walketh in uprightness of life, and beholdeth all things in simplicity, not admitting in his eyes malice from the error of the world, lest he should see the perversion of any of the commandments of the Lord.

5. Keep therefore the law of God, my children, and get simplicity, and walk in guilelessness, not prying over-curiously into the commands of God and the business of your neighbour; but love the Lord and your neighbour, have compassion on the poor and weak. Bow down your back unto husbandry, and labour in tillage of the ground in all manner of husbandry, offering gifts unto the Lord with thanksgiving; for with the first-fruits of the earth did the Lord bless me, even as He blessed all the saints from Abel even until now. For no other portion is given to thee than of the fatness of the earth, whose fruits are raised by toil; for our father Jacob blessed me with blessings of the earth and of first-fruits. And Levi and Judah were glorified by the Lord among the sons of Jacob; for the Lord made choice of them, and to the one He gave the priesthood, to the other the kingdom. Them therefore obey, and walk in the simplicity of your father; for unto Gad hath it been given to destroy the temptations that are coming upon Israel.

6. I know, my children, that in the last times your sons will forsake simplicity, and will cleave unto avarice, and leaving guilelessness will draw near to malice, and forsaking the commandments of the Lord will cleave unto Beliar, and leaving husbandry will follow after their wicked devices, and shall be dispersed among the Gentiles, and shall serve their enemies. And do you therefore command these things to your children, that if they sin they may the more quickly return to the Lord; for He is merciful, and will deliver them even to bring them back into their land.

7. I am a hundred and twenty-two years old, and I know not against myself a sin unto death. Except my wife, I have not known any woman. I never committed fornication in the haughtiness of my eyes; I drank not wine, to be led astray thereby; I coveted not any desirable thing that was my neighbour's; guile never entered in my heart; a lie never passed through my lips; if any man grieved, I wept with him, and I

shared my bread with the poor. I never ate alone; I moved no landmark; in all my days I wrought godliness and truth. I loved the Lord with all my strength; likewise also did I love every man even as my own children. So ye also do these things, my children, and every spirit of Beliar shall flee from you, and no deed of malicious men shall rule over you; and every wild beast shall ye subdue, having with yourselves the God of heaven walking with men in simplicity of heart.

And he commanded them that they should carry him up to Hebron, and bury him there in the cave with his fathers. And he stretched out his feet and died, the fifth son of Jacob, in a good old age; and with every limb sound, and with strength unabated, he slept the eternal sleep.

THE TESTAMENT OF ZEBULUN CONCERNING COMPASSION AND MERCY.

1. The record of Zebulun, which he enjoined his children in the hundred[1] and fourteenth year of his life, thirty-two years after the death of Joseph. And he said to them: Hearken to me, sons of Zebulun, attend to the words of your father. I am Zebulun, a good gift[2] to my parents. For when I was born our father was increased very exceedingly, both in flocks and herds, when with the streaked rods he had his portion. I know not, my children, that in all my days I have sinned, save only in thought. Nor do I remember that I have done any iniquity, except the sin of ignorance which I committed against Joseph; for I screened my brethren, not telling to my father what had been done. And I wept sore in secret, for I feared

---

[1] The Ox. MS. reads 150, and refers the event to two years after Joseph's death. The text of the Cam. MS. gives an impossible result here, as it would make Zebulun twenty-eight years younger than Joseph, who died at the age of 110. According to the Ox. MS., Reuben (cf. c. 1) and Zebulun would die in the same year, the former at 125, the latter 150. A comparison of *Test. Reub.* c. 1, shows the most probable solution to be to give the numerals, ριδ΄, β΄.

[2] The derivation of Zebulun seems to be from זָבַל, a collateral form of זָבַד, to give. Hence Leah plays on the double meaning of the former verb, Gen. xxx. 20.

my brethren, because they had all agreed together, that if any one should declare the secret, he should be slain with the sword. But when they wished to kill him, I adjured them much with tears not to be guilty of this iniquity.

2. For Simeon and Gad came against Joseph to kill him. And Joseph fell upon his face, and said unto them, Pity me, my brethren, have compassion upon the bowels of Jacob our father: lay not upon me your hands to shed innocent blood, for I have not sinned against you; yea, if I have sinned, with chastening chastise me, but lay not upon me your hand, for the sake of Jacob our father. And as he spoke these words, I pitied him and began to weep, and my heart melted within me, and all the substance of my bowels was loosened within my soul. And Joseph also wept, and I too wept with him; and my heart throbbed fast, and the joints of my body trembled, and I was not able to stand. And when he saw me weeping with him, and them coming against him to slay him, he fled behind me, beseeching them. And Reuben rose and said, My brethren, let us not slay him, but let us cast him into one of these dry pits which our fathers digged and found no water. For for this cause the Lord forbade that water should rise up in them, in order that Joseph might be preserved; and the Lord appointed it so, until they sold him to the Ishmaelites.

3. For in the price of Joseph, my children, I had no share; but Simeon and Gad and six other of our brethren took the price of Joseph, and bought sandals[1] for themselves, their wives, and their children, saying, We will not eat of it, for it is the price of our brother's blood, but will tread it down under foot, because he said that he was king over us, and so let us see what his dreams mean. Therefore is it written in the writing of the law of Enoch, that whosoever will not raise up seed to his brother, his sandal shall be unloosed, and they shall spit into his face. And the brethren of Joseph wished not that their brother should live, and the Lord loosed unto them the sandal of Joseph. For when they came into Egypt they were unloosed by the servants of Joseph before the gate, and so made obeisance to Joseph after the fashion of Pharaoh. And not only did they make obeisance to him, but were spit upon also, falling down before him forthwith, and so they were put to

[1] Cf. the Targum Ps. Jon. on Gen. xxxvii. 28.

shame before the Egyptians; for after this the Egyptians heard all the evils which we had done to Joseph.

4. After these things they brought forth food; for I through two days and two nights tasted nothing, through pity for Joseph. And Judah ate not with them, but watched the pit; for he feared lest Simeon and Gad should run back and slay him. And when they saw that I also ate not, they set me to watch him until he was sold. And he remained in the pit three days and three nights, and so was sold famishing. And when Reuben heard that while he was away Joseph had been sold, he rent his clothes about him, and mourned, saying, How shall I look in the face of Jacob my father? And he took the money, and ran after the merchants, and found no one; for they had left the main road, and journeyed hastily through rugged byways.[1] And Reuben ate no food on that day. Dan therefore came to him, and said, Weep not, neither grieve; for I have found what we can say to our father Jacob. Let us slay a kid of the goats, and dip in it the coat of Joseph; and we will say, Look, if this is the coat of thy son: for they stripped off from Joseph the coat of our father when they were about to sell him, and put upon him an old garment of a slave. Now Simeon had the coat, and would not give it up, wishing to rend it with his sword; for he was angry that Joseph lived, and that he had not slain him. Then we all rose up together against him, and said, If thou give it not up, we will say that thou alone didst this wickedness in Israel; and so he gave it up, and they did even as Dan had said.

5. And now, my children, I bid you to keep the commands of the Lord, and to show mercy upon your neighbour, and to have compassion towards all, not towards men only, but also towards beasts. For for this thing's sake the Lord blessed me; and when all my brethren were sick I escaped without sickness, for the Lord knoweth the purposes of each. Have therefore compassion in your hearts, my children, because even as a man doeth to his neighbour, even so also will the Lord do to him. For the sons of my brethren were sickening, were dying on account of Joseph, because they showed not mercy in their hearts; but my sons were preserved without sickness, as ye know. And when I was in Canaan, by the sea-coast, I caught

---

[1] Cam. MS. διὰ τραγλοκολπητῶν; Ox. MS. διὰ τρωγλοδυτῶν.

spoil of fish for Jacob my father; and when many were choked in the sea, I abode unhurt.

6. I was the first who made a boat to sail upon the sea, for the Lord gave me understanding and wisdom therein; and I let down a rudder behind it, and I stretched a sail on an upright mast in the midst; and sailing therein along the shores, I caught fish for the house of my father until we went into Egypt; and through compassion, I gave of my fish to every stranger. And if any man were a stranger, or sick, or aged, I boiled the fish and dressed them well, and offered them to all men as every man had need, bringing them together and having compassion upon them. Wherefore also the Lord granted me to take much fish: for he that imparteth unto his neighbour, receiveth manifold more from the Lord. For five years I caught fish, and gave thereof to every man whom I saw, and brought sufficient for all the house of my father. In the summer I caught fish, and in the winter I kept sheep with my brethren.

7. Now I will declare unto you what I did. I saw a man in distress and nakedness in winter-time, and had compassion upon him, and stole away a garment secretly from my house, and gave it to him who was in distress. Do you therefore, my children, from that which God bestoweth upon you, show compassion and mercy impartially to all men, and give to every man with a good heart. And if ye have not at the time wherewith to give to him that asketh you, have compassion for him in bowels of mercy. I know that my hand found not at the time wherewith to give to him that asked me, and I walked with him weeping for more than seven furlongs, and my bowels yearned towards him unto compassion.

8. Have therefore yourselves also, my children, compassion towards every man with mercy, that the Lord also may have compassion upon you, and have mercy upon you; because also in the last days God sendeth His compassion on the earth, and wheresoever He findeth bowels of mercy, He dwelleth in him. For how much compassion a man hath upon his neighbours, so much also hath the Lord upon him. For when we went down into Egypt, Joseph bore no malice against us, and when he saw me he was filled with compassion. And looking towards him, do ye also, my children, approve yourselves without malice, and

love one another; and reckon not each one the evil of his brother, for this breaketh unity, and divideth all kindred, and troubleth the soul: for he who beareth malice hath not bowels of mercy.

9. Mark the waters, that they flow together, and sweep along stones, trees, sand; but if they are divided into many streams, the earth sucketh them up, and they become of no account. So also shall ye be if ye be divided. Divide not yourselves into two heads, for everything which the Lord made hath but one head; He gave two shoulders, hands, feet, but all the members are subject unto the one head. I have learnt by the writing of my fathers, that in the last days ye will depart from the Lord, and be divided in Israel, and ye will follow two kings, and will work every abomination, and every idol will ye worship, and your enemies shall lead you captive, and ye shall dwell among the nations with all infirmities and tribulations and anguish of soul. And after these things ye will remember the Lord, and will repent, and He will lead you back; for He is merciful and full of compassion, not imputing evil to the sons of men, because they are flesh, and the spirits of error deceive them in all their doings. And after these things shall the Lord Himself arise to you,[1] the Light of righteousness, and healing[2] and compassion shall be upon His wings. He shall redeem all captivity of the sons of men from Beliar, and every spirit of error shall be trodden down. And He shall bring back all the nations to zeal for Him, and ye shall see God in the fashion of a man whom the Lord shall choose, Jerusalem is His name. And again with the wickedness of your words will ye provoke Him to anger, and ye shall be cast away, even unto the time of consummation.

10. And now, my children, grieve not that I am dying, nor be troubled in that I am passing away from you. For I shall arise once more in the midst of you, as a ruler in the midst of his sons; and I will rejoice in the midst of my tribe, as many as have kept the law of the Lord, and the commandments of Zebulun their father. But upon the ungodly shall the Lord bring everlasting fire, and will destroy them throughout all generations. I am hastening away unto my rest, as did my

---

[1] Mal. iv. 2.
[2] The Ox. MS. reads: "And ye shall return from your land, and ye shall see the Lord in Jerusalem for His name's sake."

fathers; but do ye fear the Lord your God with all your strength all the days of your life. And when he had said these things he fell calmly asleep, and his sons laid him in a coffin; and afterwards they carried him up to Hebron, and buried him with his fathers.

THE TESTAMENT OF DAN CONCERNING ANGER AND LYING.

1. The record of the words of Dan, which he spake to his sons in his last days. In the hundred and twenty-fifth year of his life he called together his family, and said: Hearken to my words, ye sons of Dan; give heed to the words of the mouth of your father. I have proved in my heart, and in my whole life, that truth with just dealing is good and well-pleasing to God, and that lying and anger are evil, because they teach man all wickedness. I confess this day to you, my children, that in my heart I rejoiced concerning the death of Joseph, a true and good man; and I rejoiced at the selling of Joseph, because his father loved him more than us. For the spirit of jealousy and of vainglory said to me, Thou also art his son. And one of the spirits of Beliar wrought with me, saying, Take this sword, and with it slay Joseph; so shall thy father love thee when he is slain. This is the spirit of anger that counselled me, that even as a leopard devoureth a kid, so should I devour Joseph. But the God of Jacob our father gave him not over into my hands that I should find him alone, nor suffered me to work this iniquity, that two tribes should be destroyed in Israel.

2. And now, my children, I am dying, and I tell you of a truth, that unless ye keep yourselves from the spirit of lying and of anger, and love truth and long-suffering, ye shall perish. There is blindness in anger, my children, and no wrathful man regardeth any person with truth: for though it be a father or a mother, he behaveth towards them as enemies; though it be a brother, he knoweth him not; though it be a prophet of the Lord, he disobeyeth him; though a righteous man, he regardeth him not; a friend he doth not acknowledge. For

the spirit of anger encompasseth him with the nets of deceit, and blindeth his natural eyes, and through lying darkeneth his mind, and giveth him a sight of his own making. And wherewith encompasseth he his eyes? In hatred of heart; and he giveth him a heart of his own against his brother unto envy.

3. My children, mischievous is anger, for it becometh as a soul to the soul itself; and the body of the angry man it maketh its own, and over his soul it getteth the mastery, and it bestoweth upon the body its own power, that it may work all iniquity; and whenever the soul doeth aught, it justifieth what has been done, since it seeth not. Therefore he who is wrathful, if he be a mighty man, hath a treble might in his anger; one by the might and aid of his servants, and a second by his wrath, whereby he persuadeth and overcometh in injustice: and having a third of the nature of his own body, and of his own self working the evil. And though the wrathful man be weak, yet hath he a might twofold of that which is by nature; for wrath ever aideth such in mischief. This spirit goeth always with lying at the right hand of Satan, that his works may be wrought with cruelty and lying.

4. Understand ye therefore the might of wrath, that it is vain. For it first of all stingeth him in word: then by deeds it strengtheneth him who is angry, and with bitter punishments disturbeth his mind, and so stirreth up with great wrath his soul. Therefore, when any one speaketh against you, be not[1] ye moved unto anger. And if any man praiseth you as good, be not lifted up nor elated, either to the feeling or showing of pleasure.[2] For first it pleaseth the hearing, and so stirreth up the understanding to understand the grounds for anger; and then, being wrathful, he thinketh that he is justly angry. If ye fall into any loss or ruin, my children, be not troubled; for this very spirit maketh men desire that which hath perished, in order that they may be inflamed by the desire. If ye suffer loss willingly, be not vexed, for from vexation he raiseth up wrath with lying. And wrath with lying is a twofold mischief;[3] and they speak one with another that they may disturb the mind; and when the soul is

---

[1] The reading of the Ox. MS., μὴ κινεῖσθε, is to be taken.
[2] Cam. MS. εἰς εἰδίαν; Ox. MS. εἰς ἀηδίαν.   [3] Read κακόν.

continually disturbed, the Lord departeth from it, and Beliar ruleth over it.

5. Observe, therefore, my children, the commandments of the Lord, and keep His law; and depart from wrath, and hate lying, that the Lord may dwell among you, and Beliar may flee from you. Speak truth each one with his neighbour, so shall ye not fall into lust and confusion; but ye shall be in peace, having the God of peace, so[1] shall no war prevail over you. Love the Lord through all your life, and one another with a true heart. For I know that in the last days ye will depart from the Lord, and will provoke Levi unto anger, and will fight against Judah; but ye shall not prevail against them. For an angel of the Lord shall guide them both; for by them shall Israel stand. And whensoever ye depart from the Lord, ye will walk in all evil, working the abominations of the Gentiles, going[2] astray with women of them that are ungodly; and the spirits of error shall work in you with all malice. For I have read in the book of Enoch the righteous, that your prince is Satan, and that all the spirits of fornication and pride shall be subject unto Levi, to lay a snare for the sons of Levi, to cause them to sin before the Lord. And my sons will draw near unto Levi, and sin with them in all things; and the sons of Judah will be covetous, plundering other men's goods like lions. Therefore shall ye be led away with them in captivity, and there shall ye receive all the plagues of Egypt, and all the malice of the Gentiles: and so, when ye return to the Lord, ye shall obtain mercy, and He shall bring you into His sanctuary, calling peace upon you; and there shall arise unto you from the tribe of Judah and of Levi the salvation of the Lord; and He shall make war against Beliar, and He shall give the vengeance of victory to our coasts. And the captivity shall He take from Beliar, even the souls of the saints, and shall turn disobedient hearts unto the Lord, and shall give to them who call upon Him everlasting peace; and the saints shall rest in Eden, and the righteous shall rejoice in the new Jerusalem, which shall be unto the glory of God for ever and ever. And no longer shall Jerusalem endure desolation, nor Israel be led

---

[1] The Ox. MS. omits from here to τοῖς ἔθνεσι Σωτήρ in c. 6.

[2] Ἐκπορεύοντες may be an error for ἐκπορνεύοντες, which Grabe wrongly gives as the reading of the Cam. MS.

captive; for the Lord shall be in the midst of her, dwelling among men, even the Holy One of Israel reigning over them in humility and in poverty; and he who believeth on Him shall reign in truth in the heavens.

6. And now, my children, fear the Lord, and take heed unto yourselves of Satan and his spirits; and draw near unto God, and to the Angel[1] that intercedeth for you, for He is a Mediator between God and man for the peace of Israel. He shall stand up against the kingdom of the enemy; therefore is the enemy eager to destroy all that call upon the Lord. For he knoweth that in the day on which Israel shall believe, the kingdom of the enemy shall be brought to an end; and the very angel of peace shall strengthen Israel, that it fall not into the extremity of evil. And it shall be in the time of the iniquity of Israel, that the Lord will depart from them, and will go after him that doeth His will, for unto none of His angels shall it be as unto him. And His name shall be in every place of Israel, and among the Gentiles—Saviour. Keep therefore yourselves, my children, from every evil work, and cast away wrath and all lying, and love truth and long-suffering; and the things which ye have heard from your father, do ye also impart to your children, that the Father of the Gentiles may receive you: for He is true and long-suffering, meek and lowly, and teacheth by His works the law of God. Depart, therefore, from all unrighteousness, and cleave unto the righteousness of the law of the Lord: and bury me near my fathers.

7. And when he had said these things he kissed them, and slept the long sleep. And his sons buried him, and after that they carried up his bones to the side of Abraham, and Isaac, and Jacob. Nevertheless, as Dan had prophesied unto them that they should forget the law of their God, and should be alienated from the land of their inheritance, and from the race of Israel, and from their kindred, so also it came to pass.

[1] Cf. Dorner, *Doctrine of the Person of Christ*, Introd. p. 15, Eng. transl.

THE TESTAMENT OF NAPHTALI CONCERNING NATURAL GOODNESS.

1. The record of the testament of Naphtali, what things he ordained at the time of his death in the hundred and thirty-second year of his life. When his sons were gathered together in the seventh month, the fourth day of the month, he, being yet in good health, made them a feast and good cheer. And after he was awake in the morning, he said to them, I am dying; and they believed him not. And he blessed the Lord, and affirmed that after yesterday's feast he should die. He began then to say to his sons: Hear, my children; ye sons of Naphtali, hear the words of your father. I was born from Bilhah; and because Rachel dealt craftily, and gave Bilhah in place of herself to Jacob, and she bore me upon Rachel's lap, therefore was I called Naphtali.[1] And Rachel loved me because I was born upon her lap; and when I was of young and tender form, she was wont to kiss me, and say, Would that I might see a brother of thine from my own womb, like unto thee! whence also Joseph was like unto me in all things, according to the prayers of Rachel. Now my mother was Bilhah, daughter of Rotheus the brother of Deborah, Rebecca's nurse, and she was born on one and the self-same day with Rachel. And Rotheus was of the family of Abraham, a Chaldean, fearing God, free-born and noble; and he was taken captive, and was bought by Laban; and he gave him Aena his handmaid to wife, and she bore a daughter, and called her Zilpah, after the name of the village in which he had been taken captive. And next she bore Bilhah, saying, My daughter is eager after what is new, for immediately that she was born she was eager for the breast.

2. And since I was swift on my feet like a deer, my father Jacob appointed me for all errands and messages, and as a deer[2] did he give me his blessing. For as the potter knoweth the vessel, what it containeth, and bringeth clay thereto, so also doth the Lord make the body in accordance with the spirit, and according to the capacity of the body doth He implant the

---

[1] Gen. xxx. 8. Josephus, *Ant.* i. 19. 7.
[2] Gen. xlix. 21.

spirit, and the one is not deficient from the other by a third part of a hair; for by weight, and measure, and rule is every creature of the Most High. And as the potter knoweth the use of each vessel, whereto it sufficeth, so also doth the Lord know the body, how far it is capable for goodness, and when it beginneth in evil; for there is no created thing and no thought which the Lord knoweth not, for He created every man after His own image. As man's strength, so also is his work; and as his mind, so also is his work; and as his purpose, so also is his doing; as his heart, so also is his mouth; as his eye, so also is his sleep; as his soul, so also is his word, either in the law of the Lord or in the law of Beliar. And as there is a division between light and darkness, between seeing and hearing, so also is there a division between man and man, and between woman and woman; neither is it to be said that there is any superiority in anything, either of the face or of other like things.[1] For God made all things good in their order, the five senses in the head, and He joineth on the neck to the head, the hair also for comeliness, the heart moreover for understanding, the belly for the dividing of the stomach, the calamus[2] for health, the liver for wrath, the gall for bitterness, the spleen for laughter, the reins for craftiness, the loins for power, the ribs for containing, the back for strength, and so forth. So then, my children, be ye orderly unto good things in the fear of God, and do nothing disorderly in scorn or out of its due season. For if thou bid the eye to hear, it cannot; so neither in darkness can ye do the works of light.

3. Be ye not therefore eager to corrupt your doings through excess, or with empty words to deceive your souls; because if ye keep silence in purity of heart, ye shall be able to hold fast the will of God, and to cast away the will of the devil. Sun and moon and stars change not their order; so also ye shall not change the law of God in the disorderliness of your doings. Nations went astray, and forsook the Lord, and changed their

---

[1] The Greek text here is obviously corrupt, and doubtless one or two words are wanting. The reading of the Cam. MS. is, οὐκ ἔστιν εἰπεῖν ὅτι ἐν τῷ ἑνὶ τοῖς προσώποις ἢ τῶν ὁμοίων. In the Ox. MS. the passage is wanting.

[2] It seems very doubtful what is meant by κάλαμος here. I have thought it best, therefore, to leave the matter open. The Ox. MS. punctuates στομάχου κάλ.

order, and followed stones and stocks, following after spirits of error. But ye shall not be so, my children, recognising in the firmament, in the earth, and in the sea, and in all created things, the Lord who made them all, that ye become not as Sodom, which changed the order of its nature. In like manner also the Watchers[1] changed the order of their nature, whom also the Lord cursed at the flood, and for their sakes made desolate the earth, that it should be uninhabited and fruitless.

4. These things I say, my children, for I have read in the holy writing of Enoch that ye yourselves also will depart from the Lord, walking according to all wickedness of the Gentiles, and ye will do according to all the iniquity of Sodom. And the Lord will bring captivity upon you, and there shall ye serve your enemies, and ye shall be covered with all affliction and tribulation, until the Lord shall have consumed you all. And after that ye shall have been diminished and made few, ye will return and acknowledge the Lord your God; and He will bring you back into your own land, according to His abundant mercy. And it shall be, after that they shall come into the land of their fathers, they will again forget the Lord and deal wickedly; and the Lord shall scatter them upon the face of all the earth, until the compassion of the Lord shall come, a Man working righteousness and showing mercy unto all them that are afar off, and them that are near.

5. For in the fortieth year of my life, I saw on the Mount of Olives, at the east of Jerusalem, that the sun and the moon were standing still. And behold Isaac, the father of my father, saith to us, Run and lay hold of them, each one according to his strength; and he that seizeth them, his shall be the sun and the moon. And we all of us ran together, and Levi laid hold of the sun, and Judah outstripped the others and seized the moon, and they were both of them lifted up with them. And when Levi became as a sun, a certain young man gave to him twelve branches of palm; and Judah was bright as the moon, and under his feet were twelve rays. And Levi and Judah ran, and laid hold each of the other. And, lo, a bull upon the earth, having two great horns, and an eagle's wings upon his back; and we wished to seize him, but could not. For Joseph outstripped us, and took him, and ascended up with

[1] Cf. *Reuben* 5.

him on high. And I saw, for I was there, and behold a holy writing appeared to us, saying: Assyrians, Medes, Persians, Elamites, Gelachæans, Chaldeans, Syrians, shall possess in captivity the twelve tribes of Israel.

6. And again, after seven months, I saw our father Jacob standing by the sea of Jamnia, and we his sons were with him. And, behold, there came a ship sailing by, full of dried flesh, without sailors or pilot; and there was written upon the ship, Jacob. And our father saith to us, Let us embark on our ship. And when we had gone on board, there arose a vehement storm, and a tempest of mighty wind; and our father, who was holding the helm, flew away from us. And we, being tost with the tempest, were borne along over the sea; and the ship was filled with water and beaten about with a mighty wave, so that it was well-nigh broken in pieces. And Joseph fled away upon a little boat, and we all were divided upon twelve boards, and Levi and Judah were together. We therefore all were scattered even unto afar off. Then Levi, girt about with sackcloth, prayed for us all unto the Lord. And when the storm ceased, immediately the ship reached the land, as though in peace. And, lo, Jacob our father came, and we rejoiced with one accord.

7. These two dreams I told to my father; and he said to me, These things must be fulfilled in their season, after that Israel hath endured many things. Then my father saith unto me, I believe that Joseph liveth, for I see always that the Lord numbereth him with you. And he said, weeping, Thou livest, Joseph, my child, and I behold thee not, and thou seest not Jacob that begat thee. And he caused us also to weep at these words of his, and I burned in my heart to declare that he had been sold, but I feared my brethren.

8. Behold, my children, I have shown unto you the last times, that all shall come to pass in Israel. Do ye also therefore charge your children that they be united to Levi and to Judah. For through Judah shall salvation arise unto Israel, and in Him shall Jacob be blessed. For through his tribe shall God be seen dwelling among men on the earth, to save the race of Israel, and He shall gather together the righteous from the Gentiles. If ye work that which is good, my children, both men and angels will bless you; and God will be glorified

through you among the Gentiles, and the devil will flee from you, and the wild beasts will fear you, and the angels will cleave to you. For as if a man rear up a child well, he hath a kindly remembrance thereof; so also for a good work there is a good remembrance with God. But him who doeth not that which is good men and angels shall curse, and God will be dishonoured among the heathen through him, and the devil maketh him his own as his peculiar instrument, and every wild beast shall master him, and the Lord will hate him. For the commandments of the law are twofold, and through prudence must they be fulfilled. For there is a season for a man to embrace his wife, and a season to abstain therefrom for his prayer. So then there are two commandments; and unless they be done in due order, they bring about sin. So also is it with the other commandments. Be ye therefore wise in God, and prudent, understanding the order of the commandments, and the laws of every work, that the Lord may love you.

9. And when he had charged them with many such words, he exhorted them that they should remove his bones to Hebron, and should bury him with his fathers. And when he had eaten and drunken with a merry heart, he covered his face and died. And his sons did according to all things whatsoever Naphtali their father had charged them.

THE TESTAMENT OF GAD CONCERNING HATRED.

1. The record of the testament of Gad, what things he spake unto his sons, in the hundred and twenty-seventh year of his life, saying: I was the seventh son born to Jacob, and I was valiant in keeping the flocks. I guarded at night the flock; and whenever the lion came, or wolf, or leopard, or bear, or any wild beast against the fold, I pursued it, and with my hand seizing its foot, and whirling it round, I stunned it, and hurled it over two furlongs, and so killed it. Now Joseph was feeding the flock with us for about thirty days, and being tender, he fell sick by reason of the heat. And he returned to Hebron to his father, who made him lie down near him, because he loved him. And Joseph told our father that the sons of Zilpah

and Bilhah were slaying the best of the beasts,[1] and devouring them without the knowledge of Judah and Reuben. For he saw that I delivered a lamb out of the mouth of the bear, and I put the bear to death; and the lamb I slew, being grieved concerning it that it could not live, and we ate it, and he told our father. And I was wroth with Joseph for that thing until the day that he was sold into Egypt. And the spirit of hatred was in me, and I wished not either to see Joseph or to hear him. And he rebuked us to our faces for having eaten of the flock without Judah. And whatsoever things he told our father, he believed him.

2. I confess now my sin, my children, that oftentimes I wished to kill him, because I hated him to the death, and there were in no wise in me bowels of mercy towards him. Moreover, I hated him yet more because of his dreams; and I would have devoured him out of the land of the living, even as a calf devoureth the grass from the earth. Therefore I and Judah sold him to the Ishmaelites for thirty[2] pieces of gold, and ten of them we hid, and showed the twenty to our brethren: and so through my covetousness I was fully bent on his destruction. And the God of my fathers delivered him from my hands, that I should not work iniquity in Israel.

3. And now, my children, hearken to the words of truth to work righteousness, and all the law of the Most High, and not go astray through the spirit of hatred, for it is evil in all the doings of men. Whatsoever a man doeth, that doth the hater abhor: though he worketh the law of the Lord, he praiseth him not; though he feareth the Lord, and taketh pleasure in that which is righteous, he loveth him not: he dispraiseth the truth, he envieth him that ordereth his way aright, he delighteth in evil-speaking, he loveth arrogance, for hatred hath blinded his soul; even as I also looked on Joseph.

4. Take heed therefore, my children, of hatred; for it worketh iniquity against the Lord Himself: for it will not hear the words of His commandments concerning the loving of one's neighbour, and it sinneth against God. For if a brother stumble, imme-

---

[1] Cf. Targum Ps. Jon. of Gen. xxxvii. 2.

[2] The narrative of Genesis (xxxvii. 28) gives twenty pieces of silver; the LXX. twenty pieces of gold, with which latter agrees Josephus' μνῶν εἴκοσιν (Antiq. ii. 3. 3).

diately it wisheth to proclaim it to all men, and is urgent that he should be judged for it, and be punished and slain. And if it be a servant, it accuseth him to his master, and with all affliction it deviseth against him, if it be possible to slay him. For hatred worketh in envy, and it ever sickeneth with envy against them that prosper in well-doing, when it seeth or heareth thereof. For as love would even restore to life the dead, and would call back them that are condemned to die, so hatred would slay the living, and those that have offended in a small matter it would not suffer to live. For the spirit of hatred worketh together with Satan through hastiness[1] of spirit in all things unto men's death; but the spirit of love worketh together with the law of God in long-suffering unto the salvation of men.

5. Hatred is evil, because it continually abideth with lying, speaking against the truth; and it maketh small things to be great, and giveth heed to darkness as to light, and calleth the sweet bitter, and teacheth slander, and war, and violence, and every excess of evil; and it filleth the heart with devilish poison. And these things I say to you from experience, my children, that ye may flee hatred, and cleave to the love of the Lord. Righteousness casteth out hatred, humility destroyeth hatred. For he that is just and humble is ashamed to do wrong, being reproved not of another, but of his own heart, because the Lord vieweth his intent: he speaketh not against any man, because the fear of the Most High overcometh hatred. For, fearing lest he should offend the Lord, he will not do any wrong to any man, no, not even in thought. These things I learnt at last, after that I had repented concerning Joseph. For true repentance after a godly sort destroyeth unbelief, and driveth away the darkness, and enlighteneth the eyes, and giveth knowledge to the soul, and guideth the mind to salvation; and those things which it hath not learnt from man, it knoweth through repentance. For God brought upon me a disease of the heart; and had not the prayers of Jacob my father intervened, it had hardly failed that my spirit had departed. For by what things a man transgresseth, by the same also is he punished. For in that my heart was set mercilessly against Joseph, in my heart

---

[1] For this unusual use of ὀλιγοψυχία, cf. Prov. xiv. 29, LXX., where there is the same contrast with μακροθυμία.

too I suffered mercilessly, and was judged for eleven months, for so long a time as I had been envious against Joseph until he was sold.

6. And now, my children, love ye each one his brother, and put away hatred from your hearts, loving one another in deed, and in word, and in thought of the soul. For in the presence of our father I spake peaceably with Joseph; and when I had gone out, the spirit of hatred darkened my mind, and moved my soul to slay him. [1] Love ye therefore one another from your hearts; and if a man sin against thee, tell him of it gently, and drive out the poison of hatred, and foster not guile in thy soul. And if he confess and repent, forgive him; and if he deny it, strive not with him, lest he swear, and thou sin doubly. Let not a stranger hear your secrets amid your striving, lest he hate and become thy enemy, and work great sin against thee; for ofttimes he will talk guilefully[2] with thee, or evilly overreach thee, taking his poison from thyself. Therefore, if he deny it, and is convicted and put to shame, and is silenced, do not tempt him on. For he who denieth repenteth, so that he no more doeth wrong against thee; yea also, he will honour thee, and fear thee, and be at peace with thee. But if he be shameless, and abideth in his wrongdoing, even then forgive him from the heart, and give the vengeance to God.

7. If a man prospereth more than you, be not grieved, but pray also for him, that he may have perfect prosperity. For perchance it is expedient for you thus; and if he be further exalted, be not envious, remembering that all flesh shall die: and offer praise to God, who giveth things good and profitable to all men. Seek out the judgments of the Lord, and so shall thy mind rest and be at peace. And though a man become rich by evil means, even as Esau the brother of my father, be not jealous; but wait for the end of the Lord. For either He taketh His benefits away from the wicked, or leaveth them still to the repentant, or to the unrepentant reserveth punishment for ever. For the poor man who is free from envy, giving thanks to the Lord in all things, is rich among all men, because he hath not evil jealousy of men. Put away,

---

[1] The Ox. MS. omits from here to the last clause of c. 7.

[2] For δολωφωνῆσαι, the reading of the Cam. MS. here, Grabe conjectured δολοφονήσει. Probably δολοφωνήσει is to be preferred.

therefore, hatred from your souls, and love one another with uprightness of heart.

8. And do ye also tell these things to your children, that they honour Judah and Levi, for from them shall the Lord raise up a Saviour to Israel. For I know that at the last your children shall depart from them, and shall walk in all wickedness, and mischief, and corruption before the Lord. And when he had rested for a little while, he said again to them, My children, obey your father, and bury me near to my fathers. And he drew up his feet, and fell asleep in peace. And after five years they carried him up, and laid him in Hebron with his fathers.

THE TESTAMENT OF ASHER CONCERNING TWO FACES OF VICE AND VIRTUE.

1. The record of the testament of Asher, what things he spake to his sons in the hundred and twentieth year of his life. While he was still in health, he said to them: Hearken, ye children of Asher, to your father, and I will declare to you all that is right in the sight of God. Two ways hath God given to the sons of men, and two minds, and two doings, and two places, and two ends. Therefore all things are by twos, one corresponding to the other. There are two ways of good and evil, with which are the two minds in our breasts distinguishing them. Therefore if the soul take pleasure in good, all its actions are in righteousness; and though it sin, it straightway repenteth. For, having his mind set upon righteousness, and casting away maliciousness, he straightway overthroweth the evil, and uprooteth the sin. But if his mind turn aside in evil, all his doings are in maliciousness, and he driveth away the good, and taketh unto him the evil, and is ruled by Beliar; and even though he work what is good, he perverteth it in evil. For whenever he beginneth as though to do good, he bringeth the end of his doing to work evil, seeing that the treasure of the devil is filled with the poison of an evil spirit.

2. There is then, he saith, a soul which speaketh the good for the sake of the evil, and the end of the doing leadeth to

mischief. There is a man who showeth no compassion upon him who serveth his turn in evil; and this thing hath two aspects, but the whole is evil. And there is a man that loveth him that worketh evil; he likewise dwelleth in evil, because he chooseth even to die in an evil cause for his sake: and concerning this it is clear that it hath two aspects, but the whole is an evil work. And though there is love, it is but wickedness concealing the evil, even as it beareth a name that seemeth good, but the end of the doing tendeth unto evil. Another stealeth, worketh unjustly, plundereth, defraudeth, and withal pitieth the poor: this, too, hath a twofold aspect, but the whole is evil. Defrauding his neighbour he provoketh God, and sweareth falsely against the Most High, and yet pitieth the poor: the Lord who commandeth the law he setteth at nought and provoketh, and refresheth the poor; he defileth the soul, and maketh gay the body; he killeth many, and he pitieth a few: and this, too, hath a twofold aspect. Another committeth adultery and fornication, and abstaineth from meats; yet in his fasting he worketh evil, and by his power and his wealth perverteth many, and out of his excessive wickedness worketh the commandments: this, too, hath a twofold aspect, but the whole is evil. Such men are as swine or hares;[1] for they are half clean, but in very deed are unclean. For God in the heavenly[2] tablets hath thus declared.

3. Do not ye therefore, my children, wear two faces like unto them, of goodness and of wickedness; but cleave unto goodness only, for in goodness doth God rest, and men desire it. From wickedness flee away, destroying the devil by your good works; for they that are double-faced serve not God, but their own lusts, so that they may please Beliar and men like unto themselves.

4. For good men, even they that are single of face, though they be thought by them that are double-faced to err, are just before God. For many in killing the wicked do two works, an evil by a good; but the whole is good, because he hath uprooted and destroyed that which is evil. One man hateth him that showeth mercy, and doeth wrong to the adulterer and the thief: this, too, is double-faced, but the whole work is good, because he followeth the Lord's example, in that he receiveth not

[1] Cf. Lev. xi. 5, 7.   [2] Cf. Levi 5.

that which seemeth good with that which is really bad. Another desireth not to see good days with them that riot, lest he defile his mouth and pollute his soul: this, too, is double-faced, but the whole is good, for such men are like to stags and to hinds, because in a wild condition they seem to be unclean, but they are altogether clean; because they walk in a zeal for God, and abstain from what God also hateth and forbiddeth by His commandments, and they ward off the evil from the good.

5. Ye see therefore, my children, how that there are two in all things, one against the other, and the one is hidden by the other.[1] Death succeedeth to life, dishonour to glory, night to day, and darkness to light; and all things are under the day, and just things under life: wherefore also everlasting life awaiteth death. Nor may it be said that truth is a lie, nor right wrong; for all truth is under the light, even as all things are under God. All these things I proved in my life, and I wandered not from the truth of the Lord, and I searched out the commandments of the Most High, walking with singleness of face according to all my strength unto that which is good.

6. Take heed therefore ye also, my children, to the commandments of the Lord, following the truth with singleness of face, for they that are double-faced receive twofold punishment. Hate the spirits of error, which strive against men. Keep the law of the Lord, and give not heed unto evil as unto good; but look unto the thing that is good indeed, and keep it in all commandments of the Lord, having your conversation unto Him, and resting in Him: for the ends at which men aim do show their righteousness, and know the angels of the Lord from the angels of Satan. For if the soul depart troubled, it is tormented by the evil spirit which also it served in lusts and evil works; but if quietly and with joy it hath known the angel of peace, it shall comfort him in life.

7. Become not, my children, as Sodom, which knew not the angels of the Lord, and perished for ever. For I know that ye will sin, and ye shall be delivered into the hands of your enemies, and your land shall be made desolate, and ye shall be scattered unto the four corners of the earth. And ye shall

---

[1] The Ox. MS. adds, ἐν τῇ εὐφροσύνῃ ἡ μέθη, ἐν τῷ γέλωτι τὸ πένθος, ἐν τῷ γάμῳ ἡ ἀκρασία.

be set at nought in the Dispersion as useless water, until the Most High shall visit the earth; and He shall come as man, with men eating and drinking, and in peace breaking the head of the dragon through water. He shall save Israel and all nations, God speaking in the person of man. Therefore tell ye these things to your children, that they disobey Him not. For I have read in the Heavenly Tablets that in very deed ye will disobey Him, and act ungodly against Him, not giving heed to the law of God, but to the commandments of men. Therefore shall ye be scattered as Gad and as Dan my brethren, who shall know not their own lands, tribe, and tongue. But the Lord will gather you together in faith through the hope of His tender mercy, for the sake of Abraham, and Isaac, and Jacob.

8. And when he had said these things unto them, he charged them, saying: Bury me in Hebron. And he fell into a peaceful sleep, and died; and after this his sons did as he had charged them, and they carried him up and buried him with his fathers.

THE TESTAMENT OF JOSEPH CONCERNING SOBRIETY.

1. The record of the testament of Joseph. When he was about to die he called his sons and his brethren together, and said to them: My children and brethren, hearken to Joseph the beloved of Israel; give ear, my sons, unto your father. I have seen in my life envy and death, and I wandered not in the truth of the Lord. These my brethren hated me, and the Lord loved me: they wished to slay me, and the God of my fathers guarded me: they let me down into a pit, and the Most High brought me up again: I was sold for a slave, and the Lord made me free: I was taken into captivity, and His strong hand succoured me: I was kept in hunger, and the Lord Himself nourished me: I was alone, and God comforted me: I was sick, and the Most High visited me: I was in prison, and the Saviour showed favour unto me; in bonds, and He released me; amid slanders, and He pleaded my

E

cause; amid bitter words of the Egyptians, and He rescued me; amid envy and guile, and He exalted me.

2. And thus Potiphar[1] the chief cook[2] of Pharaoh entrusted to me his house, and I struggled against a shameless woman, urging me to transgress with her; but the God of Israel my father guarded me from the burning flame. I was cast into prison, I was beaten, I was mocked; and the Lord granted me to find pity in the sight of the keeper of the prison. For He will in no wise forsake them that fear Him, neither in darkness, nor in bonds, nor in tribulations, nor in necessities. For not as man is God ashamed, nor as the son of man is He afraid, nor as one that is earth-born is He weak, or can He be thrust aside; but in all places is He at hand, and in divers ways doth He comfort, departing for a little to try the purpose of the soul. In ten temptations He showed me approved, and in all of them I endured; for endurance is a mighty charm, and patience giveth many good things.

3. How often did the Egyptian threaten me with death! How often did she give me over to punishment, and then call me back, and threaten me when I would not company with her! And she said to me, Thou shalt be lord of me, and all that is mine, if thou wilt give thyself unto me, and thou shalt be as our master. Therefore I remembered the words of the fathers of my father Jacob, and I entered into my chamber and prayed unto the Lord; and I fasted in those seven years, and I appeared to my master as one living delicately, for they that fast for God's sake receive beauty of face. And if one gave me wine, I drank it not; and I fasted for three days, and took my food and gave it to the poor and sick. And I sought the Lord early, and wept for the Egyptian woman of Memphis, for very unceasingly did she trouble me, and at night she came to me under the pretence of visiting me; and at first, because she had no male child, she feigned to count me as a

---

[1] The Greek spelling here is Φωτιμάρ, in the later chapters Πετεφρίς (Πεντεφρῆς, Cd. Oxon.). The former is more like the Hebrew, the latter really the LXX. spelling, Πετεφρῆς. We may perhaps see herein a trace of a double authorship in the *Test. Joseph.*

[2] Cf. Gen. xxxix. 1, LXX., and Josephus (*Antiq.* ii. 4. 1), who calls Potiphar μαγείρων ὁ βασιλεύς. The view of the Eng. ver. is most probably correct, though we find טבח used in the sense of cook in 1 Sam. ix. 23.

son. And I prayed unto the Lord, and she bare a male child; therefore for a time she embraced me as a son, and I knew it not. Last of all, she sought to draw me into fornication. And when I perceived it, I sorrowed even unto death; and when she had gone out I came to myself, and I lamented for her many days, because I saw her guile and her deceit. And I declared unto her the words of the Most High, if haply she would turn from her evil lust.

4. How often has she fawned upon me with words as a holy man, with guile in her talk, praising my chastity before her husband, while desiring to destroy me when we were alone! She lauded me openly as chaste, and in secret she said unto me, Fear not my husband; for he is persuaded concerning thy chastity, so that even should one tell him concerning us he would in no wise believe. For all these things I lay upon the ground in sackcloth, and I besought God that the Lord would deliver me from the Egyptian. And when she prevailed nothing, she came again to me under the plea of instruction, that she might know the word of the Lord. And she said unto me, If thou willest that I should leave my idols, be persuaded by me, and I will persuade my husband to depart from his idols, and we will walk in the law of thy Lord. And I said unto her, The Lord willeth not that those who reverence Him should be in uncleanness, nor doth He take pleasure in them that commit adultery. And she held her peace, longing to accomplish her evil desire. And I gave myself yet more to fasting and prayer, that the Lord should deliver me from her.

5. And again at another time she said unto me, If thou wilt not commit adultery, I will kill my husband, and so will I lawfully take thee to be my husband. I therefore, when I heard this, rent my garment, and said, Woman, reverence the Lord, and do not this evil deed, lest thou be utterly destroyed; for I will declare thy ungodly thought unto all men. She therefore, being afraid, besought that I would declare to no one her wickedness. And she departed, soothing me with gifts, and sending to me every delight of the sons of men.

6. And she sendeth to me food sprinkled with enchantments. And when the eunuch who brought it came, I looked up and beheld a terrible man giving me with the dish a sword, and I perceived that her scheme was for the deception of my soul.

And when he had gone out I wept, nor did I taste that or any other of her food. So then after one day she came to me and observed the food, and said unto me, What is this, that thou hast not eaten of the food? And I said unto her, It is because thou filledst it with death; and how saidst thou, I come not near to idols, but to the Lord alone? Now therefore know that the God of my father hath revealed unto me by an angel thy wickedness, and I have kept it to convict thee, if haply thou mayest see it and repent. But that thou mayest learn that the wickedness of the ungodly hath no power over them that reverence God in chastity, I took it and ate it before her, saying, The God of my fathers and the Angel of Abraham shall be with me. And she fell upon her face at my feet, and wept; and I raised her up and admonished her, and she promised to do this iniquity no more.

7. But because her heart was set upon me to commit lewdness, she sighed, and her countenance fell. And when her husband saw her, he said unto her, Why is thy countenance fallen? And she said, I have a pain at my heart, and the groanings of my spirit do oppress me; and so he comforted her who was not sick. Then she rushed in to me while her husband was yet without, and said unto me, I will hang myself, or cast myself into a well or over a cliff, if thou wilt not consent unto me. And when I saw the spirit of Beliar was troubling her, I prayed unto the Lord, and said unto her, Why art thou troubled and disturbed, blinded in sins? Remember that if thou killest thyself, Sethon, the concubine of thy husband, thy rival, will beat thy children, and will destroy thy memorial from off the earth. And she said unto me, Lo then thou lovest me; this alone is sufficient for me, that thou carest for my life and my children: I have expectation that I shall enjoy my desire. And she knew not that because of my God I spake thus, and not because of her. For if a man hath fallen before the passion of a wicked desire, then by that hath he become enslaved, even as also was she. And if he hear any good thing with regard to the passion whereby he is vanquished, he receiveth it unto his wicked desire.

8. I declare unto you, my children, that it was about the sixth hour when she departed from me; and I knelt before the Lord all that day, and continued all the night; and about dawn

I rose up weeping, and praying for a release from the Egyptian. At last, then, she laid hold of my garments, forcibly dragging me to have connection with her. When, therefore, I saw that in her madness she was forcibly holding my garments, I fled away naked. And she falsely accused me to her husband, and the Egyptian cast me into the prison in his house; and on the morrow, having scourged me, the Egyptian[1] sent me into the prison in his house. When, therefore, I was in fetters, the Egyptian woman fell sick from her vexation, and listened to me how I sang praises unto the Lord while I was in the abode of darkness, and with glad voice rejoiced and glorified my God only because by a pretext I had been rid of the Egyptian woman.

9. How often hath she sent unto me, saying, Consent to fulfil my desire, and I will release thee from thy bonds, and I will free thee from the darkness! And not even in thoughts did I ever incline unto her. For God loveth him who in a den of darkness fasteth with chastity, rather than him who in secret chambers liveth delicately without restraint. And whosoever liveth in chastity, and desireth also glory, and if the Most High knoweth that it is expedient for him, he bestoweth this also upon him, even as upon me. How often, though she were sick, did she come down to me at unlooked-for times, and listened to my voice as I prayed! And when I heard her groanings I held my peace. For when I was in her house she was wont to bare her arms, and breasts, and legs, that I might fall before her; for she was very beautiful, splendidly adorned for my deception. And the Lord guarded me from her devices.

10. Ye see therefore, my children, how great things patience worketh, and prayer with fasting. And if ye therefore follow after sobriety and purity in patience and humility of heart, the Lord will dwell among you, because He loveth sobriety. And wheresoever the Most High dwelleth, even though a man fall into envy, or slavery, or slander, the Lord who dwelleth in him, for his sobriety's sake not only delivereth him from evil, but also exalteth and glorifieth him, even as me. For in every way the man is guarded, whether in deed, or in word, or in thought. My brethren know how my father loved me, and I

---

[1] This repetition of a clause seems like the slip of a copyist. The Ox. MS. reads, εἰς τὴν εἱρκτὴν τοῦ Φαραώ.

was not exalted in my heart; although I was a child, I had the fear of God in my thoughts. For I knew that all things should pass away, and I kept myself within bounds, and I honoured my brethren; and through fear of them I held my peace when I was sold, and revealed not my family to the Ishmaelites, that I was the son of Jacob, a great man and a mighty.

11. Do ye also, therefore, have the fear of God in your works, and honour your brethren. For every one who worketh the law of the Lord shall be loved by Him. And when I came to the Indocolpitæ with the Ishmaelites, they asked me, and I said that I was a slave from their house, that I might not put my brethren to shame. And the eldest of them said unto me, Thou art not a slave, for even thy appearance doth make it manifest concerning thee. And he threatened me even unto death. But I said that I was their slave. Now when we came into Egypt, they strove concerning me, which of them should buy me and take me. Therefore it seemed good to all that I should remain in Egypt with a merchant of their trade, until they should return bringing merchandise. And the Lord gave me favour in the eyes of the merchant, and he entrusted unto me his house. And the Lord blessed him by my means, and increased him in silver and gold, and I was with him three months and five days.

12. About that time the Memphian wife of Potiphar passed by with great pomp, and cast her eyes upon me, because her eunuchs told her concerning me. And she told her husband concerning the merchant, that he had become rich by means of a young Hebrew, saying, And they say that men have indeed stolen him out of the land of Canaan. Now therefore execute judgment with him, and take away the youth to be thy steward; so shall the God of the Hebrews bless thee, for grace from heaven is upon him.

13. And Potiphar was persuaded by her words, and commanded the merchant to be brought, and said unto him, What is this that I hear, that thou stealest souls out of the land of the Hebrews, and sellest them for slaves? The merchant therefore fell upon his face, and besought him, saying, I beseech thee, my lord, I know not what thou sayest. And he said, Whence then is thy Hebrew servant? And he said, The

Ishmaelites entrusted him to me until they should return. And he believed him not, but commanded him to be stripped and beaten. And when he persisted, Potiphar said, Let the youth be brought. And when I was brought in, I did obeisance to the chief of the eunuchs (for he was third in rank with Pharaoh, being chief of all the eunuchs, and having wives and children and concubines). And he took me apart from him, and said unto me, Art thou a slave or free? And I said, A slave. And he said unto me, Whose slave art thou? And I said unto him, The Ishmaelites'. And again he said unto me, How becamest thou their slave? And I said, They bought me out of the land of Canaan. And he believed me not, and said, Thou liest: and he commanded me to be stripped and beaten.

14. Now the Memphian woman was looking through a window while I was being beaten, and she sent unto her husband, saying, Thy judgment is unjust; for thou dost even punish a free man who hath been stolen, as though he were a transgressor. And when I gave no other answer though I was beaten, he commanded that we should be kept in guard, until, said he, the owners of the boy shall come. And his wife said unto him, Wherefore dost thou detain in captivity this noble child, who ought rather to be set at liberty, and wait upon thee? For she wished to see me in desire of sin, and I was ignorant concerning all these things. Then said he to his wife, It is not the custom of the Egyptians to take away that which belongeth to others before proof is given. This he said concerning the merchant, and concerning me, that I must be imprisoned.

15. Now, after four and twenty days came the Ishmaelites; and having heard that Jacob my father was mourning because of me, they said unto me, How is it that thou saidst that thou wert a slave? and lo, we have learnt that thou art the son of a mighty man in the land of Canaan, and thy father grieveth for thee in sackcloth. And again I would have wept, but I restrained myself, that I should not put my brethren to shame. And I said, I know not, I am a slave. Then they take counsel to sell me, that I should not be found in their hands. For they feared Jacob, lest he should work upon them a deadly vengeance. For it had been heard that he was mighty with the Lord and with men. Then said the merchant unto them,

Release me from the judgment of Potiphar. They therefore came and asked for me, saying, He was bought by us with money. And he sent us away.

16. Now the Memphian woman pointed me out to her husband, that he should buy me; for I hear, said she, that they are selling him. And she sent a eunuch to the Ishmaelites, and asked them to sell me; and since he was not willing to traffic with them, he returned. So when the eunuch had made trial of them, he made known to his mistress that they asked a large price for their slave. And she sent another eunuch, saying, Even though they demand two minæ of gold, take heed not to spare the gold; only buy the boy, and bring him hither. And he gave them eighty pieces of gold for me, and told his mistress that a hundred had been given for me. And when I saw it I held my peace, that the eunuch should not be punished.

17. Ye see, my children, what great things I endured that I should not put my brethren to shame. Do ye also love one another, and with long-suffering hide ye one another's faults. For God delighteth in the unity of brethren, and in the purpose of a heart approved unto love. And when my brethren came into Egypt, and learnt that I returned their money unto them, and upbraided them not, yea, that I even comforted them, and after the death of Jacob I loved them more abundantly, and all things whatsoever he commanded I did very abundantly, then they marvelled. For I suffered them not to be afflicted even unto the smallest matter; and all that was in my hand I gave unto them. Their children were my children, and my children were as their servants; their life was my life, and all their suffering was my suffering, and all their sickness was my infirmity. My land was their land, my counsel their counsel, and I exalted not myself among them in arrogance because of my worldly glory, but I was among them as one of the least.

18. If ye also therefore walk in the commandments of the Lord, my children, He will exalt you there, and will bless you with good things for ever and ever. And if any one seeketh to do evil unto you, do ye by well-doing pray for him, and ye shall be redeemed of the Lord from all evil. For, behold, ye see that through long-suffering I took unto wife even the

daughter of my[1] master. And a hundred talents of gold were given me with her; for the Lord made them to serve me. And He gave me also beauty as a flower above the beautiful ones of Israel; and He preserved me unto old age in strength and in beauty, because I was like in all things to Jacob.

19. Hear ye also, my children, the visions which I saw. There were twelve deer feeding, and the nine were divided and scattered in the land, likewise also the three. And I saw that from Judah was born a virgin wearing a linen[2] garment, and from her went forth a Lamb, without spot, and on His left hand there was as it were a lion; and all the beasts rushed against Him, and the lamb overcame them, and destroyed them, and trod them under foot. And because of Him the angels rejoiced, and men, and all the earth. And these things shall take place in their season, in the last days. Do ye therefore, my children, observe the commandments of the Lord, and honour Judah and Levi; for from them shall arise unto you the Lamb of God, by grace saving all the Gentiles and Israel. For His kingdom is an everlasting kingdom, which shall not be shaken; but my kingdom among you shall come to an end as a watcher's[3] hammock, which after the summer will not appear.

20. I know that after my death the Egyptians will afflict you, but God will undertake your cause, and will bring you into that which He promised to your fathers. But carry ye up my bones with you;[4] for when my bones are taken up, the Lord will be with you in light, and Beliar shall be in darkness with the Egyptians. And carry ye up Zilpah your mother, and lay her near Bilhah, by the hippodrome, by the side of

---

[1] Another account is given in the *Targ. Ps. Jon.* of Gen. xli. 45: "And he gave him to wife Asenath, whom Dinah bare to Shechem, and the wife of Potipherah prince of Tanes brought up."

[2] This wearing of a linen garment would seem to imply a connection with the priestly tribe. St. Luke (i. 36) indeed calls the Virgin the kinswoman of Elisabeth. On this tendency to associate the old sacerdotal tribe with the new royalty of Messiah, cf. *e.g. Protevangel. Jacobi*, cc. 6, 7, 9; Augustine, *contra Faustum*, xxiii. 4; Epiphanius, *Hær.* lxxviii. 13.

[3] Isa. i. 8, xxiv. 20.

[4] Cf. *Test. Simeon* 8, and *Jubilees* 46. The account of Joseph's burial in the *Targ. Ps. Jon.* on Gen. l. 26 is: "And Joseph died, a hundred and ten years old; and they embalmed him, and placed him in a coffin, and sank him in the middle of the Nile of Egypt."

Rachel.[1] And when he had said these things, he stretched out his feet, and slept the long sleep. And all Israel bewailed him, and all Egypt, with a great lamentation. For he felt even for the Egyptians even as his own members, and showed them kindness, aiding them in every work, and counsel, and matter.

THE TESTAMENT OF BENJAMIN CONCERNING A PURE MIND.

1. The record of the words of Benjamin, which he set forth to his sons, after he had lived a hundred and twenty years. And he kissed them, and said: As Isaac was born to Abraham in his hundredth year, so also was I to Jacob. Now since Rachel died in giving me birth, I had no milk; therefore I was suckled by Bilhah her handmaid. For Rachel remained barren for twelve years after that she had born Joseph: and she prayed the Lord with fasting twelve days, and she conceived and bare me. For our father loved Rachel dearly, and prayed that he might see two sons born from her: therefore was I called the son of days, which is Benjamin.[2]

2. When therefore I went into Egypt, and Joseph my brother recognised me, he said unto me, What did they tell my father in that they sold me? And I said unto him, They dabbled thy coat with blood and sent it, and said, Look if this is the coat of thy son. And he said to me, Even so, brother; for when the Ishmaelites took me, one of them stripped off my coat, and gave me a girdle, and scourged me, and bade me run. And as he went away to hide my garment, a lion met him, and slew him; and so his fellows were afraid, and sold me to their companions.

3. Do ye also therefore, my children, love the Lord God of

---

[1] Cf. Gen. xlviii. 7, LXX.

[2] The ordinary theory as to the meaning of Benjamin is comparatively late, and seems doubtful. The *Targum Jerushalmi* (on Gen. xxxv. 18), and the *Breshith Rabba*, § 82, make Benjamin and Benoni synonymous. Cf. Josephus, *Antiq.* i. 21. 3; Cyril, *Glaph. in Gen.* lib. iv. With the view mentioned in the text, cf. Arethas on Rev. vii. 8 (Cramer's *Catena*, viii. 289).

heaven, and keep His commandments, and be followers of the good and holy man Joseph; and let your mind be unto good, even as ye know me. He that hath his mind good seeth all things rightly. Fear ye the Lord, and love your neighbour; and even though the spirits of Beliar allure you into all troublous wickedness, yet shall no troublous wickedness have dominion over you, even as it had not over Joseph my brother. How many men wished to slay him, and God shielded him! For he that feareth God and loveth his neighbour cannot be smitten by Beliar's spirit of the air, being shielded by the fear of God; nor can he be ruled over by the device of men or of beasts, for he is aided by the love of the Lord which he hath towards his neighbour. For he even besought our father Jacob that he would pray for our brethren, that the Lord would not impute to them the evil that they devised concerning Joseph. And thus Jacob cried out, My child Joseph, thou hast prevailed over the bowels of thy father Jacob. And he embraced him, and kissed him for two hours, saying, In thee shall be fulfilled the prophecy of heaven concerning the Lamb of God, even the Saviour of the world, that spotless shall He be delivered up for transgressors, and sinless[1] shall He be put to death for ungodly men in the blood of the covenant, for the salvation of the Gentiles and of Israel, and shall destroy Beliar, and them that serve him.

4. Know ye, my children, the end of the good man? Be followers of his compassion in a good mind, that ye also may wear crowns of glory. The good man hath not a dark eye; for he showeth mercy to all men, even though they be sinners, even though they devise evil concerning him. So he that doeth good overcometh the evil, being shielded by Him that is good; and he loveth the righteous as his own soul. If any one is glorified, he envieth him not; if any one is enriched, he is not jealous; if any one is valiant, he praiseth him; he trusteth and laudeth him that is sober-minded; he showeth mercy to the poor; he is kindly disposed toward the weak; he singeth the praises of God; as for him who hath the fear of God, he protecteth him as with a shield; him that loveth God he aideth; him that rejecteth the Most High he admonisheth

---

[1] This would seem to be the earliest instance of the application of the word ἀναμάρτητος to our Lord.

and turneth back; and him that hath the grace of a good spirit, he loveth even as his own soul.

5. If ye have a good mind, my children, then will both wicked men be at peace with you, and the profligate will reverence you and turn unto good; and the covetous shall not only cease from their inordinate desire, but shall even give the fruits of their covetousness to them that are afflicted. If ye do well, even the unclean spirits shall flee from you; yea, the very beasts shall flee from you in dread. For where the reverence for good works is present unto the mind, darkness fleeth away from him. For if any one is injurious to a holy man, he repenteth; for the holy man showeth pity on his reviler, and holdeth his peace. And if any one betray a righteous soul, and the righteous man, though praying, be humbled for a little while, yet not long after he appeareth far more glorious, even as was Joseph my brother.

6. The mind of the good man is not in the power of the deceit of the spirit of Beliar, for the angel of peace guideth his soul. He gazeth not passionately on corruptible things, nor gathereth together riches unto desire of pleasure; he delighteth not in pleasure, he hurteth not his neighbour, he pampereth not himself with food, he erreth not in the pride of his eyes, for the Lord is his portion. The good mind admitteth not the glory and dishonour of men, neither knoweth it any guile or lie, fighting or reviling; for the Lord dwelleth in him and lighteth up his soul, and he rejoiceth towards all men at every time. The good mind hath not two tongues, of blessing and of cursing, of insult and of honour, of sorrow and of joy, of quietness and of trouble, of hypocrisy and of truth, of poverty and of wealth; but it hath one disposition, pure and uncorrupt, concerning all men. It hath no double sight, nor double hearing; for in everything which he doeth, or speaketh, or seeth, he knoweth that the Lord watcheth his soul, and he cleanseth his mind that he be not condemned by God and men. But of Beliar every work is twofold, and hath no singleness.

7. Flee ye therefore, my children, the evil-doing of Beliar; for it giveth a sword to them that obey it, and the sword is the mother of seven evils. First the mind conceiveth through Beliar, and first there is envy; secondly, desperation; thirdly, tribulation; fourthly, captivity; fifthly, neediness; sixthly,

trouble; seventhly, desolation. Therefore also Cain is delivered over to seven vengeances by God, for in every hundred years the Lord brought one plague upon him. Two hundred years he suffered, and in the nine hundredth year he was brought to desolation at the flood, for Abel his righteous brother's sake. In seven[1] hundred years was Cain judged, and Lamech in seventy times seven; because for ever those who are likened unto Cain in envy unto hatred of brethren shall be judged with the same punishment.

8. Do ye also therefore, my children, flee ill-doing, envy, and hatred of brethren, and cleave to goodness and love. He that hath a pure mind in love, looketh not after a woman unto fornication; for he hath no defilement in his heart, because the Spirit of God resteth in him. For as the sun is not defiled by shining over dung and mire, but rather drieth up both and driveth away the ill smell; so also the pure mind, constrained among the defilements of the earth, rather edifieth, and itself suffereth no defilement.

9. Now I suppose, from the words of the righteous Enoch, that there will be also evil-doings among you: for ye will commit fornication with the fornication of Sodom, and shall perish all save a few, and will multiply inordinate lusts with women; and the kingdom of the Lord shall not be among you, for forthwith He will take it away. Nevertheless the temple of God shall be built in your portion, and shall be glorious among you. For He shall take it, and the twelve tribes shall be gathered together there, and all the Gentiles, until the Most High shall send forth His salvation in the visitation of His only-begotten one. And He shall enter into the front[2] of the temple, and there shall the Lord be treated with outrage, and He shall be lifted up upon a tree. And the veil of the temple shall be rent, and the Spirit of God shall descend upon the Gentiles as fire poured forth. And He shall arise from the grave, and shall ascend from earth into heaven: and I know how lowly He shall be upon the earth, and how glorious in the heaven.

10. Now when Joseph was in Egypt, I longed to see his visage and the form of his countenance; and through the

---

[1] For ἑπτακοσίοις ἔτεσιν the Ox. MS. reads simply ἑπτά.
[2] This would seem to be the meaning of πρῶτος ναός.

prayers of Jacob my father I saw him, while awake in the daytime, in his full and perfect shape. Know ye therefore, my children, that I am dying. Work therefore truth and righteousness each one with his neighbour, and judgment unto faithful doing, and keep the law of the Lord and His commandments; for these things do I teach you instead of all inheritance. Do ye also therefore give them to your children for an everlasting possession; for so did both Abraham, and Isaac, and Jacob. All these things they gave us for an inheritance, saying, Keep the commandments of God until the Lord shall reveal His salvation to all nations. Then shall ye see Enoch, Noah, and Shem, and Abraham, and Isaac, and Jacob, arising on the right hand in gladness. Then shall we also arise, each one over our tribe, worshipping the King of heaven, who appeared upon the earth in the form of a man of humility. And as many as believed on Him on the earth shall rejoice with Him; and then shall all men arise, some unto glory and some unto shame. And the Lord shall judge Israel first, even for the wrong they did unto Him; for when He appeared as a deliverer, God in the flesh, they believed Him not. And then shall He judge all the Gentiles, as many as believed Him not when He appeared upon earth. And He shall reprove Israel among the chosen ones of the Gentiles, even as He reproved Esau among the Midianites, who deceived their brethren, so that they fell into fornication and idolatry; and they were alienated from God, and became as they that were no children in the portion of them that fear the Lord. But if ye walk in holiness in the presence of the Lord, ye shall dwell in hope again in me, and all Israel shall be gathered unto the Lord.

11. And I shall no longer be called a ravening wolf[1] on account of your ravages, but a worker of the Lord, distributing food to them that work what is good. And one[2] shall rise up from my seed in the latter times, beloved of the Lord, hearing upon the earth His voice, enlightening with new knowledge all the Gentiles, bursting in upon Israel for salvation with the light of knowledge, and tearing it away from it like

[1] Gen. xlix. 27.
[2] This passage, referring to St. Paul (who was of the tribe of Benjamin, Rom. xi. 1, Phil. iii. 5), is quoted by Tertullian, *Adversus Marcionem*, v. 1; cf. *Scorpiace*, 13.

a wolf, and giving it to the synagogue of the Gentiles. And until the consummation of the ages shall he be in the synagogues of the Gentiles, and among their rulers, as a strain of music in the mouth of all; and he shall be inscribed in the holy books, both his work and his word, and he shall be a chosen one of God for ever; and because of him my father Jacob instructed me, saying, He shall fill up that which lacketh of thy tribe.

12. And when he finished his words, he said: I charge you, my children, carry up my bones out of Egypt, and bury me at Hebron, near my fathers. So Benjamin died a hundred and twenty-five years old, in a good old age, and they placed him in a coffin. And in the ninety-first year of the departure of the children of Israel from Egypt, they and their brethren brought up the bones of their fathers secretly in a place which is called Canaan; and they buried them in Hebron, by the feet of their fathers. And they returned from the land of Canaan, and dwelt in Egypt until the day of their departing from the land of Egypt.

FRAGMENTS

OF THE

SECOND AND THIRD CENTURIES.

F

THE translation of the Syriac pieces contained in this volume is based on a careful examination of that made by Dr. Cureton, the merits of which are cordially acknowledged. It will, however, be seen that it differs from that in many and important particulars.

Many thanks are due to the Dean of Canterbury for his kindness in giving much valuable help.

B. P. P.

INTRODUCTORY NOTICE.

THE fragments that follow are the productions of writers who lived during the second century or the beginning of the third. Little is known of the writers, and the statements made in regard to them are often very indefinite, and the result of mere conjecture.

Bardesan, or Bardesanes, according to one account, was born at Edessa in 154 A.D., and it is supposed that he died sometime between 224 and 230. Eusebius says that he flourished in the time of Marcus Aurelius. He was for some time resident at the court of Abgar VI., King of Edessa, with whom he was on intimate terms. He at first belonged to the gnostic sect of the Valentinians; but abandoning it, he seemed to come nearer the orthodox beliefs; but in reality, it is said, he devised errors of his own. He wrote many works. Eusebius attributes the work now translated, *The Book of Laws*, or *On Fate*, to Bardesanes; but many modern critics have come to the conclusion that it was written by a scholar of Bardesanes, but that it gives us the genuine opinions and reasonings of Bardesanes. The question is of interest in connection with the Clementine *Recognitions*, which contain a large portion of the work. The Syriac was first published by Cureton in his *Spicilegium*.

Melito was Bishop of Sardis, and flourished in the reign of Marcus Aurelius. He wrote many works, but all of them have perished except a few fragments. The genuineness of the Syriac fragments is open to question.

Quadratus was one of the first of the Christian apologists. He is said to have presented his apology to Hadrian, while the emperor was in Athens, attending the celebration of the Eleusinian mysteries.

Aristo of Pella, a Jew, was the author of a work called *The Disputation of Jason and Papiscus*. Nothing further is known of him. He flourished in the first half of the second century.

Claudius Apollinaris was Bishop of Hierapolis, and presented a defence of the Christians to Marcus Aurelius. He wrote many important works, of which we have only a few fragments.

Hegesippus also flourished in the time of Antoninus Pius and Marcus Aurelius. He is the first ecclesiastical historian, but his book was rather notes for an ecclesiastical history than a history.

Pantænus, probably a Sicilian by birth, passed from Stoicism to Christianity, and went to India to proclaim the truth. He returned to Alexandria, and became president of the catechetical school there, in which post he remained till his death, which took place about the year 212 A.D.

Rhodo went from Asia to Rome, and became a pupil of Tatian. After the lapse of his master into heresy, he remained true to the faith, and wrote against heretics.

Maximus flourished about the same time as Rhodo, under the Emperors Commodus and Severus.

Polycrates was Bishop of Ephesus. He took a part in the controversy on the Passover question. He died about 200 A.D.

Theophilus was Bishop of Cæsarea. He was contemporary with Polycrates, and, like him, engaged in the Passover controversy.

Serapion was ordained Bishop of Antioch in 190 A.D., but almost no other fact of his life is known. He wrote several works.

Apollonius wrote a work against the Montanists, probably in the year 210 A.D. This is all that is known of him.

Dionysius was Bishop of Corinth in the reign of Marcus Aurelius. He wrote letters to various churches.

The letter of the churches in Vienne and Lyons was written shortly after the persecution in Gaul, that took place in A.D. 177. It is not known who is the author. Some have supposed that Irenæus wrote it; but there is no historical testimony to this effect.

FRAGMENTS OF THE SECOND AND THIRD CENTURIES.

BARDESAN.[1]

THE BOOK OF THE LAWS OF [VARIOUS] COUNTRIES.[2]

SOME days since we were calling[3] to pay a visit to our brother Shemashgram, and Bardesan came and found us there. And when he had made inquiries after his health,[4] and ascertained that he was well, he asked us, "What were you talking about? for I heard your voice outside as I was coming in." For it was his habit, whenever he found us talking about anything before he came,[5] to ask us, "What were you saying?" that he might talk with us about it.

"Avida here," said we to him, "was saying to us, 'If God is one, as ye say, and if He is the creator of men, and if it is His will that you should do that which you are commanded, why did He not so create men that they should not be able to do wrong, but should constantly be doing that which is right? for in this way His will would have been accomplished.'"

"Tell me, my son Avida," said Bardesan to him, "why it has come into thy mind that the God of all is not One; or that

---

[1] Lit. "Son of Daisan," from a river so called near Edessa.—HAHN.
[2] Called by Eusebius, *Hist. Eccl.* iv. 30, *The Discourse on Fate* (Ὁ περὶ εἱμαρμένης διάλογος). This is more correct than the title above given: the "Laws" are adduced only as illustrations of the argument of the piece. The subject would, however, be more properly given as "The Freedom of the Will."
[3] Lit. "going in." Cureton renders, "we went up."
[4] Lit. "felt him."   [5] Lit. "before him." Merx: "ehe er kam."

He is One, but doth not will that men should behave themselves justly and uprightly?"

"I, sir," said Avida, "have asked these [brethren], persons of my own age, in order that *they* may return me an answer."

"If," said Bardesan to him, "thou wishest to learn, it were for thy advantage to learn from some one who is older than they; but if to teach, it is not requisite for *thee* to ask *them*, but [rather] that thou shouldst induce *them* to ask *thee* what they wish. For teachers are *asked* questions, and do not themselves ask them; or, if they ever do ask a question, it is to direct the mind of the questioner, so that he may ask properly, and they may know what his desire is. For it is a good thing that a man should know how to ask questions."

"For my part," said Avida, "I wish to learn; but I began first of all to question my brethren here, because I was too bashful to ask thee."

"Thou speakest becomingly,"[1] said Bardesan. "But know, nevertheless, that he who asks questions properly, and wishes to be convinced, and approaches the way of truth without contentiousness, has no need to be bashful; because he is sure by means of the things I have mentioned to please him to whom his questions are addressed. If so be, therefore, my son, thou hast any opinion of thy own[2] respecting this matter about which thou hast asked, tell it to us all; and, if we too approve of it, we shall express our agreement with thee; and, if we do not approve of it, we shall be under obligation to show thee why we do not approve of it. But if thou wast simply desirous of becoming acquainted with this subject, and hast no opinion of thy own about it, as a man who has but lately joined the disciples and is a recent inquirer, I will tell thee [respecting it]; so that thou mayest not go from us empty away. If, moreover, thou art pleased with those things which I shall say to thee, we have other things besides to tell thee[3] concerning this matter; but, if thou art not pleased, we on our part shall have stated our views without any personal feeling."

"I too," said Avida, "shall be much gratified[4] to hear and

---

[1] The word used is formed from the Greek εὐσχημόνως.

[2] Lit. "hast anything in thy mind."

[3] Lit. "there are for thee other things also."

[4] ܠܡܫ is here substituted for the ܘܫܠ of the text, which yields no sense.

to be convinced: because it is not from another that I have heard of this subject, but I have spoken of it to my brethren here out of my own mind; and they have not cared to convince me; but they say, 'Only believe, and thou wilt [then] be able to know everything.' But for my part, I cannot believe unless I be convinced."

"Not only," said Bardesan, "is Avida unwilling to believe, but there are many [others] also who, because there is no faith in them, are not even capable of being convinced; but they are always pulling down and building up, and [so] are found destitute of all knowledge of the truth. But notwithstanding, since Avida is not willing to believe, lo! I will speak to you who do believe, concerning this matter about which he asks; and [thus] he too will hear something further [about it]."

He began accordingly to address us [as follows]: "Many men are there who have not faith, and have not received knowledge from the True Wisdom.[1] In consequence of this, they are not competent to speak and give instruction [to others], nor are they readily inclined themselves to hear. For they have not the foundation of faith to build upon, nor have they any confidence on which to rest their hope. Moreover, because they are accustomed to doubt even concerning God, they likewise have not in them the fear of Him, which would of itself deliver them from all [other] fears: for he in whom there is no fear of God is the slave of all [sorts of] fears. For, even with regard to those things of various kinds which they disbelieve, they are not certain that they disbelieve them rightly, but they are unsettled in their opinions, and have no fixed belief,[2] and the taste of their thoughts is insipid in their [own] mouth; and they are always haunted with fear, and flushed with excitement, and reckless.

"But with regard to what Avida has said: 'How is it that God did not so make us that we should not sin and incur condemnation?'—if man had been made so, he would not have belonged to himself, but would have been the instrument of him that moved him; and it is evident also, that he who moves [an instrument] as he pleases, moves it either for good or for evil. And how, in that case, would a man differ from a harp, on

---

[1] Lit. "the wisdom of the truth."
[2] Lit. "are not able to stand."

which another plays; or from a ship, which another guides: where the praise and the blame reside in the hand of the performer or the steersman,[1] and the harp itself knows not what is played on it, nor the ship itself whether it be well steered and guided [or ill], they being only instruments made for the use of him in whom is the [requisite] skill? But God in His benignity chose not so to make man; but by freedom He exalted him above many [of His] creatures, and [even] made him equal with the angels. For look at the sun, and the moon, and the signs of the zodiac,[2] and all the other creatures which are greater than we in some points, [and see] how individual freedom has been denied them, and how they are all fixed [in their course] by decree, so that they may do that only which is decreed for them, and nothing else. For the sun never says, I will not rise at my appointed time; nor the moon, I will not change, nor wane, nor wax; nor does any one of the stars say, I will not rise nor set; nor the sea, I will not bear up the ships, nor stay within my boundaries; nor the mountains, We will not continue in the places in which we are set; nor do the winds say, We will not blow; nor the earth, I will not bear up and sustain whatsoever is upon me. But all these things are servants, and are subject to one decree: for they are the instruments of the wisdom of God, which erreth not.

"[Not so, however, with man]: for, if everything ministered, who would be he that is ministered to? And, if everything were ministered to, who would be he that ministered? [In that case], too, there would not be one thing diverse from another: yet that which is one, and in which there is no diversity [of parts], is a being[3] which up to this time has not been fashioned. But those things which are destined[4] for ministering have been fixed in the power of man: because in

---

[1] Or, "in the hand of the operator:" but it is better to employ two words.

[2] Or, "and the sphere."

[3] The word ܠܙܐ, here used, occurs subsequently as a designation of the Gnostic Æons. Here, as Merx observes, it can hardly go beyond its original meaning of *ens, entia, Wesen, that which is*. It evidently refers, however, in this passage to a *system* of things, a world.

[4] Lit. "required."

the image of Elohim¹ was he made. Therefore have these things, in the benignity [of God], been given to him, that they may minister to him for a season. It has also been given to him to be guided by his own will; so that whatever he is able to do, if he will he may do it, and if he do not will he may not do it, and [that so] he may justify himself or condemn. For, had he been made so as not to be able to do evil and thereby incur condemnation, in like manner also the good which he did would not have been his own, and he could not have been justified by it. For, if any one should not of his own will do that which is good or that which is evil, his justification and his condemnation would rest simply with that Fortune to which he is subjected.²

"It will therefore be manifest to you, that the goodness of God is great toward man, and that freedom has been given to him in greater measure than to any of those elemental bodies³ of which we have spoken, in order that by this freedom he may justify himself, and order his conduct in a godlike manner, and be copartner with angels, who are likewise possessed of personal freedom. For we are sure that, if the angels likewise had not been possessed of personal freedom, they would not have consorted with the daughters of men, and sinned, and fallen from their places. In like manner, too, those other [angels], who did the will of their Lord, were, by reason of their self-control, raised to higher rank, and sanctified, and received noble gifts. For every being in existence is in need of the Lord of all; of His gifts also there is no end.

Know ye, however, notwithstanding [what I have said], that even those things of which I have spoken as subsisting by decree are not absolutely destitute of all freedom; and on this account, at the last day, they will all be made subject to judgment."

"But how," said I to him, "should those things which are fixed [and regulated by decree] be judged?"

"Not inasmuch as they are fixed, O Philip," said he, "will the elements be judged, but inasmuch as they are endowed with

---

¹ Gen. i. 27. The Hebrew itself, בצלם אלהים, is given in Syriac characters, without translation.

² Cureton renders, "for which he is created." Merx has, "das ihn gemacht hat."

³ The Greek στοιχεῖα.

power. For beings[1] are not deprived of their natural properties[2] when they come to be fashioned, but [only] of the full exercise of their strength,[3] suffering a decrease[4] [of power] through their intermingling one with another, and being kept in subjection by the power of their Maker; and in so far as they are in subjection they will not be judged, but in respect of that [only] which is [under] their own [control]."

"Those things," said Avida to him, "which thou hast said, are very 'good; but, lo! the commands which have been given to men are severe, and they cannot perform them."

"This," said Bardesan, "is the saying of one who has not the will to do that which is right; nay, more, of him who has [already] yielded obedience and submission to his foe. For men have not been commanded to do anything but that which they are able to do. For the commandments set before us are [only] two, [and they are] such as are compatible with freedom and consistent with equity: one, that we refrain from everything which is wrong, and which we should not like to have done to ourselves; and the other, that we should do that which is right, and which we love and are pleased to have done to us likewise. Who, then, is the man that is too weak to avoid stealing, or to avoid lying, or to avoid acts of profligacy, or to avoid hatred and deception? For, lo! all these things are under [the control of] the mind of man; and are not dependent on[5] the strength of the body, but on the will of the soul. For even if a man be poor, and sick, and old, and disabled in his limbs, he is able to avoid doing all these things. And, as he is able to avoid doing these things, so is he able to love, and to bless, and to speak the truth, and to pray for what is good for every one with whom he is acquainted; and if he be in health,

---

[1] ܐܝܬ, that which exists, especially that which has an independent existence, is used here of the Gnostic Æons. They were so called in respect of their pre-existence, their existence independent of time or creation. When they came to be "created," or more properly "fashioned," they were called "emanations."

[2] Lit. " of their nature."

[3] Lit. "the strength of their exactness," i.e. their exact (or complete) strength. Cureton has, "their force of *energy*."

[4] Lit. "being lessened," or "lowered."

[5] Lit. "do not take place by."

and capable [of working],[1] he is able also to give of that which he has; moreover, to support with strength of body him that is sick and enfeebled—this also he can do.

"Who, then, it is that is not capable of doing that which men destitute of faith complain of, I know not. For my part, I think that it is precisely in respect to these commandments that man has more power than in anything [else]. For they are easy, and there are no circumstances that can hinder their performance. For we are not commanded to carry heavy loads of stones, or of timber, or of anything else, which those only who have [great] bodily strength can do; nor to build fortresses[2] and found cities, which kings only can do; nor to steer a ship, which mariners only have the skill to steer; nor to measure and divide land, which [land-] measurers only know how to do; nor [to practise] any one of those arts which are possessed by some, while the rest are destitute of them. But there have been given to us, in accordance with the benignity of God, commandments having no harshness in them[3]—such as any living man whatsoever[4] may rejoice to do.[5] For there is no man that does not rejoice when he does that which is right, nor any one that is not gladdened within himself if he abstains from things that are bad—except those who were not created for this good thing, and are called tares.[6] For would not the judge be unjust who should censure a man with regard to any such thing as he has not the ability to do?"

"Sayest thou of these deeds, O Bardesan," said Avida to him, "that they are easy to do?"

"To him that hath the will," said Bardesan, "I have said, and do [still] say, that they are easy. For this [obedience I contend for] is the proper behaviour of a free mind,[7] and of the soul which has not revolted against its governors. As for the action of the body, there are many things which hinder it: especially old age, and sickness, and poverty."

"Possibly," said Avida, "a man may be able to abstain from

---

[1] Cureton renders, "have the use of his hands:" Merx gives "etwas erwirbt."
[2] Or "towns."
[3] Lit. "without ill-will."
[4] Lit. "every man in whom there is a soul."
[5] Lit. "can do rejoicing."
[6] The Greek ζιζάνια.
[7] Lit. "a mind the son of the free."

the things that are bad; but as for doing the things that are good, what man is capable [of this]?"

"It is easier," said Bardesan, "to do good than to abstain from evil. For the good comes from the man himself,[1] and therefore he rejoices whenever he does good; but the evil is the work of the Enemy, and therefore [it is that, only] when a man is excited [by some evil passion], and is not in his sound natural condition,[2] he does the things that are bad. For know, my son, that for a man to praise and bless his friend is an easy thing; but for a man to refrain from taunting and reviling one whom he hates is not easy: nevertheless, it is possible. When, too, a man does that which is right, his mind is gladdened, and his conscience at ease, and he is pleased for every one to see what he does. But, when a man behaves amiss and commits wrong, he is troubled and excited, and full of anger and rage, and distressed in his soul and in his body; and, when he is in this [state of] mind, he does not like to be seen by any one; and even those things in which he rejoices, and which are accompanied with praise and blessing [from others], are spurned from his thoughts, while those things by which he is agitated and disturbed are [rendered more distressing to him because] accompanied by the curse of [conscious] guilt.

"Perhaps, however, some one will say that fools also are pleased when they do abominable things. [Undoubtedly]: but not because they do them [as such], nor because they receive any commendation [for them], nor because [they do them] with a good hope;[3] nor does the pleasure itself stay long with them. For the pleasure which is [experienced] in a healthy state [of the soul], with a good hope, is one thing; and the pleasure of a diseased state [of the soul], with a bad hope, is another. For lust is one thing, and love is another; and friendship is one thing, and good-fellowship another; and we ought without any difficulty to understand that the false counterfeit of affection which is called lust, even though there be in it the enjoyment of the moment, is nevertheless widely different from true affection, whose enjoyment is for ever, incorruptible and indestructible."

---

[1] Lit. "is the man's own."   [2] Lit. "is not sound in his nature."

[3] Cureton, "for good hope." But ܒܣܒܪ is a common expression for "in hope," as in Rom. viii. 20.

"Avida here," said I to him, "has also been speaking thus: 'It is from his nature that man does wrong; for, were he not naturally formed to do wrong, he would not do it.'"

"If all men," said Bardesan, "acted alike,[1] and followed one bias,[2] it would [then] be manifest that it was their nature that guided them, and that they had not that freedom of which I have been speaking to you. That you may understand, however, what is nature and what is freedom, I will proceed to inform you.

"The nature of man is, that he should be born, and grow up, and rise to his full stature, and produce children, and grow old, eating and drinking, and sleeping and waking, and that [then] he should die. These things, because they are of nature, belong to all men; and not to all men only, but also to all animals whatsoever,[3] and some of them also to trees. For this is the work of physical nature,[4] which makes and produces and regulates everything just as it has been commanded. Nature, I say, is found to be maintained among animals also in their actions. For the lion eats flesh, in accordance with his nature; and therefore all lions are eaters of flesh. The sheep eats grass; and therefore all sheep are eaters of grass. The bee makes honey, by which it is sustained; therefore all bees are makers of honey. The ant collects for herself a store in summer, from which to sustain herself in winter; and therefore do all ants act likewise. The scorpion strikes with its sting him who has not hurt it; and thus do all scorpions strike. Thus all animals preserve their nature: the eaters of flesh do not eat herbage; nor do the eaters of herbage eat flesh.

"Men, on the contrary, are not governed thus; but, whilst in the matters pertaining to their bodies they preserve their nature like animals, in the matters pertaining to their minds they do that which they choose, as those who are free,[5] and endowed with power, and as [made in] the likeness of God. For there are some of them that eat flesh, and do not touch bread; and there are some of them that make a distinction between the [several] kinds of flesh-food; and there are some

---

[1] Lit. "did one deed."
[2] Lit. "used one mind."
[3] Lit. "in whom there is a soul."
[4] Φύσις.
[5] Lit. "as children of the free."

of them that do not eat the flesh of any animal whatever.[1] There are some of them that become the husbands of their mothers, and of their sisters, and of their daughters; and there are some who do not consort with women at all. There are those who take it upon *themselves* to inflict vengeance, like lions and leopards; and there are those who strike him that has not done them any wrong, like scorpions; and there are those that are led like sheep, and do not harm their conductors. There are some that behave themselves with kindness, and some with justice, and some with wickedness.

"If any one should say that each one of them has a nature so to do, let him be assured[2] that it is not so. For there are those who [once] were profligates and drunkards; and, when the admonition of good counsels reached them, they became pure and sober,[3] and spurned their bodily appetites. And there are those who [once] behaved with purity and sobriety; and when they turned away from right admonition, and dared to set themselves against the commands of Deity and of their teachers, they fell from the way of truth, and became profligates and revellers. And there are those who after their fall repented again, and fear [came and] abode upon them, and they turned themselves [afresh] towards the truth which they had [before] held.[4]

"What, therefore, is the nature of man? For, lo! all men differ one from another in their conduct and in their aims,[5] and such [only] as are of[6] one mind and of one purpose resemble one another. But those men who, up to the present moment, have been enticed by their appetites and governed by their anger, are resolved to ascribe any wrong they do to their Maker, that they themselves may be found faultless, and that He who made them may, in the idle talk [of men],[7] bear the blame. They do not consider that nature is amenable to no law. For a man is not found fault with for being tall or short in his stature, or white or black, or because his eyes are large or small, or for any bodily defect whatsoever; but he is found

---

[1] Lit. "in which there is a soul."   [2] Lit. "let him see."
[3] Lit. "patient," *i.e.* tolerant of the craving which seeks gratification.
[4] Lit. "in which they had stood."   [5] Or "volitions."
[6] Lit. "have stood in."
[7] So Merx, "in eitler Rede." Cureton, "by a vain plea."

fault with if he steal, or lie, or practise deceit, or poison [another], or be abusive, or do [any other] such-like things.

"From hence, lo! it will be evident, that for those things which are not in our own hands, but which we have from nature, we are in no wise condemned, nor are we in any wise justified; but by those things which we do in [the exercise of] our personal freedom, if they be right we are justified and entitled to praise, and if they be wrong we are condemned and subjected to blame."

Again we questioned him, and said to him: "There are others who say that men are governed by the decree of Fate, [so as to act] at one time wickedly, and at another time well."

"I too am aware, O Philip and Baryama," said he to us, "that there are [such] men: those who are called Chaldæans, and also others who are fond of this subtle knowledge,[1] as I myself also once was. For it has been said by me in another place,[2] that the soul of man longs[3] to know that which the many are ignorant of, and those men make it their aim to do [this];[4] and [that] all the wrong which [men] commit, and all that they do aright, and all those things which happen to them, as regards riches and poverty, and sickness and health, and blemishes of the body, come to them through the governance of those stars which are called the Seven;[5] and that they are, [in fact], governed by them. But there are others who affirm the opposite of these things,—how that this art is a lying invention of the astrologers;[6] or that Fate has no existence whatever, but is an empty name; that, [on the contrary], all things, great and small, are placed in the hands of man; and that bodily blemishes and faults simply befall and happen to him by chance. But others, [again], say that whatsoever a man does he does of his own will, in [the exercise of] the freedom which has been given to him, and that the faults and blemishes and

---

[1] Lit. "this knowledge of art (or skill)."

[2] To what other work of his he refers is not known.

[3] Cureton, "is capable." Dr. Payne Smith (*Thes. Syr. s.v.*) says, referring to ܥܒܕ as used in this passage: "*eget, cupit, significare videtur.*"

[4] So Dr. Payne Smith. Merx renders, "Even that [which] men desire to do." Cureton has, "and the same men meditate to do."

[5] Lit. "the sevenths."   [6] Lit. "Chaldæans."

[other] untoward things which befall him he receives as punishment from God.

"For myself, however, according to my weak judgment,[1] the matter appears to stand [thus]: that these three opinions[2] are partly to be accepted as true, and partly to be rejected as false;—accepted as true, because men speak after the appearances which they see, and also because these men see how things come upon them [as if] accidentally; to be set aside as fallacious, because the wisdom of God is too profound[3] for them—that [wisdom] which founded the world, and created man, and ordained Governors, and gave to all things the [degree of] pre-eminence which is suited to every one of them. What I mean is, that this power is possessed by God, and the Angels, and the Potentates,[4] and the Governors,[5] and the Elements, and men, and animals; but that [this] power has not been given to all these orders [of beings] of which I have spoken in respect to everything (for He that has power over everything is One); but over some things they have power, and over some things they have not power, as I have been saying: in order that in those things over which they have power the goodness of God may be seen, and in those over which they have no power they may know that they have a Superior.

"There is, then, [such a thing as] Fate, as the astrologers say. That everything, moreover, is not under the control of our will, is apparent from this—that the majority of men have had the will to be rich, and to exercise dominion over their fellows, and to be healthy in their bodies, and to have things in subjection to them as they please; but that wealth is not found except with a few, nor dominion except with one here and another there, nor health of body with all men; and that [even] those who are rich do not have complete possession of their riches, nor do those who are in power have things in subjection to them as they wish, but that sometimes things are disobedient [to them] as they do not wish; and that at one time the rich are rich as they desire, and at another time they

---

[1] Lit. "my weakness."
[2] Or "sects" (αἱρέσεις).
[3] Lit. "rich."
[4] ܫܠܝܛܢܐ, Shlitâne.
[5] ܡܕܒܪܢܐ, Medabhrâne. Merx, p. 74, referring to the Peshito of Gen. i. 16, thinks that by the Potentates are meant the sun and moon, and by the Governors the five planets.

become poor as they do not desire; and that those who are thoroughly poor have dwellings such as they do not wish, and pass their lives in the world as they do not like, and covet [many] things which [only] flee from them. Many have children, and do not rear them; others rear them, and do not retain possession of them; others retain possession of them, and they become a disgrace and a sorrow [to their parents]. Some are rich, as they wish, and are afflicted with ill-health, as they do not wish; others are blest with good health, as they wish, and afflicted with poverty, as they do not wish. There are those who have in abundance the things they wish for, and but few of those things for which they do not wish; and there are others who have in abundance the things they do not wish for, and but few of those for which they do wish.

"And so the matter is found [to stand] thus: that wealth, and honours, and health, and sickness, and children, and [all the other] various objects of desire, are placed under [the control of] Fate, and are not in our own power; but [that, on the contrary], while we are pleased and delighted with such things as are in accordance with our wishes, towards such as we do not wish for we are drawn by force; and, from those things which happen to us when we are not pleased, it is evident that those things also with which we are pleased do not happen to us because we desire them; but that things happen as they do happen, and with some of them we are pleased, and with others not.

"And [thus] we men are found to be governed by Nature all alike, and by Fate variously, and by our freedom each as he chooses.

"But let us now proceed to show with respect to Fate that it has not power over everything. [Clearly not]: because that which is called Fate is itself [nothing more than] a [certain] order of procession,[1] which has been given to the Potentates and Elements by God; and, in conformity with this said pro-

[1] Merx renders ܣܘܼܪܥܵܢܵܐ by "emanation," quoting two passages from Eph. Syr. where the root ܢܒܥ is used of the issuing of water from a fountain. Dr. Payne Smith says: "The word seems to mean no more than *cursus*: cf. Euseb. *Theoph.* i. 31. 5, 55. 1, 83. 22, where it is used of the stars; and i. 74. 13, where it means the course of nature."

cession and order, intelligences[1] undergo change when they descend[2] to [be with] the soul, and souls undergo change when they descend[2] to [be with] bodies; and this [order], under the name of Fate and γένεσις,[3] is the agent of the changes[4] that take place in this assemblage [of parts of which man consists],[5] which is being sifted and purified for the benefit of whatsoever by the grace of God and by goodness has been benefited, and is being [and will continue to be] benefited until the close of all [things].

"The body, then, is governed by Nature, the soul also sharing in its experiences and sensations; and the body is neither hindered nor helped by Fate in the several acts it performs. For a man does not become a father before the age of fifteen, nor does a woman become a mother before the age of thirteen. In like manner, too, there is a law for old age: for women [then] become incapable of bearing, and men cease to possess the natural power of begetting children; while other animals, which are likewise governed by their nature, do, [even] before those ages I have mentioned, not only produce offspring, but also become too old to do so, just as the bodies of men also, when they are grown old, cease to propagate: nor is Fate able to give them offspring at a time when the body has not the natural power to give them. Neither, again, is Fate able to preserve the body of man in life without meat and drink; nor yet, even when it has meat and drink, to grant it exemption from death: for these and many other things belong exclusively to Nature.[6]

"But, when the times and methods of Nature have had their

---

[1] Read ܡܕܥܐ for ܡܕܥܐ.   [2] Lit. "in their descents."

[3] Or "nativity," "natal hour" (ܒܝܬ ܝܠܕܐ = place of birth, "Geburtshaus:" Merx).

[4] Lit. "this agent of change." Cureton, "this alternation." "Das diese Veränderung bewirkende Agens" is the rendering of Merx.

[5] Dr. Payne Smith thinks the reference to be to the Gnostic νοῦς, ψυχή, and σῶμα, which seem to be spoken of just before. This difficult passage is rendered by Cureton: "And this alternation itself is called the Fortune, and the Nativity of this assemblage, which is being sifted and purified for the assistance of that which," etc. Merx has, ". . . zur Unterstützung des Dinges, welches . . . unterstützt worden ist und unterstützt bleibt bis zur Vernichtung des Weltalls."

[6] Lit. "are Nature's own."

full scope, then does Fate come and make its appearance among them, and produce effects of various kinds: at one time helping Nature and augmenting [its power], and at another crippling and baffling it. Thus, from Nature comes the growth and perfecting of the body; but apart from Nature, that is by Fate, come diseases and blemishes in the body. From Nature comes the union of male and female, and the unalloyed happiness of them both; but from Fate comes hatred and the dissolution of the union, and, [moreover], all that impurity and lasciviousness which by reason of [the natural propensity to] intercourse men practise in their lust. From Nature comes birth and children; and from Fate, that sometimes the children are deformed, and sometimes are cast away, and sometimes die before their time. From Nature comes a supply [of nourishment] sufficient for the bodies of all [creatures];[1] and from Fate comes the want of sustenance, and [consequent] suffering in those bodies; and so, again, from the same Fate comes gluttony and unnecessary luxury. Nature ordains that the aged shall be judges for the young, and the wise for the foolish, and that the strong shall be set over[2] the weak, and the brave over the timid; but Fate brings it to pass that striplings are set over the aged, and the foolish over the wise, and that in time of war the weak command the strong, and the timid the brave.

"You must distinctly understand[3] that, in all cases in which Nature is disturbed from its direct course, its disturbance comes by reason of Fate; [and this happens] because the Chiefs[4] and Governors, with whom rests that agency of change[5] which is called Nativity, are opposed to one another. Some of them, which are called Dexter, are those which help Nature, and add to its predominance,[6] whenever the procession is favourable to them, and they stand in those regions of the zodiac which are in the ascendant, in their own portions.[7] Those, on the contrary, which are called Sinister are evil, and whenever they in their turn are in possession of the ascendant they act in opposition to Nature; and not on men only do they inflict

---

[1] Lit. "a sufficiency in measure for all bodies."
[2] Lit. "be heads to."   [3] Lit. "know ye distinctly."
[4] Or "heads."
[5] Lit. "agent of change," as above. Merx: "das Veränderungsprincip."
[6] Lit. "excellence."   [7] i.e. zones of the earth. See p. 107.

harm, but at times on animals also, and trees, and fruits, and the produce of the year, and fountains of water, and, [in short], on everything that is comprised within Nature, which is under their government.

"And in consequence of this,—[namely], the divisions and parties which exist among the Potentates,—some men have thought that the world is governed [by these contending powers] without any superintendence [from above]. [But that is] because they do not understand that this very thing—[I mean] the parties and divisions [subsisting among them],—and the justification and condemnation [consequent on their behaviour], belong to that constitution of things founded in freedom which has been given by God, to the end that these agents likewise, by reason of their self-determining power,[1] may be either justified or condemned. Just as we see that Fate crushes Nature, so can we also see the freedom of man defeating and crushing Fate itself,—not, however, in everything,—just as also Fate itself does not in everything defeat Nature. For it is proper that the three things, Nature, and Fate, and Freedom, should be continued in existence until the procession [of which I before spoke] be completed, and the [appointed] measure and number [of its evolutions] be accomplished, even as it seemed good to Him who ordains of what kind shall be the mode of life and the end of all creatures, and the condition of all beings and natures."

"I am convinced," said Avida, "by the arguments thou hast brought forward, that it is not from his nature that a man does wrong, and also that all men are not governed alike. If thou canst further prove also that it is not from Fate and Destiny that those who do wrong so act, then will it be incumbent on us to believe that man possesses personal freedom, and by his nature has the power [both] to follow that which is right and to avoid that which is wrong, and will therefore also justly be judged at the last day."

"Art thou," said Bardesan, "by the fact that all men are not governed alike, convinced that it is not from their nature that they do wrong? Why, then, thou canst not possibly escape the conviction[2] that neither also from Fate exclusively

---

[1] Or, "power as to themselves."
[2] Lit. "the matter compels thee to be convinced."

do they do wrong, if we are able to show thee that the sentence of the Fates and Potentates does not influence all men alike, but that we have freedom in our own selves, so that we can avoid serving physical nature and being influenced by the control of the Potentates."

"Prove me this," said Avida, "and I will be convinced by thee, and whatsoever thou shalt enjoin upon me I will do."

"Hast thou," said Bardesan, "read the books of the astrologers[1] who are in Babylon, in which is described what effects the stars have in their [various] combinations at the Nativities of men; and the books of the Egyptians, in which are described all the [various] characters which men happen to have?"

"I have read books of astrology,"[2] said Avida, "but I do not know which are those of the Babylonians and which those of the Egyptians."

"The teaching of both countries," said Bardesan, "is the same."

"It is well known to be so," said Avida.

"Listen, then," said Bardesan, "and observe, that that which the stars decree by their Fate and their portions is not practised by all men alike who are in all [parts of] the earth. For men have made laws [for themselves] in various countries, in [the exercise of] that freedom which was given them by God: forasmuch as this gift is in its very nature opposed to that Fate emanating from the Potentates, who assume to themselves that which was not given them. I will begin my enumeration [of these laws], so far as I can remember [them], from the East, the beginning of the whole world:—

"*Laws of the Seres.*—The Seres have laws forbidding to kill, or to commit impurity, or to worship idols; and in the whole of Serica there are no idols, and no harlots, nor any one that kills a man, nor any that is killed: although they, like other men, are born at all hours and on all days. Thus the fierce Mars, whensoever he is 'posited' in the zenith, does not overpower the freedom of the Seres, and compel a man to shed the blood of his fellow with an iron weapon; nor does Venus, when posited with Mars, compel any man whatever among the Seres to consort with his neighbour's wife, or with any [other] woman. Rich and poor, however, and sick people and healthy,

[1] Lit. "Chaldæans."   [2] Lit. "Chaldaism."

and rulers and subjects, are there: because such matters are given into the power of the Governors.

"*Laws of the Brahmans who are in India.*—Again, among the Hindoos, the Brahmans, of whom there are many thousands and tens of thousands, have a law forbidding to kill at all, or to pay reverence to idols, or to commit impurity, or to eat flesh, or to drink wine; and among these people not one of these things [ever] takes place. Thousands of years, too, have elapsed, during which these men, lo! have been governed by this law which they made for themselves.

"*Another Law which is in India.*—There is also another law in India, and in the same zone,[1] prevailing among those who are not of the caste[2] of the Brahmans, and do not embrace their teaching, bidding them serve idols, and commit impurity, and kill, and do other bad things, which by the Brahmans are disapproved. In the same zone of India, too, there are men who are in the habit of eating the flesh of men, just as all other nations eat the flesh of animals. Thus the evil stars have not compelled the Brahmans to do evil and impure things; nor have the good stars prevailed on the rest of the Hindoos to abstain from doing evil things; nor have those stars which are well 'located' in the regions which properly belong to them,[3] and in the signs of the zodiac favourable to a humane disposition,[4] prevailed on those who eat the flesh of men to abstain from using this foul and abominable food.

"*Laws of the Persians.*—The Persians, again, have made themselves laws permitting them to take as wives their sisters, and their daughters, and their daughters' daughters; and there are some who go yet further, and take even their mothers. Some of these said Persians are scattered abroad, [away from their

---

[1] The Greek κλίμα, denoting one of the seven belts (see p. 107 below) into which the earth's latitude was said to be divided. The Arabs also borrowed the word.

[2] Or "family."

[3] That is, their own "houses," as below. Each house had one of the heavenly bodies as its "lord," who was stronger, or better "located" in his own house than in any other. Also, of two planets equally strong in other respects, that which was in the strongest house was the stronger. The strength of the houses was determined by the order in which they rose, the strongest being that about to rise, which was called the ascendant.

[4] Lit. "the signs of humanity."

country], and are [found] in Media, and in the country of the Parthians,[1] and in Egypt, and in Phrygia (they are called Magi); and in all the countries and zones in which they are [found], they are governed by this law which was made for their fathers. Yet we cannot say that for all the Magi, and for the rest of the Persians, Venus was posited with the Moon and with Saturn in the house of Saturn in her portions, while the aspect of Mars was toward them.[2] There are many places, too, in the kingdom of the Parthians, where men kill their wives, and their brothers, and their children, and incur no penalty; while among the Romans and the Greeks, he that kills one of these incurs capital punishment, the severest of penalties.

"*Laws of the Geli.*—Among the Geli the women sow and reap, and build, and perform all the tasks of labourers, and wear no raiment of colours, and put on no shoes, and use no pleasant ointments; nor does any one find fault with them when they consort with strangers, or cultivate intimacies with their household slaves. But the husbands of these Gelæ are dressed in garments of colours, and ornamented with gold and jewels, and anoint themselves with pleasant ointments. Nor is it on account of any effeminacy on their part that they act in this manner, but on account of the law which has been made for them: in fact, all the men are fond of hunting and addicted to war. But we cannot say that for all the women of the Geli Venus was posited in Capricorn or in Aquarius, in a position of ill luck; nor can we possibly say that for all the Geli Mars and Venus were posited in Aries, where it is written that brave and wanton[3] men are born.

"*Laws of the Bactrians.*—Among the Bactrians, who are

---

[1] The text adds ܟܘܫܝܐ.

[2] Lit. "while Mars was witness to them."

[3] The difficult word ܡܠܝܨܐ is not found in the lexicons. Dr. Payne Smith remarks that it could only come from ܠܥܣ, which verb, however, throws away its ܠ, so that the form would be ܡܥܨܐ. He suggests, doubtfully, that the right reading is ܡܢܝܫܐ, from ܢܥܣ, which is used occasionally for *appetite*, and forms such an adjective in the sense of *animosus, animâ præditus;* and that if so, it may, like ܢܥܣܢܐ in Jude 19 and 1 Cor. xv. 44, 46, be = ψυχικοί, *having an animal nature, sensual.* Eusebius and Cæsarius have στατάλους, a word of similar force.

called Cashani, the women adorn themselves with the goodly raiment of men, and with much gold, and with costly jewels; and the slaves and handmaids minister to them more than to their husbands; and they ride on horses decked out with trappings of gold and with precious stones.[1] These women, moreover, do not practise continency, but have intimacies with their slaves, and with strangers who go to that country; and their husbands do not find fault with them, nor have the women themselves any fear [of punishment], because the Cashani look upon [2] their wives [only] as mistresses. Yet we cannot say that for all the Bactrian women Venus and Mars and Jupiter are posited in the house of Mars in the middle of the heavens,[3] the place where women are born that are rich and adulterous, and that make their husbands subservient to them in everything.

"*Laws of the Racami, and of the Edessæans, and of the Arabians.*—Among the Racami, and the Edessæans, and the Arabians, not only is she that commits adultery put to death, but she also upon whom rests the suspicion [4] of adultery suffers capital punishment.

"*Laws in Hatra.*—There is a law in force[5] in Hatra, that whosoever steals any little thing, even though it were worthless as water, shall be stoned. Among the Cashani, [on the contrary], if any one commits such a theft as this, they [merely] spit in his face. Among the Romans, [too], he that commits a small theft is scourged and sent about his business. On the other side of the Euphrates, and [as you go] eastward, he that is stigmatized as either a thief or a murderer does not much resent it;[6] but, if a man be stigmatized as an arsenocœte, he will avenge himself even to the extent of killing [his accuser].

---

[1] Cureton's rendering, "*and some* adorn themselves," etc., is not so good, as being a repetition of what has already been said. It is also doubtful whether the words can be so construed. The Greek of Eusebius gives the sense as in the text: κοσμοῦσαι πολλῷ χρυσῷ καὶ λίθοις βαρυτίμοις τοὺς ἵππους. If ܠܐܣ̈ܐ, *horses*, be masc., or masc. only, as Bernstein gives it, the participle should be altered to the same gender. But Dr. Payne Smith remarks that Amira in his Grammar makes it fem. Possibly the word takes both genders; possibly, too, the women of Bactria rode on mares.

[2] Lit. "possess." [3] The zenith.
[4] Lit. "name," or "report." [5] Lit. "made."
[6] Lit. "is not very angry."

"*Laws*......—Among[1]............boys.....to us, and are not...... Again, in all the region of the East, if any persons are [thus] stigmatized, and are known [to be guilty], their [own] fathers and brothers put them to death; and very often[2] they do not even make known the graves [where they are buried].

"[Such are] the laws of the people of the East. But *in the North, and in the country of the Gauls*[3] and their neighbours, such youths among them as are handsome the men take as wives, and they even have feasts [on the occasion]; and it is not considered by them as a disgrace, nor as a reproach, because of the law which prevails among them. But it is a thing impossible that all those in Gaul who are branded with this disgrace should at their Nativities have had Mercury posited with Venus in the house of Saturn, and within the limits of Mars, and in the signs of the zodiac to the west. For, concerning such men as are born under these conditions, it is written that they are branded with infamy, [as being] like women.

"*Laws of the Britons.*—Among the Britons many men take one [and the same] wife.

"*Laws of the Parthians.*—Among the Parthians, [on the other hand], one man takes many wives, and all of them keep to him only, because of the law which has been made there in that country.

"*Laws of the Amazons.*—As regards the Amazons, they, all of them, the entire nation, have no husbands; but like animals, once a year, in the spring-time, they issue forth from their territories and cross the river; and, having crossed it, they hold a great festival on a mountain, and the men from those parts come and stay with them fourteen days, and associate with them, and they become pregnant by them, and pass over again to their own country; and, when they are delivered, such [of the children] as are males they cast away, and the females they bring up. Now it is evident that, according to the ordinance of Nature, since they all became pregnant in one month, they also in one month are [all] delivered, a little sooner or a

---

[1] Eusebius has, Παρ' Ἕλλησι δὲ καὶ οἱ σοφοὶ ἐρωμένους ἔχοντες οὐ ψέγονται.
[2] Lit. "how many times."
[3] The text of Eusebius and the *Recognitions* is followed, which agrees better with the context. The Syriac reads "Germans."

little later; and, as we have heard, all of them are robust and warlike; but not one of the stars is able to help any of those males who are born so as to prevent their being cast away.

"*The Book of the Astrologers.*—It is written in the book of the astrologers, that, when Mercury is posited with Venus in the house of Mercury, he produces painters, sculptors, and bankers; but that, when they are in the house of Venus, they produce perfumers, and dancers, and singers, and poets. And [yet], in all the country of the Tayites and of the Saracens, and in Upper Libya, and among the Mauritanians, and in the country of the Nomades, which is at the mouth of the Ocean, and in outer Germany, and in Upper Sarmatia, and in Spain, and in all the countries to the north of Pontus, and in all the country of the Alanians, and among the Albanians, and among the Zazi, and in Brusa, which is beyond the Douro, one sees neither sculptors, nor painters, nor perfumers, nor bankers, nor poets; but, [on the contrary], this decree of Mercury and Venus is prevented from [influencing] the entire circumference of the world. In the whole of Media, all men when they die, [and even] while life is still remaining in them, are cast to the dogs, and the dogs eat the dead of the whole of Media. Yet we cannot say that all the Medians are born having the Moon posited with Mars in Cancer in the day-time beneath the earth: for it is written that those whom dogs eat are so born. The Hindoos, when they die, are all of them burnt with fire, and many of their wives are burnt along with them alive. But we cannot say that all those women of the Hindoos who are burnt had at their Nativity Mars and the Sun posited in Leo in the night-time beneath the earth, as those persons are born who are burnt with fire. All the Germans die by strangulation,[1] except those who are killed in battle. But it is a thing impossible, that, at the Nativity of all the Germans, the Moon and Hora should have been posited between Mars and Saturn. The truth is, that in all countries, every day, and at all hours, men are born under Nativities diverse from one another, and the laws of men prevail over the decree [of the stars], and they are governed by their customs. Fate does not compel the Seres to commit murder against their wish, nor the Brahmans to eat flesh; nor does it hinder the Persians from taking [as wives] their

---

[1] So Eusebius: ἀγχονιμαίῳ μόρῳ. Otherwise "suffocation."

daughters and their sisters, nor the Hindoos from being burnt, nor the Medes from being devoured by dogs, nor the Parthians from taking many wives, nor among the Britons many men from taking one [and the same] wife, nor the Edessæans from cultivating chastity, nor the Greeks from practising gymnastics, ..., nor the Romans from perpetually seizing upon [other] countries, nor the [men of the] Gauls from marrying one another; nor [does it compel] the Amazons to rear the males; nor does his Nativity compel any man within the circumference of the [whole] world to cultivate the art of the Muses; but, as I have [already] said, in every country and in every nation all men avail themselves of the freedom of their nature in any way they choose, and, by reason of the body with which they are clothed, do service to Fate and to Nature, sometimes as they wish, and at other times as they do not wish. For in every country and in every nation there are rich and poor, and rulers and subjects, and people in health and those who are sick—each one according as Fate and [his] Nativity have affected him."

"Of these things, Father Bardesan," said I to him, "thou hast convinced us, and we know that they are true. But knowest thou that the astrologers say that the earth is divided into seven portions, which are called Zones; and that over the said portions those seven [stars] have authority, each of them [over one]; and that in each one of the said portions the will of its own Potentate prevails; and that this is called [its] law?"

"First of all, know thou, my son Philip," said he to me, "that the astrologers have invented this statement as a device [for the promotion] of error. For, although the earth be divided into seven portions, yet in every one of the seven portions many laws are to be found differing from one another. For there are not seven [kinds of] laws [only] found in the world, according to the number of the seven stars; nor yet twelve, according to the number of the signs of the zodiac; nor yet thirty-six, according to the number of the Decani.[1] But there are many [kinds of] laws [to be seen as you go] from kingdom to kingdom, from country to country, from district to district, and in every abode [of man], differing one from another. For ye remember what

---
[1] So called from containing each ten of the parts or degrees into which the zodiacal circle is divided. Cf. Hahn, *Bardesanes Gnosticus*, p. 72.

I said to you—that in one zone, [that] of the Hindoos, there are many men that do not eat the flesh of animals, and there are others that [even] eat the flesh of men. And again, I told you, [in speaking] of the Persians and the Magi, that it is not in the zone of Persia only that they have taken [for wives] their daughters and their sisters, but that in every country to which they have gone they have followed the law of their fathers, and have preserved the mystic arts contained in that [teaching] which they delivered to them. And again, remember that I told you of many nations spread abroad over the entire circuit of the world,[1] who have not been confined to any one zone, but have dwelt in every quarter from which the wind blows,[2] and in all the zones, and who have not the arts which Mercury and Venus [are said to] have given when in conjunction with each other. Yet, if laws were regulated by zones, this could not be; but they clearly are not: because those men [I have spoken of] are at a wide remove from having anything in common with many [other] men in their habits of life.

"[Then, again], how many wise men, think ye, have abolished from their countries laws which appeared to them not well made? How many laws, also, are there which have been set aside through necessity? And how many kings are there who, when they have got possession of countries which did not belong to them, have abolished their established laws, and made such [other] laws as they chose? And, whenever these things occurred, no one of the stars was able to preserve the law. Here is an instance at hand for you to see [for yourselves]: it is but as yesterday since the Romans took possession of Arabia, and they abolished all the laws previously existing [there], and especially the circumcision which they practised. The truth is,[3] that he who is his own master is [sometimes] compelled to obey the law imposed on him by another, who himself [in turn] becomes possessed of the power to do as he pleases.

"But let me mention to you a fact which more than anything [else] is likely[4] to convince the foolish, and such as are wanting

---

[1] Lit. "who surround the whole world."
[2] Lit. "have been in all the winds."
[3] Lit. "for."   [4] Lit. "able."

in faith. All the Jews, who received the law through Moses, circumcise their male children on the eighth day, without waiting for the coming of the [proper] stars, or standing in fear of the law of the country [where they are living]. Nor does the star which has authority over the zone govern them by force; but, whether they be in Edom, or in Arabia, or in Greece, or in Persia, or in the north, or in the south, they carry out this law which was made for them by their fathers. It is evident that what they do is not from Nativity: for it is impossible that for all the Jews, on the eighth day, on which they are circumcised, Mars should 'be in the ascendant,' so that steel should pass upon them, and their blood be shed. Moreover, all of them, wherever they are, abstain from paying reverence to idols. One day in seven, also, they and their children cease from all work,—from all building, and from all travelling, and from all buying and selling; nor do they kill an animal on the Sabbath-day, nor kindle a fire, nor administer justice; and there is not found among them any one whom Fate compels,[1] either to go to law on the Sabbath-day and gain his cause, or to go to law and lose it, or to pull down, or to build up, or to do any one of those things which are done by all those men who have not received this law. They have also other things in respect to which they do not [on the Sabbath] conduct themselves like the rest of mankind, though on this same day they both bring forth and are born, and fall sick and die: for these things do not pertain to the power of man.

"In Syria and in Edessa men used to part with their manhood in honour of Tharatha; but, when King Abgar[2] became a believer he commanded that every one that did so should have his hand cut off, and from that day until now no one does so in the country of Edessa.

"And what shall we say of the new race of us Christians, whom Christ at His advent planted in every country and in every region? for, lo! wherever we are, we are all called after the one name of Christ—Christians. On one day, the first of the week, we assemble ourselves together, and on the days of the

[1] Lit. "commands."

[2] According to Neander, *General Church History*, i. 109, this was the Abgar Bar Manu with whom Bardesan is said to have stood very high. His conversion is placed between 160 and 170 A.D.

readings¹ we abstain from [taking] sustenance. The brethren who are in Gaul do not take males [for wives], nor those who are in Parthia two wives; nor do those who are in Judea circumcise themselves; nor do our sisters who are among the Geli consort with strangers; nor do those [brethren] who are in Persia take their daughters [for wives]; nor do those who are in Media abandon their dead, or bury them alive, or give them as food to the dogs; nor do those who are in Edessa kill their wives or their sisters when they commit impurity, but they withdraw from them, and give them over to the judgment of God; nor do those who are in Hatra² stone thieves [to death]; but, wherever they are, and in whatever place they are [found], the laws of the [several] countries do not hinder them from obeying the law of their [Sovereign], Christ; nor does the Fate of the [celestial] Governors compel them to make use of things which they regard as impure.

"On the other hand, sickness and health, and riches and poverty, things which are not within the scope of their freedom, befall them wherever they are. For although the freedom of man is not influenced by the compulsion of the Seven, or, if at any time it is influenced, it is able to withstand the influences exerted upon it, yet, [on the other hand], this [same] man, externally regarded,³ cannot on the instant liberate himself from the command of his Governors: for he is a slave and in subjection. For, if we were able to do everything, we should ourselves be everything; and, if we had not the power to do anything, we should be the tools of others.

"But, when God wills [them], all things are possible, [and they may take place] without hindrance: for there is nothing that can stay that Great and Holy Will. For even those who think that they [successfully] withstand it, do not withstand it by strength, but by wickedness and error. And this may go on for a little while, because He is kind and forbearing towards all beings that exist,⁴ so as to let them remain as they are, and be governed by their own will, whilst notwithstanding they are held in check by the works which have been done and by the

---

¹ For ܩܪܝܢܐ, Merx, by omitting one ܐ, gives ܩܪܝܢܐ, "readings." But what is meant is not clear. Ephraem Syrus ascribes certain compositions of this name to Bardesanes. Cf. Hahn, *Bard. Gnost.* p. 28.

² Or "Hutra."   ³ Lit. "this man who is seen."   ⁴ Lit. "all natures."

arrangements which have been made for their help. For this well-ordered constitution of things[1] and [this] government which have been instituted, and the intermingling of one with another, serve to repress the violence of [these] beings,[2] so that they should not inflict harm [on one another] to the full, nor yet to the full suffer harm, as was the case with them before the creation of the world. A time is also coming when this [propensity to inflict] harm which still remains in them shall be brought to an end, through the teaching which shall be [given them] amidst intercourse of another kind. And at the establishment of that new world all evil commotions shall cease, and all rebellions terminate, and the foolish shall be convinced, and all deficiencies shall be filled up, and there shall be quietness and peace, through the gift of the Lord of all existing beings."

[Here] endeth the Book of the Laws of Countries.

Bardesan, therefore, an aged man, and one celebrated for [his] knowledge of events, wrote, in a certain work which was composed by him, concerning the synchronisms[3] with one another of the luminaries of heaven, speaking as follows:—

"Two revolutions of Saturn,[4] 60 years;
5 revolutions of Jupiter, 60 years;
40 revolutions of Mars, 60 years;
60 revolutions of the Sun, 60 years;
72 revolutions of Venus, 60 years;
150 revolutions of Mercury, 60 years;
720 revolutions of the Moon, 60 years.

And this," says he, "is one synchronism of them all; that is, the time of one [such] synchronism of them. So that from hence [it appears that] to [complete] 100 such synchronisms there will be [required] six thousands of years. Thus:—

200 revolutions of Saturn, six thousands of years;
500 revolutions of Jupiter, 6 thousands of years;
4 thousand revolutions of Mars, 6 thousands of years;
Six thousand revolutions of the Sun, 6 thousands of years;

---

[1] Lit. "this order." [2] Lit. "natures." [3] The Greek σύνοδοι.
[4] The five planets are called by their Greek names, Κρόνος, κ.τ.λ.

7 thousand and 200 revolutions of Venus, 6 thousands of years;
12 thousand revolutions of Mercury, 6 thousands of years;
72 thousand revolutions of the Moon, 6 thousands of years."
These things did Bardesan thus compute when desiring to show that this world would stand only six thousands of years.

A DISCOURSE OF MELITO,

THE PHILOSOPHER;

WHICH WAS [DELIVERED] IN THE PRESENCE OF ANTONINUS CÆSAR, AND [IN WHICH] HE EXHORTED [1] THE SAID CÆSAR TO ACQUAINT HIMSELF WITH GOD, AND SHOWED TO HIM THE WAY OF TRUTH.

He began to speak as follows:—

"It is not easy," said Melito, "speedily to bring into the right way the man who has a long time previously been held fast by error. It may, however, be effected: for, when a man turns away ever so little from error, the mention of the truth is acceptable to him. For, just as when the cloud breaks ever so little there comes fair weather, even so, when a man turns toward God, the thick cloud of error which deprived him of true vision is quickly withdrawn from before him. For error, like disease [2] and sleep, long holds fast those who come under its influence; [3] but truth uses the word as a goad, and smites the slumberers, and awakens them; and when they are awake they look at the truth, and also understand it: they hear, and distinguish that which is from that which is not. For there are men who call iniquity righteousness: they think, for

---

[1] This appears to be the sense intended, and is that given by M. Renan: "Sermo qui factus est." Cureton renders, "Who was in the presence, etc.," and supposes that Melito first saw and conversed with the emperor, and afterwards wrote this discourse (Melito speaks of it more than once as written). This view, however, does not dispose of the fact that Melito is here affirmed to have "exhorted (lit. *said to*) Cæsar, etc." It was clearly meant to be understood that the discourse (or *speech*) was spoken: the references to writing merely show that it was written, either before or after the delivery.

[2] Cureton: "passion." The word ܠܐܘ takes both meanings.

[3] Lit. "sojourn beneath it."

example, that it is righteousness for a man to err with the many. But I, for my part, affirm that it is not a good excuse [for error] that a man errs with the many. For, if one man only sin,[1] his sin is great: how much greater will be the sin when many sin [together]!

"Now, the sin of which I speak is this: when a man abandons that which really exists, and serves that which does not really exist. There *is* that which really exists, and it is called GOD. He, [I say], really exists, and by His power doth everything subsist. This being is in no sense made, nor did He ever come into being; but He has existed from eternity, and will [continue to] exist for ever and ever. He changeth not, while everything [else] changes. No eye[2] can see Him, nor thought apprehend Him, nor language describe Him; and those who love Him speak of Him thus: *Father, and God of Truth.*

"If, therefore, a man forsake the light, and say that there is another God, it is plain from what he himself says that it is some created thing which he calls God. For, if a man call fire God, it is not God, because it is fire; and, if a man call water God, it is not God, because it is water; and, if [he so call] this earth on which we tread, or these heavens which are seen by us, or the sun, or the moon, or some one of these stars which run their course without ceasing by [Divine] command, and do not speed along by their own will, [neither are these gods]; and, if a man call gold and silver gods, are not these objects things which we use as we please? and, if [he so call] those pieces of wood which we burn, or those stones which we break, how can these things be gods? For, lo! they are [for] the use of man. How can *they* escape the commission of great sin, who in their speech change the great God into those things which, so long as they continue, continue by [Divine] command?

"But, notwithstanding this, I say that so long as a man does not hear, and [so] does not discern or understand that there is a Lord over these creatures, he is not perhaps to be blamed: because no one finds fault with a blind man though he walk ever so badly. For, in the same manner [as the blind, so] men also, when they were seeking after God, stumbled upon stones and blocks of wood; and such of them as were rich stumbled upon gold and silver, and were prevented by their stumblings

[1] Cureton: "act foolishly." [2] Lit. "sight."

from [finding] that which they were seeking after. But, now that a voice has been heard through all the earth,[1] [declaring] that there is a God of truth, and there has been given to every man an eye wherewith to see, those persons are without excuse who are ashamed of [incurring the censure of] their former companions in error, and yet desire to walk in the right way. For those who are ashamed to be saved must of necessity perish. I therefore counsel them to open their eyes and see: for, lo! light is given abundantly[2] to us all to see thereby; and if, when light has arisen upon us, any one close his eyes so as not to see, into the ditch he must go.[3] But why is a man ashamed of [the censure of] those who have been in error along with himself? Rather does it behove him to persuade them to follow in his steps; and, if they should not be persuaded by him, [then] to disengage himself from their society. For there are some men who are unable to rise from their mother earth, and therefore also do they make them gods from the earth their mother; and they are condemned by the judgments of truth, forasmuch as they apply the name [of Him] who is unchangeable to those objects which are subject to change, and shrink not from calling those things gods which have been made by the hands of man, and dare to make an image of God whom they have not seen.

"But I [have to] remark further, that the Sibyl[4] also has said concerning them that it is the images of deceased kings that they worship. And this is easy to understand: for, lo! even now they worship and honour the images of those of Cæsarean rank[5] more than their former [gods]; for from those their former gods both [pecuniary] tribute and produce

---

[1] Comp. Rom. x. 18.
[2] Cureton: "light without envy." But the expression resembles the Gk. ἀφθόνως, ungrudgingly, without stint.
[3] Lit. "to the ditch is his way." Comp. Matt. xv. 14.
[4] See *A. N. Christ. Lib.* vol. ii. p. 303, where the following lines are quoted by Justin Martyr from the *Sybilline Oracles*:

"But we have strayed from the Immortal's ways,
And worship with a dull and senseless mind
Idols, the workmanship of our own hands,
And images and figures of dead men."

[5] Cureton: "those belonging to the Cæsars." But the Cæsars themselves are clearly meant.

accrue to Cæsar, as to one who is greater than they. On this account, those who despise them, and [so] cause Cæsar's revenue to fall short, are put to death. But to the treasury of other kings also it is appointed how much the worshippers in various places shall pay, and how many vesselfuls[1] of water from the sea they shall supply. Such is the wickedness of the world—of those who worship and fear that which has no sensation. Many of them, too, who are crafty, either for the sake of gain, or for vainglory, or for dominion over the multitude, both themselves worship, and incite those who are destitute of understanding to worship, that which has no sensation.

"I will further write and show, as far as my ability goes, how and for what causes images were made to kings and tyrants, and [how] they came to be regarded[2] as gods. The people of Argos made images to Hercules, because he belonged to their city, and was strong, and by his valour slew noxious beasts, and more especially because they were afraid of him. For he was subject to no control, and carried off the wives of many: for his lust was great, like that of Zuradi the Persian, his friend. Again, the people of Acte worshipped Dionysus,[3] a king, because he had recently[4] planted the vine in their country. The Egyptians worshipped Joseph the Hebrew, who was called Serapis, because he supplied them with corn during the years of famine. The Athenians worshipped Athene, the daughter of Zeus, king of the island of Crete, because she built the town of Athens, and made Ericthippus her son king there, whom she had by adultery with Hephæstus, a blacksmith, son of a wife of her father. She was, too, always courting the society of Hercules, because he was her brother on her father's side. For Zeus the king became enamoured of Alcmene, the wife of Electryon, who was from Argos, and committed adultery with her, and she gave birth to Hercules. The people of Phœnicia worshipped Balthi,[5] queen of Cyprus,

---

[1] Cureton: "sacks full." The first word is used of a leathern pouch or wallet, as in Luke x. 4 (Peshito) for πήρα.

[2] Lit. "they became."

[3] Cureton, without necessity, reads the word "Dionysius."

[4] Cureton renders "originally." But comp. Judith iv. 3, where the same word answers to προσφάτως.

[5] Venus.

because she fell in love with Tamuz, son of Cuthar king of the Phœnicians, and left her own kingdom and came and dwelt in Gebal, a fortress of the Phœnicians, and at the same time made all the Cyprians subject to King Cuthar. Also, before Tamuz she had fallen in love with Ares, and committed adultery with him; and Hephæstus, her husband, caught her, and his jealousy was roused against her, and he came and killed Tamuz in Mount Lebanon, as he was hunting[1] wild boars; and from that time Balthi remained in Gebal, and she died in the city of Aphiki,[2] where Tamuz was buried. The Elamites worshipped Nuh, daughter of the king of Elam: when the enemy had carried her captive, her father made for her an image and a temple in Shushan, a royal residence which is in Elam. The Syrians worshipped Athi, a Hadibite, who sent the daughter of Belat, a person skilled in medicine, and she healed Simi, the daughter of Hadad king of Syria; and some time afterwards, when Hadad himself had the leprosy upon him, Athi entreated Elisha the Hebrew, and he came and healed him of his leprosy. The people of Mesopotamia also worshipped Cuthbi, a Hebrew woman, because she delivered Bakru, the paternal [king][3] of Edessa, from his enemies. With respect to Nebo, who is [worshipped] in Mabug, why should I write to you? For, lo! all the priests who are in Mabug know that it is the image of Orpheus, a Thracian Magus. Hadran, again, is the image of Zaradusht, a Persian Magus. For both of these Magi practised magic at a well which was in a wood in Mabug, in which was an unclean spirit, and it assaulted and disputed the passage of every one who passed by in all that

---

[1] Cureton's conjecture of ܢܨܝܕ or ܕܨܝܕ for ܨܝܕܝܢ has been adopted.

[2] Some have identified it with Aphek, Josh. xix. 30. The rites observed here were specially abominable.

[3] Cureton: "the patrician." Dr. Payne Smith, *Thes. Syr. s.v.*, regards the word as equivalent to πατὴρ τῆς πόλεως, *pater civitatis*, "a title of honour found in the Byzantine writers," and is inclined to think it a term belonging to the dialect of Edessa. A similar use of the same adjective is quoted from Buxtorf, *Lex. Chald. Talm.* p. 12: "אבי cognomen R. Nachmanis, qui a celebritate familiæ sic cognominatus est, quasi *Patritius*." This view appears to be supported by the similar use of an adjective for a substantive above: "(persons) of Cæsarean rank," for "Cæsars."

country in which the town of Mabug is situated; and these Magi, in accordance with what was a mystery in their Magian system, bade Simi, the daughter of Hadad, to draw water from the sea and pour it into the well, so that the spirit should not come up and commit assault. In like manner, the rest of mankind made images to their kings and worshipped them; of which matter I will not write further.

"But thou, a [person of] liberal mind, and familiar with the truth, if thou wilt [properly] consider these matters, commune with thine own self;[1] and, though they should clothe thee in the garb of a woman, remember that thou art a man. Believe in Him who is in reality God, and to Him lay open thy mind, and to Him commit thy soul, and He is able to give thee immortal life for ever, for everything is possible to Him;[2] and let all other things be esteemed by thee just as they are—images as images, and sculptures as sculptures; and let not that which is only made be put by thee in the place of Him who is not made, but let Him, the ever-living God, be constantly present to thy mind.[3] For thy mind itself is His likeness: for it too is invisible and impalpable,[4] and not to be represented by any form, yet by its will is the whole bodily frame moved. Know, therefore, that, if thou constantly serve Him who is immoveable, even He exists for ever, so thou also, when thou shalt have put off this [body], which is visible and corruptible, shalt stand before Him for ever, endowed with life and knowledge, and thy works shall be to thee wealth inexhaustible and possessions

---

[1] Lit. "be (or, get to be) with thyself." Cureton: "enter into thyself." The meaning appears to be, "think for thyself."

[2] Cureton: "everything cometh through His hands." It should rather be, "*into* His hands," *i.e.* "He has power to do everything." See note 1, p. 91.

[3] Lit. "be running in thy mind."

[4] The text has ܡܬܬܙܝܥ, which M. Renan derives from the root ܙܘܥ and translates "*commovetur*." This, although correct in grammar, does not suit the sense. The grammars recognise the form as a possible Eshtaphel of ܢܓܥ "*tangere*," but it is not found in actual use. Dr. Payne Smith thinks the right reading to be ܡܬܡܫܐ, which gives the required sense.

unfailing. And know that the chief of thy good works is this: that thou know God, and serve Him. Know, too, that He asketh not anything of thee: He needeth not anything.

"Who is this God? He who is Himself truth, and His word truth. And what is truth? That which is not fashioned, nor made, nor represented by art: that is, which has never been brought into existence, and is [on that account] called truth.[1] If, therefore, a man worship that which is made with hands, it is not the truth that he worships, nor yet the word of truth.

"I have very much to say on this subject; but I feel ashamed for those who do not understand that they are superior to the work of their own hands, nor perceive how they give gold to the artists that they may make for them gods, and give them silver for their adornment and honour, and move their riches about from place to place, and [then] worship them. And what infamy can be greater than this, that a man should worship his riches, and forsake Him who bestowed those riches upon him? and that he should revile man, yet worship the image of man; and slay a beast, yet worship the likeness of a beast? This also is evident, that it is the workmanship of their fellow-men that they worship: for they do not worship the treasures [2] while they are laid by in the bag, but when the artists have fashioned images out of them they worship them; neither do they worship the gold or the silver considered as property,[3] but when the gravers have sculptured them then they worship them. Senseless man! what addition has been made to thy

---

[1] Or, "that which is fixed and invariable." There seems to be a reference to the derivation of ܩܘܫܬܐ (truth) from ܩܡ, *firmus (stabilis) fuit*. Cureton has strangely mistranslated ܗܘܐ ܗܘܝܘ ܗܘܐ ܠܐ, by "that which, without having been brought into existence, does exist." The first ܗܘܐ is nothing but the sign of emphatic denial which is frequently appended to ܠܐ, and ܗܘܝܘ is the infinitive of emphasis belonging to the second ܗܘܐ.

[2] Cureton: "materials." The printed text has ܣܡܡܢܐ, "drugs." The correct reading, there can hardly be a doubt, is ܣܝܡܬܐ.

[3] Lit. "the property of the gold or silver," if the word ܢܣܒܬܐ is rightly taken. Although no such derivative of ܢܣܒ is found in the lexicons, the form is possible from the Palel of that verb: e.g. ܩܘܒܠܬܐ from ܩܒܠ. See Hoffmann, *Gram. Syr.* sec. 87, 19.

gold, that now thou worshippest it? If it is because it has
been made to resemble a winged animal, why dost thou not
worship the winged animal [itself]? And if because it has
been made like a beast of prey, lo! the beast of prey itself is
before thee. And if it is the workmanship itself that pleases
thee, let the workmanship of God please thee, who made all
things, and in His own likeness made the workmen, who strive
to do like Him, but resemble Him not.

"But perhaps thou wilt say: How is it that God did not so
make me that I should serve Him, and not images? In speaking thus, thou art seeking to become an idle instrument, and
not a living man. For God made thee as perfect as it seemed
good to Him. He has given thee a mind endowed with freedom; He has set before thee objects in great number, that
thou on thy part mayest distinguish [the nature of] each thing
and choose for thyself that which is good; He has set before thee
the heavens, and placed in them the stars; He has set before
thee the sun and the moon, and they too every day run their
course therein; He has set before thee the multitude of waters,
and restrained them by His word; He has set before thee the
wide earth, which remains at rest, and continues before thee
without variation:[1] yet, lest thou shouldst suppose that of its
own nature it [so] continues, He makes it also to quake when
He pleaseth; He has set before thee the clouds, which by
[His] command bring water from above and satisfy the earth—
that from hence thou mayest understand that He who puts
these things in motion is superior to them all, and mayest accept
[thankfully] the goodness of Him who has given thee a mind
whereby to distinguish these things from one another.

Wherefore I counsel thee to know thyself, and to know God.
For understand how that there is within thee that which is called
the soul—by it the eye seeth, by it the ear heareth, by it the
mouth speaketh; and how it makes use of the whole body;
and [how], whenever He pleaseth to remove the soul from the
body, this falleth [to decay] and perisheth. From this, therefore, which exists within thyself and is invisible, understand
how God also moveth the whole by His power, like the body;
[and] that, whenever it pleases Him to withdraw His power, the
whole world also, like the body, will fall [to decay] and perish.

[1] Lit. "in one fashion."

"But why this world was made, and why it passes away, and why the body exists, and why it falls [to decay], and why it continues, thou canst not know until thou hast raised thy head from this sleep in which thou art sunk, and hast opened thine eyes and seen that God is One, the Lord of all, and hast come to serve Him with all thy heart. Then will He grant thee to know His will: for every one that is severed from the knowledge of the living God is dead and buried [even while] in his body. Therefore [is it that] thou dost wallow on the ground before demons and shadows, and askest vain petitions from that which has not anything to give. But thou, stand thou up from among those who are lying on the earth and caressing stones, and giving their substance as food for the fire, and offering their raiment to idols, and, while [themselves] possessed of senses, are bent on serving that which has no sensation; and offer thou for thy imperishable soul petitions [for that] which decayeth not, to God who suffers no decay—and thy freedom will be at once apparent; and be thou careful of it,[1] and give thanks to God who made thee, and gave thee the mind of the free, that thou mightest shape thy conduct even as thou wilt. He hath set before thee all these things, and showeth thee that, if thou follow after evil, thou shalt be condemned for thy evil deeds; but that, if after goodness, thou shalt receive from Him abundant good,[2] together with immortal life for ever.

"There is, therefore, nothing to hinder thee from changing thy evil manner of life, because thou art a free man; or from seeking and finding out who is the Lord of all; or from serving Him with all thy heart: because with Him there is no reluctance to give the knowledge of Himself to those that seek it, according to the measure of their capacity to know Him.

"Let it be thy first care not to deceive thyself. For, if thou sayest of that which is not God: This is God, thou deceivest thyself, and sinnest before the God of truth. Thou fool! is that God which is [bought and] sold? Is that God which is in want? Is that God which must be watched over? How buyest thou him as a slave, and servest him as a master? How askest thou of him, as of one that is rich, to give to thee, and thyself givest to him as to one that is poor? How dost

---

[1] Or, "of what pertains to it."   [2] Lit. "many good things."

thou expect of him that he will make thee victorious in battle? for, lo! when thy enemies have conquered thee, they strip him likewise.

"Perhaps one who is a king may say: I cannot behave myself aright, because I am a king; it becomes me to do the will of the many. He who speaks thus really deserves to be laughed at: for why should not the king himself lead the way[1] to all good things, and persuade the people under his rule to behave with purity, and to know God in truth, and in his own person set before them the patterns of all things excellent—since thus it becomes him to do? For it is a shameful thing that a king, however badly he may conduct himself, should [yet] judge and condemn those who do amiss.

"My opinion is this: that in *this* way a kingdom may be governed in peace—when the sovereign is acquainted with the God of truth, and is withheld by fear of Him from doing wrong[2] to those who are his subjects, and judges everything with equity, as one who knows that he himself also will be judged before God; while, at the same time, those who are under his rule[3] are withheld by the fear of God from doing wrong to their sovereign, and are restrained by [the same] fear from doing wrong to one another. By this knowledge of God and fear of Him all evil may be removed from the realm. For, if the sovereign abstain from doing wrong to those who are under his rule, and they abstain from doing wrong to him and to each other, it is evident that the whole country will dwell in peace. Many blessings, too, will be [enjoyed] there, because amongst them all the name of God will be glorified. For what blessing is greater than this, that a sovereign should deliver the people that are under his rule from error, and by this good deed render himself pleasing to God? For from error arise all those evils [from which kingdoms suffer]; but the greatest of all errors is this: when a man is ignorant of God, and in God's stead worships that which is not God.

[1] Lit. "be the beginner."
[2] Cureton is probably right in so taking the words, although the construction is not quite the same as in the similar sentence a little below. If so, for ܚܠܦ we must read ܚܠܦ.
[3] Lit. "hand."

"There are, however, persons who say: It is for the honour of God that we make the image: in order, that is, that we may worship the God who is concealed from our view. But they are unaware that God is in every country, and in every place, and is never absent, and that there is not anything done and He knoweth it not. Yet thou, despicable man! within whom He is, and without whom He is, and above whom He is, hast nevertheless gone and bought thee wood from the carpenter's, and it is carved and made into an image insulting to God.[1] To this thou offerest sacrifice, and knowest not that the all-seeing eye seeth thee, and that the word of truth reproves thee, and says to thee: How can the unseen God be sculptured? Nay, it is the likeness of thyself that thou makest and worshippest. Because the wood has been sculptured, hast thou not the insight to perceive that it is [still] wood, or [that the stone] is [still] stone? The gold also the workman[2] taketh according to its weight in the balance. And when thou hast had it made[3] [into an image], why dost thou weigh it? Therefore thou art a lover of gold, and not a lover of God. And art thou not ashamed, perchance it be deficient, to demand of the maker of it why he has stolen some of it? Though thou hast eyes, dost thou not see? And though thou hast intelligence,[4] dost thou not understand? Why dost thou wallow on the ground, and offer supplication to things which are without sense? Fear Him who shaketh the earth, and maketh the heavens to revolve, and smiteth the sea, and removeth the mountain from its place—Him who can make Himself like a fire, and consume all things; and, if thou be not able to clear thyself of guilt, yet add not to thy sins; and, if thou be not able to know God, yet doubt not[5] that He exists.

"Again, there are persons who say: Whatsoever our fathers have bequeathed to us, [that] we reverence. Therefore, of course, it is, that those whose fathers have bequeathed them

---

[1] Lit. "into an insult of God." So M. Renan, "in opprobrium Dei." Cureton, admitting that this *may* be the sense, renders, "an abomination of God," and refers to the circumstance that in Scripture an idol is frequently so spoken of. But ܒܗܬܐ is not used in such passages (it is either ܬܘܩܠܬܐ, or, less frequently, ܛܘܠܩܐ), nor does it appear ever to have the meaning which Cureton assigns to it.

[2] Lit. "he." [3] Lit. "hast made it."
[4] Lit. "heart." [5] Lit. "be of opinion."

poverty strive to become rich! and those whose fathers did not instruct them, desire to be instructed, and to learn that which their fathers knew not! And why, forsooth, do the children of the blind see, and the children of the lame walk? Nay, it is not well for a man to follow [his] predecessors, [if they be] those whose course was evil; but [rather] that we should turn from that path of theirs, lest that which befell [our] predecessors should bring disaster upon us also. Wherefore, inquire whether thy father's course was good: and, [if so], do thou also follow in his steps; but, if thy father's course was very evil, let thine be good, and so let it be with thy children after thee.[1] Be grieved also for thy father because his course is evil, so long as thy grief may avail to help him. But, as for thy children, speak to them thus: There is a God, the Father of all, who never came into being, neither was ever made, and by whose will all things subsist. He also made the luminaries, that His works may see one another; and He conceals Himself in His power from all His works: for it is not permitted to any being subject to change to see Him who changes not. But such as are mindful [of His words], and are admitted into that covenant which is unchangeable, *they* see God—so far as it is possible for them to see Him. These also will have power to escape destruction, when the flood of fire comes upon all the world. For there was once a flood and a wind,[2] and the great[3] men were swept away by a violent blast from the north, but the just were left, for a demonstration of the truth. Again, at another time there was a flood of water, and all men and

---

[1] This seems preferable to Cureton's, "and let thy children also follow after thee." Had this been the meaning, probably the verb ܢܗܘܐ would have been used, as in the preceding sentence, not ܢܗܘܘܢ.

[2] So the Sibylline oracle, as quoted by Cureton in the Greek:
"And, when he would the starry steep of heaven
Ascend, the Sire Immortal did his works
With mighty blasts assail: forthwith the winds
Hurled prostrate from its height the towering pile,
And bitter strife among the builders roused."

[3] Lit. "chosen." The same expression, except that the similar ܓܒܝܐ is used for ܓܒܪܐ, occurs Sap. Sol. xiv. 6, as a translation of ὑπερηφάνων γιγάντων, *gigantes superbi*. See *Thes. Syr.*, s.v. ܓܒܐ.

animals perished in the multitude of waters, but the just were preserved in an ark of wood by the command of God. So also will it be at the last time: there shall be a flood of fire, and the earth shall be burnt up, together with its mountains; and mankind shall be burnt up, along with the idols which they have made, and the carved images which they have worshipped; and the sea shall be burnt up, together with its islands; but the just shall be preserved from wrath, like as [were] their fellows of the ark from the waters of the deluge. And then shall those who have not known God, and those who have made them idols, bemoan themselves, when they shall see those idols of theirs being burnt up, together with themselves, and nothing shall be found to help them.

"When thou, Antoninus[1] Cæsar, shalt become acquainted with these things, and thy children also with thee, [then] wilt thou bequeath to them an inheritance for ever which fadeth not away, and thou wilt deliver thy soul, and the souls of thy children also, from that which shall come upon the whole earth in the judgment of truth [and] of righteousness. For, according as thou hast acknowledged Him here, [so] will He acknowledge thee there; and, if thou account Him here superfluous, He will not account thee one of those who have known Him and confessed Him.

"These [may] suffice thy Majesty; and, if they be [too] many, yet deign to accept them."[2]

[Here] endeth Melito.

BY MELITO, BISHOP OF SARDIS.

FROM THE DISCOURSE ON SOUL AND BODY.

For this reason did the Father send His Son from heaven without a bodily form, that, when He should put on a body by means of the Virgin's womb, and be born man, He might save

---

[1] The MS. has "Antonius."

[2] Cureton, for the last clause, gives "as thou wilt," remarking that the sense is obscure. The literal rendering is, "if thou wilt," the consequent clause being unexpressed. "If you please, [accept them]," seems what is meant.

man, and gather together those members of His which death had scattered when he divided man.

And further on:—The earth shook, and its foundations trembled; the sun fled away, and the elements turned back, and the day was changed [into night]: for they could not endure [the sight of] their Lord hanging on a tree. The [whole] creation was amazed, marvelling and saying, "What new mystery, then, is this? The Judge is judged, and holds his peace; the Invisible One is seen, and is not ashamed; the Incomprehensible is laid hold upon, and is not indignant; the Illimitable is circumscribed, and doth not resist; the Impassible suffereth, and doth not avenge; the Immortal dieth, and answereth not a word; the Celestial is laid in the grave, and endureth! What new mystery is this?" The [whole] creation, [I say], was astonished; but, when our Lord arose from the place of the dead, and trampled death under foot, and bound the strong one, and set man free, then did the whole creation see clearly that for man's sake the Judge was condemned, and the Invisible was seen, and the Illimitable was circumscribed, and the Impassible suffered, and the Immortal died, and the Celestial was laid in the grave. For our Lord, when He was born man, was condemned in order that He might show mercy, was bound in order that He might loose, was seized in order that He might release, suffered in order that He might feel compassion,[1] died in order that He might give life, was laid in the grave that He might raise [from the dead].

BY THE SAME, FROM THE DISCOURSE ON THE CROSS.

On these accounts He came to us; on these accounts, though He was incorporeal, He formed for Himself a body after our fashion,[2]—appearing as a sheep, yet still remaining the Shepherd; being esteemed a servant, yet not renouncing the Sonship; being carried [in the womb] of Mary, yet arrayed in [the nature of] His Father; treading upon the earth, yet filling

---

[1] ܚܢܢ seems to be the true reading, not the ܚܢܢ of the printed MS.
[2] Or "wove—a body from our material."

heaven; appearing as an infant, yet not discarding the eternity of His nature; being invested with a body, yet not circumscribing the unmixed simplicity of His Godhead; being esteemed poor, yet not divested of His riches; needing sustenance inasmuch as He was man, yet not ceasing to feed the entire world inasmuch as He is God; putting on the likeness of a servant, yet not impairing[1] the likeness of His Father. He sustained every character[2] [belonging to Him] in an immutable nature: He was standing before Pilate, and [at the same time] was sitting with His Father; He was nailed upon the tree, and [yet] was the Lord of all things.

[FROM THE TREATISE] OF MELITO THE BISHOP, ON FAITH.

We have collected together [extracts] from the Law and the Prophets relating to those things which have been declared concerning our Lord Jesus Christ, that we may prove to your love that this [Being] is perfect reason, the Word of God; He who was begotten before the light; He who is Creator together with the Father; He who is the Fashioner of man; He who is all in all; He who among the patriarchs is Patriarch; He who in the law is the Law; among the priests, Chief Priest; among kings, the Ruler; among prophets, the Prophet; among the angels, Archangel; in the voice [of the preacher], the Word; among spirits, the Spirit; in the Father, the Son; in God, God; King for ever and ever. For this is He who was pilot to Noah; He who was guide to Abraham; He who was bound with Isaac; He who was in exile with Jacob; He who was sold with Joseph; He who was captain of the host with Moses; He who was the divider of the inheritance with Jesus the son of Nun; He who in David and the prophets announced His own sufferings; He who put on a bodily form in the Virgin; He who was born in Bethlehem; He who was wrapped in swaddling-clothes in the manger; He who was seen by the shepherds; He who was glorified by the angels; He who was worshipped by the Magi; He who was pointed out by John; He who gathered

---

[1] Lit. "changing." [2] Lit. "He was everything."

together the apostles; He who preached the kingdom; He who cured the lame; He who gave light to the blind; He who raised the dead; He who appeared in the temple; He who was not believed on by the people; He who was betrayed by Judas; He who was apprehended by the priests; He who was condemned by Pilate; He who was pierced in the flesh; He who was hanged on the tree; He who was buried in the earth; He who rose from the place of the dead; He who appeared to the apostles; He who was carried up to heaven; He who is seated at the right hand of the Father; He who is the repose of those that are departed; the recoverer of those that are lost; the light of those that are in darkness; the deliverer of those that are captive; the guide of those that go astray; the asylum of the afflicted; the bridegroom of the church; the charioteer of the cherubim; the captain of the angels; God who is from God; the Son who is from the Father; Jesus Christ the King for evermore. Amen.

BY MELITO, BISHOP OF (THE CITY OF) ATTICA.

This is He who took a bodily form in the Virgin, and was hanged upon the tree, and was buried within the earth, and suffered not dissolution; He who rose from the place of the dead, and raised up men from the earth—from the grave below to the height of heaven. This is the Lamb that was slain; this is the Lamb that opened not His mouth.[1] This is He who was born of Mary, fair sheep [of the fold]. This is He that was taken from the flock, and was led to the slaughter, and was slain in the evening, and was buried at night; He who had no bone of Him broken on the tree; He who suffered not dissolution within the earth; He who rose from the place of the dead, and raised up the race of Adam from the grave below. This is He who was put to death. And where was He put to death? In the midst of Jerusalem. By whom? By Israel: because He cured their lame, and cleansed their lepers, and gave light to their blind, and raised their dead! This was the cause of His death. Thou, [O Israel], wast giving commands, and He

[1] Lit. "the Lamb without voice."

was being crucified; thou wast rejoicing, and He was being buried; thou wast reclining on a soft couch, and He was watching in the grave and the shroud.¹ O Israel, transgressor of the law, why hast thou committed this new iniquity, subjecting the Lord to new sufferings—thine own Lord, Him who fashioned thee, Him who made thee, Him who honoured thee, who called thee Israel? But thou hast not been found to be Israel: for thou hast not seen God, nor understood the Lord. Thou hast not known, O Israel, that this was the first-born of God, who was begotten before the sun, who made the light to shine forth, who lighted up the day, who separated the darkness, who fixed the first foundations, who poised the earth, who collected the ocean, who stretched out the firmament, who adorned the world. Bitter [were] thy nails, and sharp; bitter thy tongue, which thou didst whet; bitter [was] Judas, to whom thou gavest hire; bitter thy false witnesses, whom thou stirredst up; bitter thy gall, which thou preparedst; bitter thy vinegar, which thou madest; bitter thy hands, filled with blood. Thou slewest thy Lord, and He was lifted up upon the tree; and an inscription was fixed [above], to show who He was that was slain. And who was this? (that which we shall not say is [too] shocking [to hear], and that which we shall say is very dreadful: nevertheless hearken, and tremble.) [It was] He because of whom the earth quaked. He that hung up the earth [in space] was [Himself] hanged up; He that fixed the heavens was fixed [with nails]; He that bore up the earth was borne up on a tree; the Lord [of all] was subjected to ignominy in a naked body—God put to death! the King of Israel slain with Israel's right hand! Alas for the new wickedness of the new murder! The Lord was exposed with naked body: He was not deemed worthy even of covering; and, in order that He might not be seen, the luminaries turned away, and the day became darkened, because they slew God, who hung naked on the tree. It was not the body of our Lord that the luminaries covered with darkness when they set,² but the eyes of men. For, because the people quaked not, the earth quaked; because

---

¹ The Greek γλωσσόκομον.

² This is the rendering of ܐܥܪܒ ; but Cureton has "fled," as though he read ܥܪܩ.

they were not affrighted, the earth was affrighted. Thou smotest thy Lord: thou also hast been smitten upon the earth. And thou indeed liest dead; but He is risen from the place of the dead, and ascended to the height of heaven, having suffered for the sake of those who suffer, and having been bound for the sake of Adam's race which was imprisoned, and having been judged for the sake of him who was condemned, and having been buried for the sake of him who was buried.

And further on:—This is He who made the heaven and the earth, and in the beginning, together with the Father, fashioned man; who was announced by means of the law and the prophets; who put on a bodily form in the Virgin; who was hanged upon the tree; who was buried in the earth; who rose from the place of the dead, and ascended to the height of heaven, and sitteth on the right hand of the Father.

BY THE HOLY MELITO, BISHOP OF THE CITY OF ITTICA.

He that bore up the earth was borne up on a tree. The Lord was subjected to ignominy with naked body—God put to death, the King of Israel slain!

[*The following Fragments of Melito are translated from the Greek, except No. IX., which is taken from the Latin.*]

I.

FROM THE WORK ON THE PASSOVER.

[In Eusebius, *Hist. Eccl.* iv. 26.]

When Servilius Paulus was proconsul of Asia, at the time that Sagaris[1] suffered martyrdom, there arose a great controversy at Laodicea concerning [the time of the celebration of]

---

[1] He was Bishop of Laodicea, and suffered martyrdom during the persecution under M. Aurelius Antoninus.—MIGNE.

the Passover, which on that occasion had happened to fall at the proper season;[1] and this [treatise] was [then] written.[2]

II.

FROM THE APOLOGY ADDRESSED TO MARCUS AURELIUS ANTONINUS.

[In Eusebius, *Hist. Eccl. l.c.*]

For the race of the pious is now persecuted in a way contrary to all precedent, being harassed by a new kind of edicts[3] everywhere in Asia. For unblushing informers, and such as are greedy of other men's goods, taking occasion from the orders [issued], carry on their robbery without any disguise, plundering of their property night and day those who are guilty of no wrong.

. . . . . .

If these proceedings take place at thy bidding,[4] well and good.[5] For a just sovereign will never take unjust measures; and we, on our part, gladly accept the honour of such a death. This request only we present to thee, that thou wouldst first of all examine for thyself into the behaviour of these [reputed] agents of so much strife, and then come to a just decision as to whether they merit death and punishment, or deserve to live in safety and quiet. But if, on the contrary, it shall turn out

---

[1] The churches of Asia Minor kept Easter on the fourteenth day from the new moon, whatever day of the week that might be; and hence were called *Quartodecimans*. Other churches, chiefly those of the West, kept it on the Sunday following the day of the Jewish passover. In the case here referred to, the 14th of the month occurred on the Sunday in question.

[2] Migne, not so naturally, punctuates otherwise, and renders, "which had happened [then] to fall at the proper season, and on that occasion this [treatise] was written."

[3] Migne thinks that by these are meant the orders given by magistrates of cities on their own authority, in distinction from those which issued from emperors or governors of provinces.

[4] The reference must be to private letters: for in any of the leading cities of Asia a mandate of the emperor would have been made public before the proconsul proceeded to execute it.—MIGNE.

[5] *Ἔστω καλῶς γενόμενον* seems to be here used in the sense of *καλῶς* alone. The correctness of Migne's translation, *recte atque ordine facta sunto*, is open to doubt.

that this measure, and this new sort of command, which it
would be unbecoming to employ even against barbarian foe-
men, do not proceed from thee, then all the more do we entreat
thee not to leave us thus exposed to the spoliation of the
populace.

* * * * * *

For the philosophy current with us flourished in the first
instance among barbarians;[1] and, when it afterwards sprang
up among the nations under thy rule, during the distinguished
reign of thy ancestor Augustus, it proved to be a blessing of
most happy omen to thy empire. For from that time the
Roman power has risen to greatness and splendour. To this
power thou hast succeeded as the much desired[2] possessor; and
such shalt thou continue, together with thy son,[3] if thou protect that philosophy which has grown up with thy empire, and
which took its rise with Augustus; to which also thy [more
recent] ancestors paid honour, along with the other religions
[prevailing in the empire]. A very strong proof, moreover,
that it was for good that the system we profess came to prevail
at the same time that the empire of such happy commencement
was established, is this—that ever since the reign of Augustus
nothing untoward has happened; but, on the contrary, everything has contributed to the splendour and renown [of the
empire], in accordance with the devout wishes[4] of all. Nero
and Domitian alone of all [the emperors], imposed upon by
certain calumniators, have cared to bring any impeachment
against our doctrines. They, too, are the source from which it
has happened that the lying slanders on those who profess them
have, in consequence of the senseless habit which prevails [of
taking things on hearsay], flowed down to our own times.[5]
But the course which they in their ignorance pursued was set
aside by thy pious progenitors, who frequently and in many

---

[1] The Jews. Porphyry calls the doctrines of the Christians βάρβαρον
τόλμημα. See Euseb. *Hist. Eccl.* vi. 19.—MIGNE.

[2] Εὐκταῖος.

[3] Commodus, who hence appears to have not yet been associated with
his father in the empire.—MIGNE.

[4] Εὐχάς.

[5] Ἀφ' ὧν καὶ τὸ τῆς συκοφαντίας ἀλόγῳ συνηθείᾳ περὶ τοὺς τοιούτους
ῥυῆναι συμβέβηκε ψεῦδος.

instances rebuked by their rescripts¹ those who dared to set on foot any hostilities against them. It appears, for example, that thy grandfather Adrian wrote, among others, to Fundanus, the proconsul then in charge of the government of Asia. Thy father, too, when thou thyself wast associated with him² in the administration of the empire, wrote to the cities, forbidding them to take any measures adverse to us: among the rest to the people of Larissa, and of Thessalonica, and of Athens, and, [in short], to all the Greeks. And as regards thyself, seeing that thy sentiments respecting the Christians³ are not only the same as theirs, but even much more generous and wise, we are the more persuaded that thou wilt do all that we ask of thee.

III.

FROM THE SAME APOLOGY.

[In the *Chronicon Alexandrinum.*]

We are not those who pay homage to stones, that are without sensation; but of the only God, who is before all and over all, and, moreover, of His Christ, who is veritably God the Word⁴ [that existed] before all time, are we worshippers.

IV.

FROM THE BOOK OF EXTRACTS.

[In Eusebius, *l.c.*]

Melito to his brother Onesimus, greeting:

As you have often, prompted by your regard for the word [of God], expressed a wish to have some extracts made from the Law and the Prophets concerning the Saviour, and concerning our faith in general, and have desired, moreover, to obtain an accurate account of the Ancient Books, as regards their number and their arrangement, I have striven to the best of my ability to perform this task: well knowing your zeal for the faith, and your eagerness to become acquainted with the

---

¹ Ἐγγράφως.
² The reading of Valesius, σοῦ τὰ πάντα συνδιοικοῦντος αὐτῷ, is here adopted.
³ Περὶ τούτων.   ⁴ Ὄντως Θεοῦ Λόγου.

word, and especially because [I am assured that], through your yearning after God, you esteem these things beyond all things else, engaged as you are in a struggle for eternal salvation.

I accordingly proceeded to the East, and went to the very spot where [the things in question] were preached and took place; and, having made myself accurately acquainted with the books of the Old Testament, I have set them down below, and herewith send you [the list]. Their names are as follows:—

The five [books] of Moses—Genesis, Exodus, Leviticus, Numbers, Deuteronomy; Joshua,[1] Judges, Ruth, the four [books] of Kings, the two of Chronicles, the [book of the] Psalms of David, the Proverbs of Solomon, also called [the Book of] Wisdom, Ecclesiastes, the Song of Songs, Job, [the books of] the prophets Isaiah, Jeremiah, of the twelve contained in a single book, Daniel, Ezekiel, Esdras. From these I have made my extracts, dividing them into six books.

V.

FROM THE CATENA ON GENESIS.

From Melito of Sardis.

In place of Isaac the just, a ram appeared for slaughter, in order that Isaac might be liberated from [his] bonds. The slaughter of this [animal] redeemed Isaac [from death]. In like manner, the Lord, being slain, saved us; being bound, He loosed us; being sacrificed, He redeemed us. . . .

For the Lord was a lamb, like the ram which Abraham saw caught in the bush Sabec.[2] But this bush represented the cross, and that place Jerusalem, and the lamb the Lord bound for slaughter.

. . . .

For as a ram was He bound, says he concerning our Lord Jesus Christ, and as a lamb was He shorn, and as a sheep was He led to the slaughter, and as a lamb was He crucified; and He carried the cross[3] on His shoulders when He was led up [to the hill] to be slain, as was Isaac by his father. But Christ

---

[1] Ἰησοῦς Ναυῆ.
[2] The Hebrew word סְבָךְ, *thicket*, is not found as a proper name.
[3] Τὸ ξύλον.

suffered, and Isaac did not suffer: for he was [but] a type of Him who should suffer. Yet, even when serving [only] for a type of Christ, he smote men with astonishment and fear.

For a new mystery was presented to view,—a son led by his father to a mountain to be slain, whose feet he bound together, and laid him on the wood of the sacrifice, preparing with care[1] whatever was necessary to his immolation. Isaac on his part is silent, bound like a ram, not opening his mouth, nor uttering a sound with his voice. For, not fearing the knife, nor quailing before the fire, nor troubled by [the prospect of] suffering, he sustained bravely [the character of] the type of the Lord. Accordingly there lies Isaac before us, with his feet bound like a ram, his father standing by, with the knife all bare in his hand, not shrinking from shedding the blood of his son.

VI.

TWO SCHOLIA ON GEN. XXII. 18.

[In the edition of the LXX. published by Card. Caraffe, 1581.]

The Syriac and the Hebrew [text] use the word "suspended" (κρεμάμενος),[2] as more clearly typifying the cross.

The word Sabek[3] some have rendered "remission" (ἄφεσις), others "upright" (ὄρθιος), as if the meaning, agreeing with the popular belief, were—a goat walking erect up to a bush, and there standing erect caught by his horns, so as to be a plain type of the cross. For this reason it is not translated, because the single Hebrew word signifies in other languages[4] many things. To those, however, who ask [the meaning] it is proper to give an answer, and to say that Sabek denotes "lifted up" (ἐπηρμένος).

VII.

ON THE NATURE OF CHRIST.

[In Anastasius of Sinai, *The Guide*, ch. 13.]

For there is no need, to persons of intelligence, to attempt to

---

[1] Μετὰ σπουδῆς. Migne: *cum festinatione*.
[2] The Hebrew is נאחז, the Syriac ܐܚܝܕ, both meaning simply "caught."
[3] See note on the fragment just before.
[4] Lit. "when translated."

prove, from the deeds of Christ subsequent to His baptism, that His soul and His body, His human nature[1] like ours, were real, and no phantom of the imagination. For the deeds done by Christ after His baptism, and especially His miracles, gave indication and assurance to the world of the Deity hidden in His flesh. For, being at once both God and perfect man likewise, He gave us sure indications of His two natures:[2] of His Deity, by His miracles during the three years that elapsed after His baptism; of his humanity, during the thirty [similar] periods which preceded His baptism, in which, by reason of His low estate[3] as regards the flesh, He concealed the signs of His Deity, although He was the true God existing before all ages.

VIII.

FROM THE ORATION ON OUR LORD'S PASSION.

[*Ibid.* ch. 12.]

God has suffered from the right hand of Israel.

IX.

From *The Key*.

Head of the Lord—[His] simple Divinity; because He is the Beginning and Creator of all things: in Daniel.[4]

The white hair of the Lord, because He is "the Ancient of Days:" as above.

The eyes of the Lord—the Divine inspection: because He sees all things. Like that in the apostle: "For all things are naked and open in His eyes."[5]

The eyelids of the Lord—hidden spiritual mysteries in the Divine precepts. In the Psalm: "His eyelids question, that is prove, the children of men."[6]

The smelling of the Lord—His delight in the prayers or works of the saints. In Genesis: "And the Lord smelled an odour of sweetness."[7]

---

[1] Or, according to Migne's punctuation, "His soul, and the body of His human nature." The words are, τὸ ἀληθὲς καὶ ἀφάνταστον τῆς ψυχῆς αὐτοῦ καὶ τοῦ σώματος τῆς καθ' ἡμᾶς ἀνθρωπίνης φύσεως.

[2] Οὐσίας.   [3] Τὸ ἀτελὲς.   [4] Dan. vii. 9, 13, 22.
[5] Heb. iv. 13.   [6] Ps. xi. 4.   [7] Gen. viii. 21.

The mouth of the Lord—His Son, or word [addressed] to men. In the prophet, "The mouth of the Lord hath spoken;"[1] and elsewhere, "They provoked His mouth to anger."[2]

The tongue of the Lord—His Holy Spirit. In the Psalm: "My tongue is a pen."[3]

The face of the Lord—His manifestation. In Exodus, "My face shall go before thee;"[4] and in the prophet, "The face of the Lord divided them."[5]

The word of the Lord—[His] Son. In the Psalm: "My heart hath uttered a good word."[6]

The arm of the Lord—[His] Son, by whom He hath wrought all His works. In the prophet Isaiah: "And to whom is the arm of the Lord revealed?"[7]

The right hand of the Lord—that is, [His] Son; as also above in the Psalm: "The right hand of the Lord hath done valiantly."[8]

The right hand of the Lord—electio omnis. As in Deuteronomy: "In His right hand [is] a fiery law."[9]

The wings of the Lord—Divine protection. In the Psalm: "In the shadow of Thy wings will I hope."[10]

The shoulder of the Lord—the Divine power, by which He condescends to carry the feeble. In Deuteronomy: "He took them up, and put them on His shoulders."[11]

The hand of the Lord—Divine operation. In the prophet: "Have not my hands made all these things?"[12]

The finger of the Lord—the Holy Spirit, by whose operation the tables of the law in Exodus are said to have been written;[13] and in the Gospel: "If I by the finger of God cast out demons."[14]

The fingers of the Lord—the lawgiver Moses, or the prophets. In the Psalm: "I will regard the heavens," that is, the books of the Law and the Prophets, "the works of Thy fingers."[15]

The wisdom of the Lord—[His] Son. In the apostle: "Christ the power of God, and the wisdom of God;"[16] and in

---

[1] Isa. i. 20.
[2] Lam. i. 18.
[3] Ps. xlv. 1.
[4] Ex. xxxiii. 14.
[5] Lam. iv. 16.
[6] Ps. xlv. 1.
[7] Isa. liii. 1.
[8] Ps. cxviii. 16.
[9] Deut. xxxiii. 2.
[10] Ps. lvii. 1.
[11] Deut. xxxiii. 12.
[12] Isa. lxvi. 2.
[13] Ex. xxxiv. 1.
[14] Luke xi. 20.
[15] Ps. viii. 3.
[16] 1 Cor. i. 24.

Solomon: "The wisdom of the Lord reacheth from one end to the other mightily."[1]

The womb of the Lord—the hidden recess of Deity out of which He brought forth His Son. In the Psalm: "Out of the womb, before Lucifer, have I borne Thee."[2]

The feet of the Lord—[His] immoveableness and eternity. In the Psalm: "And thick darkness [was] under His feet."[3]

The throne of the Lord—angels, or saints, or simply sovereign dominion.[4] In the Psalm: "Thy throne, O God, is for ever and ever."[5]

Seat—the same as above, angels or saints, because the Lord sits upon these. In the Psalm: "The Lord sat upon His holy seat."[6]

The descent of the Lord—His visitation of men. As in Micah: "Behold, the Lord shall come forth from His place; He shall come down trampling under foot the ends of the earth."[7] Likewise in a bad sense. In Genesis: "The Lord came down to see the tower."[8]

The ascent of the Lord—the raising up of man, who is taken from earth to heaven. In the Psalm: "Who ascendeth above the heaven of heavens to the east."[9]

The standing of the Lord—the patience of the Deity, by which He bears with sinners that they may come to repentance. As in Habakkuk: "He stood and measured the earth;"[10] and in the Gospel: "Jesus stood, and bade him be called,"[11] that is, the blind man.

The transition of the Lord—[His] assumption of [our] flesh, through which by His birth, His death, His resurrection, His ascent into heaven, He made transitions, so to say. In the Song of Songs: "Behold, He cometh, leaping upon the mountains, bounding over the hills."[12]

The going[13] *of the Lord*—His coming or visitation. In the Psalm.

The way of the Lord—the operation of the Deity. As in Job, in speaking of the devil: "He is the beginning of the ways of the Lord."[14]

---

[1] Sap. viii. 1.   [2] Ps. cx. 3.   [3] Ps. xviii. 9.
[4] Ipsa regnandi potestas.   [5] Ps. xlv. 6; comp. Ps. v. xxix.
[6] Ps. xlvii. 8.   [7] Mic. i. 3.   [8] Gen. xi. 3.
[9] Ps. lxviii. 33.   [10] Hab. iii. 6.   [11] Mark x. 49.
[12] Cant. Cant. ii. 8.   [13] Gressus.   [14] Job xl. 19.

Again: *The ways of the Lord*—His precepts. In Hosea: "For the ways of the Lord are straight, and the just shall walk in them."[1]

The footsteps of the Lord—the signs of [His] secret operations. As in the Psalm: "And Thy footsteps shall not be known."[2]

The knowledge of the Lord—that which makes [men] to know Him. To Abraham [He says]: "Now I know that thou fearest the Lord;"[3] that is, I have made thee to know.

The ignorance of God[4] is [His] disapproval. In the Gospel: "I know you not."[5]

The remembrance of God—His mercy, by which He rejects and has mercy on whom He will. So in Genesis: "The Lord remembered Noah;"[6] and in another passage: "The Lord hath remembered His people."[7]

The repentance of the Lord—[His] change of procedure.[8] As in the book of Kings: "It repenteth me that I have made Saul king."[9]

The anger and wrath of the Lord—the vengeance of the Deity upon sinners, when He bears with them with a view to punishment, does not [at once] judge them according to [strict] equity. As in the Psalm: "In His anger and in His wrath will He trouble them."[10]

The sleeping of the Lord—when, in the thoughts of some, His faithfulness is not sufficiently wakeful. In the Psalm: "Awake, why sleepest Thou, O Lord?"[11]

The watches of the Lord—in the guardianship of His elect He is always at hand by the presence of [His] Deity. In the Psalm: "Lo! He will not slumber nor sleep."[12]

The sitting of the Lord—[His] ruling. In the Psalm: "The Lord sitteth upon His holy seat."[13]

The footstool of the Lord—man assumed by the Word; or His saints, as some think. In the Psalm: "Worship ye His footstool, for it is holy."

The walking of the Lord—the delight of the Deity in the

---

[1] Hos. xiv. 10.
[2] Ps. lxxvii. 19.
[3] Gen. xxii. 12.
[4] Nescire Dei.
[5] Luke xiii. 25.
[6] Gen. viii. 1.
[7] Esther x. 12.
[8] Rerum mutatio.
[9] 1 Sam. xv. 11.
[10] Ps. ii. 5.
[11] Ps. xliv. 23.
[12] Ps. cxxi. 4.
[13] Ps. xlvii. 8.

walks of His elect. In the prophet: "I will walk in them, and will be their Lord."[1]

The trumpet of the Lord—His mighty voice. In the apostle: "At the command, and at the voice of the archangel, and at the trumpet of God, shall He descend from heaven."[2]

QUADRATUS, BISHOP OF ATHENS.

FROM THE APOLOGY FOR THE CHRISTIAN RELIGION.

[In Eusebius, *Hist. Eccl.* iv. 3.]

Our Saviour's works, moreover, were always present: for they were real, [consisting of] those who had been healed of their diseases, those who had been raised from the dead; who were not only seen whilst they were being healed and raised up, but were [afterwards] constantly present. Nor did they remain only during the sojourn of the Saviour [on earth], but also a considerable time after His departure; and, indeed, some of them have survived even down to our own times.

ARISTO OF PELLA.

FROM THE DISPUTATION OF JASON AND PAPISCUS.

"I remember," says Jerome (Comm. ad Gal. cap. iii. comm. 13), "in the *Dispute between Jason and Papiscus*, which is composed in Greek, to have found it written: 'The execration of God is he that is hanged.'"

FROM THE SAME WORK.

Jerome likewise, in his *Hebrew Questions on Genesis*, says: "*In the beginning God made the heaven and the earth.* The majority believe, as it is affirmed also in the *Dispute between Jason and Papiscus,* and as Tertullian in his book *Against Praxeas* contends, and as Hilarius too, in his exposition of one of the Psalms, declares, that in the Hebrew it is: 'In the

[1] Ezek. xxxvii. 27.   [2] 1 Thess. iv. 15.

Son God made the heaven and the earth.' But that this is false, the nature of the case itself proves."

PERHAPS FROM THE SAME WORK.

... And when the man himself[1] who had instigated them[2] to this folly had paid the just penalty (says Eusebius, *Hist.* iv. 6), "the whole nation from that time was strictly forbidden to set foot on the region about Jerusalem, by the formal decree and enactment of Adrian, who commanded that they should not even from a distance look on their native soil!" So writes Aristo of Pella.

FROM THE SAME WORK.

I have found this expression *Seven heavens* (says Maximus, in *Scholia on the work concerning the Mystical Theology*, ascribed to Dionysius the Areopagite, cap. i.) also in the *Dispute between Papiscus and Jason*, written by Aristo of Pella, which Clement of Alexandria, in the sixth book of the *Outlines*,[3] says was composed by Saint Luke.

CONCERNING THE SAME WORK.

(Thus writes Origen, *contra Celsum*, iv. 52.)

... in which [book] a Christian is represented disputing with a Jew from the Jewish Scriptures, and showing that the prophecies concerning the Christ apply to Jesus: although his opponent addresses himself to the argument with no common ability,[4] and in a manner not unbefitting his Jewish character.

CLAUDIUS APOLLINARIS, BISHOP OF HIERAPOLIS, AND APOLOGIST.

FROM AN UNKNOWN BOOK.

"This narration (says Eusebius, *Hist.* v. 5) is given" (it relates to that storm of rain which was sent to the army of the Emperor M. Antoninus, to allay the thirst of the soldiers, whilst

---

[1] Barchochebas.
[2] The Jews.
[3] Ὑποτυπώσεις.
[4] Οὐκ ἀγεννῶς.

the enemy was discomfited by thunderbolts hurled upon them) "even by those historians who are at a wide remove from the doctrines that prevail among us, and who have been simply concerned to describe what related to [the emperors who are] the subjects of their history; and it has been recorded also by our own writers. But historians without [the pale of the church], as being unfriendly to the faith, while they have recorded the prodigy, have refrained from acknowledging that it was sent in answer to our prayers. On the other hand, our writers, as lovers of truth, have reported the matter in a simple and artless way. To this number Apollinaris must be considered as belonging. 'Thereupon,' he says, 'the legion which had by its prayer caused the prodigy received from the emperor a title suitable to the occurrence, and was called in the Roman language the *Thunder-hurling* [*Legion*].'"

FROM THE BOOK CONCERNING THE PASSOVER.[1]

There are, then, some who through ignorance raise disputes about these things (though their conduct is pardonable: for ignorance is no subject for blame—it rather needs further instruction), and say that on the fourteenth day the Lord ate the lamb with the disciples, and that on the great day of the [feast of] unleavened bread He Himself suffered; and they quote Matthew as speaking in accordance with their view. Wherefore their opinion is contrary to the law, and the Gospels seem to be at variance with them.

FROM THE SAME BOOK.

The fourteenth day, the true Passover of the Lord; the great sacrifice, the Son of God instead of the lamb, who was bound, who bound the strong, and who was judged, [though] Judge of living and dead, and who was delivered into the hands of sinners to be crucified, who was lifted up on the horns of the unicorn, and who was pierced in His holy side, who poured forth from His side the two purifying elements,[2] water and blood, word and spirit, and who was buried on the day of the passover, the stone being placed upon the tomb.

---

[1] This extract and the following are taken from the preface to the *Chronicon Paschale*.

[2] Πάλιν καθάρσια, qu. παλινκαθάρσια = "re-purifiers."

HEGESIPPUS.

FRAGMENTS FROM HIS FIVE BOOKS OF COMMENTARIES ON THE ACTS OF THE CHURCH.

I.

CONCERNING THE MARTYRDOM OF JAMES, THE BROTHER OF THE LORD, FROM BOOK V.

[In Eusebius, *Hist. Eccl.* ii. 23.]

James, the Lord's brother, succeeds to the government of the church, in conjunction with the apostles. He has been universally called *the Just*, from the days of the Lord down to the present time. For many bore the name of James; but this one was holy from his mother's womb. He drank no wine or [other] intoxicating liquor,[1] nor did he eat flesh; no razor came upon his head; he did not anoint himself with oil, nor make use of the bath. He alone was permitted to enter the holy place:[2] for he did not wear any woollen garment, but fine linen [only]. He alone, [I say], was wont to go into the temple: and he used to be found kneeling on his knees, begging forgiveness for the people—so that the skin of his knees became horny like that of a camel's, by reason of his constantly bending the knee in adoration to God, and begging forgiveness for the people. Therefore, in consequence of his pre-eminent justice, he was called *the Just*, and *Oblias*,[3] which signifies in Greek *Defence of the People*, and *Justice*, in accordance with what the prophets declare concerning him.

Now some persons belonging to the seven sects existing among the people, which have been before described by me in the Notes, asked him: "What is the door of Jesus?" And he replied that He was the Saviour. In consequence of this answer, some believed that Jesus is the Christ. But the sects

---

[1] Σίκερα.   [2] Τὰ ἅγια.

[3] The reference appears to be to the Hebrew word עֹפֶל, *a rising ground*, which was applied as a proper name to a fortified ridge of Mount Zion. See 2 Chron. xxvii. 3. It has been proposed to read ἐκαλεῖτο Σαδδὶκ καὶ 'Ωζλιὰμ ['Ωβλίας?], ὅ ἐστιν δίκαιος καὶ περιοχὴ τοῦ λαοῦ. The text, in which not only a Hebrew word but also a Greek (Δίκαιος) is explained *in Greek*, can hardly give the correct reading.

before mentioned did not believe, either in a resurrection or in the coming of One to requite every man according to his works; but those who did believe, believed because of James. So, when many even of the ruling class believed, there was a commotion among the Jews, and scribes, and Pharisees, who said: "A little more, and we shall have all the people looking for Jesus as the Christ."

They came, therefore, in a body to James, and said: "We entreat thee, restrain the people: for they are gone astray in their opinions about Jesus, as if he were the Christ. We entreat thee to persuade all who have come hither for the day of the passover, concerning Jesus. For we all listen to thy persuasion; since we, as well as all the people, bear thee testimony that thou art just, and showest partiality to none. Do thou, therefore, persuade the people not to entertain erroneous opinions concerning Jesus: for all the people, and we also, listen to thy persuasion. Take thy stand, then, upon the summit[1] of the temple, that from that elevated spot thou mayest be clearly seen, and thy words may be plainly audible to all the people. For, in order to attend the passover, all the tribes have congregated [hither], and some of the Gentiles also."

The aforesaid scribes and Pharisees accordingly set James on the summit of the temple, and cried aloud to him, and said: "O just one, whom we are all bound to obey, forasmuch as the people is in error, and follows Jesus the crucified, do thou tell us what is the door of Jesus, the crucified." And he answered with a loud voice: "Why ask ye me concerning Jesus the Son of man? He Himself sitteth in heaven, at the right hand of the Great Power, and shall come on the clouds of heaven."

And, when many were fully convinced [by these words], and offered praise for the testimony of James, and said, "Hosanna to the son of David," then again the said Pharisees and scribes said to one another, "We have not done well in procuring this testimony to Jesus. But let us go up and throw him down, that they may be afraid, and not believe him." And they cried aloud, and said: "Oh! oh! the just man himself is in error." Thus they fulfilled the Scripture written in Isaiah: "Let us away with the just man, because he is troublesome to us: therefore shall they eat the fruit of their doings." So they went up

[1] Πτερύγιον.

and threw down the just man, and said to one another: "Let
us stone James the Just." And they began to stone him: for
he was not killed by the fall; but he turned, and kneeled down,
and said: "I beseech Thee, Lord God [our] Father, forgive
them; for they know not what they do."

And, while they were thus stoning him to death, one of the
priests, the sons of Rechab, the son of Rechabim, to whom testimony is borne by Jeremiah the prophet, began to cry aloud,
saying: "Cease, what do ye? The just man is praying for
us." But one among them, one of the fullers, took the staff
with which he was accustomed to wring out the garments [he
dyed], and hurled it at the head of the just man.

And so he suffered martyrdom; and they buried him on the
spot, and the pillar erected to his memory still remains, close by
the temple. This man was a true witness to both Jews and
Greeks that Jesus is the Christ.

And shortly after Vespasian besieged Judea, taking them
captive.

CONCERNING THE RELATIVES OF OUR SAVIOUR.

[Also in Eusebius, *Hist. Eccl.* iii. 20.]

There still survived of the kindred of the Lord the grandsons
of Judas, who according to the flesh was called his brother.
These were informed against, as belonging to the family of
David, and Evocatus brought them before Domitian Cæsar:
for [that emperor] dreaded the advent of Christ, as Herod had
done.

So he asked them whether they were of [the family of]
David; and they confessed they were. Next he asked them
what property they had, or how much money they possessed.
They both replied that they had only 9000 denaria [between
them], each of them owning half that sum; but even this they
said they did not possess in cash, but as the estimated value of
some land, consisting of thirty-nine plethra only, out of which
they had to pay the dues, and that they supported themselves
by their own labour. And then they began to hold out their
hands, exhibiting, as proof of their manual labour, the rough-
ness of their skin, and the corns raised on their hands by constant work.

Being then asked concerning Christ and His kingdom, what was its nature, and when and where it was to appear, they returned answer that it was not of this world, nor of the earth, but belonging to the sphere of heaven and angels, and would make its appearance at the end of time, when He shall come in glory, and judge living and dead, and render to every one according to the course of his life.[1]

Thereupon Domitian passed no condemnation upon them, but treated them with contempt, as too mean for notice, and let them go free. At the same time he issued a command, and put a stop to the persecution against the church.

When they were released they became leaders[2] of the churches, as was natural in the case of those who were at once martyrs and of the kindred of the Lord. And, after the establishment of peace [to the church], their lives were prolonged to [the reign of] Trajan.

CONCERNING THE MARTYRDOM OF SYMEON THE SON OF CLOPAS, BISHOP OF JERUSALEM.

[Also in Eusebius, *Hist. Eccl.* iii. 32.]

Some of these heretics, forsooth, laid an information against Symeon the son of Clopas, as being of [the family of] David, and a Christian. And on these charges he suffered martyrdom when he was 120 years old, in the reign of Trajan Cæsar, when Atticus was consular legate[3] [in Syria]. And it so happened, says the same writer, that, while inquiry was then being made for those belonging to the royal tribe of the Jews, the accusers themselves were convicted of belonging to it. With show of reason could it be said that Symeon was one of those who actually saw and heard the Lord, on the ground of his great age, and also because the Scripture of the Gospels makes mention of Mary the [daughter] of Clopas, who, as our narrative has shown already, was his father.

[The same historian mentions] others also, of the family of one of the reputed brothers of the Saviour, named Judas, as having survived until this same reign, after the testimony they bore for the faith of Christ in the time of Domitian, as already recorded.

[1] Τὰ ἐπιτηδεύματα αὐτοῦ.   [2] Ἡγήσασθαι.   [3] Ὑπατικοῦ.

[He writes as follows:] They came, then, and took the presidency of every church, as witnesses [for Christ], and as being of the kindred of the Lord. And, after profound peace had been established in every church, they remained down to the reign of Trajan Cæsar: [that is], until the time when he who was sprung from an uncle of the Lord, the afore-mentioned Symeon son of Clopas, was informed against by the [various] heresies, and subjected to an accusation like the rest, and for the same cause, before the legate Atticus; and, while suffering outrage during many days, he bore testimony [for Christ]: so that all, including the legate himself, were astonished above measure that a man 120 years old should have been able to endure [such torments]. He was finally condemned to be crucified.

... Up to that period the church had remained like a virgin pure and uncorrupted: for, if there were any persons who were disposed to tamper with the wholesome rule of the preaching of salvation,[1] they still lurked in some dark place of concealment or other. But, when the sacred band of apostles had in various ways closed their lives, and that generation of men to whom it had been vouchsafed to listen to the Godlike Wisdom with their own ears had passed away, then did the confederacy of godless error take its rise through the treachery of false teachers, who, seeing that none of the apostles any longer survived, at length attempted with bare [and uplifted] head to oppose the preaching of the truth by preaching "knowledge falsely so called."

CONCERNING HIS JOURNEY TO ROME, AND THE JEWISH SECTS.

[Also in Eusebius, *Hist. Eccl.* iv. 22.]

And the church of the Corinthians continued in the orthodox faith[2] up to the time when Primus was bishop in Corinth. I had some intercourse with these [brethren] on my voyage to Rome, when I spent several days with the Corinthians, during which we were mutually refreshed by the orthodox faith.

On my arrival at Rome, I drew up a list of the succession [of bishops] down to Anicetus, whose deacon was Eleutherus. To Anicetus succeeded Soter, and after him [came] Eleutherus. But in the case of every succession, and in every city, the state

---

[1] Τοῦ σωτηρίου κηρύγματος.   [2] Ἐν τῷ ὀρθῷ λόγῳ.

of affairs is in accordance with the teaching of the Law and of the Prophets and of the Lord. . . .

And after James the Just had suffered martyrdom, as had the Lord also [and] on the same account, again Symeon the son of Clopas, descended from [the Lord's] uncle, is made bishop, his election being promoted by all as being a kinsman of the Lord.

Therefore was the church called a virgin, for she was not as yet corrupted by worthless teaching.[1] Thebulis it was who, [displeased] because he was not made bishop, first began to corrupt her by stealth. He too was connected with the seven sects which existed among the people, like Simon, from whom come the Simoniani; and Cleobius, from whom come the Cleobiani; and Doritheus, from whom come the Dorithiani; and Gorthæus, from whom come the Gortheani; and Masbothæus, from whom come the Masbothæi. From these [men] also come the Menandrianists, and the Marcionists, and the Carpocratians, and the Valentinians, and the Basilidians, and the Saturnilians. Each [of these leaders] in his own private and distinct capacity brought in his own private opinion. From these have come false Christs, false prophets, false apostles— men who have split up the one church into parts[2] through their corrupting doctrines, [uttered] in disparagement of God and of His Christ. . . .

There were, moreover, various opinions in the matter of circumcision among the children of Israel, held by those who were opposed to the tribe of Judah and to Christ: such as the Essenes, the Galileans, the Hemerobaptists, the Masbothæi, the Samaritans, the Sadducees, the Pharisees.

PANTÆNUS,

AN ALEXANDRIAN PHILOSOPHER.

[In *Extracts from the Prophets*, written probably by Theodotus, and collected by Clement of Alexandria or some other writer.]

"In the sun hath He set His tent."[3] Some affirm that the reference is to the Lord's body, which He Himself places in the

---

[1] Ἀκοαῖς ματαίαις. [2] Ἐμέρισαν τὴν ἕνωσιν τῆς ἐκκλησίας. [3] Ps. xix. 4.

sun:[1] Hermogenes, for instance. As to His body, some say it is His tent, others the church of the faithful. But our Pantænus said: "The language employed by prophecy is for the most part indefinite, the present tense being used for the future, and again the present for the past."

[In the Scholia of Maximus on St. Gregory the Divine.]

This mode of speaking Saint Dionysius the Areopagite declares to be used in Scripture to denote predeterminations and expressions of the divine will.[2] In like manner also the followers of Pantænus,[3] who became the preceptor of the great Clement the Stromatist, affirm that they are commonly used in Scripture for expressions of the divine will. Accordingly, when asked by some who prided themselves on the outside learning,[4] in what way the Christians supposed God to become acquainted with the universe,[5] their own opinion being that He obtains His knowledge of it [in different ways],—of things falling within the province of the understanding by means of the understanding, and of those within the region of the senses by means of the senses,—they replied: "Neither [does He gain acquaintance with] sensible things by the senses, nor with things within the sphere of the understanding by the understanding: for it is not possible that He who is above all existing things should apprehend them by means of existing things. We assert, on the contrary, that He is acquainted with existing things as the products of His own volition."[6] They added, by way of showing the reasonableness of their view: "If He has made all things by an act of His will (and no argument will be adduced to gainsay this), and if it is ever a matter of piety and rectitude to say that God is acquainted with His own will, and if He has voluntarily made every several thing that has come into existence, then surely God must be acquainted with all existing things as the products of His own will, seeing that it was in the exercise of that will that He made them."

---

[1] Φασὶ τὸ σῶμα τοῦ Κυρίου ἐν τῷ ἡλίῳ αὐτὸν ἀποτίθεσθαι.
[2] Θελήματα.   [3] Οἱ περὶ Πάνταινον.   [4] Τὴν ἔξω παίδευσιν.
[5] Τὰ ὄντα.   [6] Ὡς ἴδια θελήματα.

RHODO.

[In Eusebius, *Hist. Eccl.* v. 13.]

Wherefore also they [1] disagree among themselves, maintaining as they do an opinion which has no consistency with itself. For one of their herd, Apelles, who prides himself on the strictness of his life,[2] and on his age, admits that there is [only] one first principle,[3] yet says that the prophecies [have come] from an opposing spirit, in which opinion he is influenced by the responses of a soothsaying[4] maid named Philumene. But others, among whom are Potitus and Basilicus, like Marcion[5] himself, introduce two first principles. These men, following the Pontic wolf, and not being able to discover any more than he the division of things, have had recourse to rash assertion, and declared the existence of two first principles simply and without proof. Others of them, again, drifting [from bad] to worse, assume not two only, but even three natures. Of these men the leader and champion is Syneros, as those who adopt his teaching say. . . .

For the old man Apelles entered into conversation with us, and was convicted of uttering many false opinions. For example, he asserted that men should on no account examine into their creed,[6] but that every one ought to continue to the last in the belief he has once adopted. For he declared that those who had rested their hope on the Crucified One would be saved, provided only they were found living in the practice of good works. But the most perplexing of all the doctrines laid down by him was, as we have remarked before, what he said concerning God: for he affirmed that there was [only] one first principle, precisely as our own faith teaches. . . .

On my asking him, "Where do you get proof of this? or how are you able to assert that there is [only] one first principle? tell us,"—he said that the prophecies refuted themselves, because they had uttered nothing at all that was true: for that they were discordant and false, and self-contradictory.

---

[1] The Marcionites.   [2] Πολιτείᾳ. See Migne's note.
[3] Ἀρχήν.   [4] Δαιμονώσης.
[5] Some copies have "Marcion *the sailor*," and so Tertullian (*de Præscriptionibus*) speaks of him.
[6] Τὸν λόγον.

As to the question, "How does it appear that there is [only] one first principle?" he said he could not tell, only he was impelled to that belief. On my thereupon conjuring him to speak the truth, he solemnly declared that he was expressing his real sentiments; and that he did not know *how* there could be one uncreated God, but that he believed the fact. Here I burst into laughter and rebuked him, because he professed to be a teacher, and yet was unable to confirm what he taught [by arguments].

MAXIMUS, BISHOP OF JERUSALEM.

FROM THE BOOK CONCERNING MATTER, OR IN DEFENCE OF THE PROPOSITION THAT MATTER IS CREATED, AND IS NOT THE CAUSE OF EVIL.

[In Eusebius, *Præp. Evang.* vii. 22.]

"That there cannot exist two uncreated [substances] at one and the same time, I presume that you hold equally [with myself]. You appear, however, very decidedly to have assumed, and to have introduced into the argument, this [principle], that we must of unavoidable necessity maintain one of two things: either that God is separate from matter; or else, on the contrary, that He is indissolubly connected with it.

"If, then, any one should choose to assert that He exists in union [with matter], that would be saying that there is [only] one uncreated [substance]. For either of the two must constitute a part of the other; and, since they form parts of each other, they cannot be two uncreated [substances]. Just as, in speaking of man, we do not describe him as subdivided into a number of distinct parts, each forming a separate created [substance], but, as reason requires us to do, assert that he was made by God a single created [substance] consisting of many parts,—so, in like manner, if God is not separate from matter, we are driven to the conclusion that there is [only] one uncreated [substance].

"If, on the other hand, it be affirmed that He is separate [from matter], it necessarily follows that there is some [other substance] intermediate between the two, by which their separation is made apparent. For it is impossible that one thing should be shown to be severed by an interval from another, unless there be something else by which the interval between the two is produced. This [principle], too, holds good not only with regard to this or any other single case, but in any number of cases you please. For the same argument which we have employed in dealing with the two uncreated [substances] must in like manner be valid if the substances [in question] be given as three. For in regard to these also I should [have to] inquire whether they are separate from one another, or whether, on the contrary, each of them is united to its fellow. For, if you should say that they are united, you would hear from me the same argument as before; but if, on the contrary, you should say that they are separate, you could not escape the unavoidable assumption of a separating [medium].

"If, again, perchance any one should think that there is a third view which may be consistently maintained with regard to uncreated [substances],—namely, that God is not separate from matter, nor yet, on the other hand, united to it as a part, but that God exists in matter as in a place, or possibly matter exists in God,—let such a person observe the consequence:—

"That, if we make matter God's place, we must of necessity admit that He can be contained,[1] and that He is circumscribed by matter. Nay, further, he must grant that He is, in the same way as matter, driven about hither and thither, unable to maintain His place and to stay where He is, since that in which He exists is perpetually being driven about in one direction or another. Beside this, he must also admit that God has had His place among the worse [kind of elements]. For if matter was once in disorder, and if He reduced it to order for the purpose of rendering it better, there was a time when God existed among [the] disordered [elements of matter].

"I might also fairly put this question: whether God filled the whole of matter, or was in some part of it. If any one should choose to say that God was in some part of matter, he would be making Him indefinitely smaller than matter, inasmuch as a

[1] Χωρητόν, the reading of one MS., instead of χωρητικόν.

part of it contained the whole of Him;[1] but, if he maintained that He pervaded the whole of matter, I need to be informed how He became the Fashioner of this [matter]. For we must necessarily assume, either that there was on the part of God a contraction, so to speak,[2] of Himself, [and a withdrawal from matter], whereupon He proceeded to fashion that from which He had retired; or else that He fashioned Himself in conjunction with matter, in consequence of having no place to retire to.

"But suppose it to be maintained, on the other hand, that matter is in God, it will behove us similarly to inquire, whether we are to understand by this that He is sundered from Himself, and that, just like the air, which contains [various] kinds of animals, so is He sundered and divided into parts for the reception of those [creatures] which from time to time exist in[3] Him; or whether [matter is in God] as in a place,—for instance, as water is contained in earth. For should we say 'as in air,' we should perforce be speaking of God as divisible into parts; but if 'as water in earth,' and if matter was, [as is admitted], in confusion and disorder, and moreover also contained what was evil, we should have to admit that God is the place of disorder and evil. But this it does not seem to me consistent with reverence to say, but hazardous rather. For you contend that matter is uncreated,[4] that you may not have to admit that God is the author of evil; and yet, while aiming to escape this [difficulty], you make Him the receptacle of evil.

"If you had stated that your suspicion that matter was uncreated arose from the nature of created things as we find them,[5] I should have employed abundant argument in proof that it cannot be so. But, since you have spoken of the existence of evil as the cause of such suspicion, I am disposed to enter upon a [separate] examination of this point. For, when once it has been made clear how it is that evil exists, and when it is seen to be impossible to deny that God is the author of evil, in consequence of His having had recourse to matter for

---

[1] For εἰ δὲ μέρος αὐτῆς, ὅλον ἐχώρησεν αὐτόν, Migne reads, εἴ γε (or εἰ δὴ) μέρος αὐτῆς ὅλον, κ.τ.λ.
[2] Συστολήν τινα. [3] Τῶν γινομένων [ἐν] αὐτῷ, Migne.
[4] This word, ἀγέννητον, is added from Migne's conjecture.
[5] Ἐκ τῶν ὑποστάντων γενητῶν.

His materials,[1] it seems to me that a suspicion of this kind disappears.

"You assert, then, that matter, destitute of all qualities [good or bad], co-existed at the outset with God, and that out of it He fashioned the world as we now find it."

"Such is my opinion."

"Well, then, if matter was without any qualities, and the world has come into existence from God, and if the world possesses qualities, the author of those qualities must be God."

"Exactly so."

"Since, too, I heard you say yourself just now that out of nothing[2] nothing can possibly come, give me an answer to the question I am about to ask you. You seem to me to think that the qualities of the world have not sprung from pre-existing[3] qualities, and moreover that they are something different from the substances [themselves]."

"I do."

"If, therefore, God did not produce the qualities [in question] from qualities already existing, nor yet from substances, by reason that they are not substances, the conclusion is inevitable, that they were made by God out of nothing. So that you seemed to me to affirm more than you were warranted to do, [when you said] that it had been proved impossible to hold the opinion[4] that anything was made by God out of nothing.

"But let us put the matter thus. We see persons among ourselves making certain things out of nothing, however true it may be that they make them by means of something.[5] Let us take our illustration, say, from builders. These men do not make cities out of cities; nor, similarly, temples out of temples. Nay, if you suppose that, because the substances [necessary] for these [constructions] are already provided, therefore they make them out of that which already exists, your reasoning is fallacious. For it is not the substance that makes the city or the temples, but the art which is employed about the substance.

---

[1] Ἐκ τοῦ ὕλην αὐτὸν ὑποτιθέναι.   [2] Ἐξ οὐκ ὄντων.   [3] Ὑποκειμένων.

[4] For συλλελόγισται ὡς οὐκ ἀδύνατον εἶναι δοξάζειν, Migne reads, ὡς συλλελόγισται ἀδύνατον εἶναι δοξάζειν.

[5] Lit. "in something." Whether the materials or the art is meant is not very clear. Possibly there is a play of words in the use of the two prepositions, ἐκ and ἐν.

Neither, [again], does the art proceed from any art inhering in the substances, but it arises independently of any such art in them.

"But I fancy you will meet the argument by saying that the artist produces the art which is [manifest] in the substance [he has fashioned] out of the art which he [himself already] has. In reply to this, however, I think it may be fairly said, that neither in man does art spring from any already existing art. For we cannot possibly allow that art exists by itself, since it belongs to the class of things which are accidentals, and which receive their existence only when they appear in [connection with] substance. For man will exist though there should be no architecture, but the latter will have no existence unless there be first of all man. Thus we cannot avoid the conclusion, that it is the nature of art to spring up in man out of nothing. If, then, we have shown that this is the case with man, we surely must allow that God can make not only the qualities [of substances] out of nothing, but also the substances [themselves]. For, if it appears possible that anything [whatever] can be made out of nothing, it is proved that this may be the case with substances also.

"But, since you are specially desirous of inquiring about the origin of evil, I will proceed to the discussion of this topic. And I should like to ask you a few questions. Is it your opinion that things evil are substances, or that they are qualities of substances?"

"Qualities of substances, I am disposed to say."

"But matter was destitute of qualities and of form: this I assumed at the outset of the discussion. Therefore, if things evil are qualities of substances, and matter was destitute of qualities, and you have called God the author of qualities, God will also be the former of that which is evil. Since, then, it is not possible, on this supposition any more than on the other, to speak of God as not the cause of evil, it seems to me superfluous to add matter to Him, [as if that were the cause of evil]. If you have any reply to make to this, begin your argument."

"If, indeed, our discussion had arisen from a love of contention, I should not be willing to have the inquiry raised a second time about [the origin of] evil; but, since we are prompted rather by friendship and the good of our neighbour to engage in controversy, I readily consent to have the question raised afresh on this subject. You have no doubt long been aware of the character of my mind, and of the object at which I aim in dispute: that I have no wish to vanquish falsehood by plausible reasoning, but rather that truth should be established in connection with thorough investigation. You yourself, too, are of the same mind, I am well assured. Whatever method, therefore, you deem successful for the discovery of truth, do not shrink from using it. For, by following a better course of argument, you will not only confer a benefit on yourself, but most assuredly on me also, [instructing me] concerning matters of which I am ignorant."

"You seem clearly to agree with [1] me, that things evil are in some sort substances: [2] for, apart from substances, I do not see them to have any existence. Since, then, my good friend, you say that things evil are substances, it is necessary to inquire into the nature of substance. Is it your opinion that substance is a kind of bodily structure?"[3]

"It is."

"And does that bodily structure exist by itself, without the need of any one to come and give it existence?"

"Yes."

"And does it seem to you that things evil are connected with certain [courses of] action?"

"That is my belief."

"And do actions come into existence only when an actor is there?"

"Yes."

"And, when there is no actor, neither will his action ever take place?"

"It will not."

"If, therefore, substance is a kind of bodily structure, and this does not stand in need of some one in and through whom it may receive its existence, and if things evil are actions of some one, and actions require some one in and through whom they receive their existence,—things evil will *not* be substances.

[1] Migne, instead of παραστῆναι, conjectures παραστῆσαι, which, however, would not suit what appears to be the meaning.
[2] Οὐσίας τινάς.   [3] Σωματικήν τινα σύστασιν.

And if things evil are not substances, and murder is an evil, [and] is the action of some one, it follows that murder is not a substance. But, if you insist that agents are substance, then I myself agree with you. A man, for instance, who is a murderer, is, in so far as he is a man, a substance; but the murder which he commits is not a substance, but a work of the substance. Moreover, we speak of a man sometimes as bad because he commits murder; and sometimes, again, because he performs acts of beneficence, as good: and these names adhere to the substance, in consequence of the things which are accidents of it, which, [however], are not [the substance] itself. For neither is the substance murder, nor, again, is it adultery, nor is it any [other] similar evil. But, just as the grammarian derives his name from grammar, and the orator from oratory, and the physician from physic, though the substance is not physic, nor yet oratory, nor grammar, but receives its appellation from the things which are accidents of it, from which it popularly receives its name, though it is not any one of them,—so in like manner it appears to me that the substance receives name from things regarded as evil, though it is not [itself] any one of them.

"I must beg you also to consider that, if you represent some other being as the cause of evil to men, he also, in so far as he acts in them, and incites them to do evil, is himself evil, by reason of the things he does. For he too is said to be evil, for the simple reason that he is the doer of evil things; but the things which a being does are not the being himself, but his actions, from which he receives his appellation, and is called evil. For if we should say that the things he does are himself, and these consist in murder, and adultery, and theft, and such-like, these things will be himself. And if these things are himself, and if when they take place they get to have a substantial existence,[1] but by not taking place they also cease to exist, and if these things are done by men,—men will be the doers of these things, and the causes of existing and of no longer existing. But, if you affirm that these things are his actions, he gets to be evil from the things he does, not from those things of which the substance [of him] consists.

"Moreover, we have said that he is called evil from those things which are accidents of the substance, which are not

---

[1] Τὴν σύστασιν ἔχει.

[themselves] the substance: as a physician from the art of physic. But, if he receives the beginning of his existence from the actions he performs, he too began to be evil, and these evil things likewise began to exist. And, if so, an evil being will not be without a beginning, nor will evil things be unoriginated, since we have said that they are originated by him."

"The argument relating to the opinion I before expressed, you seem to me, my friend, to have handled satisfactorily: for, from the premisses you assumed in the discussion, I think you have drawn a fair conclusion. For, beyond doubt, if matter was [at first] destitute of qualities, and if God is the fashioner of the qualities [it now has], and if evil things are qualities, God is the author of those evil things. The argument, then, relating to that [opinion] we may consider as well discussed, and to me it [now] seems false to speak of matter as destitute of qualities. For it is not possible to say of any substance[1] whatsoever that it is without qualities. For, in the very act of saying that it is destitute of qualities, you do [in fact] indicate its quality, representing of what kind matter is, which of course is [ascribing to it] a species of quality. Wherefore, if it is agreeable to you, rehearse the argument to me from the beginning: for, to me, matter seems to have had qualities from all eternity.[2] For in this way I [can] affirm that evil things also come from it in the way of emanation, so that the cause of evil things may not be ascribed to God, but that matter may be [regarded as] the cause of all such things."

"I approve your desire, my friend, and praise the zeal you manifest in the discussion of opinions. For it assuredly becomes every one who is desirous of knowledge, not simply and out of hand to agree with what is said, but to make a careful examination of the arguments [adduced]. For, though a disputant, by laying down false premisses, may make his opponent draw the conclusion he wishes, yet he will not convince a hearer of this; but only when he says that which[3] it seems possible to say with fairness. So that one of two things will happen: either he will, as he listens, be decisively helped to reach that [conclusion] towards which he [already] feels himself impelled, or he will convict his adversary of not speaking the truth.

---

[1] Migne reads οὐσίας for αἰτίας.   [2] Ἀνάρχως.
[3] Reading, with Migne, εἰ ὅ τι for εἴ τι.

"Now, it seems to me that you have not sufficiently discussed the statement that matter has qualities from the first. For, if this is the case, what will God be the maker of? For, if we speak of substances, we affirm these to exist beforehand; or if again of qualities, we declare these also to exist already. Since, therefore, both substance and qualities exist, it seems to me unreasonable to call God a creator.

"But, lest I should seem to be constructing an argument [to suit my purpose], be so good as to answer the question: In what way do you assert God to be a creator? Is He such because He changed the substances, so that they should no longer be the same as they had once been, but become different from what they were; or because, while He kept the substances the same as they were before that period, He changed their qualities?"

"I do not at all think that any alteration took place in substances: for it appears to me absurd to say this. But I affirm that a certain change was made in their qualities; and it is in respect of these that I speak of God as a creator. Just as we might happen to speak of a house as made out of stones, in which case we could not say that the stones no longer continue to be stones as regards their substance, now that they are made into a house (for I affirm that the house owes its existence to the quality of its construction, forasmuch as the previous quality of the stones has been changed),—so does it seem to me that God, while the substance remains [the same], has made a certain change in its qualities; and it is in respect of such change that I speak of the origin of this world as having come from God."

"Since, then, you maintain that a certain change—namely, of qualities—has been produced by God, answer me briefly what I am desirous to ask you."

"Proceed, pray, with your question."

"Do you agree in the opinion that evil things are qualities of substances?"

"I do."

"Were these qualities in matter from the first, or did they begin to be?"

"I hold that these qualities existed in combination with matter, without being originated."

"But do you not affirm that God has made a certain change in the qualities?"

"That is what I affirm."

"For the better, or for the worse?"

"For the better, I should say."

"Well, then, if evil things are qualities of matter, and if the Lord [of all] changed its qualities for the better, whence, it behoves us to ask, come evil things? For either the qualities remained the same in their nature as they previously were, or, if they were not evil before, but you assert that, in consequence of a change wrought on them by God, the first qualities of this kind came into existence in connection with matter,—God will be the author of evil, inasmuch as He changed the qualities which were not evil, so as to make them evil.

"Possibly, however, it is not your view that God changed evil qualities for the better; but you mean that all those other qualities which happened to be neither good nor bad,[1] were changed by God with a view to the adornment [of the creation]."

"That has been my opinion from the outset."

"How, then, can you say that He has left the qualities of bad things just as they were? Is it that, although He was able to destroy those qualities as well as the others, He was not willing; or [did He refrain] because He had not the power? For, if you say that He had the power, but not the will, you must admit Him to be the cause of these [qualities]: since, when He could have put a stop to the existence of evil, He chose to let it remain as it was, and that, too, at the very time when He began to fashion matter. For, if He had not concerned Himself at all with matter, He would not have been the cause of those things which He allowed to remain. But, seeing that He fashioned a certain part of it, and left a certain part as we have described it, although He could have changed that also for the better, it seems to me that He deserves to have the blame cast on Him, for having permitted a part of matter to be evil, to the ruin of that [other] part which He fashioned.

"Nay, more, it seems to me that the most serious wrong has been committed as regards this part, in that He constituted this part of matter so as to be now affected by evil. For, if we were to examine carefully into things, we should find that the

---

[1] Or "indifferent:" ἀδιάφοροι.

condition of matter is worse now than in its former state, before it was reduced to order. For, before it was separated into parts, it had no sense of evil; but now every one of its parts is afflicted with a sense of evil.

"Take an illustration from man. Before he was fashioned, and became a living being through the art of the Creator, he was by nature exempt from any contact whatever with evil; but, as soon as ever he was made by God a man, he became liable to the sense of even approaching evil: and thus that very thing which you say was brought about by God for the benefit of matter,[1] is found to have turned out rather to its detriment.

"But, if you say that evil has not been put a stop to, because God was unable to do away with it, you will be making God powerless. But, if He is powerless, it will be either because He is weak by nature, or because He is overcome by fear, and reduced to subjection by a stronger. If, then, you go so far as to say that God is weak by nature, it seems to me that you imperil your salvation itself; but, if [you say that He is weak] through being overcome by the fear of a greater, things evil will be greater than God, since they frustrate the carrying out of His purpose. But this, as it seems to me, it would be absurd to say of God. For why should not *they* rather be [considered] gods, since according to your account they are able to overcome God: if, that is to say, we mean by God that which has a controlling power over all things?

"But I wish to ask you a few questions concerning matter itself. Pray tell me, therefore, whether matter was something simple or compound. I am induced to adopt this method of investigating the subject before us by [considering] the diversity that obtains in existing things. For, if perchance matter was something simple and uniform, how comes it that the world is compound,[2] and consists of divers substances and combinations? For by 'compound' we denote a mixture of certain simple [elements]. But if, on the contrary, you prefer to call matter compound, you will, of course, be asserting that it is compounded of certain simple elements. And, if it was compounded of simple elements, these simple elements must

---

[1] Migne reads ἐπ' εὐεργεσίᾳ for ἐστὶν εὐεργεσία.
[2] The text has, σύνθετος δὲ ὁ κόσμος; which Migne changes to, πῶς δὴ σύνθετός ἐστιν ὁ κόσμος;

have existed at some time or other separately by themselves, and when they were compounded together matter came into being: from which it of course follows that matter is created. For, if matter is compound, and compound things are constituted from simple, there was once a time when matter had no existence,—namely, before the simple elements came together. And, if there was once a time when matter was not, and there was never a time when the uncreated was not, matter cannot be uncreated. And hence there will be many uncreated [substances]. For, if God was uncreated, and the simple elements out of which matter was compounded [were also uncreated], there will not be two uncreated things only,—not to discuss the question what it is which constitutes objects simple, whether matter or form.

"Is it, further, your opinion that nothing in existence is opposed to itself?"

"It is."

"Is water, then, opposed to fire?"

"So it appears to me."

"Similarly, is darkness opposed to light, and warm to cold, and moreover moist to dry?"

"It seems to me to be so."

"Well, then, if nothing in existence is opposed to itself, and these things are opposed to each other, they cannot be one and the same matter; no, nor yet be made out of one and the same matter.

"I wish further to ask your opinion on a matter kindred to that of which we have been speaking. Do you believe that the parts [of a thing] are not mutually destructive?"

"I do."

"And you believe that fire and water, and so on, are parts of matter?"

"Quite so."

"Do you not also believe that water is subversive of fire, and light of darkness, and so of all similar things?"

"Yes."

"Well, then, if the parts [of a whole] are not mutually destructive, and yet the parts of matter are mutually destructive, they cannot be parts of one matter. And, if they are not parts of one another, they cannot be composed of one and the same matter; nay, they cannot be matter at all, since nothing in existence is destructive of itself, as we learn from the doctrine of opposites: for nothing is opposed to itself—an opposite being by nature opposed to something else. White, for example, is not opposed to itself, but is said to be the opposite of black; and, similarly, light is shown not to be opposed to itself, but is considered an opposite in relation to darkness; and so of a very great number of things besides. If, then, matter were some one thing, it could not be opposed to itself. This, then, being the nature of opposites, it is proved that matter has no existence."

POLYCRATES, BISHOP OF EPHESUS.

FROM HIS EPISTLE TO VICTOR AND THE ROMAN CHURCH CONCERNING THE DAY OF KEEPING THE PASSOVER.

[In Eusebius, *Hist. Eccl.* v. 24.]

As for us, then, we scrupulously observe the exact day,[1] neither adding nor taking away. For in Asia great luminaries[2] have gone to their rest, who shall rise again in the day of the coming of the Lord, when He cometh with glory from heaven and shall raise again all the saints. [I speak of] Philip, one of the twelve apostles, who is laid to rest at Hierapolis; and his two daughters, who arrived at old age unmarried;[3] his other daughter also, who passed her life[4] under the influence of the Holy Spirit, and reposes at Ephesus; John, moreover, who reclined on the Lord's bosom, and who became a priest wearing the mitre,[5] and a witness and a teacher—he rests at Ephesus. Then there is Polycarp, both bishop and martyr at Smyrna; and Thraseas from Eumenia, both bishop and martyr, who rests at Smyrna. Why should I speak of Sagaris, bishop and martyr, who rests at Laodicea? of the blessed Papirius, moreover? and of Melito the eunuch, who performed all his actions under the influence of the Holy Spirit, and lies at Sardis,

---

[1] Ἀρραδιούργητον ἄγομεν τὴν ἡμέραν.
[2] Στοιχεῖα.
[3] Δύο θυγατέρες αὐτοῦ γεγηρακυῖαι παρθένοι.
[4] Πολιτευσαμένη.
[5] Πέταλον.

awaiting the visitation[1] from heaven, when he shall rise again from the dead? These all kept the passover on the fourteenth day [of the month], in accordance with the Gospel, without ever deviating from it, but keeping to the rule of faith.

Moreover I also, Polycrates, who am the least of you all, in accordance with the tradition of my relatives, some of whom I have succeeded—seven of my relatives were bishops, and I am the eighth, and my relatives always observed the day when the people put away[2] the leaven—I myself, brethren, I say, who am sixty-five years old in the Lord, and have fallen in with the brethren in all parts of the world, and have read through all Holy Scripture, am not frightened at the things which are said to terrify us. For those who are greater than I have said, "We ought to obey God rather than men."[3] . . .

I might also have made mention of the bishops associated with me, whom it was your own desire to have called together by me, and I called them together: whose names, if I were to write them down, would amount to a great number. These [bishops], on coming to see me, unworthy as I am,[4] signified their united approval of the letter, knowing that I wore [these] grey hairs not in vain, but have always regulated my conduct in [obedience] to the Lord Jesus.

THEOPHILUS, BISHOP OF CÆSAREA IN PALESTINE.

FROM HIS EPISTLE ON THE QUESTION OF THE PASSOVER, WRITTEN IN THE NAME OF THE SYNOD OF CÆSAREA.

[In Eusebius, *Hist. Eccl.* v. 25.]

Endeavour also to send abroad copies of our epistle among all the churches, so that those who easily deceive their own souls may not be able to lay the blame on us. We would have you know, too, that in Alexandria also they observe [the festival] on the same day as ourselves. For the [Paschal] letters are sent from us to them, and from them to us: so that we observe the holy day in unison and together.

[1] Ἐπισκοπήν.   [2] Ἤρνυσι. Some read ἤρτυσι.
[3] Acts v. 29.   [4] Τὸν μικρόν.

SERAPION, BISHOP OF ANTIOCH.

I.

FROM THE EPISTLE TO CARICUS AND PONTICUS.

[In Eusebius, *Hist. Eccl.* v. 19.]

That ye may see also that the proceedings of this lying confederacy,[1] to which is given the name of New Prophecy, is abominated among the whole brotherhood throughout the world, I have sent you letters of the most blessed Claudius Apollinarius, who was made bishop of Hierapolis in Asia.

II.

FROM THE BOOK CONCERNING THE GOSPEL OF PETER.

[In Eusebius, *Hist. Eccl.* v. 12.]

For we, brethren, receive both Peter and the rest of the apostles as Christ [Himself]. But those writings which are falsely inscribed with their name,[2] we as experienced persons reject, knowing that no such writings have been handed down to us.[3] When, indeed, I came to see you, I supposed that all were in accord with the orthodox faith; and, although I had not read through the Gospel inscribed with the name of Peter which was brought forward by them, I said: If this is the only thing which threatens[4] to produce ill-feeling among you, let it be read. But, now that I have learnt from what has been told me that their mind was secretly cherishing some heresy,[5] I will make all haste to come to you again. Expect me therefore, brethren, shortly. Moreover, brethren, we, having discovered to what kind of heresy Marcion adhered, and seen how he contradicted himself, not understanding of what he was speaking, as you will gather from what has been written to you[6]—for, having borrowed this said Gospel from those who

---

[1] Ψευδοῦς τάξεως.
[2] The reading of Migne, ὀνόματι, is adopted instead of ὀνόματα.
[3] Τὰ τοιαῦτα οὐ παρελάβομεν.   [4] Δοκοῦν.
[5] Αἱρέσει τινὶ ὁ νοῦς αὐτῶν ἐπεφώλευεν.
[6] The construction is not again resumed.

were familiar with it from constant perusal, namely from the successors of those who were his leaders [in the heresy], whom we call Docetæ (for most of the opinions held by him are derived from their teaching), we were able to read it through; and while we found most of its contents to agree with the orthodox account of the Saviour, we found some things inconsistent with that, and these we have set down below for your inspection.

APOLLONIUS.
[In Eusebius, *Hist. Eccl.* v. 18.]

I.

But who is this new teacher? His works and teaching inform [us]. This is he who taught the dissolution of marriage; who inculcated fasting; who called Peruga and Tymius, small towns of Phrygia, Jerusalem, because he wished to collect thither people from all parts; who set up exactors of money; who craftily contrives the taking of gifts under the name of voluntary offerings; who grants stipends to those who publish abroad his doctrine, that by means of gluttony the teaching of the doctrine may prevail.

II.

We declare to you, then, that these first prophetesses, as soon as they were filled with the spirit, left their husbands. Of what falsehood, then, were they guilty in calling Prisca a maiden! Do you not think that all Scripture forbids a prophet to receive gifts and money? When, therefore, I see that the prophetess has received gold and silver and expensive articles of dress, how can I avoid treating her with disapproval?

III.

Moreover, Themiso also, who was clothed in a garb of plausible[1] covetousness, who declined to bear the sign of confessorship, but by a large sum of money put away from him the chains [of martyrdom], although after such conduct it was his duty to conduct himself with humility, yet had the

[1] ἀξιόπιστον.

hardihood to boast that he was a martyr, and, in imitation of the apostle, to compose a general epistle, in which he attempted to instruct in the elements of the faith[1] those who had believed to better purpose than he, and defended the doctrines of the new-fangled teaching,[2] and moreover uttered blasphemy against the Lord and the apostles and the holy church.

IV.

But, not to dwell further on these matters, let the prophetess tell us concerning Alexander, who calls himself a martyr, with whom she joins in banqueting; who himself also is worshipped by many;[3] whose robberies and other deeds of daring, for which he has been punished, it is not necessary for us to speak of, since the treasury[4] has him in keeping. Which of them, then, condones the sins of the other? The prophet the robberies of the martyr, or the martyr the covetousness of the prophet? For whereas the Lord has said, "Provide not gold, nor silver, nor two coats [a-piece],"[5] these men have, on the flat contrary, transgressed the command by the acquisition of these forbidden things. For we shall show that those who are called among them prophets and martyrs obtain money not only from the rich, but also from the poor, from orphans and widows. And if they are confident [that they are right] in so doing, let them stand [forward] and discuss [the point], in order that, if they be refuted, they may cease for the future so to transgress. For the fruits of the prophet must needs be brought to the test: for "from its fruit is the tree known."[6] But that those who desire it may become acquainted with what relates to Alexander, he was condemned by Æmilius Frontinus, proconsul at Ephesus, not on account of the name [of Christ], but for the daring robberies he committed when he was already a transgressor.[7] Afterwards, when he had spoken falsely of the name of the Lord, he was released, having

---

[1] κατηχεῖν.   [2] συναγωνίζεσθαι τοῖς τῆς καινοφωνίας λόγοις.
[3] Or, "whom many of them (the Montanists—reading αὐτῶν for αὐτῷ) worship."
[4] ὀπισθόδομος, a chamber at the back of the temple of Minerva, in which public money was kept.
[5] Matt. x. 9.   [6] Matt. xii. 33.
[7] παραβάτης, here meaning an *apostate*.

deceived the faithful there;[1] and [even the brethren of] his own district,[2] from which he came, did not receive him, because he was a robber. Thus, those who wish to learn what he is, have the public treasury of Asia to go to. And yet the prophet, although he spent many years with him, knows [forsooth] nothing about him! By convicting *him*, we by his means clearly convict of misrepresentation[3] the prophet likewise. We are able to prove the like in the case of many [others] besides. And if they are confident [of their innocence], let them abide the test.

V.

If they deny that their prophets have taken gifts, let them confess thus much, that if they be convicted of having taken them, they are not prophets; and we will adduce ten thousand proofs [that they have]. It is proper, too, that all the fruits of a prophet should be examined. Tell me: does a prophet dye [his hair]? Does a prophet use stibium [on his eyes]? Is a prophet fond of dress? Does a prophet play at gaming-tables and dice? Does a prophet lend money on interest?[4] Let them confess whether these things are allowable or not. For my part, I will prove that these practices have occurred among them.

FRAGMENTS FROM A LETTER OF DIONYSIUS, BISHOP OF CORINTH, TO THE ROMAN CHURCH.

I.

For this has been your custom from the beginning, to do good to all the brethren in various ways, and to send resources to many churches which are in every city, thus refreshing the poverty of the needy, and granting subsidies to the brethren who are in the mines. Through the resources which ye have sent from the beginning, ye Romans, keep up the custom of

[1] This is explained by Rufinus to mean: "When certain brethren who had influence with the judge interceded for him, he pretended that he was suffering for the name of Christ, and by this means he was released."

[2] παροικία.

[3] ὑπόστασιν, from ὑφίστημι, probably in the sense of *substituting one thing for another*.

[4] τάβλαις καὶ κύβοις.

the Romans handed down by the fathers, which your blessed Bishop Soter has not only preserved, but added to, sending a splendid gift to the saints, and exhorting with blessed words those brethren who go up to Rome, as an affectionate father his children.

II.

We passed this holy Lord's day, in which we read your letter, from the constant reading of which we shall be able to draw admonition, even as from the reading of the former one you sent us written through Clement.

III.

Therefore you also have by such admonition joined in close union (the churches) that were planted by Peter and Paul, that of the Romans and that of the Corinthians: for both of them went[1] to our Corinth, and taught us in the same way as they taught you when they went to Italy; and having taught you, they suffered martyrdom at the same time.[2]

IV.

For I wrote letters when the brethren requested me to write. And these letters the apostles of the devil have filled with tares, taking away some things and adding others, for whom a woe is in store. It is not wonderful, then, if some have attempted to adulterate the Lord's writings, when they have formed designs against those which are not such, [*i.e.* of such importance or of such a character].

THE LETTER OF THE CHURCHES OF VIENNA AND LUGDUNUM TO THE CHURCHES OF ASIA AND PHRYGIA.[3]

It began thus:—" The servants of Christ who sojourn in Vienna and Lugdunum of Gaul to the brethren throughout Asia and Phrygia, who have the same faith and hope of redemption as ourselves, peace, grace, and glory from God the Father, and from Christ Jesus our Lord."

After some further preliminary remarks the letter proceeds:

---

[1] MSS. "planted." [2] The text is evidently very corrupt.
[3] This letter has come down to us in fragments quoted by Eusebius. We have used the translation of Lord Hailes as the basis of ours.

—" The greatness of the tribulation in this region, and the exceeding anger of the heathen [nations] against the saints, and the sufferings which the blessed Witnesses endured,¹ neither are we competent to describe accurately, nor indeed is it possible to detail them in writing. For with all his strength did the adversary assail us, even then giving a foretaste of his activity among us which is to be without restraint; and he had recourse to every means, accustoming his own subjects and exercising them beforehand against the servants of God, so that not only were we excluded from houses,² baths, and the forum, but a universal prohibition was laid against any one of us appearing in any place whatsoever. But the grace of God acted as our general against him. It rescued the weak; it arrayed against him men like firm pillars, who could through patience bear up against the whole force of the assaults of the wicked one. These came to close quarters with him, enduring every form of reproach and torture; and, making light of grievous trials, they hastened on to Christ, showing in reality that the ' sufferings of the present time are not worthy to be compared with the glory that is to be revealed in us.'³ And first they nobly endured the evils which were heaped on them by the populace, — namely, hootings and blows, draggings, plunderings, stonings, and confinements,⁴ and everything that an infuriated mob is wont to perpetrate against those whom they deem bitter enemies. And at length, being brought to the forum by the tribune of the soldiers, and the magistrates that had charge of the city, they were examined in presence of the whole multitude; and having confessed, they were shut up in prison until the arrival of the governor.

" After this, when they were brought before the governor, and when he displayed a spirit of savage hostility to us, Vettius Epagathus, one of the brethren, interposed. For he was a man who had contained the full measure of love towards God and

---

¹ We have translated μάρτυρες "witnesses" and μαρτυρία "testimony" throughout.

² Houses of friends and relatives. Olshausen takes them to be public buildings.

³ Rom. viii. 18.

⁴ By "confinements" in this passage evidently is meant that the populace prevented them from resorting to public places, and thus shut them up in their own houses.

his neighbours. His mode of life had been so strict, that though he was a young man, he deserved to be described in the words used in regard to the elderly Zacharias: 'He had walked therefore in all the commandments and ordinances of the Lord blameless.'[1] He was also eager to serve his neighbour in any way, he was very zealous for God, and he was fervent in spirit. Such being the character of the man, he could not bear that judgment should be thus unreasonably passed against us, but was moved with indignation, and requested that he himself should be heard in defence of his brethren, undertaking to prove that there is nothing ungodly or impious amongst us. On this, those who were round the judgment-seat cried out against him, for he was a man of distinction; and the governor, not for a moment listening to the just request thus made to him, merely asked him if he himself were a Christian. And on his confessing in the clearest voice that he was, he also was taken up into the number of the Witnesses, receiving the appellation of the Advocate of the Christians,[2] and having himself the Advocate, the Spirit,[3] more abundantly than Zacharias; which he showed in the fulness[4] of his love, in that he had of his own good-will offered to lay down his own life in defence of the brethren. For he was and is a genuine disciple of Christ, 'following the Lamb whithersoever He goeth.'[5]

"After this the rest began to be distinguished,[6] for the proto-martyrs were decided and ready, and accomplished the confession of their testimony with all alacrity. But there appeared also those who were unprepared and unpractised, and who were still feeble, and unable to bear the tension of a great contest. Of these about ten in number proved abortions; causing great grief and immeasurable sorrow amongst us, and damping the ardour of the rest who had not yet been apprehended. For these, although they suffered every kind of cruelty, remained nevertheless in the company of the Witnesses,

[1] Luke i. 6.   [2] From the heathen judge.   [3] Luke i. 67.
[4] The writer refers to St. John's Gospel (xv. 13): "Greater love hath no man than this, that a man lay down his life for his friends."
[5] Rev. xiv. 4.
[6] This expression seems to refer to what took place in athletic combats. The athletes were tested before fighting, and those in every way qualified were permitted to fight, while the others were rejected. This testing, Valesius supposes, was called διάκρισις.

and did not forsake them. But then the whole of us were greatly alarmed on account of our uncertainty as to confession, not because we feared the tortures inflicted, but because we looked to the end, and dreaded lest any one should fall away. Those who were worthy, however, were daily apprehended, filling up the number of the others : so that out of the two churches all the excellent, and those to whom the churches owed most of all their establishment and prosperity, were collected together in prison. Some heathen household slaves belonging to our people were also apprehended, since the governor had given orders publicly that all of us should be sought out. These, through the instigation of Satan, and through fear of the tortures which they saw the saints enduring, urged on also by the soldiers, falsely accused us of Thyestean banquets and Œdipodean connections, and other crimes which it is lawful for us neither to mention nor think of ; and, indeed, we shrink from believing that any such crimes have ever taken place among men. When the rumour of these accusations was spread abroad, all raged against us like wild beasts; so that if any formerly were temperate in their conduct to us on account of relationship, they then became exceedingly indignant and exasperated against us. And thus was fulfilled that which was spoken by our Lord : ' The time shall come when every one who slayeth you shall think that he offereth service to God.' [1]

"Then at last the holy Witnesses suffered tortures beyond all description, Satan striving eagerly that some of the evil reports might be acknowledged by them.[2] But in an exceeding degree did the whole wrath of mob, general, and soldiers fall on Sanctus, a deacon from Vienna, and on Maturus, a newly-enlightened but noble combatant, and on Attalus, a native of Pergamus, who had always been the pillar [3] and foundation of the church there, and on Blandina, through whom Christ showed that the things that to men appear mean and deformed

---

[1] John xvi. 2.

[2] The words here admit of two meanings : that something blasphemous might be uttered by them—such as speaking against Christ and swearing by Cæsar ; or that some accusation against the Christians might be uttered by them—confirming, for instance, the reports of infanticide and incest prevalent against the Christians. The latter in this passage seems unquestionably to be the meaning.

[3] 1 Tim. iii. 15.

and contemptible, are with God deemed worthy of great glory, on account of love to Him,—a love which is not a mere boastful appearance, but shows itself in the power which it exercises over the life. For while we were all afraid, and especially her mistress in the flesh, who was herself one of the combatants among the Witnesses, that she would not be able to make a bold confession on account of the weakness of her body, Blandina was filled with such power, that those who tortured her one after the other in every way from morning till evening were wearied and tired, confessing that they had been baffled, for they had no other torture they could apply to her; and they were astonished that she remained in life, when her whole body was torn and opened up, and they gave their testimony[1] that one only of the modes of torture employed was sufficient to have deprived her of life, not to speak of so many excruciating inflictions. But the blessed woman, like a noble athlete, recovered her strength in the midst of the confession; and her declaration, 'I am a Christian, and there is no evil done amongst us,' brought her refreshment, and rest, and insensibility to all the sufferings inflicted on her.

"Sanctus also nobly endured all the excessive and *superhuman*[2] tortures which man could possibly devise against him; for the wicked hoped, on account of the continuance and greatness of the tortures, to hear him confess some of the unlawful practices. But he opposed them with such firmness that he did not tell them even his own name, nor that of his nation or city, nor if he were slave or free; but in answer to all these questions, he said in Latin, 'I am a Christian.' This was the confession he made repeatedly, instead of giving his name, his city, his race, and indeed in reply to every question that was put to him; and other language the heathens heard not from him. Hence arose in the minds of the governor and the torturers a determined resolution to subdue him; so that, when

---

[1] Heinichen construes differently. He makes the "torturers astonished that Blandina gave her testimony that one kind of torture was sufficient to deprive her of life." Perhaps the right construction is to make ὅτι mean "because" or "for:" "They were astonished at Blandina bearing her testimony, for one kind of torture was sufficient to have killed her."

[2] The words ὑπερβεβλημένως καὶ ὑπὲρ πάντα ἄνθρωπον naturally go with ὑπομένων, and therefore intimate that Sanctus' endurance was greater than human; but we doubt if this is intended by the writer.

every other means failed, they at last fixed red-hot plates of brass to the most delicate parts of his body. And these indeed were burned, but he himself remained inflexible and unyielding, firm in his confession, being bedewed and strengthened by the heavenly fountain of the water of life which issues from the belly of Christ.[1] But his body bore witness to what had happened; for it was all wounds and weals, shrunk and torn up, and had lost externally the human shape. In him Christ suffering wrought great wonders, destroying the adversary, and showing for an example to the rest that there is nothing fearful where there is the Father's love, and nothing painful where there is Christ's glory. For the wicked after some days again tortured the Witness, thinking that, since his body was swollen and inflamed, if they were to apply the same tortures they would gain the victory over him, especially since the parts of his body could not bear to be touched by the hand, or that he would die in consequence of the tortures, and thus inspire the rest with fear. Yet not only did no such occurrence take place in regard to him, but even, contrary to every expectation of man, his body unbent itself and became erect in the midst of the subsequent tortures, and resumed its former appearance and the use of its limbs, so that the second torture turned out through the grace of Christ a cure, not an affliction.

"Among those who had denied was a woman of the name of Biblias. The devil, thinking that he had already swallowed her, and wishing to damn her still more by making her accuse falsely, brought her forth to punishment, and employed force to constrain her, already feeble and spiritless, to utter accusations of atheism against us. But she, in the midst of the tortures, came again to a sound state of mind, and awoke as it were out of a deep sleep; for the temporary suffering reminded her of the eternal punishment in Gehenna, and she contradicted the accusers of Christians, saying, 'How can children be eaten by those who do not think it lawful to partake of the blood of even brute beasts?' And after this she confessed herself a Christian, and was added to the number of Witnesses.

"But when the tyrannical tortures were rendered by Christ

[1] John vii. 38: "He that believeth on me, as the Scripture hath said, out of his belly shall flow rivers of living water."

of no avail through the patience of the blessed, the devil devised other contrivances—confinement in the darkest and most noisome cells of the prison, the stretching of the feet on the stocks,[1] even up to the fifth hole, and the other indignities which attendants stirred up by wrath and full of the devil are wont to inflict on the imprisoned. The consequence was, that very many were suffocated in prison, as many at least as the Lord, showing His glory, wished to depart in this way. For there were others who were tortured so bitterly, that it seemed impossible for them to survive even though they were to obtain every kind of attention; and yet they remained alive in prison, destitute indeed of care from man, but strengthened by the Lord, and invigorated both in body and soul, and they animated and consoled the rest. But the new converts who had been recently apprehended, and whose bodies had not previously been tortured, could not endure the confinement, but died in the prison.

"Now the blessed Pothinus, who had been entrusted with the service of the bishopric in Lugdunum, was also dragged before the judgment-seat. He was now upwards of ninety years of age, and exceedingly weak in body. Though he breathed with difficulty on account of the feebleness of the body, yet he was strengthened by the eagerness of his spirit, on account of his earnest desire to bear his testimony. His body, indeed, was already dissolved through old age and disease, yet the life was preserved in him, that Christ might triumph through him. When he was brought by the soldiers to the judgment-seat, under a convoy of the magistrates of the city, and amid exclamations of every kind from the whole population, as if he himself were the Christ, he gave the good testimony. Being asked by the governor who was the God of the Christians, he said, 'If thou art worthy, thou shalt know.' Thereupon he was unmercifully dragged about, and endured many blows; for those who were near maltreated him in every way with their hands and feet, showing no respect for his age, while those at a distance hurled against him each one whatever came

---

[1] The holes were placed in a line, so that the further the hole in which one leg was put from the hole in which the other leg was put, the more nearly would the two legs form a straight line, and the greater would be the pain.

to hand, all of them believing that they would sin greatly and act impiously if they in any respect fell short in their insulting treatment of him. For they thought that in this way they would avenge their gods. And Pothinus, breathing with difficulty, was cast into prison, and two days after he expired.

"Upon this a grand dispensation [1] of God's providence took place, and the immeasurable mercy of Jesus was made manifest,—such an occurrence as but rarely happens among the brotherhood, yet one that does not fall short of the art of Christ. For those who in the first apprehension had denied, were imprisoned along with the others, and shared their hardships. Their denial, in fact, turned out at this time to be of no advantage to them. For while those who confessed what they really were, were imprisoned simply as Christians, no other accusation being brought against them, those who denied were detained as murderers and profligates. They, moreover, were doubly punished. For the confessors were lightened by the joy of their testimony and their hope in the promises, and by their love to Christ, and by the Father's Spirit. But the deniers were tormented greatly by their own consciences, so that when they were led forth their countenances could be distinguished among all the rest. For the confessors went forth joyous, with a mingling of glory and abundant grace in their looks, so that their chains lay like becoming ornaments around them, as around a bride adorned with golden fringes wrought with divers colours.[2] And they breathed at the same time the fragrance of Christ,[3] so that some even thought that they were anointed with this world's perfume. But the deniers were downcast, humbled, sad-looking, and weighed down with every kind of disgrace. They were, moreover, reproached even by the heathens with being base and cowardly, and charged with the crime of murder; they had lost the altogether honourable, glorious, and life-giving appellation.[4] When the rest saw this, they were strengthened, and those who were

---

[1] The dispensation is, that those who denied were not set free, but confined with the others; and that this harsh treatment and sad state of mind confirmed the resolution of those not yet apprehended to confess Christ. Various other explanations have been given, but this seems the most reasonable.

[2] Ps. xlv. 13.   [3] 2 Cor. ii. 15.   [4] Of Christian.

apprehended confessed unhesitatingly, not allowing the reasoning of the devil to have even a place in their thoughts."

Eusebius omits something, saying that after a little the letter proceeded as follows:—

"After these things, then, their testimonies took every shape through the different ways in which they departed.[1] For, plaiting a crown from different colours and flowers of every kind, they presented it to the Father. It was right therefore that the noble athletes, after having endured divers contests and gained grand victories, should receive the great crown of incorruption.

"Maturus, therefore, and Sanctus, and Blandina, and Attalus were publicly[2] exposed to the wild beasts—that common spectacle of heathen barbarity; for a day was expressly assigned to fights with wild beasts on account of our people. And Maturus and Sanctus again endured every form of torture in the amphitheatre, as if they had had no suffering at all before. Or rather, like athletes who had overthrown their adversary several times,[3] and were now contending for the crown itself, again they endured the lashes[4] which were usual there; and they were dragged about by the wild beasts, and suffered every indignity which the maddened populace demanded in cries and exhortations proceeding from various parts of the amphitheatre. And last of all they were placed in the iron chair, on which their bodies were roasted, and they themselves were filled with the fumes of their own flesh. But the heathens did not stop even here, but became still more frantic in their desire to overcome the endurance of the Christians.

---

[1] We have adopted here an emendation of Routh's. The literal version of the common text is: "The testimonies of their departure were divided into every form."

[2] The Greek is εἰς τὸ δημόσιον, was led "to the public [building]" to the wild beasts. The public [building] is taken to be the amphitheatre.

[3] The words "several times" are represented in Greek by διὰ πλειόνων κλήρων, lit. "through several lots." When there were several athletes to contend, the pairs were determined by lot. After the first contest the victors were again formed into pairs by lot, until finally there should be but one pair left. See the process at the Olympic games described in Lucian Hermotimus, c. xl. p. 782.

[4] The bestiarii, before fighting with wild beasts, had to run the gauntlet.

But not even thus did they hear anything else from Sanctus than the utterance of the confession which he had been accustomed to make from the beginning. These, then, after life had lasted a long time throughout the great contest, were at last sacrificed,[1] after they alone had formed a spectacle to the world, throughout that day, instead of all the diversity which usually takes place in gladiatorial shows.

"Blandina[2] was hung up fastened to a stake, and exposed, as food to the wild beasts that were let loose against her; and through her presenting the spectacle of one suspended on something like a cross, and through her earnest prayers, she inspired the combatants with great eagerness: for in the combat they saw, by means of their sister, with their bodily eyes, Him who was crucified for them, that He might persuade those who trust in Him that every one that has suffered for the glory of Christ has eternal communion with the living God. When none of the wild beasts at that time touched her, she was taken down from the stake and conveyed back to prison. She was thus reserved for another contest, in order that, gaining the victory in many preparative conflicts, she might make the condemnation of the Crooked Serpent[3] unquestionable, and that she might encourage the brethren. For though she was an insignificant, weak, and despised woman, yet she was clothed with the great and invincible athlete Christ. On many occasions she had overpowered the adversary, and in the course of the contest had woven for herself the crown of incorruption.

"Attalus also was vehemently demanded by the mob, for he was a man of mark. He entered the lists a ready combatant on account of his good conscience, since he had been truly practised in the Christian discipline, and had always been a Witness of the truth among us. He was led round the amphitheatre, a tablet going before him, on which was written in Latin, 'This is Attalus the Christian;' and the people swelled

---

[1] Rufinus translates *jugulati sunt*. Probably, "killed with the sword." The term may have been a technical one, being applied to the gladiators or bestiarii, whose death may have been looked on as a sacrifice to a god or a dead hero.

[2] Blandina was a slave: hence the mode of punishment. On this matter see Lipsius, *De Cruce*.

[3] Lord Hailes remarks that this alludes to Isa. xxvii. 1.

with indignation against him. But the governor, learning that he was a Roman, ordered him to be taken back to prison and kept with the rest who were there, with regard to whom he had written to the Cæsar, and was now awaiting his determination.

"The intervening time did not prove barren or unfruitful to the Witnesses, but through their patient endurance the immeasurable love of Christ was made manifest. For through the living the dead were made alive; and the Witnesses conferred favours on those who were not Witnesses, and the Virgin Mother had much joy in receiving back alive those whom she had given up as dead abortions. For through the Witnesses the greater number of those who had denied returned, as it were, into their mother's womb, and were conceived again and re-quickened; and they learned to confess. And being now restored to life, and having their spirits braced, they went up to the judgment-seat to be again questioned by the governor, while that God who wishes not the death of the sinner,[1] but mercifully calls to repentance, put sweetness into their souls. This new examination took place because the Cæsar had given orders that the Witnesses should be punished, but that if any denied they should be set free. And as now was commencing here the fair, which is attended by vast numbers of men assembling from all nations, he brought the blessed up to the judgment-seat, exhibiting them as a theatrical show and spectacle to the mobs. Wherefore also he again questioned them, and whoever appeared to have had the rights of Roman citizenship he beheaded, and the rest he sent to the wild beasts.

"Now Christ was greatly glorified in those who formerly denied; for, contrary to every expectation of the heathen, they confessed. For these were examined separately, under the belief that they were to be set free; but confessing, they were added to the number of the Witnesses. But there were also some who remained without; namely, those who had no trace of faith, and no perception of the marriage garment,[2] nor

---

[1] Ezek. xxxiii. 11.

[2] Heinichen renders "the bride's garment," and explains in the following manner. The bride is the church, the garment Christ; and the sons of perdition had no idea what garment the church of Christ should wear, had no idea that they should be clothed with Christ, and be filled with His Spirit. It is generally taken to be the marriage garment of Matt. xxii. 12.

notion of the fear of God, but through their conduct caused evil reports of our way of life, that is, sons of perdition. But all the rest were added to the church.

"Present at the examination of these was one Alexander, a native of Phrygia, a physician by profession. He had lived for many years in Gaul, and had become well known to all for his love to God and his boldness in proclaiming the truth, for he was not without a share of apostolic grace. He stood near the judgment-seat, and, urging by signs those who had denied to confess, he looked to those who stood round the judgment-seat like one in travail. But the mobs, enraged that those who had formerly denied should now confess, cried out against Alexander as if he were the cause of this change. Then the governor summoned him before him, and inquired of him who he was; and when Alexander said that he was a Christian, the governor burst into a passion, and condemned him to the wild beasts. And on the next day he entered the amphitheatre along with Attalus; for the governor, wishing to gratify the mob, again exposed Attalus to the wild beasts. These two, after being tortured in the amphitheatre with all the instruments devised for that purpose, and having undergone an exceedingly severe contest, at last were themselves sacrificed. Alexander uttered no groan or murmur of any kind, but conversed in his heart with God; but Attalus, when he was placed on the iron chair, and all the parts of his body were burning, and when the fumes from his body were borne aloft, said to the multitude in Latin, 'Lo! this which ye do is eating men. But as for us, we neither eat men nor practise any other wickedness.' And being asked what name God has, he answered, 'God has not a name as men have.'

"After all these, on the last day of the gladiatorial shows, Blandina was again brought in along with Ponticus, a boy of about fifteen years of age. These two had been taken daily to the amphitheatre to see the tortures which the rest endured, and force was used to compel them to swear by the idols of the heathen; but on account of their remaining stedfast, and setting all their devices at nought, the multitude were furious against them, so as neither to pity the tender years of the boy nor to respect the sex of the woman. Accordingly they exposed them to every terror, and inflicted on them every torture, repeatedly trying to compel them to swear. But they failed in effecting this; for Ponticus, encouraged by his sister,[1] so plainly indeed that even the heathens saw that it was she that encouraged and confirmed him, after enduring nobly every kind of torture, gave up the ghost; while the blessed Blandina, last of all, after having like a noble mother encouraged her children, and sent them on before her victorious to the King, trod the same path of conflict which her children had trod, hastening on to them with joy and exultation at her departure, not as one thrown to the wild beasts, but as one invited to a marriage supper. And after she had been scourged and exposed to the wild beasts, and roasted in the iron chair, she was at last enclosed in a net and cast before a bull. And after having been well tossed by the bull, though without having any feeling of what was happening to her, through her hope and firm hold of what had been entrusted to her and her converse with Christ, she also was sacrificed, the heathens themselves acknowledging that never among them did woman endure so many and such fearful tortures.

"Yet not even thus was their madness and their savage hatred to the saints satiated. For wild and barbarous tribes, when excited by the Wild Beast, with difficulty ceased from their rage, and their insulting conduct found another and peculiar subject in the bodies of the Witnesses. For they felt no shame that they had been overcome, for they were not possessed of human reason; but their defeat only the more inflamed their rage, and governor and people, like a wild beast, showed a like unjust hatred of us, that the Scripture might be fulfilled, 'He that is unjust, let him be unjust still; and he that is righteous, let him be righteous still.'[2] For they threw to the dogs those who had been suffocated in prison, carefully watching them day and night, lest any one should receive burial from us. They then laid out the mangled remains left by the wild beasts, and the scorched remains left by the fire, and the heads of the rest along with their trunks, and in like manner

---

[1] She may have been his sister by birth, as some have supposed, but the term "sister" would have been applied had she been connected by no other tie than that of a common faith.

[2] Rev. xxii. 11. Lardner thinks the passage is quoted from Dan. xii. 10. *Credib.* part ii. c. 16.

for many days watched them lying unburied with a military guard. There were some who raged and gnashed their teeth at them, seeking to get from them further vengeance. Others derided and insulted them, at the same time magnifying their own idols, and ascribing to them the punishment inflicted on the Christians. There were persons also of a milder disposition, who to some extent seemed to sympathize; yet they also frequently upbraided, saying, 'Where now is their God, and what good have they got from that religion which they chose in preference to their life?' Such was the diversity which characterized the conduct of the heathens. But our state was one of deep sorrow that we could not bury the bodies. For night aided us not in this matter; money failed to persuade, and entreaty did not shame them into compliance; but they kept up the watch in every way, as if they were to gain some great advantage from the bodies of the Christians not obtaining burial."

Something is omitted. The letter then goes on:—

"The bodies of the Witnesses, after having been maltreated in every way, and exposed in the open air for six days, were burned, reduced to ashes, and swept by the wicked into the river Rhone, which flows past, in order that not even a vestige of them might be visible on earth. And these things they did, as if they had been able to overcome God, and deprive them of their second birth,[1] in order, as they said, that 'they may not have hope in a resurrection, trusting to which they introduce some strange and new mode of worship, and despise dangers, and go readily and with joy to death. Now let us see if they will rise again, and if their God can help them, and rescue them out of our hands.'"

Eusebius here breaks off his series of continuous extracts, but he makes a few more for special purposes. The first is the account which the churches gave of the character of the Witnesses:—

"Who also were to such an extent zealous followers and imitators of Christ, who, being in the shape of God, thought it not an object of desire to be treated like God;[2] that though

---

[1] παλιγγενεσία. The term refers here to the new state of affairs at the end of the world.
[2] Phil. ii. 6.

they were in such glory, and had borne their testimony not once, nor twice, but often, and had been again taken back to prison after exposure to the wild beasts, and bore about with them the marks of the burnings and bruises and wounds all over their bodies, yet did they neither proclaim themselves Witnesses, nor indeed did they permit us to address them by this name; but if any one of us on any occasion, either by letter or in conversation, called them Witnesses, they rebuked him sharply. For they willingly gave the title of Witness to Christ, 'the faithful and true Witness,'[1] and first-born from the dead, and the leader to the divine life. And they reminded us of those Witnesses who had already departed, and said: 'These indeed are now Witnesses, whom Christ has vouchsafed to take up to Himself in the very act of confession, thus putting His seal upon their testimony through their departure. But we are mean and humble confessors.' And with tears they besought the brethren that earnest prayers might be made for their being perfected. They in reality did all that is implied in the term 'testimony,' acting with great boldness towards all the heathen; and their nobleness they made manifest through their patience, and fearlessness, and intrepidity. But the title of Witness, as implying some superiority to their brethren,[2] they refused, being filled with the fear of God."

After a little they say:—

"They humbled themselves[3] under the powerful hand by which they are now highly exalted. Then they pleaded for all,[4] but accused none; they absolved all, they bound none; and they prayed for those who inflicted the tortures, even as Stephen the perfect Witness, 'Lord, lay not this sin to their charge.'[5] But if he prayed for those who stoned him, how much more for the brethren!"

---

[1] Rev. i. 5 and iii. 14.

[2] The Greek is τὴν πρὸς τοὺς ἀδελφοὺς τῶν μαρτύρων προσηγορίαν, generally translated, "offered to them by their brethren."

[3] 1 Pet. v. 6.

[4] The Greek is, πᾶσι μὲν ἀπελογοῦντο. Rufinus translated, "Placabant omnes, neminem accusabant." Valesius thought that the words ought to be translated, "They rendered an account of their faith to all;" or, "They defended themselves before all." Heinichen has justified the translation in the text by an appeal to a passage in Eusebius, *Hist. Eccl.* iv. 15.

[5] Acts vii. 60.

After other things, again they say :—

"For they had this very great conflict with him [the devil] on account of their genuine love, in order that the Beast being choked, might vomit forth those whom he thought he had already swallowed. For they assumed no airs of superiority over the fallen, but with those things in which they themselves abounded they aided the needy, displaying towards them the compassion of a mother. And pouring out many tears for them to the Father, they begged life;[1] and He gave it to them, and they shared it with their neighbours. And departing victorious over all to God, having always loved peace, and having recommended peace to us, in peace they went to God, leaving no sorrow to their Mother, nor division and dissension to their brethren, but joy and peace, and concord and love."

"The same writing of the fore-mentioned martyrs," says Eusebius, "contains a story worth remembrance.

"For there was one of them of the name of Alcibiades, who lived an exceedingly austere life, confining his diet to bread and water, and partaking of nothing else whatsoever. He tried to continue this mode of life in prison; but it was revealed to Attalus after the first conflict which he underwent in the amphitheatre that Alcibiades was not pursuing the right course in refusing to use the creatures of God, and in leaving an example which might be a stumbling-block to others. And Alcibiades was persuaded, and partook freely of all kinds of food, and thanked God. For they were not without the oversight of the grace of God, but the Holy Spirit was their counsellor."

[1] Ps. xx. 4.

CLEMENS ALEXANDRINUS

ON THE

SALVATION OF THE RICH MAN.

TRANSLATED BY

REV. WILLIAM WILSON, M.A.

WHO IS THE RICH MAN THAT SHALL BE SAVED?

I. THOSE who bestow laudatory addresses on the rich appear to me to be rightly judged not only flatterers and base, in vehemently pretending that things which are disagreeable give them pleasure, but also godless and treacherous; godless, because neglecting to praise and glorify God, who is alone perfect and good, "of whom are all things, and by whom are all things, and for whom are all things" (Rom. xi. 35), they invest[1] with divine honours men wallowing in an execrable and abominable life, and, what is the principal thing, liable on this account to the judgment of God; and treacherous, because, although wealth is of itself sufficient to puff up and corrupt the souls of its possessors, and to turn them from the path by which salvation is to be attained, they stupefy them still more, by inflating the minds of the rich with the pleasures of extravagant praises, and by making them utterly despise all things except wealth, on account of which they are admired; bringing, as the saying is, fire to fire, pouring pride on pride, and adding conceit to wealth, a heavier burden to that which by nature is a weight, from which somewhat ought rather to be removed and taken away as being a dangerous and deadly disease. For to him who exalts and magnifies himself, the change and downfall to a low condition succeeds in turn, as the divine word teaches. For it appears to me to be far kinder, than basely to flatter the rich and praise them for what is bad, to aid them in working out their salvation in every possible way; asking this of God, who surely and sweetly bestows such things on His own children; and thus by the grace of the Saviour healing their souls, en-

[1] This clause is defective in the MS., and is translated as supplemented by Fell from conjecture.

lightening them and leading them to the attainment of the truth; and whosoever obtains this and distinguishes himself in good works shall gain the prize of everlasting life. Now prayer that runs its course till the last day of life needs a strong and tranquil soul; and the conduct of life needs a good and righteous disposition, reaching out towards all the commandments of the Saviour.

II. Perhaps the reason of salvation appearing more difficult to the rich than to poor men, is not single but manifold. For some, merely hearing, and that in an off-hand way, the utterance of the Saviour, "that it is easier for a camel to go through the eye of a needle than for a rich man to enter into the kingdom of heaven" (Matt. xix. 24), despair of themselves as not destined to live, surrender all to the world, cling to the present life as if it alone was left to them, and so diverge more from the way to the life to come, no longer inquiring either whom the Lord and Master calls rich, or how that which is impossible to man becomes possible to God. But others rightly and adequately comprehend this, but attaching slight importance to the works which tend to salvation, do not make the requisite preparation for attaining to the objects of their hope. And I affirm both of these things of the rich who have learned both the Saviour's power and His glorious salvation. With those who are ignorant of the truth I have little concern.

III. Those then who are actuated by a love of the truth and love of their brethren, and neither are rudely insolent towards such rich as are called, nor, on the other hand, cringe to them for their own avaricious ends, must first by the word relieve them of their groundless despair, and show with the requisite explanation of the oracles of the Lord that the inheritance of the kingdom of heaven is not quite cut off from them if they obey the commandments; then admonish them that they entertain a causeless fear, and that the Lord gladly receives them, provided they are willing; and then, in addition, exhibit and teach how and by what deeds and dispositions they shall win the objects of hope, inasmuch as it is neither out of their reach, nor, on the other hand, attained without effort; but, as is the case with athletes—to compare things small and perishing with things great and immortal—let the man who is endowed with worldly wealth reckon that this depends on himself. For among those, one man, because he despaired of being able to conquer and gain crowns, did not give in his name for the contest; while another, whose mind was inspired with this hope, and yet did not submit to the appropriate labours, and diet, and exercises, remained uncrowned, and was balked in his expectations. So also let not the man that has been invested with worldly wealth proclaim himself excluded at the outset from the Saviour's lists, provided he is a believer and one who contemplates the greatness of God's philanthropy; nor let him, on the other hand, expect to grasp the crowns of immortality without struggle and effort, continuing untrained, and without contest. But let him go and put himself under the Word as his trainer, and Christ the President of the contest; and for his prescribed food and drink let him have the New Testament of the Lord; and for exercises, the commandments; and for elegance and ornament, the fair dispositions, love, faith, hope, knowledge of the truth, gentleness, meekness, pity, gravity: so that, when by the last trumpet the signal shall be given for the race and departure hence, as from the stadium of life, he may with a good conscience present himself victorious before the Judge who confers the rewards, confessedly worthy of the Fatherland on high, to which he returns with crowns and the acclamations of angels.

IV. May the Saviour then grant to us that, having begun the subject from this point, we may contribute to the brethren what is true, and suitable, and saving, first touching the hope itself, and, second, touching the access to the hope. He indeed grants to those who beg, and teaches those who ask, and dissipates ignorance and dispels despair, by introducing again the same words about the rich, which become their own interpreters and infallible expounders. For there is nothing like listening again to the very same statements, which till now in the Gospels were distressing you, hearing them as you did without examination, and erroneously through puerility: "And going forth into the way, one approached and kneeled, saying, Good Master, what good thing shall I do that I may inherit everlasting life? And Jesus saith, Why callest thou me good? There is none good but one, *that is*, God. Thou knowest the commandments. Do not commit adultery, Do not kill, Do not steal, Do not bear false witness, Defraud not, Honour thy father and thy mother. And he answering saith to Him, All these have I observed. And Jesus, looking upon him, loved him, and said, One thing thou lackest. If thou wouldest be perfect, sell what thou hast and give to the poor, and thou shalt have treasure in heaven: and come, follow me. And he was sad at that saying, and went away grieved: for he was rich, having great possessions. And Jesus looked round about, and saith to His disciples, How hardly shall they that have riches enter into the kingdom of God! And the disciples were astonished at His words. But Jesus answereth again, and saith unto them, Children, how hard is it for them that trust in riches to enter into the kingdom of God! More easily shall a camel enter through the eye of a needle than a rich man into the kingdom of God. And they were astonished out of measure, and said, Who then can be saved? And He, looking upon them, said, What is impossible with men is possible with God. For with God all things are possible. Peter began to say to Him, Lo, we have left all and followed Thee. And Jesus answered and said, Verily I say unto you, Whosoever shall leave what is his own, parents, and brethren, and possessions, for my sake and the gospel's, shall receive an hundred-fold now in this world, lands, and possessions, and house, and brethren, with persecutions; and in the world to come is life everlasting. But many that are first shall be last, and the last first."[1]

V. These things are written in the Gospel according to Mark; and in all the rest correspondingly; although perchance the expressions vary slightly in each, yet all show identical agreement in meaning.

But well knowing that the Saviour teaches nothing in a merely human way, but teaches all things to His own with divine and mystic wisdom, we must not listen to His utterances carnally; but with due investigation and intelligence must search out and learn the meaning hidden in them. For even those things which seem to have been simplified to the disciples by the Lord Himself are found to require not less, even more, attention than what is expressed enigmatically, from the surpassing superabundance of wisdom in them. And whereas the things which are thought to have been explained by Him to those within—those called by Him the children of the kingdom—require still more consideration than the things which

[1] Mark x. 17-31. Clement does not give always Mark's *ipsissima verba*.

seemed to have been expressed simply, and respecting which therefore no questions were asked by those who heard them, but which, pertaining to the entire design of salvation, and to be contemplated with admirable and supercelestial depth of mind, we must not receive superficially with our ears, but with application of the mind to the very spirit of the Saviour, and the unuttered meaning of the declaration.

VI. For our Lord and Saviour was asked pleasantly a question most appropriate for Him,—the Life respecting life, the Saviour respecting salvation, the Teacher respecting the chief doctrines taught, the Truth respecting the true immortality, the Word respecting the word of the Father, the Perfect respecting the perfect rest, the Immortal respecting the sure immortality. He was asked respecting those things on account of which He descended, which He inculcates, which He teaches, which He offers, in order to show the essence of the gospel, that it is the gift of eternal life. For He foresaw as God, both what He would be asked, and what each one would answer Him. For who should do this more than the Prophet of prophets, and the Lord of every prophetic spirit? And having been called "good," and taking the starting note from this first expression, He commences His teaching with this, turning the pupil to God, the good, and first and only dispenser of eternal life, which the Son, who received it of Him, gives to us.

VII. Wherefore the greatest and chiefest point of the instructions which relate to life must be implanted in the soul from the beginning,—to know the eternal God, the giver of what is eternal, and by knowledge and comprehension to possess God, who is first, and highest, and one, and good. For this is the immutable and immoveable source and support of life, the knowledge of God, who really is, and who bestows the things which really are, that is, those which are eternal, from whom both being and the continuance[1] of it are derived to other beings. For ignorance of Him is death; but the knowledge and appropriation of Him, and love and likeness to Him, are the only life.

VIII. He then who would live the true life is enjoined first to know Him "whom no one knows, except the Son reveal (Him)" (Matt. xi. 17). Next is to be learned the greatness

[1] Instead of μεῖναι Fell here suggests μὴ εἶναι, non-being.

of the Saviour after Him, and the newness of grace; for, according to the apostle, "the law was given by Moses, grace and truth came by Jesus Christ" (John i. 17); and the gifts granted through a faithful servant are not equal to those bestowed by the true Son. If then the law of Moses had been sufficient to confer eternal life, it were to no purpose for the Saviour Himself to come and suffer for us, accomplishing the course of human life from His birth to His cross; and to no purpose for him who had done all the commandments of the law from his youth to fall on his knees and beg from another immortality. For he had not only fulfilled the law, but had begun to do so from his very earliest youth. For what is there great or pre-eminently illustrious in an old age which is unproductive of faults? But if one in juvenile frolicsomeness and the fire of youth shows a mature judgment older than his years, this is a champion admirable and distinguished, and hoary pre-eminently in mind.

But, nevertheless, this man being such, is perfectly persuaded that nothing is wanting to him as far as respects righteousness, but that he is entirely destitute of life. Wherefore he asks it from Him who alone is able to give it. And with reference to the law, he carries confidence; but the Son of God he addresses in supplication. He is transferred from faith to faith. As perilously tossing and occupying a dangerous anchorage in the law, he makes for the Saviour to find a haven.

IX. Jesus, accordingly, does not charge him with not having fulfilled all things out of the law, but loves him, and fondly welcomes his obedience in what he had learned; but says that he is not perfect as respects eternal life, inasmuch as he had not fulfilled what is perfect, and that he is a doer indeed of the law, but idle at the true life. Those things, indeed, are good. Who denies it? For "the commandment is holy" (Rom. vii. 12), as far as a sort of training with fear and preparatory discipline goes, leading as it did to the culmination of legislation and to grace (Gal. iii. 24). But Christ is the fulfilment "of the law for righteousness to every one that believeth;" and not as a slave making slaves, but sons, and brethren, and fellow-heirs, who perform the Father's will.

X. "If thou wilt be perfect" (Matt. xix. 21). Consequently he was not yet perfect. For nothing is more perfect than what is perfect. And divinely the expression "if thou wilt" showed the self-determination of the soul holding converse with Him. For choice depended on the man as being free; but the gift on God as the Lord. And He gives to those who are willing and are exceedingly earnest, and ask, that so their salvation may become their own. For God compels not (for compulsion is repugnant to God), but supplies to those who seek, and bestows on those who ask, and opens to those who knock. If thou wilt, then, if thou really willest, and art not deceiving thyself, acquire what thou lackest. One thing is lacking thee,—the one thing which abides, the good, that which is now above the law, which the law gives not, which the law contains not, which is the prerogative of those who live. He forsooth who had fulfilled all the demands of the law from his youth, and had gloried in what was magnificent, was not able to complete the whole[1] with this one thing which was specially required by the Saviour, so as to receive the eternal life which he desired. But he departed displeased, vexed at the commandment of the life, on account of which he supplicated. For he did not truly wish life, as he averred, but aimed at the mere reputation of the good choice. And he was capable of busying himself about many things; but the one thing, the work of life, he was powerless, and disinclined, and unable to accomplish. Such also was what the Lord said to Martha, who was occupied with many things, and distracted and troubled with serving; while she blamed her sister, because, leaving serving, she set herself at His feet, devoting her time to learning: "Thou art troubled about many things, but Mary hath chosen the good part, which shall not be taken away from her" (Luke x. 41). So also He bade him leave his busy life, and cleave to One and adhere to the grace of Him who offered everlasting life.

XI. What then was it which persuaded him to flight, and made him depart from the Master, from the entreaty, the hope, the life, previously pursued with ardour?—"Sell thy possessions." And what is this? He does not, as some conceive offhand, bid him throw away the substance he possessed, and abandon his property; but bids him banish from his soul his

---

[1] The reading of the MS. is πραθῆναι, which is corrupt. We have changed it into περιθεῖναι. Various other emendations have been proposed. Perhaps it should be προσθεῖναι, "to add."

notions about wealth, his excitement and morbid feeling about it, the anxieties, which are the thorns of existence, which choke the seed of life. For it is no great thing or desirable to be destitute of wealth, if without a special object,—not except on account of life. For thus those who have nothing at all, but are destitute, and beggars for their daily bread, the poor dispersed on the streets, who know not God and God's righteousness, simply on account of their extreme want and destitution of subsistence, and lack even of the smallest things, were most blessed and most dear to God, and sole possessors of everlasting life.

Nor was the renunciation of wealth and the bestowment of it on the poor or needy a new thing; for many did so before the Saviour's advent,—some because of the leisure (thereby obtained) for learning, and on account of a dead wisdom; and others for empty fame and vain-glory, as the Anaxagorases, the Democriti, and the Crateses.

XII. Why then command as new, as divine, as alone life-giving, what did not save those of former days? And what peculiar thing is it that the new creature[1] the Son of God intimates and teaches? It is not the outward act which others have done, but something else indicated by it, greater, more godlike, more perfect, the stripping off of the passions from the soul itself and from the disposition, and the cutting up by the roots and casting out of what is alien to the mind. For this is the lesson peculiar to the believer, and the instruction worthy of the Saviour. For those who formerly despised external things relinquished and squandered their property, but the passions of the soul, I believe, they intensified. For they indulged in arrogance, pretension, and vain-glory, and in contempt of the rest of mankind, as if they had done something superhuman. How then would the Saviour have enjoined on those destined to live for ever what was injurious and hurtful with reference to the life which He promised? For although such is the case, one, after ridding himself of the burden of wealth, may none

---

[1] The application of the words ἡ καινὴ κτίσις to Christ has been much discussed. Segaar has a long note on it, the purport of which he thus sums up: ἡ καινὴ κτίσις is a creature to whom nothing has ever existed on earth equal or like, man but also God, through whom is true light and everlasting life.

the less have still the lust and desire for money innate and living; and may have abandoned the use of it, but being at once destitute of and desiring what he spent, may doubly grieve both on account of the absence of attendance, and the presence of regret. For it is impossible and inconceivable that those in want of the necessaries of life should not be harassed in mind, and hindered from better things in the endeavour to provide them somehow, and from some source.

XIII. And how much more beneficial the opposite case, for a man, through possessing a competency, both not himself to be in straits about money, and also to give assistance to those to whom it is requisite so to do! For if no one had anything, what room would be left among men for giving? And how can this dogma fail to be found plainly opposed to and conflicting with many other excellent teachings of the Lord? "Make to yourselves friends of the mammon of unrighteousness, that when ye fail, they may receive you into the everlasting habitations" (Luke xvi. 9). "Acquire treasures in heaven, where neither moth nor rust destroys, nor thieves break through" (Matt. vi. 19). How could one give food to the hungry, and drink to the thirsty, clothe the naked, and shelter the houseless, for not doing which He threatens with fire and the outer darkness, if each man first divested himself of all these things? Nay, He bids Zaccheus and Matthew, the rich tax-gatherers, entertain Him hospitably. And He does not bid them part with their property, but, applying the just and removing the unjust judgment, He subjoins, "To-day salvation has come to this house, forasmuch as he also is a son of Abraham" (Luke v. 29, xix. 5). He so praises the use of property as to enjoin, along with this addition, the giving a share of it, to give drink to the thirsty, bread to the hungry, to take the houseless in, and clothe the naked. But if it is not possible to supply those needs without substance, and He bids people abandon their substance, what else would the Lord be doing than exhorting to give and not to give the same things, to feed and not to feed, to take in and to shut out, to share and not to share? which were the most irrational of all things.

XIV. Riches, then, which benefit also our neighbours, are not to be thrown away. For they are possessions, inasmuch as they are possessed, and goods, inasmuch as they are useful and provided by God for the use of men; and they lie to our hand, and are put under our power, as material and instruments which are for good use to those who know the instrument. If you use it skilfully, it is skilful; if you are deficient in skill, it is affected by your want of skill, being itself destitute of blame. Such an instrument is wealth. Are you able to make a right use of it? It is subservient to righteousness. Does one make a wrong use of it? It is, on the other hand, a minister of wrong. For its nature is to be subservient, not to rule. That then which of itself has neither good nor evil, being blameless, ought not to be blamed; but that which has the power of using it well and ill, by reason of its possessing voluntary choice. And this is the mind and judgment of man, which has freedom in itself and self-determination in the treatment of what is assigned to it. So let no man destroy wealth, rather than the passions of the soul, which are incompatible with the better use of wealth. So that, becoming virtuous and good, he may be able to make a good use of these riches. The renunciation, then, and selling of all possessions, is to be understood as spoken of the passions of the soul.

XV. I would then say this. Since some things are within and some without the soul, and if the soul make a good use of them, they also are reputed good, but if a bad, bad;—whether does He who commands us to alienate our possessions repudiate those things, after the removal of which the passions still remain, or those rather, on the removal of which wealth even becomes beneficial? If therefore he who casts away worldly wealth can still be rich in the passions, even though the material [for their gratification] is absent,—for the disposition produces its own effects, and strangles the reason, and presses it down and inflames it with its inbred lusts,—it is then of no advantage to him to be poor in purse while he is rich in passions. For it is not what ought to be cast away that he has cast away, but what is indifferent; and he has deprived himself of what is serviceable, but set on fire the innate fuel of evil through want of the external means [of gratification]. We must therefore renounce those possessions that are injurious, not those that are capable of being serviceable, if one knows the right use of them. And what is managed with wisdom, and sobriety, and piety, is profitable; and what is hurtful must be cast away.

But things external hurt not. So then the Lord introduces the use of external things, bidding us put away not the means of subsistence, but what uses them badly. And these are the infirmities and passions of the soul.

XVI. The presence of wealth in these is deadly to all, the loss of it salutary. Of which, making the soul pure,—that is, poor and bare,—we must hear the Saviour speaking thus, "Come, follow me." For to the pure in heart He now becomes the way. But into the impure soul the grace of God finds no entrance. And that (soul) is unclean which is rich in lusts, and is in the throes of many worldly affections. For he who holds possessions, and gold, and silver, and houses, as the gifts of God; and ministers from them to the God who gives them for the salvation of men; and knows that he possesses them more for the sake of the brethren than his own; and is superior to the possession of them, not the slave of the things he possesses; and does not carry them about in his soul, nor bind and circumscribe his life within them, but is ever labouring at some good and divine work, even should he be necessarily some time or other deprived of them, is able with cheerful mind to bear their removal equally with their abundance. This is he who is blessed by the Lord, and called poor in spirit, a meet heir of the kingdom of heaven, not one who could not live rich.

XVII. But he who carries his riches in his soul, and instead of God's Spirit bears in his heart gold or land, and is always acquiring possessions without end, and is perpetually on the outlook for more, bending downwards and fettered in the toils of the world, being earth and destined to depart to earth,—whence can he be able to desire and to mind the kingdom of heaven,—a man who carries not a heart, but land or metal, who must perforce be found in the midst of the objects he has chosen? For where the mind of man is, there is also his treasure. The Lord acknowledges a twofold treasure,— the good: "For the good man, out of the good treasure of his heart, bringeth forth good;" and the evil: for "the evil man, out of the evil treasure, bringeth forth evil: for out of the abundance of the heart the mouth speaketh" (Matt. xii. 34, 35). As then treasure is not one with Him, as also it is with us, that which gives the unexpected great gain in the finding, but also a second, which is profitless and undesirable, an evil acquisition, hurtful; so also there is a richness in good things, and a richness in bad things, since we know that riches and treasure are not by nature separated from each other. And the one sort of riches is to be possessed and acquired, and the other not to be possessed, but to be cast away.

In the same way spiritual poverty is blessed. Wherefore also Matthew added, "Blessed are the poor" (Matt. v. 3). How? "In spirit." And again, "Blessed are they that hunger and thirst after the righteousness of God" (Matt. v. 6). Wherefore wretched are the contrary kind of poor, who have no part in God, and still less in human property, and have not tasted of the righteousness of God.

XVIII. So that (the expression) rich men that shall with difficulty enter into the kingdom, is to be apprehended in a scholarly[1] way, not awkwardly, or rustically, or carnally. For if the expression is used thus, salvation does not depend on external things, whether they be many or few, small or great, or illustrious or obscure, or esteemed or disesteemed; but on the virtue of the soul, on faith, and hope, and love, and brotherliness, and knowledge, and meekness, and humility, and truth, the reward of which is salvation. For it is not on account of comeliness of body that any one shall live, or, on the other hand, perish. But he who uses the body given to him chastely and according to God, shall live; and he that destroys the temple of God shall be destroyed. An ugly man can be profligate, and a good-looking man temperate. Neither strength and great size of body makes alive, nor does any of the members destroy. But the soul which uses them provides the cause for each. Bear then, it is said, when struck on the face (Matt. v. 39); which a man strong and in good health can obey. And again, a man who is feeble may transgress from refractoriness of temper. So also a poor and destitute man may be found intoxicated with lusts; and a man rich in worldly goods temperate, poor in indulgences, trustworthy, intelligent, pure, chastened.

If then it is the soul which, first and especially, is that which is to live, and if virtue springing up around it saves, and vice

---

[1] μαθηματικῶς. Fell suggests instead of this reading of the text, πνευματικῶς or μεμελημένως.

kills; then it is clearly manifest that by being poor in those things, by riches of which one destroys it, it is saved, and by being rich in those things, riches of which ruin it, it is killed. And let us no longer seek the cause of the issue elsewhere than in the state and disposition of the soul in respect of obedience to God and purity, and in respect of transgression of the commandments and accumulation of wickedness.

XIX. He then is truly and rightly rich who is rich in virtue, and is capable of making a holy and faithful use of any fortune; while he is spuriously rich who is rich, according to the flesh, and turns life into outward possession, which is transitory and perishing, and now belongs to one, now to another, and in the end to nobody at all. Again, in the same way there is a genuine poor man, and another counterfeit and falsely so called. He that is poor in spirit, and that is the right thing, and he that is poor in a worldly sense, which is a different thing. To him who is poor in worldly goods, but rich in vices, who is not poor in spirit[1] and rich toward God, it is said, Abandon the alien possessions that are in thy soul, that, becoming pure in heart, thou mayest see God; which is another way of saying, Enter into the kingdom of heaven. And how may you abandon them? By selling them. What then? Are you to take money for effects, by effecting an exchange of riches, by turning your visible substance into money? Not at all. But by introducing, instead of what was formerly inherent in your soul, which you desire to save, other riches which deify and which minister everlasting life, dispositions in accordance with the command of God; for which there shall accrue to you endless reward and honour, and salvation, and everlasting immortality. It is thus that thou dost rightly sell the possessions, many and superfluous, which shut the heavens against thee by exchanging them for those which are able to save. Let the former be possessed by the carnal poor, who are destitute of the latter. But thou, by receiving instead spiritual wealth, shalt have now treasure in the heavens.

XX. The wealthy and legally correct man, not understanding these things figuratively, nor how the same man can be

---

[1] ὁ κατὰ πνεῦμα οὐ πτωχός... φησί. Segaar omits οὐ, and so makes ὁ κατ' πνεῦμα, κ.τ.λ. the nominative to φησί. It seems better, with the Latin translator, to render as above, which supposes the change of ὁ into ὅς.

both poor and rich, and have wealth and not have it, and use the world and not use it, went away sad and downcast, leaving the state of life, which he was able merely to desire but not to attain, making for himself the difficult impossible. For it was difficult for the soul not to be seduced and ruined by the luxuries and flowery enchantments that beset remarkable wealth; but it was not impossible, even surrounded with it, for one to lay hold of salvation, provided he withdrew himself from material wealth,—to that which is grasped by the mind and taught by God, and learned to use things indifferent rightly and properly, and so as to strive after eternal life. And the disciples even themselves were at first alarmed and amazed. Why were they so on hearing this? Was it that they themselves possessed much wealth? Nay, they had long ago left their very nets, and hooks, and rowing boats, which were their sole possessions. Why then do they say in consternation, "Who can be saved?" They had heard well and like disciples what was spoken in parable and obscurely by the Lord, and perceived the depth of the words. For they were sanguine of salvation on the ground of their want of wealth. But when they became conscious of not having yet wholly renounced the passions (for they were neophytes and recently selected by the Saviour), they were excessively astonished, and despaired of themselves no less than that rich man who clung so terribly to the wealth which he preferred to eternal life. It was therefore a fit subject for all fear on the disciples' part; if both he that possesses wealth and he that is teeming with passions were the rich, and these alike shall be expelled from the heavens. For salvation is the privilege of pure and passionless souls.

XXI. But the Lord replies, "Because what is impossible with men is possible with God." This again is full of great wisdom. For a man by himself working and toiling at freedom from passion achieves nothing. But if he plainly shows himself very desirous and earnest about this, he attains it by the addition of the power of God. For God conspires with willing souls. But if they abandon their eagerness, the spirit which is bestowed by God is also restrained. For to save the unwilling is the part of one exercising compulsion; but to save the willing, that of one showing grace. Nor does the kingdom of heaven belong to sleepers and sluggards, "but the violent take it by force" (Matt. xi. 12). For this alone is commendable violence, to force God, and take life from God by force. And He, knowing those who persevere firmly, or rather violently, yields and grants. For God delights in being vanquished in such things.

Therefore on hearing those words, the blessed Peter, the chosen, the pre-eminent, the first of the disciples, for whom alone and Himself the Saviour paid tribute (Matt. xvii. 26), quickly seized and comprehended the saying. And what does he say? "Lo, we have left all and followed Thee." Now if by all he means his own property, he boasts of leaving four oboli perhaps in all,[1] and forgets to show the kingdom of heaven to be their recompense. But if, casting away what we were now speaking of, the old mental possessions and soul diseases, they follow in the Master's footsteps, this now joins them to those who are to be enrolled in the heavens. For it is thus that one truly follows the Saviour, by aiming at sinlessness and at His perfection, and adorning and composing the soul before it as a mirror, and arranging everything in all respects similarly.

XXII. "And Jesus answering said, Verily I say unto you, Whosoever shall leave what is his own, parents, and children, and wealth, for my sake and the gospel's, shall receive an hundred-fold" (Mark x. 29, quoted inexactly). But let neither this trouble you, nor the still harder saying delivered in another place in the words, "Whoso hateth not father, and mother, and children, and his own life besides, cannot be my disciple" (Luke xiv. 26). For the God of peace, who also exhorts to love enemies, does not introduce hatred and dissolution from those that are dearest. But if we are to love our enemies, it is in accordance with right reason that, ascending from them, we should love also those nearest in kindred. Or if we are to hate our blood-relations, deduction teaches us that much more are we to spurn from us our enemies. So that the reasonings would be shown to destroy one another. But they do not destroy each other, or are they near doing so. For from the same feeling and disposition, and on the ground of the same rule, one loving

[1] The text is the reading on the margin of the first edition. The reading of the MS., τοῦ λόγου, is amended by Segaar into τὸ τοῦ λόγου, "as the saying is."

his enemy may hate his father, inasmuch as he neither takes vengeance on an enemy, nor reverences a father more than Christ. For by the one word he extirpates hatred and injury, and by the other shamefacedness towards one's relations, if it is detrimental to salvation. If then one's father, or son, or brother, be godless, and become a hindrance to faith and an impediment to the higher life, let him not be friends or agree with him, but on account of the spiritual enmity, let him dissolve the fleshly relationship.

XXIII. Suppose the matter to be a law-suit. Let your father be imagined to present himself to you and say, "I begot and reared thee. Follow me, and join with me in wickedness, and obey not the law of Christ;" and whatever a man who is a blasphemer and dead by nature would say.

But on the other side hear the Saviour: "I regenerated thee, who wert ill born by the world to death. I emancipated, healed, ransomed thee. I will show thee the face of the good Father God. Call no man thy father on earth. Let the dead bury the dead; but follow thou me. For I will bring thee to a rest[1] of ineffable and unutterable blessings, which eye hath not seen, nor ear heard, nor have entered into the heart of men; into which angels desire to look, and see what good things God hath prepared for the saints and the children who love Him (1 Cor. ii. 9; 1 Pet. i. 12). I am He who feeds thee, giving myself as bread, of which he who has tasted experiences death no more, and supplying day by day the drink of immortality. I am teacher of supercelestial lessons. For thee I contended with Death, and paid thy death, which thou owedst for thy former sins and thy unbelief towards God."

Having heard these considerations on both sides, decide for thyself and give thy vote for thine own salvation. Should a brother say the like, should a child, should a wife, should any one whosoever, in preference to all let Christ in thee be conqueror. For He contends in thy behalf.

XXIV. You may even go against wealth. Say, "Certainly Christ does not debar me from property. The Lord does not envy." But do you see yourself overcome and overthrown by it? Leave it, throw it away, hate, renounce, flee. "Even if thy right eye offend thee," quickly "cut it out" (Matt. v. 29).

---

[1] Segaar amends ἀνάπαυσιν to ἀπόλαυσιν, "enjoyment."

Better is the kingdom of God to a man with one eye, than the fire to one who is unmutilated. Whether hand, or foot, or soul, hate it. For if it is destroyed here for Christ's sake, it will be restored to life yonder.

XXV. And to this effect similarly is what follows. "Now at this present time not to have lands, and money, and houses, and brethren, with persecutions." For it is neither penniless, nor homeless, nor brotherless people that the Lord calls to life, since He has also called rich people; but, as we have said above, also brothers, as Peter with Andrew, and James with John the sons of Zebedee, but of one mind with each other and Christ. And the expression "with persecutions" rejects the possessing of each of those things. There is a persecution which arises from without, from men assailing the faithful, either out of hatred, or envy, or avarice, or through diabolic agency. But the most painful is internal persecution, which proceeds from each man's own soul being vexed by impious lusts, and diverse pleasures, and base hopes, and destructive dreams; when, always grasping at more, and maddened by brutish loves, and inflamed by the passions which beset it like goads and stings, it is covered with blood, (to drive it on) to insane pursuits, and to despair of life, and to contempt of God.

More grievous and painful is this persecution, which arises from within, which is ever with a man, and which the persecuted cannot escape; for he carries the enemy about everywhere in himself. Thus also burning which attacks from without works trial, but that from within produces death. War also made on one is easily put an end to, but that which is in the soul continues till death.

With such persecution, if you have worldly wealth, if you have brothers allied by blood and other pledges, abandon the whole wealth of these which leads to evil; procure peace for yourself, free yourself from protracted persecution; turn from them to the gospel; choose before all the Saviour and Advocate and Paraclete of your soul, the Prince of life. "For the things which are seen are temporary; but the things which are not seen are eternal" (2 Cor. v. 18). And in the present time are things evanescent and insecure, but in that to come is eternal life.

XXVI. "The first shall be last, and the last first" (Mark x.

31). This is fruitful in meaning and exposition,[1] but does not demand investigation at present; for it refers not only to the wealthy alone, but plainly to all men, who have once surrendered themselves to faith. So let this stand aside for the present. But I think that our proposition has been demonstrated in no way inferior to what we promised, that the Saviour by no means has excluded the rich on account of wealth itself, and the possession of property, nor fenced off salvation against them; if they are able and willing to submit their life to God's commandments, and prefer them to transitory objects, and if they would look to the Lord with steady eye, as those who look for the nod of a good helmsman, what he wishes, what he orders, what he indicates, what signal he gives his mariners, where and whence he directs the ship's course. For what harm does one do, who, previous to faith, by applying his mind and by saving has collected a competency? Or what is much less reprehensible than this, if at once by God, who gave him his life, he has had his home given him in the house of such men, among wealthy people, powerful in substance, and pre-eminent in opulence? For if, in consequence of his involuntary birth in wealth, a man is banished from life, rather is he wronged by God, who created him, in having vouchsafed to him temporary enjoyment, and in being deprived of eternal life. And why should wealth have ever sprung from the earth at all, if it is the author and patron of death?

But if one is able in the midst of wealth to turn from its power, and to entertain moderate sentiments, and to exercise self-command, and to seek God alone, and to breathe God and walk with God, such a poor man submits to the commandments, being free, unsubdued, free of disease, unwounded by wealth. But if not, "sooner shall a camel enter through a needle's eye, than such a rich man reach the kingdom of God" (Mark x. 25).

Let then the camel, going through a narrow and strait way before the rich man, signify something loftier; which mystery of the Saviour is to be learned in the "Exposition of first Principles and of Theology."[2]

XXVII. Well, first let the point of the parable, which is

---

[1] σαφηνισμόν, here adopted instead of the reading σοφισμόν, which yields no suitable sense.
[2] A work mentioned elsewhere.

evident, and the reason why it is spoken, be presented. Let it teach the prosperous that they are not to neglect their own salvation, as if they had been already fore-doomed, nor, on the other hand, to cast wealth into the sea, or condemn it as a traitor and an enemy to life, but learn in what way and how to use wealth and obtain life. For since neither does one perish by any means by fearing because he is rich, nor is by any means saved by trusting and believing that he shall be saved, come let them look what hope the Saviour assigns them, and how what is unexpected may become ratified, and what is hoped for may come into possession.

The Master accordingly, when asked, "Which is the greatest of the commandments?" says, "Thou shalt love the Lord thy God with all thy soul, and with all thy strength" (Matt. xxii. 36, 37, 38) : that no commandment is greater than this (He says), and with exceeding good reason; for it gives command respecting the First and the Greatest, God Himself, our Father, by whom all things were brought into being, and exist, and to whom what is saved returns again. By Him, then, being loved beforehand, and having received existence, it is impious for us to regard ought else older or more excellent; rendering only this small tribute of gratitude for the greatest benefits; and being unable to imagine anything else whatever by way of recompense to God, who needs nothing and is perfect; and gaining immortality by the very exercise of loving the Father to the extent of one's might and power. For the more one loves God, the more he enters within God.

XXVIII. The second in order, and not any less than this, He says, is, "Thou shalt love thy neighbour as thyself" (Matt. xxii. 39), consequently God above thyself. And on His interlocutor inquiring, "Who is my neighbour?" (Luke x. 29), He did not, in the same way with the Jews, specify the blood-relation, or the fellow-citizen, or the proselyte, or him that had been similarly circumcised, or the man who uses one and the same law. But He introduces one on his way down from the upland region from Jerusalem to Jericho, and represents him stabbed by robbers, cast half-dead on the way, passed by by the priest, looked sideways at by the Levite, but pitied by the vilified and excommunicated Samaritan; who did not, like those, pass casually, but came provided with such things as the man in danger required, such as oil, bandages, a beast of burden, money for the inn-keeper, part given now, and part promised. "Which," said He, "of them was neighbour to him that suffered these things?" and on his answering, "He that showed mercy to him," (replied), (Luke x. 29, 31), Go thou also, therefore, and do likewise, since love buds into well-doing.

XXIX. In both the commandments, then, He introduces love; but in order distinguishes it. And in the one He assigns to God the first part of love, and allots the second to our neighbour. Who else can it be but the Saviour Himself? or who more than He has pitied us, who by the rulers of darkness were all but put to death with many wounds, fears, lusts, passions, pains, deceits, pleasures? Of these wounds the only physician is Jesus, who cuts out the passions thoroughly by the root,—not as the law does the bare effects, the fruits of evil plants, but applies His axe to the roots of wickedness. He it is that poured wine on our wounded souls (the blood of David's vine), that brought the oil which flows from the compassions of the Father,[1] and bestowed it copiously. He it is that produced the ligatures of health and of salvation that cannot be undone,—Love, Faith, Hope. He it is that subjected angels, and principalities, and powers, for a great reward, to serve us. For they also shall be delivered from the vanity of the world through the revelation of the glory of the sons of God. We are therefore to love Him equally with God. And he loves Christ Jesus who does His will and keeps His commandments. "For not every one that saith unto me, Lord, Lord, shall enter into the kingdom of heaven; but he that doeth the will of my Father" (John xiv. 23; Matt. vii. 21). And "Why call ye me Lord, Lord, and do not the things which I say?" (Luke vi. 40). "And blessed are ye who see and hear what neither righteous men nor prophets" (have seen or heard) (Matt. xiii. 23), if ye do what I say.

XXX. He then is first who loves Christ; and second, he who loves and cares for those who have believed on Him. For whatever is done to a disciple, the Lord accepts as done to Himself, and reckons the whole as His. "Come, ye blessed of my Father, inherit the kingdom prepared for you from the foundation of the world. For I was an hungered, and ye gave

---

[1] Combefisius reads 'Spirit.'

me to eat: I was thirsty, and ye gave me to drink: and I was a stranger, and ye took me in: I was naked, and ye clothed me: I was sick, and ye visited me: I was in prison, and ye came to me. Then shall the righteous answer, saying, Lord, when saw we Thee hungry, and fed Thee? or thirsty, and gave Thee drink? And when saw we Thee a stranger, and took Thee in? or naked, and clothed Thee? Or when saw we Thee sick, and visited Thee? or in prison, and came to Thee? And the King answering, shall say to them, Verily I say unto you, inasmuch as ye have done it unto one of the least of these my brethren, ye have done it unto me."

Again, on the opposite side, to those who have not performed these things, "Verily I say unto you, inasmuch as ye have not done it unto one of the least of these, ye have not done it to me" (Matt. xxv. 34, etc.). And in another place, "He that receiveth you, receiveth me; and he that receiveth not you, rejecteth me" (Matt. x. 40; Luke x. 16).

XXXI. Such He names children, and sons, and little children, and friends, and little ones here, in reference to their future greatness above. "Despise not," He says, "one of these little ones; for their angels always behold the face of my Father in heaven" (Matt. xviii. 10). And in another place, "Fear not, little flock, for it is your Father's good pleasure to give you the kingdom of heaven" (Luke xii. 32). Similarly also He says that "the least in the kingdom of heaven" that is His own disciple "is greater than John, the greatest among those born of women" (Matt. xi. 11). And again, "He that receiveth a righteous man or a prophet in the name of a righteous man or a prophet, shall receive their reward; and he that giveth to a disciple in the name of a disciple a cup of cold water to drink, shall not lose his reward" (Matt. x. 41). Wherefore this is the only reward that is not lost. And again, "Make to you friends of the mammon of unrighteousness, that, when ye fail, they may receive you into everlasting habitations" (Luke xvi. 9); showing that by nature all property which a man possesses in his own power is not his own. And from this unrighteousness it is permitted to work a righteous and saving thing, to refresh some one of those who have an everlasting habitation with the Father.

See then, first, that He has not commanded you to be

solicited or to wait to be importuned, but yourself to seek those who are to be benefited and are worthy disciples of the Saviour. Excellent, accordingly, also is the apostle's saying, "For the Lord loveth a cheerful giver" (2 Cor. ix. 7); who delights in giving, and spares not, sowing so that he may also thus reap, without murmuring, and disputing, and regret, and communicating, which is pure[1] beneficence. But better than this is the saying spoken by the Lord in another place, "Give to every one that asketh thee" (Luke vi. 30). For truly such is God's delight in giving. And this saying is above all divinity,[2]—not to wait to be asked, but to inquire oneself who deserves to receive kindness.

XXXII. Then to appoint such a reward for liberality,— an everlasting habitation! O excellent trading! O divine merchandise! One purchases immortality for money; and, by giving the perishing things of the world, receives in exchange for these an eternal mansion in the heavens! Sail to this mart, if you are wise, O rich man! If need be, sail round the whole world.[3] Spare not perils and toils, that you may purchase here the heavenly kingdom. Why do transparent stones and emeralds delight thee so much, and a house that is fuel for fire, or a plaything of time, or the sport of the earthquake, or an occasion for a tyrant's outrage? Aspire to dwell in the heavens, and to reign with God. This kingdom a man imitating God will give thee. By receiving a little here, there through all ages He will make thee a dweller with Him. Ask that you may receive; haste; strive; fear lest He disgrace thee. For He is not commanded to receive, but thou to give. The Lord did not say, Give, or bring, or do good, or help, but make a friend. But a friend proves himself such not by one gift, but by long intimacy. For it is neither the faith, nor the love, nor the hope, nor the endurance of one day, but "he that endureth to the end shall be saved" (Matt. x. 22).

XXXIII. How then does man give these things? For I will give not only to friends, but to the friends of friends.

---

[1] καθαρα, Segaar, for καθα of the MS.
[2] This, the reading of the MS., has been altered by several editors, but is justly defended by Segaar.
[3] γῆν ὅλην, for which Fell reads τὴν ὅλην.

And who is it that is the friend of God? Do not you judge who is worthy or who is unworthy. For it is possible you may be mistaken in your opinion. As in the uncertainty of ignorance it is better to do good to the undeserving for the sake of the deserving, than by guarding against those that are less good to fail to meet in with the good. For through sparing, and aiming at testing, who will receive meritoriously or not, it is possible for you to neglect some[1] that are loved by God; the penalty for which is the punishment of eternal fire. But by offering to all in turn that need, you must of necessity by all means find some one of those who have power with God to save. "Judge not, then, that ye be not judged. With what measure ye mete, it shall be measured to you again (Matt. vii. 1; Luke vi. 38); good measure, pressed and shaken, and running over, shall be given to you." Open thy compassion to all who are enrolled the disciples of God; not looking contemptuously to personal appearance, nor carelessly disposed to any period of life. Nor if one appears penniless, or ragged, or ugly, or feeble, do thou fret in soul at this and turn away. This form is cast around us from without, the occasion of our entrance into this world, that we may be able to enter into this common school. But within dwells the hidden Father, and His Son,[2] who died for us and rose with us.

XXXIV. This visible appearance cheats death and the devil; for the wealth within, the beauty, is unseen by them. And they rave about the carcase, which they despise as weak, being blind to the wealth within; knowing not what a "treasure in an earthen vessel" (2 Cor. v. 7) we bear, protected as it is by the power of God the Father, and the blood of God the Son,[3] and the dew of the Holy Spirit. But be not deceived, thou who hast tasted of the truth, and been reckoned worthy of the great redemption. But contrary to what is the case with the rest of men, collect for thyself an unarmed, an unwarlike, a bloodless, a passionless, a stainless host, pious old men, orphans dear to God, widows armed with meekness, men adorned with love. Obtain with thy money such guards, for body and for soul, for whose sake a sinking ship is made buoyant, when steered by the prayers of the saints alone; and disease at its height is subdued, put to flight by the laying on of hands; and the attack of robbers is disarmed,

---

[1] τινῶν, for which the text has τιμῶν.   [2] ταῖς.   [3] παιδός.

spoiled by pious prayers; and the might of demons is crushed, put to shame in its operations by strenuous commands.

XXXV. All these warriors and guards are trusty. No one is idle, no one is useless. One can obtain your pardon from God, another comfort you when sick, another weep and groan in sympathy for you to the Lord of all, another teach some of the things useful for salvation, another admonish with confidence, another counsel with kindness. And all can love truly, without guile, without fear, without hypocrisy, without flattery, without pretence. O sweet service of loving [souls]! O blessed thoughts of confident [hearts]! O sincere faith of those who fear God alone! O truth of words with those who cannot lie! O beauty of deeds with those who have been commissioned to serve God, to persuade God, to please God, not to touch thy flesh! to speak, but[1] to the King of eternity dwelling in thee.

XXXVI. All the faithful, then, are good and Godlike, and worthy of the name by which they are encircled as with a diadem. There are, besides, some, the elect of the elect, and so much more or less distinguished by drawing themselves, like ships to the strand, out of the surge of the world and bringing themselves to safety; not wishing to seem holy, and ashamed if one call them so; hiding in the depth of their mind the ineffable mysteries, and disdaining to let their nobleness be seen in the world; whom the Word calls "the light of the world, and the salt of the earth" (Matt. v. 13, 14). This is the seed, the image and likeness of God, and His true son and heir, sent here as it were on a sojourn, by the high administration and suitable arrangement of the Father, by whom the visible and invisible things of the world were created; some for their service, some for their discipline, some for their instruction; and all things are held together so long as the seed remains here; and when it is gathered, these things shall be very quickly dissolved.

XXXVII. For what further need has God of the mysteries of love?[2] And then thou shalt look into the bosom of the Father, whom God the only-begotten Son alone hath declared.

[1] Perhaps ἀλλά has got transposed, and we should read, "but to speak to the king," etc.
[2] Segaar reads: For what more should I [say]? Behold the mysteries of love.

And God Himself is love; and out of love to us became feminine.[1] In His ineffable essence He is Father; in His compassion to us He became Mother. The Father by loving became feminine: and the great proof of this is He whom He begot of Himself; and the fruit brought forth by love is love.

For this also He came down. For this He clothed Himself with man. For this He voluntarily subjected Himself to the experiences of men, that by bringing Himself to the measure of our weakness whom He loved, He might correspondingly bring us to the measure of His own strength. And about to be offered up and giving Himself a ransom, He left for us a new Covenant-testament: My love I give unto you. And what and how great is it? For each of us He gave His life,—the equivalent for all. This He demands from us in return for one another. And if we owe our lives to the brethren, and have made such a mutual compact with the Saviour, why should we any more hoard and shut up worldly goods, which are beggarly, foreign to us and transitory? Shall we shut up from each other what after a little shall be the property of the fire? Divinely and weightily John says, "He that loveth not his brother is a murderer" (1 John iii. 14), the seed of Cain, a nursling of the devil. He has not God's compassion. He has no hope of better things. He is sterile; he is barren; he is not a branch of the ever-living supercelestial vine. He is cut off; he waits the perpetual fire.

XXXVIII. But learn thou the more excellent way, which Paul shows for salvation. "Love seeketh not her own" (1 Cor. xii. 32, xiii. 5), but is diffused on the brother. About him she is fluttered, about him she is soberly insane. "Love covers a multitude of sins" (1 Pet. iv. 8). "Perfect love casteth out fear" (1 John iv. 18). "Vaunteth not itself, is not puffed up; rejoiceth not in iniquity, but rejoiceth in the truth; beareth all things, believeth all things, hopeth all things, endureth all things. Love never faileth. Prophecies are done away, tongues cease, gifts of healing fail on the earth. But these three abide, Faith, Hope, Love. But the greatest of these is Love" (1 Cor. xiii. 4–6, 13). And rightly. For Faith departs when we are convinced by vision, by seeing God. And

---

[1] 'Εθηλύνθη, which occurs immediately after this, has been suggested as the right reading here. The text has ἰθηράθη.

Hope vanishes when the things hoped for come. But Love comes to completion, and grows more when that which is perfect has been bestowed. If one introduces it into his soul, although he be born in sins, and has done many forbidden things, he is able, by increasing love, and adopting a pure repentance, to retrieve his mistakes. For let not this be left to despondency and despair by you, if you learn who the rich man is that has not a place in heaven, and what way he uses his property.

XXXIX. If one should escape the superfluity of riches, and the difficulty they interpose in the way of life, and be able to enjoy the eternal good things; but should happen, either from ignorance or involuntary circumstances, after the seal[1] and redemption, to fall into sins or transgressions so as to be quite carried away; such a man is entirely rejected by God. For to every one who has turned to God in truth, and with his whole heart, the doors are open, and the thrice-glad Father receives His truly repentant son. And true repentance is to be no longer bound in the same sins for which He denounced death against Himself, but to eradicate them completely from the soul. For on their extirpation God takes up His abode again in thee. For it is said there is great and exceeding joy and festival in the heavens with the Father and the angels when one sinner turns and repents (Luke xv. 10). Wherefore also He cries, "I will have mercy, and not sacrifice" (Hos. vi. 6; Matt. ix. 13). "I desire not the death, but the repentance of the sinner" (Ezek. xviii. 23). "Though your sins be as scarlet wool, I will make them white as snow; though they be blacker than darkness, I will wash and make them like white wool" (Isa. i. 18). For it is in the power of God alone to grant the forgiveness of sins, and not to impute transgressions; since also the Lord commands us each day to forgive the repenting brethren (Matt. vi. 14). "And if we, being evil, know to give good gifts" (Luke xi. 13), much more is it the nature of the Father of mercies, the good Father of all consolation, much pitying, very merciful, to be long-suffering, to wait for those who have turned. And to turn is really to cease from our sins, and to look no longer behind.

XL. Forgiveness of past sins, then, God gives; but of

[1] *i.e.* of baptism.

future, each one gives to himself. And this is to repent, to condemn the past deeds, and beg oblivion of them from the Father, who only of all is able to undo what is done, by mercy proceeding from Him, and to blot out former sins by the dew of the Spirit. "For by the state in which I find you will I judge,"[1] also, is what in each case the end of all cries aloud. So that even in the case of one who has done the greatest good deeds in his life, but at the end has run headlong into wickedness, all his former pains are profitless[2] to him, since at the catastrophe of the drama he has given up his part; while it is possible for the man who formerly led a bad and dissolute life, on afterwards repenting, to overcome in the time after repentance the evil conduct of a long time. But it needs great carefulness, just as bodies that have suffered by protracted disease need regimen and special attention. Thief, dost thou wish to get forgiveness? steal no more. Adulterer, burn no more. Fornicator, live for the future chastely. Thou who hast robbed, give back, and give back more than [thou tookest]. False witness, practise truth. Perjurer, swear no more, and extirpate the rest of the passions, wrath, lust, grief, fear; that thou mayest be found at the end to have previously in this world been reconciled to the adversary. It is then probably impossible all at once to eradicate inbred passions; but by God's power and human intercession, and the help of brethren, and sincere repentance, and constant care, they are corrected.

XLI. Wherefore it is by all means necessary for thee, who art pompous, and powerful, and rich, to set over thyself some man of God as a trainer and governor. Reverence, though it be but one man; fear, though it be but one man. Give yourself to hearing, though it be but one speaking freely, using harshness, and at the same time healing. For it is good for the eyes not to continue always wanton, but to weep and smart sometimes, for greater health. So also nothing is more pernicious to the soul than uninterrupted pleasure. For it is blinded by melting away, if it remain unmoved by bold speech.

---

[1] Quoted with a slight variation by Justin Martyr, *Dialogue with Trypho,* Ante-Nicene Library, vol. ii. p. 148, and supposed by Grabe to be a quotation from the Apocryphal Gospel to the Hebrews.

[2] 'Ανόνητοι, for which the text has ἀνόητοι.

Fear this man when angry; be pained at his groaning; and reverence him when making his anger to cease; and anticipate him when he is deprecating punishment. Let him pass many sleepless nights for thee, interceding for thee with God, influencing the Father with the magic of familiar litanies. For He does not hold out against His children when they beg His pity. And for you he will pray purely, held in high honour as an angel of God, and grieved not by you, but for you. This is sincere repentance. "God is not mocked" (Gal. vi. 7), nor does He give heed to vain words. For He alone searches the marrow and reins of the heart, and hears those that are in the fire, and listens to those who supplicate in the whale's belly; and is near to all who believe, and far from the ungodly if they repent not.

XLII. And that you may be still more confident, that repenting thus truly there remains for you a sure hope of salvation, listen to a tale,[1] which is not a tale but a narrative,[2] handed down and committed to the custody of memory, about the Apostle John. For when, on the tyrant's death, he returned to Ephesus from the isle of Patmos, he went away, being invited, to the contiguous territories of the nations, here to appoint bishops, there to set in order whole churches, there to ordain such as were marked out by the Spirit.

Having come to one of the cities not far off (the name of which some give[3]), and having put the brethren to rest in other matters, at last, looking to the bishop appointed, and seeing a youth, powerful in body, comely in appearance, and ardent, said, "This (youth) I commit to you in all earnestness, in the presence of the church, and with Christ as witness." And on his accepting and promising all, he gave the same injunction and testimony. And he set out for Ephesus. And the presbyter taking home the youth committed to him, reared, kept, cherished, and finally baptized him. After this he relaxed his stricter care and guardianship, under the idea that the seal of the Lord he had set on him was a complete protection to him. But on his obtaining premature freedom, some youths of his own age, idle, dissolute, and adepts in evil courses, corrupt him. First they entice him by many costly entertainments; then afterwards by night issuing forth for highway

[1] μῦθος.   [2] λόγος.   [3] Said to be Smyrna.

robbery, they take him along with them. Then they dared to execute together something greater. And he by degrees got accustomed; and from greatness of nature, when he had gone aside from the right path, and like a hard-mouthed and powerful horse, had taken the bit between his teeth, rushed with all the more force down into the depths. And having entirely despaired of salvation in God, he no longer meditated what was insignificant, but having perpetrated some great exploit, now that he was once lost, he made up his mind to a like fate with the rest. Taking them and forming a band of robbers, he was the prompt captain of the bandits, the fiercest, the bloodiest, the cruelest.

Time passed, and some necessity having emerged, they send again for John. He, when he had settled the other matters on account of which he came, said, "Come now, O bishop, restore to us the deposit which I and the Saviour committed to thee in the face of the church over which you preside, as witness." The other was at first confounded, thinking that it was a false charge about money which he did not get; and he could neither believe the allegation regarding what he had not, nor disbelieve John. But when he said, "I demand the young man, and the soul of the brother," the old man, groaning deeply, and bursting into tears, said, "He is dead." "How and what kind of death?" "He is dead," he said, "to God. For he turned wicked and abandoned, and at last a robber; and now he has taken possession of the mountain in front of the church, along with a band like him." Rending, therefore, his clothes, and striking his head with great lamentation, the apostle said, "It was a fine guard of a brother's soul I left! But let a horse be brought me, and let some one be my guide on the way." He rode away, just as he was, straight from the church. On coming to the place, he is arrested by the robbers' outpost; neither fleeing nor entreating, but crying, "It was for this I came. Lead me to your captain;" who meanwhile was waiting, all armed as he was. But when he recognised John as he advanced, he turned, ashamed, to flight. The other followed with all his might, forgetting his age, crying, "Why, my son, dost thou flee from me, thy father, unarmed, old? Son, pity me. Fear not; thou hast still hope of life. I will give account to Christ for thee. If need be, I will willingly endure thy death, as the Lord did death for us. For thee I will surrender my life. Stand, believe; Christ hath sent me."

And he, when he heard, first stood, looking down; then threw down his arms, then trembled and wept bitterly. And on the old man approaching, he embraced him, speaking for himself with lamentations as he could, and baptized a second time with tears, concealing only his right hand. The other pledging, and assuring him on oath that he would find forgiveness for himself from the Saviour, beseeching and falling on his knees, and kissing his right hand itself, as now purified by repentance, led him back to the church. Then by supplicating with copious prayers, and striving along with him in continual fastings, and subduing his mind by various utterances[1] of words, did not depart, as they say, till he restored him to the church, presenting in him a great example of true repentance and a great token of regeneration, a trophy of the resurrection for which we hope; when at the end of the world, the angels, radiant with joy, hymning and opening the heavens, shall receive into the celestial abodes those who truly repent; and before all, the Saviour Himself goes to meet them, welcoming them; holding forth the shadowless, ceaseless light; conducting them to the Father's bosom, to eternal life, to the kingdom of heaven.

Let one believe these things, and the disciples of God, and God, who is surety, the Prophecies, the Gospels, the Apostolic words; living in accordance with them, and lending his ears, and practising the deeds, he shall at his decease see the end and demonstration of the truths taught. For he who in this world welcomes the angel of penitence will not repent at the time that he leaves the body, nor be ashamed when he sees the Saviour approaching in His glory and with His army. He fears not the fire.

But if one chooses to continue and to sin perpetually in pleasures, and values indulgence here above eternal life, and turns away from the Saviour, who gives forgiveness; let him no more blame either God, or riches, or his having fallen, but his own soul, which voluntarily perishes. But to him who directs his eye to salvation and desires it, and asks with boldness and vehemence for its bestowal, the good Father who is in heaven

---

[1] ῥήσεσι λόγων, for which Cod. Reg. Gall reads σεισῆσι λόγων.

will give the true purification and the changeless life. To whom, by His Son Jesus Christ, the Lord of the living and dead, and by the Holy Spirit, be glory, honour, power, eternal majesty, both now and ever, from generation to generation, and from eternity to eternity. Amen.

INDEXES.

I.—INDEX OF TEXTS OF SCRIPTURE.

OLD TESTAMENT.

Genesis.

	PAGE
i. 27,	89
viii. 1,	138
viii. 21,	135
xi. 3,	136
xxii. 12,	138
xxiii. 9,	17
xxix. 33,	17
xxix. 35,	31
xxx. 8,	54
xxx. 14,	42
xxxv. 22,	15
xxxvii. 28,	59
xxxviii. 1,	34
xxxviii. 6,	35
xxxix. 1,	66
xxxix. 35,	29
xli. 45,	73
xlviii. 7,	74
xlix. 7,	20
xlix. 21,	54
xlix. 27,	78
l. 26,	73

Exodus.

xxviii. 27,	25
xxix. 5, 6,	25
xxxiii. 14,	130
xxxiv. 1,	130

Leviticus.

xi. 5, 7,	63

Deuteronomy.

ii. 23,	20
xxxiii. 2,	136
xxxiii. 12,	136

1 Kings.

	PAGE
xv. 11,	138

1 Chronicles.

xi. 36,	33

Esther.

x. 12,	138

Job.

xl. 19,	137

Psalms.

ii. 5,	138
viii. 3,	136
xi. 4,	135
xviii. 9,	137
xix. 4,	147
xx. 4,	183
xliv. 23,	138
xlv. 1,	136 bis
xlv. 6,	137
xlv. 13,	175
xlvii. 8,	137, 138
lvii. 1,	136
lxviii. 33,	137
lxxvii. 19,	138
cx. 3,	137
cxviii. 16,	136
cxxi. 4,	138

Proverbs.

xiv. 29,	60

Song of Solomon.

ii. 8,	137

Isaiah.

i. 8,	73
i. 18,	212
i. 20,	136
liii. 1,	136
lxvi. 2,	136

Lamentations.

	PAGE
i. 18,	136
iv. 16,	136

Ezekiel.

xviii. 23,	212
xxxiii. 11,	178
xxxvii. 27,	139

Daniel.

iv. 10, 14, 20,	16
vii. 9, 13-22,	133
x. 3,	13

Hosea.

vi. 6,	212
xiv. 10,	138

Micah.

i. 3,	137

Habakkuk.

iii. 6,	137

Malachi.

iv. 2,	49

APOCRYPHA.

Wisdom.

viii. 1,	137

NEW TESTAMENT.

Matthew.

v. 13, 14,	210
v. 29,	202
vi. 14,	212

INDEX OF SUBJECTS.

	PAGE		PAGE	2 CORINTHIANS.	
vi. 19,	195	x. 41,	193		PAGE
vii. 21,	206	xi. 13,	212	ii. 15,	175
ix. 13,	212	xi. 20,	136	v. 7,	209
x. 22,	208	xii. 32,	207	v. 18,	203
x. 40,	207	xiii. 25,	138	ix. 7,	208
x. 41,	207	xiv. 26,	201		
xi. 11,	207	xv. 10,	212	GALATIANS.	
xi. 12,	201	xvi. 9,	195, 207	iii. 24,	192
xi. 27,	191	xix. 5,	195	vi. 7,	214
xii. 34,	197	xxiv. 21,	22		
xiii. 23,	206			PHILIPPIANS.	
xv. 4,	114	JOHN.		vi. 2,	181
xvii. 26,	201	i. 17,	192		
xviii. 10,	207	vii. 38.	173	1 TIMOTHY.	
xix. 21,	192	xiv. 23,	206	iii. 15,	171
xxii. 26, 27, 28,	205	xv. 13,	170		
xxv. 34, etc.,	207	xvi. 2,	171	HEBREWS.	
xxvii. 63,	29			iv. 13,	135
		ACTS.			
MARK.		v. 29,	163	1 PETER.	
x. 17-31,	190	vii. 60,	182	i. 6,	182
x. 29,	201			i. 12,	202
x. 31,	203, 204	ROMANS.		iv. 8,	211
		vii. 12,	192		
LUKE.		viii. 18,	169		
i. 6,	170	x. 18,	114	1 JOHN.	
i. 67,	170			iv. 18,	211
v. 29,	195	1 CORINTHIANS.			
vi. 30,	208	i. 24,	136	REVELATION.	
vi. 40,	206	ii. 9,	202	i. 5,	182
x. 16,	207	xii. 32,	211	iii. 14,	182
x. 29,	205	xiii. 4-6, 13,	211	xiv. 4.	170
x. 29, 31,	206	xiii. 5,	211	xxii. 11,	174

II.—INDEX OF PRINCIPAL MATTERS.

ALCIBIADES, a martyr, 183.
Alexander, a deceiver, 166, 167.
Alexander, a martyr, 179.
Amazons, a curious account of the, 105, 106.
Anger and lying, an exhortation against, 50-53.
Antoninus, M., the emperor, his army relieved by the prayers of his Christian soldiers, 140, 141.
Apelles, a heretic, 149.
Asher, the Testament of, concerning the two faces of vice and virtue, 62, etc.
Astrologers, the book of the, 106.
Attalus, a martyr, 177.

BACTRIANS, the laws of the, 103, 104.
Bathshua, wife of Judah, her bad influence, 34, 35, 36, 37.

Benjamin, the Testament of, concerning a pure mind, 74-79.
Biblias, a martyr, 173.
Bilhah, Reuben's sin with, 15.
Blandina, the martyr, the fearful tortures inflicted on, and heroically endured by, 171, 172, 176, 177, 179, 180.
Blind, the, excusable, 115.
Brahmans, laws of the, and of other Indians, 102.
Britons, laws of the, 105.

CANON of the Old Testament, a fragment of Melito on, 132, 133.
Christ, various predictions respecting, in the *Testaments of the Twelve Patriarchs*, 17, 20 bis, 23, 26, 30, 41, 53, 73 ; amazing contrasts in the nature and history of, set forth,

INDEX OF SUBJECTS. 221

124–129; the nature of, 134; the relatives of, brought before Domitian, 144, 145; our neighbour, the compassion of, 206; accepts what is done to His disciples as done to Himself, 206, 207; the self-sacrifice of, 211.

Christians, the laws of the, everywhere the same, 109, 110.

Commandments, the, of God easy, 92, etc.; the two great, 205.

Compassion, recommended, 47; the, of Christ, 206.

DAN, the Testament of, against anger and lying, 50, etc.; predicts the Messiah, 53.

Dinah, Levi is commanded by an angel to avenge the dishonour done to, 23.

Domitian, the relatives of Jesus brought before, 144, 145.

Drunkenness and lust, an exhortation against, 36, 37, 38.

ENVY, Simeon exhorts against, 17–19.
Er and Onan, 35.
Error, the seven spirits of, 14.

FACES, the two, of vice and virtue, 62–65.

Fate, is man governed by, and how far, 95–97; has it power over everything, 97.

Fathers, are we to follow our, whether their course was right or wrong, 123.

Fishing, the success of Zebulun in, 48.

Fornication, Reuben's exhortation against, 15, 16; Judah's exhortation against, 36, 37.

Freedom, bestowed on man by God, 89; the exercise of, illustrated by the various laws made by various nations, 101, etc.

GAD, his strength in subduing beasts of prey, 60; confesses his hatred of Joseph, and exhorts his children against hatred, 59–61.

Gaula, laws of the, 105.
Geli, laws of the, 103.

God, the will of, all-powerful, 110; the sin of abandoning, for the worship of that which is not, 113; alone to be worshipped, 117; who? 118; has made Himself known in His works, 119; described––the safety of His worshippers, 123, 124; symbolical forms of speech respecting, explained, 135–139; and matter, 150; love to, 205; His love to man, 210, 211.

Gods, those worshipped by men are not, 113, 114; why men have been made, 114–117; the folly of worshipping, 118, 122.

HATRA, laws in, 104.
Hatred, exhortations against, 59–61.
Heavens, the seven, shown to Levi, and described, 21, 22.
Hercules, 115.
Heretics, showed themselves after the death of the apostles, 146; a list of, 147.

IMAGES cannot represent God, 122.
Isaac, and the ram caught in a thicket, 133, 134.
Issachar, the Testament of, the simplicity of his character, 42–45.

JAMES, the Just, absurd legendary account of, 142; and of his martyrdom, 143, 144.
Jason and Papiscus, the Disputation of, quoted, 139, 140.
Jews, the laws of the, 109.
John, the apostle, and the youth who turned robber chief, the story of, 214–216.
Joseph, Simeon confesses his hatred of, and design to kill, 18; Gad confesses his hatred of, 59; how Zebulun took no part in the selling of, but saved him from the fury of Simeon and Gad, 45, 46; Reuben's affliction because of the selling of, 46; the Testament of, his brethren's cruel treatment of, 65, etc.; harsh treatment of, by the Egyptians, 66; recounts the wiles of the Egyptian woman, his severe trial, but successful resistance, 67–70; relates how he came into the possession of Potiphar, 70–72; kindness of, to his brethren, 72; visions seen by, 73; worshipped by the Egyptians as Osiris, 115.

Judah, his account of his natural endowments, and wonderful exploits against beasts and men, 31–34; marriage and children of, 34; with his grandfather Isaac, 34, 35; gives Er, and afterwards Onan, in marriage to Thamar, 35; incest with Thamar, 36; and his wife Bathshua, 35, 36, 37; exhorts against drunkenness and fornication, 37, 38; exhorts against the love of money, 38, 39; of the two spirits which

INDEX OF SUBJECTS.

wait on man, 39; of duty to Levi, 39, 40; foretells the sin of his children, 40; foretells the coming of the Messiah, 41; of the future of his brethren, the resurrection, 41; various admonitions of, 43, 44; Naphtali's vision of, 56.

Judging, harsh, the evil of, 209.

Judgment, the, predicted by Levi, 22.

KING, the, to lead, not to be led by the people, 121.

Kingdom, how a, may be governed in peace, 121.

Kings, why images were made to, and they were regarded as gods, 115.

LAMB, the spotless, 73.

Laws made by various nations for themselves, 101-106.

Leah, and Rachel, and Reuben's mandrakes, 40.

Levi, to be hearkened to, 17; to be obeyed, 19, 20; shown the seven heavens, 21, 22; predicts judgments and the coming of Christ, 22, 23; commanded by an angel to inflict vengeance on Shechem, 23, 24; his investiture with the priesthood and the priestly robes, 24, 25; his father teaches him the law of the priesthood, 26; exhorts his children, 26, 27, 28; predicts the sin of his children, 28, 29; predicts the new priesthood, 30; Judah exhorts his own children to love, 39, 40; Naphtali's vision of the dignity of, 56.

Liberality, 206; the reward of, 207, 208.

Love to God and man, 205-207, 211, 212; of God, 210, 211.

Lying and anger, an exhortation against, 50, etc.

MAN, why created liable to sin, 14; created free, 89; and nature, distinguished, 93, etc.; is he governed by fate? 95; the body of, governed by nature, 96.

Mandrakes, and Reuben, Leah, and Rachel, 42.

Martyrs, the, of Vienna and Lugdunum, 168-183.

Matter, and God, 150, etc.; not the cause or source of evil, 154, etc.

Melito, a fragment of, on the Canon of the Old Testament, 132, 133.

Mind, a pure, enjoined, 74-78.

Money, the love of, an exhortation against, 38, 39.

NAPHTALI, the birth of, 54; predicts the sin of his children, 56; visions seen by, 56, 57.

Nature, and fate, and free-will, how far and in what respect man is governed by, 96-100.

Neighbour, who is our?—Christ is, 205, 206.

OLD TESTAMENT, Melito's list of the books of, 132, 133.

Onan and Er, 35.

PARTHIANS, laws of the, 105.

Passover, the, the time of keeping, 129, 130 and note, 141, 142, 162, 163.

Patriarchs, the twelve, the future of, 41.

Persecution of the Christians reproved, 130, etc.

Persians, laws of the, 102.

Peter, the Gospel of, 164, 165.

Ponticus, a youthful martyr, 179.

Pothinus, a martyr, 174, 175.

Potiphar and Joseph, 66, 70, 71.

Priesthood, Levi invested with the, 24, 25; ages of the, 29, 30; the new, predicted, 30.

RACAMI, laws of the, 104.

Repentance, 212, 213; a tale illustrative of, 214-216.

Reuben, his confession of his sin, and repentance, 13; concerning the seven spirits of error, 13, 14; exhorts against love of women and fornication, 15, 16; of the allurement of the Watchers by women, 16; of Judah, and Levi, and the Christ, 17.

Rich man, the, the sin of flattering, 189; who shall be saved, 188, etc., 198, etc.; the truly and spuriously rich, 199.

Riches not to be thrown away, 193, 195, 196.

SAGARIS the martyr, 129 and note.

Sanctus the martyr, his sufferings, 171, 172, 173, 176, 177.

Saviour, the, His compassion, 206.

Seres, laws of the, 101.

Shechem, Levi commissioned by an angel to destroy, 23.

Simeon, why so called, 17; confesses his hatred of Joseph, and design to kill him, 18; warns against envy, 18, 19; eulogizes Joseph, 19; warns against disobedience to Levi, 19, 20; predicts the coming of Christ, 20; Zebulun saves Joseph from the fury of, 46.

Simplicity recommended and urged, 43-45.
Spirits, the seven, given to man at his creation, 13, 14; and the seven, of error, given by Beliar, 14.
Spirits, the two, which wait on man, 39.
Sun and moon, Naphtali's vision of the, 56.
Symbols of God, explained, 135-139.
Symeon the son of Clopas, the martyrdom of, 145, 146.

TABLETS, the heavenly, 23 and note.
Thamar, Er and Onan, 35; and Judah, 36.
Thunder-hurling Legion, the, 140, 141.
Truth, 112.

VICE and virtue, the two faces of, 62-65.
Vienna and Lugdunum, the martyrs of, 168-183.

WATCHERS, the, before the flood, allured by women, 16.
Ways, the two, 62.
Weeks, the seventy, of the transgressions of the sons of Levi, 29.
Wine, moderation in, urged, 38.
Women, Reuben cautions against the society and wiles of, 15, 16.

YOUTH, the story of the, who became a highway robber, and the Apostle John, 214-216.

ZAMNIA, the vision of the sea of, 57.
Zebulun, how he had no part in the selling of Joseph, but saved him from the fury of Simeon and Gad, 45, 46; of Reuben's affliction at the selling of Joseph, 47; exhorts to compassion, 48; the first who made boats—his success in fishing, 48; exhorts to unity, 49; predicts the sins of his children, 49.

Just published, in Two Volumes 8vo, price 21s.,

HISTORY

OF

PROTESTANT THEOLOGY,

PARTICULARLY IN GERMANY.

Viewed according to its Fundamental Movement,

AND IN CONNECTION WITH THE RELIGIOUS, MORAL, AND
INTELLECTUAL LIFE.

By Dr. J. A. DORNER,
OBERCONSISTORIALRATH AND PROFESSOR OF THEOLOGY AT BERLIN.

TRANSLATED BY THE
REV. GEORGE ROBSON, M.A., INVERNESS,
AND
SOPHIA TAYLOR.

WITH A PREFACE TO THE TRANSLATION BY THE AUTHOR.

EDINBURGH:
T. & T. CLARK, 38, GEORGE STREET.
AND ALL BOOKSELLERS.

Just published, in one large 8vo volume, handsomely bound, price 12s.,

A HISTORY

OF

THE CHRISTIAN COUNCILS,

FROM THE ORIGINAL DOCUMENTS,

TO THE CLOSE OF THE COUNCIL OF NICÆA,
A.D. 325.

BY

CHARLES JOSEPH HEFELE, D.D.,

BISHOP OF ROTTENBURG,
FORMERLY PROFESSOR OF THEOLOGY IN THE UNIVERSITY OF TÜBINGEN.

Translated from the German, and Edited by

WILLIAM R. CLARK, M.A. Oxon.,

PREBENDARY OF WELLS AND VICAR OF TAUNTON.

EDINBURGH:
T. & T. CLARK, 38, GEORGE STREET.
AND ALL BOOKSELLERS.

Just published, handsomely bound, in crown 8vo, price 7s. 6d.,

THE

FOOTSTEPS OF CHRIST.

TRANSLATED FROM THE GERMAN OF

A. CASPERS,

CHURCH PROVOST AND CHIEF PASTOR AT HUSUM,

By ADELAIDE E. RODHAM.

EDITED, WITH A PREFACE, BY

REV. CHARLES H. H. WRIGHT, M.A.

EDINBURGH:
T. & T. CLARK, 38, GEORGE STREET.
AND ALL BOOKSELLERS.

Just published, demy 8vo, price 9s.,

THE OLD CATHOLIC CHURCH;

OR,

THE HISTORY, DOCTRINE, WORSHIP, AND POLITY OF THE CHRISTIANS,

TRACED FROM

THE APOSTOLIC AGE TO THE ESTABLISHMENT OF THE POPE AS A TEMPORAL SOVEREIGN, A.D. 755.

By W. D. KILLEN, D.D.,

PRESBYTERIAN COLLEGE, BELFAST.

EDINBURGH:
T. & T. CLARK, 38, GEORGE STREET.
AND ALL BOOKSELLERS.

Just published, in demy 8vo, price 10s. 6d.,

THE TRAINING OF THE TWELVE;

OR,

EXPOSITION OF PASSAGES IN THE GOSPELS

EXHIBITING THE TWELVE DISCIPLES OF JESUS UNDER
DISCIPLINE FOR THE APOSTLESHIP.

BY THE

REV. ALEXANDER BALMAIN BRUCE,
BROUGHTY-FERRY.

EDINBURGH:
T. & T. CLARK, 38, GEORGE STREET.
AND ALL BOOKSELLERS.

RECENT PUBLICATIONS.

In crown 8vo, price 7s. 6d.,

Lectures, Exegetical and Practical, on the Epistle of James: With a New Translation of the Epistle, and Notes on the Greek Text. By the Rev. ROBERT JOHNSTONE, LL.B., Arbroath.

'Mr. Johnstone has produced a most instructive and interesting work, embodying the fruit of years of laborious study, which will not only be greatly useful to students and ministers, but be much prized by Christian readers generally.'—*North British Daily Mail.*

'Our judgment is, that it is an able and excellent commentary, and a real accession to our not too bulky stores of exegetical literature on this epistle.'—*Weekly Review.*

In crown 8vo, price 4s. 6d.,

Things to Come. By the Rev. William Reid, Lothian Road U. P. Church, Edinburgh.

CONTENTS: The Millennium—The Intermediate State—The Resurrection—The Judgment—Future Punishments—Heaven.

'Composed of solid and sober teaching.'—*Sword and Trowel.*
'We can commend very heartily this series of discourses.'—*Scottish Congregational Magazine.*

In extra foolscap, price 3s.,

Scripture Stories in Verse; with Sacred Songs and Miscellaneous Pieces. By the Rev. JOHN EDMOND, D.D., London.

The Life of Sir Walter Scott, Bart. By the Rev. GEORGE GILFILLAN, of Dundee. In neat crown 8vo, with beautiful Steel Frontispiece and Vignette, price 5s.

Cheap Edition, just out, price 2s. 6d.

'It is a healthy, natural, and vigorous piece of literary workmanship, not overloaded with details, giving prominence to the main characteristics of the novelist as a writer and as a man, and presenting to us Scott, not from a professional, but from a genuinely human standpoint.'—*Edinburgh Courant.*
'Mr. Gilfillan invests his book with an interest which cannot fail to make it popular.'—*Leeds Mercury.*

Thomas Chalmers: A Biographical Study. By James DODDS, Esq., Author of 'The Fifty Years' Struggle of the Scottish Covenanters.' In crown 8vo, price 5s.

'The book presents us with a most lovable picture of Chalmers throughout almost every page. It is a book that will please all who know Chalmers—and all who knew him love him—by its keen appreciation and exhibition of his works and virtues; it will inspire all who are here introduced to him with earnest admiration, and a desire to know more of a character so amiable and remarkable.'—*Scotsman.*
'The writer has seized with remarkable ability the salient points in his hero's character; and although the portrait is in miniature, it is thoroughly effective.'—*Pall Mall Gazette.*

Lectures on the Epistles to the Thessalonians. By JOHN LILLIE, LL.D., Kingston, N.Y. Large 8vo, 9s.

'We heartily recommend the work as one adapted not only to enlighten the judgment, but to warm the heart with Christian sentiment.'—*Homilist.*
'Every one who knows the author's antecedents would be prepared for ripe scholarship, a reverend appreciation of the sacred word in its import and connections; and they will find all this interwoven with the more popular elucidation of the text in a singularly suggestive and edifying way.'—*British and Foreign Evangelical Review.*

A Book for Governesses. By One of them. In fcap. 8vo, price 2s. 6d.

'We recommend this little book for governesses to all whom it may concern. It is a healthy, sensible, and invigorating work,—likely to strengthen the hands and inspire the hearts of young governesses with a cheerful view of their labour, and a respect for themselves, which is a wholesome element in all work.'—*Athenæum.*

EDINBURGH: WILLIAM OLIPHANT & CO.   LONDON: HAMILTON & CO.

BOOKS PUBLISHED BY JOHN MACLAREN.

Published Monthly, demy 8vo, 48 pp., price 4d.,

'THE PRESBYTERIAN:'
A MAGAZINE FOR THE CHURCH AND FAMILY.

Conducted by Members of the Free Church of Scotland.

The following are the main objects the 'Presbyterian' will keep steadily in view:—

1. THE CULTIVATION OF THE SPIRIT OF UNITY AMONG ALL PRESBYTERIAN CHURCHES, WITH AN EYE TO INCORPORATION.
2. THE EXTENSION OF PRESBYTERIANISM IN ENGLAND, IRELAND, AND THE COLONIES. AND
3. THE REVIVAL, AMONG ALL THOSE WHO LOOK TO THE ANCIENT CHURCH OF SCOTLAND AS THEIR MOTHER CHURCH, OF THE KINSHIP FEELING SO AS TO BRING ABOUT A CONFEDERATION OF ENGLISH-SPEAKING PRESBYTERIANS THROUGHOUT THE WORLD.

Life of John Welsh, Minister of Ayr, 1568-1622, including Illustrations of the Contemporary Ecclesiastical History of Scotland and France. By the late Rev. JAMES YOUNG. With a Biographical Sketch of the Author, by the Rev. JAMES ANDERSON. Crown 8vo, cloth, 6s. 6d.

The Epistles of our Lord to the Seven Churches of Asia. By the Rev. MARCUS DODS, A.M., Renfield Free Church, Glasgow, Author of 'The Prayer that Teaches to Pray,' etc. Crown 8vo, cloth, 2s. 6d.

BY THE SAME AUTHOR.

The Prayer that Teaches to Pray: Being Short Expositions on 'The Lord's Prayer.' Second Edition, crown 8vo, cloth, 2s. 6d.

Manual of Devotion. From the Writings of Saint Augustine. Translated by the Rev. MARCUS DODS, Glasgow. 12mo, cloth, 2s. 6d.

Christ's Presence in the Gospel History. By the Rev. Hugh MARTIN, A.M., Edinburgh, Author of the 'Prophet Jonah,' etc. Second Edition, with Additional Chapter on the Dogmatic Element in ULLMANN's 'Sinlessness of Jesus.' 8vo, cloth, 5s.

The Cross and the Crown; or, the Trials and Triumphs of the Scottish Kirk. A Poem in Ten Books. By the Rev. JOHN JOHNSTON, Balmaghie. Crown 8vo, cloth, 6s.

A Missionary's Wife among the Wild Tribes of South Bengal: Extracts from the Journal of Mrs. MURRAY MITCHELL. With Introduction and Supplement by Dr. GEORGE SMITH. Crown 8vo, cloth, 1s.

Views of Faith. By the Rev. A. L. R. Foote, D.D., Brechin, Author of 'Incidents in the Life of Christ,' 'Closing Scenes in the Life of Christ,' etc. etc. Crown 8vo, cloth, 3s.

The Days of the Fathers in Ross-shire. By the Rev. John KENNEDY, Dingwall. Crown 8vo, cloth, 3s. 6d.

BY THE SAME AUTHOR.

Man's Relations to God Traced in the Light of 'The Present Truth.' Crown 8vo, cloth, 2s. 6d.

The Shorter Catechism Illustrated and Practically Applied: Adapted for Public and Private Instruction. By GEORGE DONALDSON, Edinburgh. With Introductory Notice, by the Rev. ROBERT RAINY, D.D., Professor of Church History, New College, Edinburgh. Third Edition, fcap. 8vo, cloth, 1s. 6d.

Farewell Addresses. By the Rev. J. A. Wallace, Author of 'Pastoral Recollections,' 'Communion Services,' 'Pastor's Legacy,' etc. etc. Crown 8vo, cloth, 2s. 6d.

JOHN MACLAREN, 138, PRINCES STREET (WEST), EDINBURGH.

COMMENTARIES.

I.
On the Holy Bible. By the late Rev. Thomas Scott. Six Volumes. 50s.

II.
On the Gospel according to St. Matthew. By the Rev. J. A. ALEXANDER. 5s.

III.
On the Gospel according to St. Mark. By the same. 5s.

IV.
On the Acts of the Apostles. By the same. Two Vols. 15s.

V.
On the Epistle to the Galatians. By the Rev. E. Bayley, B.D. 7s. 6d.

VI.
On Leviticus: Expository and Practical. By the Rev. A. A. BONAR. 8s. 6d.

VII.
On the Epistle to the Romans. By the late Rev. Dr. MARSH. 2s. 6d.

VIII.
On the Holy Bible. By Matthew Henry. Nine Vols. 63s.

IX.
On the Epistle to the Ephesians. By the Rev. Charles HODGE, D.D. 9s. 6d.

X.
On the First Epistle to the Corinthians. By the same. 5s.

XI.
On the Second Epistle to the Corinthians. By the same. 5s.

XII.
On the Gospel according to St. Matthew. In Simple and Familiar Language. By G. B. 8s. 6d.

XIII.
On the Gospel according to St. Mark. By the same. 3s.

XIV.
On the Gospel according to St. John. By the same. 3s. 6d.

XV.
On the Gospel according to St. Luke. By the same. 3s. 6d.

XVI.
On the Song of Solomon. By the Rev. A. M. Stuart, M.A. 12s.

XVII.
The Bible Manual. By Dr. C. G. Barth, of Calw. Translated from the German. 12s.

LONDON: JAMES NISBET & CO., 21, BERNERS STREET, W.

www.ingramcontent.com/pod-product-compliance
Lightning Source LLC
Chambersburg PA
CBHW051856300426
44117CB00006B/423